Readings, Issues,
and Questions
in Public Finance

# THE IRWIN SERIES IN ECONOMICS

Atkinson
ECONOMICS: THE SCIENCE OF
CHOICE
First Edition

Baldwin
MARKET POWER, COMPETITION
AND ANTITRUST POLICY
First Edition

Blair and Kaserman
ANTITRUST ECONOMICS
First Edition

Bornstein
COMPARATIVE ECONOMIC
SYSTEMS: MODELS AND CASES
Fifth Edition

Brown
READINGS, ISSUES, AND
QUESTIONS
IN PUBLIC FINANCE
First Edition

Buchanan and Flowers
THE PUBLIC FINANCES
Sixth Edition

Colberg and Forbush
BUSINESS ECONOMICS
Seventh Edition

Daly
MANAGERIAL MACROECONOMICS:
A CANADIAN PERSPECTIVE
First Edition

Gould and Lazear
MICROECONOMIC THEORY
Sixth Edition

Hagen
THE ECONOMICS OF
DEVELOPMENT
Fourth Edition

Herber
MODERN PUBLIC FINANCE
Fifth Edition

Lindert
INTERNATIONAL ECONOMICS
Eighth Edition

Marshall, Briggs, and King
LABOR ECONOMICS
Fifth Edition

Maurice and Phillips
ECONOMIC ANALYSIS
Fifth Edition

Maurice and Smithson
MANAGERIAL ECONOMICS
Third Edition

Meyer
MONEY, FINANCIAL INSTITUTIONS,
AND THE ECONOMY
First Edition

Peterson
PRINCIPLES OF ECONOMICS:
MACRO Sixth Edition

Peterson
PRINCIPLES OF ECONOMICS:
MICRO Sixth Edition

Reynolds
ECONOMICS: A GENERAL
INTRODUCTION
Fifth Edition

Reynolds
MACROECONOMICS
Sixth Edition

Reynolds
MICROECONOMICS
Sixth Edition

Rima
DEVELOPMENT OF ECONOMIC
ANALYSIS
Fourth Edition

Rosen
PUBLIC FINANCE
Second Edition

Rowan
READINGS IN LABOR ECONOMICS
AND LABOR RELATIONS
Fifth Edition

Seo
MANAGERIAL ECONOMICS
Sixth Edition

Shepherd
PUBLIC POLICIES TOWARD
BUSINESS
Seventh Edition

Steltzer and Kitt
SELECTED ANTITRUST CASES
Seventh Edition

Stigum
PROBLEMS IN MICROECONOMICS
First Edition

Tullock and McKenzie
THE NEW WORLD OF ECONOMICS
Fourth Edition

Walton and Wykoff
UNDERSTANDING ECONOMICS
TODAY
First Edition

# Irwin Publications in Economics

*Advisory Editor*
## Martin S. Feldstein
## Harvard University

# READINGS, ISSUES, AND QUESTIONS IN PUBLIC FINANCE

*Edited by*
**Eleanor Brown**
*Pomona College*

1988  Homewood, Illinois

Acquisitions editor: Gary L. Nelson
Project Editor: Joan A. Hopkins
Production manager: Carma W. Fazio
Compositor: Publication Services
Typeface: 10/12 Times Roman
Printer: Patterson Printing

ISBN 0-256-06316-8

Library of Congress Catalog Card No. 87–82926

*Printed in the United States of America*

1 2 3 4 5 6 7 8 9 0 P 5 4 3 2 1 0 9 8

# Preface

Public finance is a broad discipline whose policy relevance and theoretical structure will overflow the bounds of any textbook. In this supplementary collection of readings and questions, I try to give undergraduates and policy students a taste of, and I hope a taste for, the many interesting issues for which principal textbooks generally do not have room.

This book is not an encyclopedia of issues in public finance; nor is it a compendium of the discipline's greatest hits. In choosing among topics and articles, I have tried to include ones that are (1) interesting to students, (2) important in their implications for policy, and (3) illustrative of analytical economic reasoning. Several of the readings were written expressly for this book and its intended audience. Some of the subjects are predictable, such as the discussions of Social Security and Medicare reform and the Tax Reform Act of 1986. Others are issues that have been raised consistently over the years by my students; Rebecca Blank's research of welfare-induced migration and Jim Luckett's piece on tax shelters are examples. All of the readings have been selected and edited to be accessible to students with a good understanding of microeconomic principles. The pieces by Eisner, Prag, and Tobin touch on macroeconomic issues; they presume only a familiarity with standard macroeconomic concepts.

Students deserve to know why we think it's worth their time to read an article. To this end, I precede each article by defining and commenting upon the key issue raised by that article. Similarly, the questions that follow each reading try to elucidate the value of the text. These questions are arranged in ascending breadth of focus. In every case, the first question focuses narrowly on the text. For the student who is stumped at this point, the signal is, "Do some rereading." Further questions ask for more thoughtful reflections on the material presented. Many of these questions provide an excellent basis for classroom discussion.

Each of the book's ten sections concludes with brief discussions, including questions, of issues not covered in the principal readings. Many of these involve recent news events. For instructors, these discussions offer an expanded range of topics to consider and material to use at points in the course schedule where only a little time is available for further work. For students, these help to bridge the gap between textbook analysis and the real world. If these entries convey the subliminal message, "Newspapers deserve reading and critical reflection," so much the better.

The contents of this book are arranged in a sequence that is typical of many public finance courses, but the sections stand independently and can be used in any order. I have followed closely the pattern in which topics are introduced in Harvey Rosen's text, *Public Finance*. Courses arranged around individual expenditure programs may wish to skip around in the readings; besides the expenditure entries under social insurance and income redistribution, education is treated in the section on public goods, and housing policies appear in the section on tax preferences.

Many people helped bring this book to fruition. My first round of thanks goes to those people who wrote pieces specifically for this project; I am deeply grateful to Rebecca Blank, Edward Golding, Jim Luckett, Steve Marks, Jay Prag, Jim Wyckoff, Nadja Zalokar, and Steve Zuckerman. I am also grateful to the authors reprinted here for their cooperation and to their original publishers for reprint permission. Many people suggested materials to be included; among the many deserving thanks are Edgar Browning, Alicia Kamenca, Hans Palmer, and Harvey Rosen. Harvey Rosen also made useful comments throughout the development of this book (no blame for its shortcomings should rest with him, of course) and generously gave me access to his files of newspaper clippings. The text makes frequent references to current research distributed as working papers in taxation by the National Bureau of Economic Research; I remain grateful to David Bradford and the NBER for my place on their mailing list. R. Bruce Billings of University of Arizona, John H. Goddeeris of Michigan State University, Eric B. Herzik of Arizona State University, and Dennis Sullivan of Miami University provided helpful reviews of a preliminary draft of the manuscript. The manuscript was capably produced by Cindy James, who somehow kept its pieces from being lost by its disorganized editor or eaten by the one-year-olds attending its compilation.

Finally, I could not have finished this project without the support of my colleagues at Pomona College and my family. This book is dedicated to my lucky seven—father, husband, son, and brothers—whose ubiquitous masculine presence makes everyday life in academic economics seem almost eerily normal.

# Contents

*of pp 61–63*

# PART I

# Market Failure

**Issue:** *If efficiency dictates that resources are allocated to private goods through competitive markets and to public goods by a collective mechanism such as government, what do we do with mixed goods?*

*"To What Extent Is Education a Public Good?"* James Wyckoff

**Issue:** *Is acid rain an important externality that should be the focus of federal policy?*

*"What Do We Know About Acid Rain?"*

*Further Issues and Questions in Market Failure*

**Issue:** *Privatization.*

**Issue:** *Regulating drivers in smoggy Denver.*

*If efficiency dictates that resources are allocated to private goods through competitive markets and to public goods by a collective mechanism such as government, what do we do with mixed goods?*

When units of a good are consumed collectively, decentralized markets do not generally provide the good in efficient amounts. Government provision is a common alternative, as in the case of national defense. Many goods have public good characteristics alongside private ones; these "mixed goods" are also frequent objects of government provision. Consider, for example, police protection: Lowering the level of crime reduces the private costs borne by victims, and everyone becomes less apprehensive as the level of public safety improves.

When a large portion of the benefit derived from a mixed good is private, there arises the question of whether to charge consumers for their consumption. The government may run the post office because universal service provides option value and national pride to all of us, but we still pay for the private benefit we get when we use the mail.

The government's approach to a mixed good might reasonably depend on the relative importance of its public and private characteristics.

The article deals with education as a mixed good, presenting a methodology for quantifying the public-good dimension of a good that is, at least at the margin, primarily private.

# TO WHAT EXTENT IS EDUCATION A PUBLIC GOOD?

*James Wyckoff\**

Recently, the issue of "privatizing" various aspects of government has received a great deal of attention. Responsibility for the provision of a good can be shifted between the public and private sectors in a number of different ways. Society could "privatize" the production, the finance, or the determination of price and quantity of a good, or any combination of these. While much has been made of getting

*Assistant Professor of Public Policy, State University of New York at Albany.

the government out of the provision of goods and services by shifting those responsibilities to the private sector, the discussion seems to have ignored the public finance theory that could form the basis for such decisions. First we will address the issue of how to define and measure the degree of "publicness" of a good or service; then we will empirically estimate the publicness of primary and secondary education.

For economists, the decision of the appropriate division between public and private responsibility frequently rests with the criterion of efficiency. The theory of public goods is often employed to justify public expenditures, or the lack thereof, for particular activities. Public goods are defined as goods that are consumed in a nonrival and nonexcludable manner. Nonrivalness implies that the cost of an additional consumer is close to zero, while nonexcludability suggests that an individual cannot be easily prevented from receiving the benefits of the good. An example of a public good would be the flood control benefits produced by a dam. Additional down-river residents can consume the benefits without reducing the benefits of others (nonrivalness), and once the dam is built they cannot be prevented from receiving the benefits (nonexcludability). Goods that are either nonrival or nonexcludable in consumption may not be allocated efficiently by the private market because the marginal unit benefits many people. Decentralized markets do not have a mechanism to sum the benefits of the marginal unit, and thus marginal benefits do not equal the costs of the marginal unit.

## THE DEGREE OF PUBLICNESS IN A MIXED GOOD

While some goods may be public goods in the strict sense of being nonrival and nonexcludable, others may only be partially nonexcludable and/or nonrival. To understand the appropriate financial role for government in such circumstances, we need to understand the relative extent of these public and private good attributes. This article concentrates on defining a measure of publicness for goods that are nonexcludable and applies that measure to the socially and financially important case of primary and secondary education.[1]

Primary and secondary education is often modeled as a mixed good—one that embodies both private and public benefits. Students and their parents receive direct benefits from education, such as increased earnings potential, child care, and improved quality of life. These benefits are rival and excludable in that additional resources are required to educate another child and society could exclude children from receiving an education. The benefits that accrue to the child and parents are reflected in the private demand for education. It has also been suggested that there are benefits to society that are not captured solely by the educated child and the child's family. For example, education causes individuals to be better informed voters and citizens, reduces crime and other antisocial behaviors, and redistributes wealth. These benefits accrue to everyone in society, whether or not they have children in school. Individuals with children in school will have both a private demand for the education of their own child and a public demand for the education of all school children.[2] Individuals without children in school would express only public demand for education.

Public and private demands are shown in Figure 1. The aggregate public demand is obtained by summing the individual public demands vertically, since the nonexcludability of the benefits allows each unit produced to satisfy the demands of all consumers for that unit. The aggregate private demand is the horizontal sum of the individual private demands. The total demand for education is obtained by vertically summing the aggregate public demand and the aggregate private demand.

The publicness of education is measured as the willingness to pay for the aggregate public benefits divided by the total willingness to pay for the marginal unit. This is the proportion of total demand that is public at the margin. In Figure 1 the publicness coefficient at $Q_1$ is OS/OT. A pure private good, one with no public externality at the margin, would have a publicness coefficient of zero (as at $Q_2$), while a pure public good, one with no private benefit component, would have a publicness coefficient of one.

It is important to note that the definition of publicness is calculated at the marginal unit. In the case of education, for example, there are likely to be substantial inframarginal externalties. That is, citizens may place a high value on children learning to read, write, and perform basic computations. They may see less value to society of children learning calculus, which may be in the child's own self-interest to pursue. A publicness coefficient of zero does not imply that society does not value education; rather, it means that, at the margin, society does not receive any benefits from education, illustrated at $Q_2$.

Many goods are neither purely public nor private, but are likely to have an element of publicness to them. The measure of publicness defined above allows us to broaden the debate from the appropriateness of public versus private finance to what proportion of public finance is appropriate. It may

be appropriate, for example, to charge some tuition for children to attend public schools.[3] The portion of costs paid for by tuition could depend on the magnitude of the publicness coefficient.

## ESTIMATING THE PUBLICNESS OF EDUCATION

To estimate the publicness of primary and secondary education we must be able to determine the willingness to pay for the public aspects of education separately from willingness to pay for the private components of education. Figure 2 represents an individual's demand for education. The cost of an extra unit of education is distributed among property taxpayers according to the assessed value of their property. So there is a price, a tax price, that each property owner pays to finance an extra unit of education. The tax price varies from person to person, due to variation in assessed value. By estimating the relationship between price and quantity of local education preferred for a number of otherwise identical individuals we will be able to trace out the demand curve shown in Figure 2. It is assumed that the demand revealed by individuals without children in school is only the public demand for education. Individuals with children in school

Figure 1

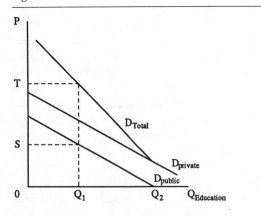

Figure 2

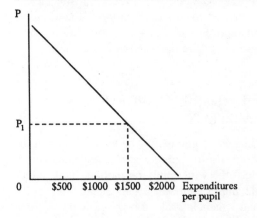

reveal a demand that is the sum of their public and private demands for education. The private demand for education can be inferred as the difference between the demand estimated for individuals with children in school and the demand estimated for individuals with no children in school.

There are at least three potential problems with this delineation of private and social demands. A child's relatives or family friends may, like the parents, express what is most properly defined as a private demand, but it will be recorded as part of the social demand if these interested parties have no school-attending children of their own. Second, parents of preschoolers may express higher than otherwise expected demands in the belief that it takes time to develop school quality. Again, this is most appropriately thought of as a private demand for education.[4] Finally, nonparents may express a willingness to pay for education in the belief that the higher expenditures will be attractive to individuals considering where to live and thus would be favorably capitalized into the value of their property. Such behavior should be included as part of the private demand. Each of these possibilities is ignored in the estimates presented below.

To obtain data to estimate the individual's private and social demands for education, a mail survey was conducted immediately following a referendum on school operating expenditures in a Michigan community. Referenda are one of several collective choice mechanisms for determining the quantities of publicly provided goods and services. The preference revelation problem typically associated with determination of demands for public goods (people refuse to admit their willingness to pay for a public good if they think they will then be forced to pay for it based on their expressed interest) is not an issue in this context because individuals decide on quantity with the knowledge that price is given. In Figure 2, an individual with a price of $P_1$ would like to choose a quantity as close to

$1500 as possible.[5] Revealing more or less than the desired quantity at the given price may make the individual worse off if the collectively chosen quantity is changed as a result.

Individuals in the community, both those who voted and those who did not, were asked how they voted (or would have) on six proposed levels of expenditure per pupil ($875, $939, $1004, $1684, $1749, or $1813). Expenditures per pupil is employed as a proxy for the quantity (quality?) of education since defining a measure of output for education is difficult.

The survey collected information on the individual's choice of expenditures per pupil; the assessed value of property; the number of children in school; and the education, sex, occupation, and age of the individual—as well as some other information. Knowledge of variables other than price and quantity are important so that in constructing estimates of the private and public demands, other variables that may affect demand can be controlled for. Expenditures per pupil is the dependent variable; price, income, number of children in school, education, sex, occupation, age, and other characteristics are independent variables. Using the data collected in the survey, a statistical estimation technique called an ordered probit model, which is similar to regression analysis, estimates the shape of the private and public demand functions.[6]

## EMPIRICAL RESULTS

The estimates suggest several interesting relationships. With the recognition that expenditures per pupil may not represent the quantity of education demanded very well, individuals were asked whether they believed that increased expenditures affected the quality of education. Those who answered yes to this question are estimated to have demands for education that are 25 percent greater than those who said no. An individual employed by the school district has a private demand that is estimated to be 40 percent greater than a similar individual who is not employed by the school district. These individuals may value education more highly than others, but it is also likely that self-interest is at work here. Individuals who have some college education are estimated to have demands that are 13 percent greater than those who did not attend college. Someone who has two children in school has a private demand that is nearly 25 percent greater than an individual with only one child in school and over 50 percent greater than someone with no children in school. The estimated coefficients on price and income imply that the public demand for education is inelastic with respect to both price and income. The price elasticity is −0.21, and the income elasticity is 0.46. The private demand for education is not statistically affected by price or income. This may indicate that families place a high priority on the education of their own children and are unwilling to reduce quantity with increases in price or decreases in income over the ranges of those variables represented in the sample.

Employing the estimates of individual private and public demands, we can compare the size of the aggregate private demand for education with the aggregate public demand and compute an estimate of the publicness coefficient for primary and secondary education. As noted before, the private demands are summed horizontally and the public demands are summed vertically to arrive at the aggregate demands. The estimated aggregate curves are then used to compute the publicness coefficient at various levels of education expenditures per pupil.

The publicness coefficient for the level of expenditures desired by the median voter[7] is estimated to be 0.09. This estimate implies that at an expenditure level of about $1500 per pupil, roughly 10 percent of the marginal benefits are social, with about 90 percent being

private. Reasonable bounds on this estimate are from 0.0 to 0.50.

While the estimate of the publicness of education is only illustrative, because of the limited nature of the sample employed in the estimates, it does suggest that efficient allocation of primary and secondary education may be achieved with less than complete public finance. To date, little empirical research has been done to address the issue of the appropriate financial role of government in the provision of mixed goods and services. Building upon traditional public finance theory, further empirical work can contribute to our economic perspective on this increasingly important set of public policy issues.

# Notes

1. The nonrival dimension of publicness is addressed in Borcherding and Deacon (1972) and Bergstrom and Goodman (1973).

2. The public demand may be spatially limited to one's own town or state. This would be an example of a local public good.

3. As with other goods, such as food, health care, or higher education, society would likely want to ensure the poor would not be excluded from receiving an education due to the cost.

4. However, in preliminary estimates of demand, a dummy variable indicating the presence of preschoolers in the household was statistically insignificant.

5. The referendum stated how much each quantity of education would affect the milleage (tax) rate; $P_1$ is calculated as the per-unit milleage rate increase times the individual's assessed property value.

6. Estimation by ordinary least squares regression is inappropriate in this case because the dependent variable is limited to one of six values rather than continuously varying. Employing OLS would cause the errors to be heteroskedastic and would lead to inefficient estimates.

7. The median voter is the voter whose quantity demanded is in the middle of all voters when voters' demands are arrayed in ascending order. In an election employing a majority rule decision criterion, the median voter is the decisive voter.

# References

Bergstrom, T. and Goodman, R. "Private Demands for Public Goods," *American Economic Review* 63 (June 1973):280-296.

Borcherding, T. and Deacon, R. "The Demand for the Services of Non-Federal Governments," *American Economic Review* 62 (December 1972): 891-901.

Wyckoff, J. "The Nonexcludable Publicness of Primary and Secondary Public Education," *Journal of Public Economics* 24 (1984): 331-351.

## QUESTIONS

1. (a) What is Wyckoff's measure of the degree of publicness of the mixed good "education"? (b) Other mixed goods sometimes provided by the government include the post office and railroad transportation. Explain the private and public aspects of each. Does the publicness have to do with nonrivalry, nonexcludability, or both?

2. The quantity of education is measured by levels of inputs (dollars) rather than output. List a couple of possible measures of the output "education" and discuss their shortcomings in measuring this variable.

3. To see how Wyckoff's measure of publicness relates to people's willingness to pay for the efficient level of education, consider the simple case of a homogeneous community of N households that are identical in all ways, including tax price, except that some have one school-aged child and others have none. Suppose that, at the efficient level of provision, 10 percent of demand at the margin reflects the public good nature of education.

Suppose we set tuition at 90 percent of costs. This is the fraction representing private benefits at the margin. Taxes will pay for the remaining 10 percent.
(a) Measuring the quantity of education as dollars spent per pupil, what will be the tax price to a nonparent when there are N households and S students?
(b) A parent pays tuition and taxes. What is the total price to a parent of another dollar spent per pupil?

The efficient level of education sets marginal costs equal to marginal benefit. In a community with S students, the cost of raising expenditure per pupil by one dollar is S. Wyckoff estimates the aggregated demand (marginal benefit) function; the efficient output level is where this aggregated MB equals S.
(c) Our measure of publicness says that the sum of everyone's valuations of the marginal unit of public good represents 10 percent of its value. At the efficient level, its total value is S. What is the MB to a nonparent at the efficient level of education? To a parent?
(d) With taxes subsidizing 10 percent of the cost of education, is each household's education bill equal to its marginal benefit?

*Is acid rain an important externality that should be the focus of federal policy?*

When valuable resources can be used at no cost to the user, markets will not make efficient use of them. Our natural environment is a frequent victim of this kind of market failure. One serious form of environmental degradation is acid rain. Policymakers are still struggling to find coherent and effective approaches to deal with this externality.

In theory, the solution is simple. Allowable levels of contributing emissions should be reduced until the marginal benefit from further reduction no longer exceeds the marginal cost of reduc-ing emissions. Implementing this rule is tough. As always, politics can interfere when one constituency (for example, the higher-sulfur coalmining industry) will be hurt even though society as a whole will gain. The tougher issues, though, are ones of measurement. Estimating the benefits of lower health risks from environmental pollution is hard. An accurate assessment of the causal link between acid rain and damaged forests would involve more scientific information than we have. These two steps in evaluating the benefits of pollution reduction—defining the physical relationship between pollutants and damage and then assigning an economic value to that damage—are unavoidably difficult and controversial.

# WHAT DO WE KNOW ABOUT ACID RAIN?

Scientific studies are largely in agreement over some, but not all, aspects of the nature and effects of acid rain. Human activities are a substantial cause of acid rain. Electric utilities represent the major source of sulfur dioxide; electric utilities, transportation, and industry all emit significant amounts (and perhaps roughly equal amounts) of nitrous oxides. These emissions are the precursors to acid rain.

Winds can carry these emissions long distances before they are deposited as acid rain. It has been estimated that two thirds of acid rain damage to structures is caused by pollutants originating more than 30 miles away. Paths from sources to deposits are hard (impossible?) to trace, and there is no agreement on whether the relationship between emissions levels and deposits is a linear one. (This means that, for example, the 50 percent reduction in pollutants being called for by Canada might not imply a 50 percent reduction in acid rain.)

On land, acid rain has been blamed for the decline of large forests. One of the most pernicious effects of acid deposition on land is that the acids allow toxic metals, perhaps most significantly aluminum, to leach into groundwaters. Concentrations of aluminum are harmful to vegetation on land; aluminum is also washed from the soil into the aquatic ecosystem.

In lakes and rivers, it is clear that increased acidity damages fish populations. Sudden increases in acidity, such as those caused when "acid snow" melts, appear to have especially deleterious effects on aquatic life. There is little agreement over whether liming (to increase alkalinity) aquatic ecosystems could feasibly offset the effects of acid rain.

There is debate over the amount of damage that will ultimately result from current emission levels. Soils have limited capacities for neutralizing acid. A report by scientists advising the Environmental Protection Agency (EPA) reported that, in 1987, northeastern soil samples showed no buildup of unneutralized acidic sulfates. The implication is that an equilibrium has been reached, with current levels of emissions consistent with current levels of acidification. Whereas earlier findings predicted that 300 to 1500 additional northeastern lakes could become acidic in the next few decades, the new study sets the figures at zero to "a few hundred." On the other hand, preliminary evidence shows that southeastern soils (for example, in the southern Blue Ridge Mountains) are retaining some acidic sulfates, suggesting that the southeast may be more vulnerable than previously believed.

Acid rain also causes damage to the built environment. Because we know how to repair architectural damage, this damage—largely in deteriorated surfaces that need repainting, resurfacing, or reinforcement—is the most easily quantified. For 17 northeastern states, the cost to structures of acid rain is estimated conservatively at $5 billion annually. The cost of visibility losses in the eastern United States has been estimated by the EPA at $2 billion.

The many fuzzy spots in our picture of the links from emissions to deposition, and from deposition to damage, render studies of the costs and benefits of various anti-acid-rain policies speculative at best. Under such circumstances, it is not unusual for the political process to decide upon a goal (for example, the 50 percent emissions reduction suggested by Canada) and then to ask economic analysis to find the most cost-effective (that is, the cheapest) way of reaching the stated goal. If the policy goal lies beyond the influence of marginal improvements in economic estimates of marginal benefits and costs, it makes some sense to focus resources on other pieces of the puzzle, for example, on developing and assessing relevant pollution-control technologies. Accordingly, President Reagan in early 1987 pledged to seek $2.5 billion for the development of anti-acid-rain technology.

# References

Schmandt, Jurgen, and Hilliard Roderick, eds. *Acid Rain and Friendly Neighbors: The Policy Dispute between Canada and the United States,* Duke University Press, 1985.

Sims, Calvin. "Fighting Acid Rain: The New Research," *New York Times,* April 8, 1987.

Taylor, Robert E. "Acid-Rain Damage to Lakes Minimal, EPA Advisors Find," *Wall Street Journal,* March 26, 1987.

———. "Southeast Faces Acid-Rain Threat, Advisors Tell EPA," *Wall Street Journal,* June 10, 1987.

# QUESTIONS

1. What technical information do we need in order to assess the marginal costs at environmental site A of pollution from point B? How much of this information is available?

2. The high-sulfur coal industry and electric utilities would be the big losers economically if a massive anti-acid-rain campaign were to move forward. In the absence of improved abatement technologies, stricter emission standards would be met mainly by switching to fuels cleaner than high-sulfur coal or by installing expensive flue scrubbers. How do you suppose representatives from these industries responded to Reagan's announced choice of a way to begin to deal with acid rain?

3. When the government lacks adequate information for designing a program, it sometimes runs experimental projects to see what happens. If you were asked to design a demonstration project to help resolve some of the uncertainties you listed in your answer to question 1, what features would your setup have? (For example, you probably wouldn't study a lake polluted by many sources or an area of unusual soil composition.) What design features would be hard to control for?

---

# Further Issues and Questions in Market Failure

## *Privatization*

Public goods are not provided in efficient amounts through private markets. Government can increase available quantities of public goods either by producing them directly or by demanding them from private producers. One argument for limiting the government's role to that of consumer is that the profit motive makes private production more efficient. Government may want to produce goods directly when it cares about the distribution of the product, as in education, or when the product has strategic importance, as in training military forces.

From Brazil to Africa, in western Europe and the United States, the 1980s have seen a trend toward "privatization," putting ownership of previously government-controlled companies into private hands. In virtually all cases, the activities being "privatized" were money-losers for the governments who owned them. There are some success stories: Richard Alm reports in *U.S. News and World Report* ("When the Government Sells Out," November 10, 1986) that the sale of Jaguar in 1984 brought doubled sales, 1000 new jobs, and a profit of $170 million in 1985.

A. The Reagan administration is no fan of big government. Each of the government's businesses or assets listed below has been suggested for privatization. For each, can you see any reason for the government to act as owner?

 1. Conrail, a freight railroad formed in 1976 when the government took over seven bankrupt railroads.

 2. The Federal Housing Administration,

an agency that guarantees mortgages for first-time home buyers with low to moderate incomes.

3. The Department of Energy's uranium enrichment facilities.

4. Naval oil reserves.

B. Advanced U.S. military weapons systems are privately produced. There are scandalous stories of overcharging by some defense contractors. Are such charges necessarily reflections of true economic inefficiency in production? Should the government respond by nationalizing the weapons industry?

### Regulating drivers in smoggy Denver.

Los Angeles, long the site of the country's worst carbon monoxide air pollution, has now lost this distinction to Denver. On June 30, 1987, the Colorado Air Quality Control Commission mandated wintertime use and supply of high-oxygen fuels for automobiles. The extra oxygen in gasoline mixtures containing ethanol (to make "gasohol") or the compound methyl tertiary butyl ether (MTBE) allows more complete fuel combustion and hence less pollution. The program is expected to reduce carbon monoxide levels by as much as 20 percent.

The new rule was met with anxiety and opposition. The *New York Times* ("Plan on Pollution Stirs Ire in Denver," July 27, 1987) reported that a Colorado Springs television station asked its viewers to answer the question, "Should the state mandate the use of oxygenated fuels in the wintertime to reduce carbon monoxide?" Only 164 viewers phoned in their support; 1778 said no. The opposition to the plan focuses not on the added cost of fuel, which should range from three to eight cents a gallon, but on worries that the new fuels will harm people's cars. Early formulations of gasohol clogged fuel injectors, caused vapor lock, and were blamed for engine damage.

A. For four months prior to the scheduled wintertime fuel switch, Colorado state troopers will test oxygenated fuels in their patrol cars. What else might the Colorado government do to assuage drivers' fears? (Would you suggest they collect and disseminate certain information? Are there reasonable risk-sharing arrangements that might be considered?)

B. Suppose Denver had mandated that oil companies provide oxygenated fuels but made their use voluntary. Regular fuels would be available at stations with the capacity to provide them, but their prices would include a wintertime pollution tax.

1. How would you determine the size of the pollution tax?

2. Would anyone be better off under the new-fuel-or-tax system than under the mandated-fuel regime? Who would choose to pay the tax? Who would buy the new fuels? Would the proportions change over time?

3. If there were significant economies of scale in providing fuels, would this affect your evaluation of the new-fuel-or-tax proposal?

C. Because supplies of ethanol have been unreliable, some oil companies are planning to use MTBE, a petroleum distillate, instead. Also, MTBE has not been associated with the car problems blamed on early versions of gasohol. If the new gasohols are really trouble-free in cool weather, evaluate from the standpoint of economic efficiency each of these criteria, reliability and reputation, for choosing a gas additive.

# PART II

# Public Choice

### How can economists be more effective in shaping policy?

The branch of economics known as public choice shows, among other things, how the political process allocates resources. In this article Alice Rivlin, a former director of the Congressional Budget Office, suggests ways economists can play a more effective role in the political arena.

# ECONOMICS AND THE POLITICAL PROCESS[†‡]

*Alice M. Rivlin*[*§]

I want to use this once-in-a-lifetime opportunity for pontificating to the profession, to explore ways of improving the interaction

[†]Reprinted by permission of *American Economic Review*, March 1987.

[‡]Presidential address delivered at the ninety-ninth meeting of the American Economic Association, December 29, 1986, New Orleans, Louisiana.

[*]Director of Economic Studies, The Brookings Institution.

[§] The Brookings Institution, 1775 Massachusetts Avenue, N.W., Washington, D.C. 20036. The views set forth here are solely my own and do not necessarily represent the opinions of the trustees, officers, or other staff members of the Brookings Institution. I am grateful for the insights and assistance of many colleagues, especially Robert D. Reischauer, Charles L. Schultze, Mary S. Skinner, and Valerie M. Owens.

between what economists do and the political process. Tension and conflict are, of course, inherent in political decisions, especially on economic policy. Nothing can make such decisions easy. Nevertheless, it is my contention that economic policymaking in Washington in the last decade has been more frustrating, muddled, and confusing than necessary. Some of the fault lies with economists and economics; some with politicians and the political process; some in the interactions. I want to offer some suggestions for modest improvements.

Most economists probably share my premise that economics ultimately ought to be more than just challenging intellectual gymnastics. It ought to help us understand how the economy works and provide a basis for intelligent political choices among economic policies. Even those who devote their energies to resolving purely theoretical issues imagine that somehow in the end their efforts will prove socially useful.

The dedicated, idealistic young economist who aspires to advise a government may well envision herself someday as the wise and impartial adviser to the philosopher queen. In this daydream, the adviser presents the best forecasts that can be made of the future course of the economy. She explains the macroeconomic policy options and what is likely to happen if each is undertaken. She elucidates why market solutions are efficient, when markets are likely to fail, and what can be done when this occurs. She identifies risks and uncertainties, which fortunately are not overwhelming. She represents the best professional judgment of her fellow economists, indicating the major respects in which most economists agree and scrupulously pointing out that in minor respects the views of some of her professional colleagues might differ from her own. She remains above the political fray, identifying any values or distributional biases that may creep into her judgments and eschewing identification with interest groups or ideological causes.

The queen for her part listens carefully and intelligently, asks thoughtful questions, and weighs the options. She may consult other experts on noneconomic aspects of the decisions, but these can be assumed not to be very important. She then makes final decisions — even very hard ones — and sticks to them. The decisions are carried out, the economy prospers, and a grateful nation applauds the wisdom of the monarch and her economist and the usefulness of economics.

But in the real world, both economics and politics are frustratingly unlike this picture. Both are pluralistic in the extreme and appear to be getting more so. Economists and political leaders not only miscommunicate, but each accuses the other of incompetence, obfus-

cation, self-serving motives, and anti-social behavior.

Economists, of course, do not wait for others to attack them; they do it themselves. Walter Heller said in his presidential address that the "chorus of self criticism has risen to a new crescendo" (1975, p. 1), and the self- deprecation has not abated in the intervening decade. If a golden age of economists' self-confidence ever occurred, it is long past. Events of recent years have kept reminding us that our national economy is diverse and complex, battered by unpredictable shocks, and increasingly interconnected with the even more diverse and complex world outside our borders. Knowledge of how the domestic economy works and interacts with the rest of the world is imperfect. Economists keep coming up with ingeneous theories, but they have a hard time testing them. Data are inadequate and controlled experimentation nearly impossible. Modeling has greatly enhanced our understanding of the past, but shows few visible signs of improving the reliability of macroeconomic prediction. Forecasting even for short periods remains an uncertain art in which neither economists nor politicians can have much confidence.

Many of the most sophisticated and realistic members of the profession, conscious of all these difficulties, have abandoned the attempt to advise governments on policies in favor of the more manageable tasks of adding to the knowledge base. This may be understandable, but it deprives the economic policy debate of the input of some very good minds and runs the risk of leaving the job of interacting with the political arena disproportionately to those with strong ideological views.

## I. FRAGMENTATION OF THE ECONOMIC POLICY PROCESS

The pluralism of economics pales beside the pluralism of the political system that policy-minded economists aspire to assist. Even if one leaves aside the complexities of federalism, the process by which national economic policy evolves in Washington is so fragmented and complicated that it is almost impossible to explain to the uninitiated how it is supposed to work, let along how it does work.

A well-founded distrust of despots led our forefathers not only to opt for representative democracy, but to divide power among the executive and legislative and judicial branches, and between the House and the Senate. On matters of taxing and spending, they were especially protective of the power of the people's representatives, making it clear that while the president could propose taxing and spending, the ultimate authority lies with the Congress, subject only to presidential veto. This divided power creates a built-in hurdle to making and carrying out fiscal policy. The hurdle is low when the president is articulating a policy that has broad support in the country and in the Congress. It can lead to erratic shifts of policy when the president is indecisive, and to deadlock when the president is leading in a direction in which the public and its elected representatives do not wish to go. Deadlocks are rare, but can be serious. The failure to reduce the huge structural budget deficit of the mid-1980's largely reflects the fact that the president's solution—drastic reduction of the federal role in the domestic economy—does not command broad popular support.

The separation of powers between the Congress and the president is basic to our system of government and probably worth the price of occasional deadlock. The difficulties of making economic policy, however, are strongly compounded by the propensity of our pluralistic society to diffuse power and decision-making authority both within the executive branch and within Congress. With respect to taxing and spending policy, for example, the simple notion that the president proposes and the Congress disposes is greatly complicated by the fragmentation of power within each branch. Moreover, periodic efforts to make the policy process more coherent within each branch, while often temporarily success-

ful, have added new power centers without consolidating the old ones.

In the executive branch, the trend since early in the century has been to centralize power in the White House in order to make it easier for the president to formulate and articulate taxing and spending policy, and to utilize the growing skills of the economics profession to that end. But this worthy goal has been accomplished in stages, with a new institution added at each stage. The creation of what is now called the Office of Management of Budget (OMB) in the 1920's made it possible for the president to review and evaluate spending requests and impose a set of priorities on his budget proposal to Congress reflecting his administration's view of the appropriate size and role of government. The creation of the Council of Economic Advisers (CEA) in the 1940's provided a focal point for bringing the advice of the economics profession into the service of presidential decision making and a locus for creating an official forecast of economic activity.

The creation of OMB and CEA improved the president's ability to formulate and articulate macroeconomic policy. It also left the president, in addition to his other impossible duties, with the job of resolving a built-in tension over responsibility for economic policy among the CEA, OMB, and the Treasury, not to mention the White House staff and the agencies with line responsibility for implementing various aspects of economic policy.

Presidents have tried various coordination mechanisms including "troika" arrangements and an almost infinite variety of broader councils and committees with varying membership, responsibilities, and leadership. The system works tolerably well or exceedingly creakily, depending on the president's personal style and the personalities involved. But it encourages battling over turf as well as substance, and is hardly designed to minimize the amount of presidential energy needed to evolve a coherent, explainable policy on taxing and spending. One might wonder whether it is not time to do what so many other countries do and give our president the equivalent of a responsible finance minister charged with the functions now diffused to our budget director, Council of Economic Advisers, and Treasury Secretary.

The fragmentation of power and responsibility is, of course, even more extreme in the Congress. The legislative branch also has a long history of attempts to make taxing and spending policy in a more coherent fashion by adding new coordinating institutions—appropriations committees, a joint economic committee, budget committees, a congressional budget office—without eliminating or consolidating any of the old ones.

The most recent attempt to improve congressional economic decision making—one in which I was an active participant—followed the Budget Reform Act of 1974 which created the budget committees and the Congressional Budget Office. These budget reforms succeeded in their main objective of focusing the attention of the Congress on overall budget policy, not just individual taxing and spending fragments. They have forced the Congress to fit the pieces together, to debate and vote on an overall taxing and spending plan—a budget resolution—to which specific taxing and spending matters must conform. No one can say that the Congress in the last few years has ignored fiscal policy! The creation of the Congressional Budget Office, moreover, has given Congress independent access to forecasts, projections, and analysis of economic options.

The downside of the budget reforms, however, was that the budget process was superimposed on the already complex responsibilities of authorizing, appropriating, and tax committees. It has added to the layers and stages of congressional policymaking without removing any of them, has made the process of budget decision making nearly impossible even for members of Congress to understand, and increased the workload so much that decisions are routinely made late and in an atmosphere of crisis. Moreover, Congress

now frequently has to deal with two sets of estimates, those of the OMB and those of the Congressional Budget Office, which may differ because they are based on different forecasts of economic activity, or for even less obvious technical reasons.

Meanwhile, back in the separate world of the Federal Reserve, monetary policy is being decided and carried out. It is a curious paradox that a nation, which feels it needs many more hands on the tiller of fiscal policy than most countries regard as workable, is content to leave monetary policy to a central bank with fewer visible ties to the rest of the government than the central banks of most countries.

There is plenty of informal communication, of course, especially between the Federal Reserve and the hydraheaded economic establishment of the executive branch. More formal cooperation between the monetary and fiscal authorities, as in the United Kingdom, might contribute only marginally to making monetary and fiscal policy decisions part of a more coherent strategy for the economy—and at the cost of depriving the executive branch of the luxury of blaming the Federal Reserve when things go wrong. The love-hate relationship between the Congress and Federal Reserve, however, warrants more attention. Despite occasional outbursts of anxiety over escalating interest rates, Congress has shown little inclination to control monetary policy, or even to inquire into the consistency of monetary and fiscal objectives. The Fed is required to report monetary growth targets to the banking committees, as though monetary policy were a matter of banking system regulation, but has little genuine interaction with the budget committees whose job is to debate and propose fiscal policy.

## II. THE PROCESS UNDER STRESS

This whole complicated economic policy system has been subjected to enormous strain in recent years. Political economists like to harken back to the golden years of the 1950's and 1960's when economists got respect and the economic policy machinery functioned smoothly. The nostalgia is only partly a result of faulty memories. It's not hard to be satisfied with economists and policy processes when the economy is growing, productivity marches steadily upward, and even the national debt is obligingly declining in relative importance. It's much harder when productivity growth plummets for reasons that no one honestly purports fully to understand, expectations of public and private consumers have to be cut back to fit with slower income growth, and inflation and interest rates are bouncing around at unfamiliar levels.

Adjusting to the energy shocks and slower growth that began in the 1970's strained the economic policy processes of all industrial countries and made the participants feel frustrated and inadequate. It's not obvious, even with hindsight, that the fundamental difficulties facing the industrial world in the 1970's can credibly be blamed on economists or any particular structure of government or economic policy responses, but all came in for their share of the understandable hostility.

The difficulties of the U.S. economy in the 1980's, by contrast, revolve heavily around an economic policy mistake: the creation of a large structural deficit in the federal budget. I do not believe that the structure of our economic decision process was the cause of the mistake. Blaming the deficit on inherent flaws in the policy process requires an explanation of why the process did not cause similar mistakes in the past. But the events of 1981 which produced the deficit illustrate several of the difficulties of economic policymaking which make mistakes harder to avoid:

• the uncertainty of macroeconomic forecasting;

• the isolation of monetary and fiscal policy;

• the contentiousness of economists and their tendency to let their ideological positions cloud their judgments about the likely effects of particular policies.

That a tax cut unmatched by comparable spending cuts would produce a deficit should have surprised no economist. That the deficit was so large reflected both economic and political miscalculations. The Reagan Administration has been faulted for masking the deficit with a "rosy scenario," but the fact is that most of the forecasting community, including the Congressional Budget Office, expected positive real growth in the economy. The administration's official forecast differed from the rest only in its degree of optimism. Forecasters in and out of government were oversanguine about growth largely because they failed to realize how serious the Federal Reserve was about reining in the money supply to control inflation. The Fed was not defying the administration, which was touting the efficacy of monetary stringency for controlling inflation, but hardly anyone seemed to remember that the way tight money controls inflation is by slowing economic activity. Moreover, as our Association's President-elect, Robert Eisner, has pointed out (1986, p. 146), the economics community, unfamiliar with a world of high inflation rates, overestimated the stimulative effect of the existing deficit. Added to this was the enthusiasm of the ideological proponents of smaller government, some of whom exaggerated the possible effects of lower tax rates on supply and some of whom simply hoped that deficits would pressure Congress to cut back domestic spending. The size of the deficits was also masked by the assumption of unspecified future spending cuts, an assumption reflecting the view that the U.S. government was operating a lot of wasteful programs with little public support which Congress could soon be persuaded to reduce or eliminate.

Both in administration and in Congress, decisions were made at a breakneck pace, in a highly charged political atmosphere, amid conflicting claims and competing forecasts, with little attention to the consistency of monetary and fiscal policy and mostly by people with little experience in evaluating the reasonableness of any set of economic estimates. (See David Stockman, 1986, ch. 3.) When the dust settled, we found ourselves with a serious recession that nobody expected, and an escalating structural budget deficit that nobody wanted. It was hardly economic policy's finest hour.

The agonizing—and so far only partially successful—struggle to correct the mistakes of 1981 have kept the economic policy process under stress and have continued to dramatize some of its weakest aspects. The struggle between the president and the Congress over deficit solutions illustrates the price we pay for the separation of powers. The fact that fiscal policy has become an exercise in damage control, while the Federal Reserve makes all the important decisions about the economy, underlines the separation of monetary and fiscal policy. The sensitivity of deficits to the pace of the economy advertises the unreliability of macroeconomic forecasts. The fact that all the actions that could be taken to correct the deficit are unpleasant ones drags out the annual agony of budget setting interminably and dramatizes how layered and cumbersome it has become.

Small wonder that the strains of the last few years, with a little help from the press, have reinforced the negative stereotypes that economists and political decision makers have of each other. Political decision makers see economists as quarrelsome folks who cannot forecast, cannot agree, cannot express themselves clearly, and have strong ideological biases. Economists return the favor by regarding politicians as short-sighted, interested only in what is popular with the electorate, and unwilling to face hard decisions. All of the stereotypes are partly right.

Politicians embody their stereotype in economist jokes. Economists have retaliated more massively by applying the tools of their trade to the political system itself. Public choice theory essentially asks the question: what would economic policy be like if our stereotype of politicians were entirely true? The answer provides considerable insight into observed political behavior and certainly helps explain why the idealistic economist so often fails to find the system simulating the public interest motivation of the philosopher queen.

## III. SOME DRASTIC NONSOLUTIONS

Widespread concern that the economic policy process is not working well has spawned proposals for drastic change that move in two quite different directions: one toward circumscribing the discretion of elected officials by putting economic policy on automatic pilot and the other toward making elected officials more directly responsible to the voters for their policies.

The automatic pilot approach flows from the perspective of public choice theory that the decisions of democratically elected officials interested in staying in office cannot be counted on to produce economic policy in the social interest, but are likely to be biased toward excessive government spending, growing deficits, special interest tax and spending programs, and easier money. A way to overcome these biases is to agree in advance on strict rules of economic policy, such as a fixed monetary growth path or constitutionally required balance in the federal budget.

Even if one accepts the premises, however, firm rules are hard to define in a rapidly changing world—no one seems to know what "money" is anymore—and can easily lead to perverse results. Recent experience with trying to reduce the federal deficit along the fixed path specified by the Gramm-Rudman-Hollings amendment, for example, has given us a taste of some of the possible disadvantages of a balanced budget rule. There is danger that specific dollar targets for the deficit will require procyclical fiscal policy, perhaps precipitating a recession that would then make budget balance even less attainable. Moreover, the effort to reach the targets can induce cosmetic or self-defeating measures, such as moving spending from one fiscal year to another for no valid reason, selling assets to reduce a current deficit while exacerbating future ones, and accomplishing desired purposes by regulatory or other non-budgetary means.

The Gramm-Rudman-Hollings experience, however, has suggested the usefulness of a different approach to deficit reduction than a balanced budget rule; namely, a deficit neutral amendment rule. If legislators advocating a tax preference are required to propose a rate increase to pay for it, special interest tax legislation may falter. Similarly, the requirement that a proposal for additional spending be accompanied by a simultaneous proposal to raise taxes or reduce another spending program may be an effective brake on deficits.

The other direction of reform reflects the contrasting view that the separation of powers and the diffusion of responsibility in our government make it too difficult for the electorate to enforce its will by holding officials responsible for their policies. The potential for deadlock would be reduced if the United States moved toward a parliamentary system, or found a way to hold political parties more strictly accountable for proposing or carrying out identifiable policies.

Casual examination of parliamentary democracies, such as the United Kingdom and Sweden, does not provide striking evidence of the superiority of parliamentary systems for making economic choices, even if one did not have two hundred years of tradition to contend with in changing our system. The more modest notion that our system would work more smoothly if political parties had better defined positions and disciplined their elected members more strictly may well be right, but seems to fly in the face of current history. Voters are showing less strong party affiliation and more inclination to choose for themselves among

candidates, while members of Congress tend increasingly to be pragmatists willing to work out nonideological compromises across party lines. These trends seem likely to be the irreversible consequences of greater education, sophistication, and exposure to public issues among voters and elected officials alike and to make a resurgence of party discipline and loyalty unrealistic.

## IV. MAKING THE ECONOMIC POLICY SYSTEM WORK BETTER

My own proposals involve less drastic changes in the structure of our government. They reflect a strong faith in the ability of informed citizens and their elected representatives to make policy decisions for the common good, even to make substantial sacrifices and take political risks to further what they perceive as the long-run national interest—once they understand what the choices are. I also believe that the separation of powers between the executive and legislative branches works pretty well most of the time. It provides needed protection against overzealousness in either branch, albeit at some risk of occasional stalemate.

The main problem, it seems to me, is that our economic policy system has gradually become so complex, diffused, and fragmented that it impedes rather than fosters informed choices on major issues. The fragmentation imposes two kinds of costs. First, it makes the decision process itself exceedingly inefficient. Decisions are made too often, in too great detail, and reviewed by too many layers of decision makers in the executive branch and in Congress. Too much time is absorbed in procedure and in wrangling over details, not enough on major decisions. It's time to simplify the process, to weed out some of the institutions, and to tip the balance between substance and process back toward substance.

Second, decisions are made separately that ought to be made together, or at least with attention to their impact on each other. The separation of monetary and fiscal policy is one example; the separation of tax and spending decisions is another. Congress has made a good deal of progress in recent years in putting spending decisions together with their revenue or deficit consequences, but more could be done. I have seven steps to suggest that might make the economic policy process work more effectively.

*First, seek out decisions that should be made less frequently and arrange to do so.* This would economize decision-making time and enhance the chances of thoughtful, well-informed decisions. It would free up time and energy for managing the government enterprise more effectively, with a longer planning horizon. It would also reduce the inefficiency and sense of unfairness that goes with frequent changes of the rules. Making the federal budget every other year would be a major advance. Major revisions of the tax code should occur even less frequently. Big ticket acquisitions, such as major weapons systems, should be reviewed thoroughly at infrequent intervals and then put on a steady efficient track, not constantly revisited.

With a two-year budget, there would occasionally be major events, such as a sudden escalation of international tension or a sharp unexpected shift in the economic outlook, that would justify reopening the budget in midstream, but the temptation to tinker frequently should be strongly resisted. The argument that economists cannot forecast accurately two years in advance, while quite true, does not undermine the case for a multiyear budget. It simply reinforces the point that discretionary fiscal policy is hazardous and ought to be viewed with great skepticism whether the budget is annual or biennial.

*Second, seek out decisions that need not be made at all and stop making them.* Some spending programs could be consolidated into block grants or devolved to the states, not necessarily in the interest of smaller govern-

ment, but in the interest of greater responsiveness to local needs and a less cluttered federal decision schedule. In other cases, the responsibility is clearly federal—as in defense—but Congress would be doing its job more effectively if it concentrated on major policy issues rather than on details of program management.

*Third, in the executive branch, consolidate authority for tax, budget, and fiscal policy in a single cabinet department.* The department could retain the name Treasury, but might better be called the Department of Economic Affairs. The Secretary of Economic Affairs should have a high level chief economist or economic council with a strong professional staff. The chief economist should work closely with the budget director who also should report to the Secretary. The purpose would be to bring together economic decisions now made in OMB, CEA, and Treasury under one high-level responsible person, to relieve the president of the duty of adjudicating among so many potentially warring power centers, and to increase the chances of building a highly professional permanent economic staff one step removed from the short-run political concerns of the White House.

*Fourth, streamline the congressional committee structure to reduce the number of steps in the budget process.* The authorizing and appropriating functions should be combined in a single set of "program committees," one for each major area of public spending. This would imply a single defense committee, for example, and a social insurance committee. The tax committees should handle the revenue side—not additional spending programs as at present. The budget committees would be charged with considering fiscal policy and putting the spending and revenue sides together into a budget to be passed by the whole congress. The Joint Economic Committee should celebrate the important contributions it made to economic understanding in the days before the budget process and then close up shop.

*Fifth, bring monetary and fiscal policy into the same conversation.* This end could be furthered by closer formal links between the central bank and the Department of Economic Affairs to dramatize the need for consultation and interaction. The Federal Reserve chairman should make a report to the budget committees of Congress laying out recommended short- and longer-run economic goals for the nation and discussing combinations of monetary and fiscal strategies to achieve them. The Fed's report should be an important input to congressional deliberations on fiscal policy.

*Sixth, strive for a government-wide official economic forecast to be updated on a regular schedule.* The main purpose of the common forecast would be to reduce the confusion generated by conflicting estimates, but the increased interaction between the Department of Economic Affairs, the Congressional Budget Office, and the Federal Reserve necessary to create such a forecast would increase mutual understanding of what is happening to the economy and what the goals of policy should be. Occasionally, it might be necessary for one of the agencies to dissent and explain why it disagreed with the forecast, but these occasions are likely to be infrequent. There should also be more attention than at present to the consequences for policy of the forecast being wrong.

*Finally, bring choices explicitly into the decision process, both in executive branch deliberations and, especially, in Congress.* Those proposing spending increases or tax reductions should routinely be required to specify what is to be given up and to offer both the benefit and its cost as a package. In other words, proposals should be deficit neutral.

## V. WHAT ECONOMISTS CAN DO

For their part, how can economists be more useful in the policy process? The press and politicians often sound as if they are telling us to work harder: go back to your computers and don't come out until you know how the economy really works and can give us reliable forecasts. But economists know that the economic system is incredibly complicated, and that increasing global interdependence and rapidly changing technologies and public attitudes are not making it easier to understand. It is not likely in our lifetimes that anyone will happen on a paradigm that explains everything, or even that forecasting will become appreciably more accurate. Like the medical profession, which also deals with an incredibly complex system, we economists just have to keep applying our imperfect knowledge as carefully as possible and learning from the results. Both doctors and economists need humility, but neither should abandon their patients to the quacks.

The objective of economists ought to be to raise the level of debate on economic policy, to make clear what they know and do not know, and to increase the chances of policy decisions that make the economy work better. Much of the time that means telling the public and politicians what they would rather not hear: hard choices must be made. We are stuck with being the dismal science.

Increased effort in three directions would make economics more useful in the policy process. *First, economists should put much more emphasis on their areas of agreement.* The press admittedly makes this difficult. Agreement is not news, and the press' stereotype of economists' diversity of views is so entrenched that they will go to great lengths to scare up a lonely dissenter to an almost universally held economic platitude and give her equal time.

Economists realize that the breakthrough insights around which "schools" are built are at best partial visions of the truth, but our training leads us to elaborate and differentiate these insights, to explain to ourselves and to others where they lead in different directions, not where they come together. Yet areas of agreement are wide—even in macroeconomics—

and a major effort to make this clearer to ourselves and our audience would be useful.

*Second, economists should devote more serious attention to increasing the basic economic literacy of the public, the media, and the political community.* While the print media seem to me increasingly knowledgeable and sophisticated about economic issues, television, where most people get most of their information, lags far behind. Television coverage of the economy is heavily weighted to isolated economic statistics reported without context—the wholesale price index increased two-tenths of a percent in October—and talking heads disagreeing, briefly, for some obscure reason. Some of the best newscasters appear to have bad cases of economics phobia.

Media bashing is not the answer. The profession needs to take the lead in explaining more clearly what is happening to the economy, why it matters, and what the arguments are about or ought to be about. This means more than each of us taking a little time to make a luncheon speech, write an op ed piece, or appear on a talk show. It means sustained efforts on the part of teams of economists to figure out how to present economic ideas more interestingly and understandably, developing new graphics and other teaching tools and getting feedback from real audiences. The technology is available and the audiences exist— the number of people who will watch long hard-to-follow congressional debates and hearings on cable television is quite astonishing. We just need to devote the kind of effort and ingenuity that goes into explaining to audiences the complex, fast-moving, jargon-ridden game of football to our complex, fast-moving, jargon-ridden game of economics.

*Third, economists need to be more careful to sort out, for ourselves and others, what we really know from our ideological biases.* George Stigler pointed out in his presidential address (1965) that economists beginning with Adam Smith have not hesitated to make strong assertions, both positive and

negative, about the effectiveness of government intervention without offering serious evidence to support their claims. For two hundred years, "the chief instrument of empirical demonstration on the economic competence of the state has been the telling anecdote" (pp. 11-12). In the more than two decades since Stigler presided over our Association, an enormous amount of useful empirical work has been done, as he predicted it would be, on the effectiveness of government programs, the costs and benefits of regulation, and so forth. Still the arguments among economists about the merits of larger vs. smaller government too often revolve around anecdotes or, worse, misleading statistics quoted out of context. My own anecdotal evidence would lead me to believe that liberals and conservatives are about equally guilty.

My concern is not with economists taking sides on policy issues or acting as advocates of particular positions. Indeed, I think many policy debates would be clarified if there were more formal and informal opportunities for economists to marshall the evidence on each side and to examine and cross-examine each other in front of some counter-part of judge or jury.

We economists tend to be uncomfortable in the role of partisans or advocates, preferring to be seen as neutral experts whether we are or not. Lawyers move more easily among roles; and the best are able to serve with distinction at different times as prosecutors, defenders, experts, and judges. The system works well when the roles are played competently and the rules of evidence strictly observed. Economists might increase their usefulness to the policy process if they made clear at any given moment which role they were playing. More important, we need to work hard to raise the standards of evidence, to make clear to the public and the participants in the political process what we are reasonably sure we know and how we know it, and where we are guessing or expressing our preferences.

# References

Eisner, Robert, *How Real is the Federal Deficit*, New York: Free Press, 1986.

Heclo, Hugh, "OMB and the President—the Problem of 'Neutral Competence'," *The Public Interest*, 1975, *10*, 80–89.

Heller, Walter W., "What's Right With Economics," *American Economic Review*, March 1975, *65*, 1–26.

Mueller, Dennis C., *Public Choice*, Cambridge: Cambridge University Press, 1979.

Okun, Arthur M., "The Economist and Presidential Leadership," in *Economics for Policy Making*, Joseph A. Pechman, ed., Cambridge: MIT Press 1983, 577–82.

Porter, Robert B., "Economic Advice to the President: From Eisenhower to Reagan," *Political Science Quarterly*, Fall 1983, *98*, 403–06.

_____, "Organizing Economic Advice to the President: A Modest Proposal," *American Economic Review Proceedings*, May 1982, *72*, 356-60.

Schultz, George, "Reflections on Political Economy," *Challenge*, March/April 1974, *17*, 6-11.

Schultze, Charles L., "The Role and Responsibilities of the Economist in Government," *American Economic Review Proceedings*, May 1982, *72*, 62-66.

Stigler, George J., "The Economist and the State," *American Economic Review*, March 1965, *55*, 1-18.

Stockman, David A., *The Triumph of Politics*, New York: Harper and Row, 1986.

Tufte, Edward R., *Political Control of the Economy*, Princeton: Princeton University Press, 1978.

# QUESTIONS

1. Rivlin argues that the system of checks and balances has led to a fragmented structure of economic policymaking. What is her proposed solution?

2. What does Rivlin mean by a "deficit neutral amendment" rule? What is the advantage of such a rule? Can you see any likely shortcomings of this approach? (Hint: How accurate are revenue projections in general?)

3. Rivlin claims that economists need to reach the public and improve general economic literacy. Can you think of a way to use the media to get people better informed?

*What considerations affect a legislator's voting behavior?*

Rivlin remarks that economists often model politicians according to a narrow stereotype of people whose overriding concern is to win elections. Whether or not the characterization is useful hinges on its success in explaining and predicting behavior. This article shows how a model of legislators' voting behavior can be constructed and then tested empirically.

# INFLUENCES ON LEGISLATOR VOTING:

## Theory and an Example

*Stephen V. Marks**

Economists often consider expenditure, tax, and regulatory policies in a idealized economic environment that does not reflect any of the complexities of the world of politics. In the real world, however, the policy formation process can hardly ever be easily separated from politics. Legislation that appears detrimental to economic efficiency or equity often gets passed by the Congress. Why do members of the Congress vote the way they do?

This article examines the determinants of how members of Congress vote on legislation that directly affects the economic status of interest groups and of the nation as a whole. This is just one aspect of political economy in a representative democracy. The analysis will help us to understand how the public choice approach analyzes political markets and how economic concepts can be fruitfully applied to the political arena. We look at a specific vote in the U.S. Congress—the 1982 vote on the domestic content requirements that would have sharply curtailed importation of auto-

*Assistant Professor of Economics, Pomona College.

mobile components to the United States. In many important ways, this vote is typical of many tax, expenditure, or regulatory bills that the Congress votes upon that provide benefits to special interests but affect the entire nation.

The article then lays out the approach economists use to analyze legislator behavior. It considers the problem of how voters can control the actions of their representatives in legislatures and examines some of the imperfections in the political market that weaken this control. The next section identifies some of the common elements in policies like import protection or farm program expenditures that benefit relatively narrow special interests at the expense of the nation overall. The section following applies this framework to the crisis of the U.S. automobile industry in the early 1980s. The article then focuses on the domestic content vote of 1982. We see how patterns of voting by members of the Congress can be explained empirically in terms of the interests of their constituencies and of their own ideological views. The last section offers some general remarks on the strengths and weaknesses of the public choice approach to explaining legislator behavior.

## CAN VOTERS CONTROL POLITICIANS?

We have representation in legislatures because it is too costly to hold public referendums on the vast number of policy issues that must be considered in our society. To get everyone in society together to vote on all these issues would be impractical; many people would opt out of the process. As a substitute, we periodically elect representatives whom we empower to vote on our behalf.

The primary responsibility for legislators is to further the interests of their constituents—both their economic or "pocketbook" interests and their ideological views on public policy issues. A legislator who fails to uphold this responsibility can be voted out of office. It is

thus not a surprise to see the strongest advocates for tobacco price supports among congressional delegations from the South and for grain subsidies among those from the Midwest.

On the other hand, members of Congress inevitably vote all the time in ways that would be opposed by at least some of their constituents. One reason for this is of course that their constituents are not all identical, but have differing interests. Moreover, most voters are not "single-issue" voters, but rather consider many dimensions of the performance of their representatives. Members of Congress make political calculations about the consequences of adopting one position versus another. It is reasonable to suppose that they try to vote generally so as to attract a winning coalition of voters.

However, sometimes legislators may even vote in a way that would be opposed by a majority of their constituents. How can we explain this? One possibility is that there is an "investment" motive for such behavior: It may provide some alternative long-run benefit to the legislator. Voting in a way that favors some group or individual may yield campaign contributions. This may produce greater electoral support in the future, even if it initially costs some votes. Similarly, legislators may engage in "logrolling" (vote trading) within Congress in order to get voter support in the long run, even if it leads to outcomes that are harmful to their constituents in the short run. A representative from North Carolina may agree to vote for sugar price supports, if representatives from Hawaii agree to support tobacco subsidies in return. Even though North Carolina is made worse off by higher sugar prices, it gains even more from higher tobacco prices.

Legislators also have a "consumption" motive to vote in ways that further their own ideologies, even if this hurts a majority of their constituents. How do legislators resolve this conflict between their ideological preferences and the need to get reelected? The economic approach is to consider the costs of voting ideologically. If voters were perfectly well-informed, and could vote their representative out of office at any time, these costs would be very high. In effect, voters would have perfect control over their representatives. However, for a variety of reasons the operation of the political market is far from perfect.[1]

First, the periodic elections in which voters decide the fate of their representatives are held infrequently. This means that voters must make their decisions on the basis of bundles of congressional votes by the incumbent, not on any single vote: There are "indivisibilities" in the political market. Constituents can only decide whether to "throw the rascal out" based on whole bundles of issues; on specific votes representatives may have some slack. Second, voters may have short memories, and legislators may thus have more slack early in their terms than closer to their reelection bids. (Of course, opposition candidates and journalists try very hard to remind voters of any potential problems in the voting record of an incumbent!)

Third, it is costly for voters to obtain information on how their representatives have voted on specific issues. It may be individually rational for voters *not* to be informed—given the costs and benefits of gathering information—even if the collective outcome is far from ideal. There is also a free-rider problem in gathering candidate information. Once this information has been collected, it becomes a public good: The information can be provided to other voters at low cost, and it is actually hard to keep anybody from getting hold of it. Thus, each voter may wait for somebody else to gather electoral information, and it may simply end up not being provided at all.

Fourth, incumbents have many electoral advantages over their challengers. They have access to free mailing and can appear on television for free in the course of their jobs. Incumbents also find it easier to obtain campaign contributions from individuals and polit-ical action committees (PACs) because, by virtue of being in office, they have the clout to provide favors or even to wield threats. Perhaps the most important benefit enjoyed by incumbents is brandname recognition. By being in office and in the headlines, incumbents may be able to establish a reputation for reliable voting and for soundness of character.

There is a final problem of electoral control. Politicians spend only finite lengths of time in office, and as they get closer to the end of their intended careers, they tend to have less to lose by not acting in ways that enhance their chances of reelection. However, a subtle remedy is provided by legislative seniority systems. As legislators serve more and more years in office, they enjoy more and more of the privileges and power that accrue to more senior members of the legislature. Apart from the personal and political benefits this provides, senior members who chair important committees often get invited to earn outside income by speaking to various groups. Thus, as the time remaining in their political careers diminishes, their opportunity cost of being thrown out of office will not shrink as much as it would otherwise.

## SPECIAL INTEREST POLITICS

Many of the policies that Congress considers and passes provide benefits to relatively specific groups and impose costs on just about everybody else. Some of this is a result of logrolling in the Congress. There is an even more fundamental economic origin of the problem, however. For the sake of economic efficiency, we tend to specialize in production; but to enjoy the full range of goods available, we tend to diversify our consumption. Thus, workers in an munitions factory have a lot more at stake with respect to federal defense expenditure policies than with respect to federal farm programs. Their whole livelihood may depend on defense contracts, but only a small part of their food budget depends on the price of milk. This simple reality colors much of the policy formation process.[2]

Since workers and firms in an industry have more at stake than do buyers of that good, they derive greater marginal benefits from gathering political information and from lobbying the legislature on their behalf. Producers also tend to be more concentrated (geographically as well as economically) and better organized than consumers, so that their marginal costs of gathering and spreading political information are lower than for consumers. Well-organized producers are better able to overcome the free-rider problem in information gathering and in lobbying the legislature, by arranging to share the costs of these activities among themselves. In some cases, other groups may strongly oppose special-interest legislation that is harmful to them, and that is also detrimental to society overall, but this is the exception rather than the rule.

From the point of view of members of the Congress, there may thus be much more to be gained by supporting a special interest than by supporting some perception of the more general public interest. This creates a bias toward supporting bills that benefit the few at the expense of the many, even if the total cost far exceeds the total benefit provided. The few who benefit will know who in Congress supported them and will benefit greatly on a per capita basis; the many who bear the costs will tend to be less aware of the role played by their representatives and will not be hurt too much on a per capita basis. Since elections are decided over bundles of issues, not on this single issue, legislators who vote in favor of special interests tend to gain more electoral support than they lose.

## THE AUTOMOBILE DOMESTIC CONTENT BILL OF 1982

The crisis of the U.S. automobile industry in the early 1980s provides an acute example of how interest groups threatened by economic change can bring political pressure to bear

on the government. The industry actually enjoyed its peak sales year in 1978.[3] Perhaps this made its downturn over the next several years even more dramatic. One cause of the downturn was intensified foreign competition. In response to the second round of OPEC oil price increases in 1979-1980, the American public shifted its preferences in favor of smaller cars. U.S. auto producers were slow to react to this change, however, while Japanese producers moved aggressively to meet the new demand. Moreover, labor costs in the U.S. auto industry were much higher than in Japan, due to both its higher wages and lower productivity levels. Finally, in an effort to bring down inflation in the early 1980s, the Federal Reserve Board slowed the rate of monetary growth. Interest rates shot upward, the country lapsed into a long and deep recession, and the demand for automobiles and other consumer durables plummeted. As a consequence of these various factors, employment in the U.S. automobile industry fell sharply between 1978 and the end of 1982. Table 1 shows that several hundred thousand jobs were lost.

These economic dislocations caused the automobile companies and the United Auto Workers (UAW) to bring fierce political pressure on the government to limit foreign imports and to provide regulatory relief. One of the responses of the Reagan administration was to initiate a voluntary automobile export restraint agreement with Japan in April 1981. These restraints initially cut Japanese automobile exports to the United States from 1.82 million to 1.68 million cars per year, at a heavy cost to U.S. car buyers: Crandall (1984) estimates that this arrangement cost U.S. consumers about $160,000 per U.S. job saved per year.

Table 1: **Total Employment, Motor Vehicles and Equipment (thousands of workers).**

| 1960 | 1970 | 1978 | 1980 | November 1982 |
|------|------|------|------|---------------|
| 724.1 | 799.0 | 1004.9 | 788.8 | 648.7 |

Source: United Auto Workers

The UAW continued to experience severe job losses, however. Part of the problem was that the export restraint agreement was not leakproof: Although it did limit the number of cars allowed into the United States, it did not limit the importation of components for cars assembled in this country. As U.S. auto producers turned increasingly to foreign sources for components, there was renewed pressure from U.S. labor for further protection.

Sympathetic members of the Congress responded, and the domestic content bill was introduced in the House of Representatives in early 1982. The bill would have required companies selling more than 100,000 cars or light trucks in the United States per year to incur a specified percentage of their labor and parts costs in this country. The greater the quantity sold, the higher would be this domestic content requirement. At their 1982 sales rates, Toyota and Nissan would have had to incur about 75 percent of their labor and parts costs in the United States, Mazda and Honda between 20 and 40 percent of their costs. A maximum domestic content requirement of 90 percent would have gone into effect after 1984.[4]

The clear winners from the bill would have been workers in the U.S. motor vehicles and parts industries, whose jobs would have been protected.[5] The UAW claimed that the bill would save more than 800,000 U.S. jobs. Many of the industrial unions of the AFL-CIO involved directly or indirectly in producing glass, plastics, rubber, steel, and other automobile components also backed the bill.

The constellation of interests opposed to the bill was much more diffuse; it included farmers, manufactured good exporters, consumers, auto dealers, and longshoremen. Farmers and other exporters opposed domestic content primarily because of the threat of foreign retaliation. Many were also well aware that any measure that limited imports to the United States would tend to drive up the value of the dollar, making U.S. exports less competitive in the long run. U.S. consumers had experienced higher automobile prices due to the voluntary export restraint agreement with Japan, and domestic content would have driven automobile prices even higher. Auto dealers viewed higher costs of passenger cars and pickup trucks in effect as a tax. As intermediaries between auto producers and consumers, they would bear at least part of the burden of that tax. Finally, the longshoremen stood to lose jobs to the extent that U.S. imports and exports were reduced.

Representatives of all of these opposition groups made statements against the bill to House committees.[6] However, their overall lobbying effort in opposition to the bill fell far short of the effort made in favor of it by the UAW and the AFL-CIO. Given that these unions had a much more direct stake in the bill and were inherently better organized, this outcome is predicted by our theory of special-interest politics.

## EMPIRICAL ANALYSIS OF THE DOMESTIC CONTENT VOTE

How did members of the House weigh the interests of those in favor of the domestic content bill versus those opposed to it? This section provides an answer by examining the votes of 411 members of the House on the proposed legislation. It will also examine the role of ideology in the representatives' voting and will control for the effects of political parties and campaign contributions.

Analysis of the determinants of the pattern of votes on the bill in the House presents a special problem. The dependent variable is qualitative rather than quantitative: It takes the values *yes* or *no*. To represent these alternatives numerically, we use a "dummy variable" that equals 1 for a yes vote and 0 for a no vote. The predicted value of this dependent variable for each member of the House can then be interpreted as the predicted probability that the member would vote yes. However, it is not appropriate in this case to use multiple linear regression: We could easily get a predicted value less than zero or greater than one, even though by definition probabilities can never lie outside this range.

This problem is shown in figure 1 for the simplest case in which there is a single explanatory variable. The dependent variable $Y$, shown along the vertical axis, takes on the values 0 and 1. Suppose that it is positively related to the explanatory variable $X$, shown along the horizontal axis, and that we get a scattering of observations of the two variables as shown.

In linear regression analysis, we would view the vote $Y_i$ of the $i$th member of the House as a linear function of the observation $X_i$ of the explanatory variable for that member, and would estimate a line like the one shown in Figure 1. For each member of the House, the predicted value $Y_i$ is found along this line at the relevant value of $X_i$. Specifically, we could write

$$Y_i = a + bX_i$$

where $a$ is the estimated intercept and $b$ is the estimated slope of the line. Some the these $Y_i$, for very high or very low values, could be outside of the $(0,1)$ interval.

We thus need a way to force our predicted probabilities to be between 0 and 1. To do this, we use a special technique known as probit estimation, in which we fit a curve rather than a straight line to the scattering of points. Our predicted value $Y_i$ is now a nonlinear function

$F()$ of $a + bX_i$,

$$Y_i = F(a + bX_i)$$

We use an $F()$ function that is bounded below by 0 and above by 1 and that increases as a function of $a + bX_i$ as shown in figure 2. This assures that the predicted probabilities found along the curve are always between 0 and 1.[7]

Our analysis of the House vote includes ten explanatory variables, rather than one, but is otherwise identical to the above. For our purposes, there will be three useful statistics. First, the sign of an *estimated coefficient* (like $b$ above) shows whether the corresponding explanatory variable has a positive or negative effect on the predicted probability that a legislator would vote for the bill. Second, if the *t-statistic* corresponding to this coefficient is large in absolute value, then this explanatory variable can be said to have a statistically significant effect on the probability of a yes vote.[8] Third, we can determine the number of votes that our estimated model predicts correctly as a rough indicator of how well it explains the pattern of votes. We will suppose that the model predicts a *yes* vote if the predicted probability of a *yes* vote exceeds the predicted probability of a *no* vote. We can then compare these predictions to the actual pattern of votes to see how well the model does. (Flipping a coin would give the correct prediction 50 percent of the time on average, so our model had better do considerably better than that!)

Figure 1

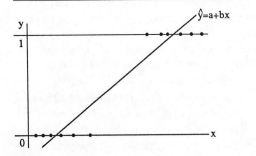

Figure 2

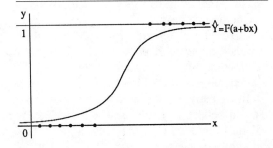

To represent the interests of workers who would directly benefit from domestic content, we include measures of *auto employment* and *steel employment* in each district as a percentage of total district employment. We expect the signs of the coefficients of both of these variables to be positive. In addition, since domestic content was being pushed as a jobs bill, we include the *unemployment rate* in each state as an explanatory variable. We expect the sign of its coefficient to also be positive. To reflect more fully the extent of labor influence, we include the percentage of employees in the state who are labor *union* members. This reflects variations in labor populations across states, but also indicates the degree of union organization per se. We expect the sign of the coefficient of *union membership* to be positive.

We will consider explicitly three opposition interests — manufactured good exporters, farmers, and consumers. The variable *export employment* is the percentage of the state civilian labor force directly involved in production of manufactures for export, while *farm employment* is the percentage of the district labor force employed in agriculture. The more important export industries are to a state or district, the lower should be the probability that their legislators vote for the bill, all else equal. We represent consumer interests in the vote through the number of *automobile registrations* per 1000 residents of the state. We expect the coefficient of this variable to be negative: The more important automobiles are to the consumers in a state, the lower should be the probability that its representatives vote for domestic content.

To control for political party affiliation, we include the *political party* of each member. This is a dummy variable, equal to 1 for Democrats and 0 for Republicans. The role of political party in legislative voting is complex: It can reflect the general ideological views of the member but can represent the effects of the party as coalition as well. Given the

common perception that Democrats have been more supportive than Republicans of import protection in recent years, we expect the sign of its coefficient to be positive. To examine the role of money in the legislative process, we include *labor contributions* (as a percentage of campaign contributions by all political action committees) to each member. Since the bill was strongly backed by labor organizations, we expect the sign of its coefficient to be positive.

Finally, we will look at two different measures of legislator *ideology*. Both measure the "liberalness" of legislators' past voting records on a scale of 0 to 100. These measures of "ideology" are not perfect, since legislators' past voting depends not just on their own ideological views, but also on their constituents' interests. However, these measures are the best we can use. The first is the rating by the Americans for Democratic Action (*ADA*), which considers a broad range of social, economic, foreign policy, and defense issues. Results using the *ADA* ratings for 1981 appear in the first column of table 2. As an alternative, we use the ratings compiled by the political magazine *National Journal* on votes on economic issues (*NJE*), which was determined in 1981 mostly by votes on general federal expenditure and tax policies. Results using the *NJE* rating for 1981 appear in the second column of table 2. To the extent that "liberal" legislators are perceived as being more sympathetic to import protection, we expect the sign of both of the ideology coefficients to be positive.

The results shown in table 2 confirm all of our expectations. Auto and steel employment in the district have significant, positive effects on the probability of a *yes* vote, as do *union membership* and *labor contributions*. The signs of *export employment, farm employment,* and *auto registrations* are all as expected, but only the effect of *export employment* is significantly different from zero. In neither column do we see that the state *unemployment*

Table 2: **Determinants of Domestic Content Voting: Coefficients and T-Statistics**

| Independent Variables | 1 (ADA) | 2 (NJE) |
|---|---|---|
| Constant | −1.99934 (−1.93412) | −2.42448 (−2.29640) |
| Auto employment | 0.11586 (2.87087) | 0.10849 (2.67809) |
| Steel Employment | 0.06973 (2.30218) | 0.07720 (2.38260) |
| Unemployment rate | 0.05379 (1.19032) | 0.06639 (1.46210) |
| Union membership | 0.03849 (2.52047) | 0.03425 (2.24785) |
| Export employment | −0.36587 (−2.12941) | −.037732 (−2.16903) |
| Farm employment | −0.02135 (−1.01462) | −0.01387 (−0.64373) |
| Auto registrations | −0.00024 (−0.13939) | −0.00015 (−0.08631) |
| Labor contributions | 0.01580 (3.04442) | 0.01311 (2.67390) |
| Political party | 0.95369 (4.05680) | 0.33518 (1.13313) |
| Measured ideology | 0.00688 (1.62029) | 0.02154 (3.83204) |
| Number of observations | 411 | 411 |
| Percent correctly predicted | 81 | 82 |

rate has a significant effect, though the coefficient is positive in each.

Our results on *political party* and *measured ideology* are dramatically different in the two columns, even though the correlation between *ADA* and *NJE* is a respectable 0.8558 for this sample. Use of *NJE* seems to suggest that ideology is of considerable significance, while use of *ADA* does not. Our conclusions on the role of political party affiliation also differ in the two cases. Use of *ADA* suggests that Democrats were significantly more likely to vote for the bill than Republicans, all else equal, while use of *NJE* does not show a significant role for political party. Overall, we see that use of *NJE* rather than *ADA* allows us to get slightly better predictions of the pattern of votes in the House: 81 percent of our predictions are correct using *ADA,* while 82 percent are correct using *NJE.*

This last set of results probably arises because *NJE* measures the economic views of the members of Congress with greater precision than does *ADA.* Both of these measures of ideology are highly correlated with political party affiliation, as well as with labor contributions.

Thus, using *NJE* appears to pick up an effect that would otherwise be attributed to political party per se. An important conclusion is that "ideology" is inherently difficult to measure. Both of our measures are correlated with political party and are at least in part functions of measured and unmeasured voter interests or special interest influences.

## CONCLUSIONS

Public choice theory provides a framework for analysis of government policy and the political process in terms of the rational actor model employed in economics. The general implications of the public choice approach seem to be well borne out for the case of the domestic content vote of 1982 in the House. We see that concentrated interest groups with a great deal at stake had significant influences on their legislators, while more diffuse interest groups were less influential. On the other hand, it appears as well that the legislators' own ideological predispositions do play some role in determining how they will vote on specific issues.

clear, since the bill would have restricted imports of foreign parts and finished products. However, there is also a subsidy to domestic automobile producers for their use of the protected domestic inputs: As a firm uses more of the domestic inputs, it is entitled to use additional units of the cheaper foreign labor and parts.

6. For details, see the U.S. House of Representatives (1982a) and (1982b).

7. $F( )$ is the cumulative standard normal probability distribution. A standard normal random variable $Z$ has a bell-shaped probability distribution, with a mean of zero and variance of one. $F(z)$ is defined over $Z$ values from negative infinity to positive infinity, and $F(a + bX_i)$ is calculated as the area under this bell-shaped curve up to the $Z$ value $a + bX_i$. To obtain the parameter estimates $a$ and $b$, we perform maximum likelihood estimation. For details, see Pindyck and Rubinfeld (1981), chapter 10.

8. Specifically, if the absolute value of the t-statistic is greater than 1.96, we are 95 percent confident that the explanatory variable does affect the probability. If it is greater than 2.575, we are 99 percent confident.

## Notes

1. Kalt and Zupan (1984) survey these reasons and provide references to the relevant public choice literature.

2. Downs (1957), Olson (1965), and Stigler (1971) have all examined the implications of this fundamental asymmetry in the policy formation process.

3. National Research Council, *The Competitive Status of the U.S. Auto Industry,* National Academy Press, Washington, DC, 1982.

4. *Congressional Quarterly Weekly Report,* September 11, 1982 and December 18, 1982.

5. Grossman (1981) shows analytically that a domestic content policy of this sort is equivalent to a combination of more familiar policies: tariff protection for the producers of intermediate goods used by the industry, plus an effective subsidy to the producer of the final good. The tariff aspect is fairly

## References

Crandall, Robert, "Import Quotas and the Automobile Industry: The Costs of Protectionism," *The Brookings Review* 2, Summer 1984, 8–16.

Downs, Anthony, *An Economic Theory of Democracy*, New York: Harper and Row, 1957.

Grossman, Gene M., [1981], "The Theory of Domestic Content Protection and Content Preference," *Quarterly Journal of Economics* 96, 1981, 583–603.

Kalt, Joseph P. and Mark A. Zupan, "Capture and Ideology in the Economic Theory of Politics," *American Economic Review* 74, 1984, 279–300.

Marks, Stephen V. and John McArthur, "Constituent Interest vs. Legislator Ideology: The Role of Political Opportunity Cost," 1987, working paper, Claremont Graduate School.

Olson, Mancur, *The Logic of Collective Action*, Cambridge: Harvard University Press, 1965.

Pindyck, Robert S. and Daniel Rubinfeld, (1981), *Econometric Models and Economic Forecasts*, second edition.

Stigler, George J., [1971], "The Theory of Economic Regulation," *Bell Journal of Economics and Management Science* 2, 1971, 3–21.

U.S. House of Representatives, *Fair Practices in Automotive Products Act*. Hearings before the Subcommittee on Trade of the Commit-tee on Ways and Means, House of Representatives, Ninety-Seventh Congress, Second Session, U.S. Government Printing Office, Washington, D.C., 1982a.

U.S. House of Representatives, *Fair Practices in Automotive Products Act*. Hearing before the Subcommittee on Commerce, Transportation, and Tourism of the Committee on Energy and Commerce, House of Representatives, Ninety-Seventh Congress, Second Session, U.S. Government Printing Office, Washington, D.C., 1982b.

## QUESTIONS

1. Using the public choice model of legislator behavior, do you predict that a legislator would vote more consistently in accord with constituents' preferences soon after being elected or after many years in Congress? Would Senators be more sensitive to their constituents' interests one year into their term or one year before their next reelection bid?

2. Of the two ideology measures used in this article, *NJE* focuses on voting records on economic issues, while *ADA* is based on social, defense, and economic issues. Describe a common or plausible set of political beliefs that might lead someone to be classified as "liberal" in some of these issue areas and "conservative" in others.

3. Which variables did not provide statistically significant explanatory power in the legislator voting estimation? In each case, do you think this is because the hypothesized effect is small, because the variable used is not a good proxy for the theoretical measure, or for some other identifiable reason?

# Further Issues and Questions in Public Choice

***Differential representation between the Senate and the House of Representatives.***

In 1987, Congress voted to allow states to raise the speed limit to 65 mph on rural stretches of interstate highways. The Senate had for some time favored the higher limit; when the measure finally passed in the House, the margin was only 217 to 206. Debate over the limit focused on the trade-off between time saved and traffic fatalities.

A. In large, sparsely populated western states, the potential time savings from a higher speed limit are high, and the contribution traffic congestion adds to mortality rates is low. Use this to explain why the measure might pass in the Senate and fail in the House.

B. Can you think of another issue likely to be much more popular in one of the houses of Congress than in the other?

### Lobbying on Capitol Hill

According to a report in the *New York Times* ("Foes of Acid-Rain Bill Led '86 Lobbyist Spending," June 1, 1987), over $60 million dollars was spent to lobby Congress in 1986. This represents a 25 percent increase over 1985 spending, perhaps due in part to the 1986 tax reform. Spending in 1985 was 16 percent higher than in the election year 1984.

The biggest spender was a coalition of electricity and coal companies opposing stricter control of emissions associated with acid rain. The bill they opposed in the House died in committee, and no acid-rain bill came up for a committee vote in the Senate. One other organization spent over $3 million; it lobbied on behalf of Social Security and Medicare and is credited with flooding Congress with eight million pieces of correspondence from its supporters.

A. Public choice theory suggests that lobbyists will be most successful if the costs of their causes are diffused across large segments of the population. Do the opponents of acid rain and supporters of programs for the elderly fit this description?
B. A group called Handgun Control Inc. spent over a million dollars promoting gun control. Do you think there was organized lobbying opposing them?
C. Interest groups sometimes counteract each other. Beer distributors in California have recently lobbied the California State Legislature to establish local beer distribution monopolies. The *Los Angeles Times,* June 11, 1987, reported that beer distributors made over $420,000 in campaign contributions to state legislators in the prior two years, primarily to keep the beer bill moving through the legislature, but that large retail chain stores had donated $360,000 in an effort to defeat the measure. What other political issues do you suspect are heavily lobbied on more than one side? Who would the contributors be?

# PART III

# The Distribution of Income and Programs for Income Redistribution

**Issue:** *Economic forces and the income distribution.*

*"A Surge in Inequality"* Lester C. Thurow

**Issue:** *Do welfare families migrate to high-welfare states?*

*"Welfare Payment Levels and the Migration of Female-Headed Families"* Rebecca M. Blank

**Issues:** *Workfare.*

*"Work for Welfare: How Much Good Will It Do?"* Frank S. Levy and Richard C. Michel

*Further Issues and Questions*

> **Issue:** *Workfare as preparation for the job market.*
>
> *"State Study Finds 57 percent on Welfare Lack Basic Skills"* Richard C. Paddock
>
> **Issue:** *Experimental projects for Medicaid.*
>
> *"After Five Years, Experimental Health Project for Medicaid Recipients Shows Mixed Results"* Clare Ansberry

### Economic forces and the income distribution.

Within the twentieth century, Americans have grown to view housing as substandard if it lacks indoor plumbing. This and many other changes in our conception of adequate living conditions reflect an increase in the average American's standard of living. Our view of poverty is partly in absolute terms and partly relative. Programs to fight hunger or to shelter the homeless address well-defined absolute standards. But much of our antipoverty effort is guided by relative concepts; we try not only to avoid destitution but also to achieve "decency," a very relative goal. Debates over whether to count catsup as a vegetable to meet school lunch nutrition goals, or whether skid- row single room occupancy hotels provide an adequate form of long-run housing, are signals that acceptable levels of poverty depend on general standards of living.

Such arguments lead us to be interested in at least part of the income distribution. Answers to the question, "What fraction of total income in a country goes to the poorest 10 percent (or 20 percent, and so on) of its households?" can tell us whether the poor are extremely poor relative to their fellow citizens. For example, the poorest 20 percent of families in the United States receive about 5 percent of total income in the United States. The share of income going to the poorest 40 percent of all households is between 16 and 17 percent. Although this may sound like substantial income inequality, it is mild compared to the inequality found in some developing nations; in Brazil, for example, the poorest 40 percent of households receive just 7 percent of the income.

To the extent that our standards of decency are relative, the distribution of income is an important, if indirect, piece of information for people interested in the design of income redistribution programs. Economists can go beyond descriptions of the income distribution, analyzing what economic forces contribute to observed inequality. This article argues that recent changes in the economic climate are leading to increased inequality in the income distribution.

# A SURGE IN INEQUALITY[†]

### Lester C. Thurow*

Since the late 1970's a significant and disturb-

*Professor of Economics at Massachusetts Institute of Technology.

ing shift has been taking place in the distribution of income and wealth in the U. S. The shares of total income going to different segments of the population have changed in such a way that the rich are getting richer, the poor are increasing in number and the middle class has trouble holding its own. The trend can be described as a surge toward inequality.

According to the U.S. Bureau of the Census, the share of total income that went to the top 20 percent of all families was 43.5 percent in 1985, the highest level recorded since the data were first collected in 1947. (In earlier periods the income share of this group had moved narrowly between 40.5 and 41.5 percent of total income.) Conversely, the income share of the bottom 60 percent of the population in 1985 was 32.4 percent, the lowest level ever recorded. (This group's share was slightly less than 36 percent in the late 1960s.)

If one looks at the data of the Federal Reserve board on income distribution, the movement toward inequality is seen to be even more pronounced. The board's set of data includes items not counted in the Census Bureau's definitions of income; among them are returns on wealth such as capital gains and retained earnings. Between 1969 and 1982 the people in the top 10 percent of the population raised their income share according to this set of data from 29 to 33 percent of total income, those between the 60th and 90th percentiles held even at 39 percent and the bottom 60 percent saw their share fall from 32 to 28 percent.

Federal Reserve board figures also show that wealth is much more unequally distributed than income. The top 2 percent of the population receive 14 percent of total income and have 28 percent of total net worth. Similarly, the top 10 percent's share of income (33 percent) almost doubles to a 57 percent share of net worth. In contrast, the bottom 50 percent of the population have 4.5 percent of total net worth. About half of the country's top wealth holders got there by inheriting their holdings and half through their own efforts. In the top wealth group 98 percent are white.

Wherever one looks—industries, occupations, age groups—the surge toward inequality is evident. From 1976 through 1985 the number of middle-income male jobs (defined here as those paying from 75 to 125 percent of median male earnings, or from $13,334

to $22,224 in 1985) declined from 23.4 to 20.3 percent of the male work force. The decline was even larger (from 38 to 32.6 percent) for males who worked full time all year. In a period when total male employment was growing by 7.4 million jobs, 400,000 middle-income male jobs were disappearing; there were small gains in jobs in the upper segments and large gains in the lower segments of the earnings distribution.

The forces underlying the distribution of income and wealth can be understood best if they are arranged in sequence. The sequence starts with the growth in output per hour of work. Productivity and hours of work, taken together, determine how much extra output is available to be divided among the economically active members of the population. This output is then divided into two separate income flows: earnings (returns on work effort and skills) and capital income (returns on the ownership of physical plant and equipment). The separate income flows are then further divided among individual earners and individual capitalists. Government takes off a share in the form of payroll taxes and corporate income taxes.

Since the same person can be both an earner and a capitalist, earnings and capital income must then be recombined to determine total individual incomes. Those incomes must be further combined into household units to determine the distribution of the ability to buy goods and services. Government takes a share of household income in the form of personal income taxes but returns part of its total tax collections to those same households in the form of social-welfare benefits such as Social Security checks. What remains is the disposable income that can be used to buy consumer goods or to augment one's wealth.

One can follow this sequential chain along its length to see exactly where greater inequality is entering the sequence. The pressures toward inequality begin with the growth of output. The rate of growth of the country's gross national product has essentially halved in the past two decades, from 3.8 percent per year in the decade 1960 through 1969 to 2 percent per year in 1979-85. With output growing much more slowly and the economy operating with much more excess capacity, competition for the smaller additions to output was bound to intensify. For example, some people who had been fully employed at good jobs would be pushed out of the labor market or squeezed down into more marginal economic positions. Indeed, unemployment has averaged 8.1 percent in the 1980's compared with 4.8 percent in the 1960's.

When one looks to see exactly who has been squeezed, the result is somewhat surprising. From 1976 through 1985 male incomes (after correcting for inflation) have fallen 8.4 percent and female incomes have risen 6.9 percent. Male incomes are still far above female incomes (median earnings of $24,999 versus $16,252 for full-time, year-round workers). Faster income gains by women are not what is closing the gap, however; in fact, their rate of increase is actually slower than it has been in the past. Instead the reason for the closing of the gap is reductions in male incomes. The most entrenched workers have lost the most.

The proximate cause of the slowdown in the growth of output is easy to find: the rate of growth of productivity declined by a factor of three, from 2.7 percent per year between 1960 and 1970 to .9 percent between 1979 and 1985. The ultimate causes of this slowdown in productivity are harder to find, somewhat mysterious and a subject of controversy among economists. What is clear is that the slowdown cannot simply be traced to a diminution in the quantity or quality of the inputs (capital, labor and technology) to the economy. Moreover, whatever is happening here is not happening to America's major international industrial competitors. The growth of productivity in countries such as West Germany and Japan is from three to five times the U.S. rate. Whatever the reason, a much slowed rate of growth of per capita income is a central reality from which

an analysis of the distribution of income and wealth must start.

In what at first glance seems paradoxical, a low growth of productivity leads to a high growth of employment, and vice versa. Europe and Japan have had good growth of productivity but little creation of jobs. European employment is no higher now than it was in the early 1970's. The U.S. has had a bad productivity performance but has created 28.4 million jobs since 1970.

In reality there is no paradox. With low productivity growth it just takes more people to produce a given volume of extra output. If output and productivity are both growing at 3 percent, no new jobs are generated, but if output is growing at 3 percent and productivity at 1 percent, employment must grow by 2 percent. The new jobs, however, will not be associated with the wage gains that would have gone with them if productivity were growing more rapidly and output were expanding at an even faster pace.

Just such an effect can be seen in the wage gains associated with the millions of new jobs. After correcting for inflation, the compensation to labor per hour of work rose 2.7 percent per year from 1960 through 1969 but fell .4 percent between 1979 and 1985. Moreover, the new jobs were associated with a much more unequal distribution of earnings. Of the 10.7 million new earners added to the economy between 1979 and 1985, 48.6 percent were paid less than $10,000 (in 1985 dollars), 30.5 percent were paid from $10,000 to $25,000 (37.6 percent of the work force was in that range in 1979) and only 20.9 percent were paid more than $25,000 (compared with 23.2 percent in 1979). Right across the earnings distribution the new jobs were inferior to those the economy had been generating before 1979.

The distribution of output into two shares—one for labor and one for capital—affects the final distribution of personal income since capital income is much more

Figure 1: **Change in pay for newly created jobs is charted for three periods. The chart shows the percentage of new jobs at the low-wage, mid-wage and high-wage levels. The wage levels are defined respectively as less that $7,400 per year, between $7,400 and $29,600 and more that $29,600. The figures are in constant 1986 dollars.**

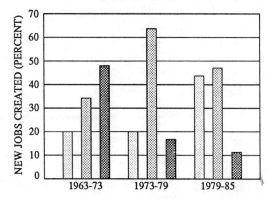

unequally distributed than labor income. If one leaves aside homes and real estate, the top 2 percent of all families are found to own 54 percent of all net financial assets (stocks, bonds, pension funds and so on), the top 10 percent to own 86 percent and the bottom 55 percent to have zero or negative financial assets. This means that if the share of total output going to capital rises, the distribution of total income will automatically become more unequal because the most unequal component (capital income) is growing at the expense of the more equal one (labor income). The data in fact show a slight shift in the functional distribution of income: labor's share of the G.N.P. fell from 60.3 to 59.5 percent between 1979 and 1985.

Sometimes the Reagan Administration's tax and social-welfare policies are given the chief responsibility for the growing inequality, but this ignores the fact that the movement toward inequality began before the president was elected. The Administration's social-welfare cutbacks have in fact turned out to be fairly modest, adding at most probably only a few hundred thousand people to the poverty roll. Most of the four million people who have been added to that roll since 1979 were not forced into poverty by the Administration's social-welfare policies; they were added by much more fundamental economic forces.

Similarly, changes in taxes have had little impact. Federal and state income taxes are progressive, meaning that the proportion of one's income paid in these taxes goes up as one's income goes up. Payroll taxes, state sales taxes and local property taxes are regressive, meaning that the proportion of one's income paid in these taxes goes down as one's income goes up. The net result is a tax system that is basically proportional. The percentage of income paid in taxes does not differ significantly from one income class to the next. The tax changes in 1981 were slightly regressive, but the changes enacted last year were slightly progressive, leaving the tax system about where it was when President Reagan took office.

Those who want a comforting explanation of inequality often point to demography. More young, unskilled and inexperienced baby boomers have entered the nation's labor force, and one should expect them to be paid less, the argument goes; when they become middle-aged and more skilled, the distribution of income will automatically reverse its current surge toward inequality. Therefore the surge need not concern policy makers; it will take care of itself eventually.

Neither part of this argument holds up under close inspection. If one keeps the age distribution of the work force constant at 1967 levels and calculates what the 1982 distribution of earnings would have been for that spectrum of ages rather than for the actual age distributions in 1982, the increase in inequality turns out to be just as large as the one actually observed. Today's inequality is being produced not by a more unequal age distribution of the population but by growing inequality in the earnings of each age group.

Nor does it automatically follow that relative incomes will rise simply because workers grow older. If the income of today's young baby-boom worker is lower than it has been in the past because of population pressures, those pressures will still exist when the baby-boom age cohort becomes middle-aged, because the cohort will still be crowded. Its members will still have lower earnings than they would have if they faced fewer contemporaries.

What, then, is the cause of the rising inequality in the distribution of earnings? There are two major forces: (1) intense international competitive pressures, coupled with high unemployment, and (2) a rising proportion of female workers.

The nation's huge balance-of-trade deficit (about $170 billion last year) is merely the most visible symbol of a much more competitive international economy. Numbers such as $170 billion are so large as to be meaningless to most people, but perhaps they can be made meaningful if one understands that it takes one million full-time, year-round employees in U.S. manufacturing to produce $42 billion worth of goods. Hence the trade deficit of some four times that amount has squeezed more than four million workers out of manufacturing and forced them to take other jobs. Because manufacturing is fairly highly paid and tends to have a more egalitarian distribution of earnings than other sectors such as services do, noncompetitiveness in manufacturing leads directly to more inequality in the distribution of earnings.

The U.S. is much more heavily involved in world trade than it used to be, but the rest of the industrial world is also much more competitive technologically than it used to be. In the past Americans did not have to compete much to export enough to pay for the small proportion of products that the nation wished to import. When the U.S. did compete, it did so on the basis of superior technology rather than lower production costs. Today's competition is among technological equals whose competition is based on which nation has the lowest production costs rather than which has the most superior technology.

With input-output techniques it is possible to isolate the earnings distributions of the industries that either export or compete with imports. This calculation reveals that both industry groups pay higher wages than the economy as a whole. In 1983 the median wage in exporting industries was $18,637 and in industries that compete with imports it was $19,583; for the entire economy the median was $16,168.

In addition to paying higher wages the exporting and import-competing industries generated a more equal distribution of earnings. In 1983, 41 percent of the entire work force worked at jobs that paid less than $12.500 per year, whereas only 31 percent of the workers in exporting industries and 30 percent of those in industries competing with imports held such jobs. Furthermore, whereas 56 percent of the total work force earned from $12,500 to $50,000 per year, 66 percent of the workers in exporting industries and 67 percent of those in the industries competing with imports were at that level. Yet at the very top of the income distribution the percentages were essentially equal: 2.6 percent of the export work force, 2.7 of

Figure 2: **Output and compensation have been diverging since 1980 in the nonfarm business sector. The data are presented on an index for which 100 represents the situation in 1977. The source of the figures is *The Economic Report of the President, 1986.***

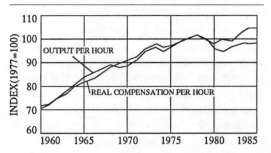

the import-competing work force and 2.7 percent of the entire work force earned more than $50,000 per year.

The meaning of these statistics is that when exports fall and imports rise to create a trade deficit, the distribution of earnings moves toward inequality. Jobs are lost in both exporting and import-competing industries and are replaced by jobs with lower, more unequal earnings in the rest of the economy. This factor is the principal reason for the observed decline in earnings of males. The industries that have been hit hardest by international competition—automobiles, steel and machine tools—are precisely the ones that have provided a large number of upper-middle-income male jobs. For women a service job does not mean a lower wage, but for men it does.

If one looks at earnings by industry or occupation, it is evident that the major effect of foreign competitive pressure has been to increase the variation in earnings within each occupation or industry and to push workers down the earnings ladder. Some of this effect might have been offset if unemployment had been low and the sectors of the economy not involved in international trade had been forced to raise productivity and wages in order to attract good workers. Instead high unemployment meant a plentiful labor supply, and wages could if anything be reduced and made more unequally distributed in those sectors that were not affected by international trade.

Another part of the surge in inequality can be traced to women, or more accurately to society's economic treatment of women. Since women are paid much less than men and are much more likely to be part-time workers, a rising proportion of female workers automatically leads to a more unequal distribution of earnings. The average female worker makes 52 percent of what the average male makes, and the average full-time, year-round female worker makes just 65 percent of what her male counterpart makes.

This phenomenon, together with an increasing proportion of households headed by females (up from 28 to 31 percent of all households in the few years between 1979 and 1985), has led to a low-income population that is increasingly dependent on the earnings of women: the feminization of poverty. Women and children account for 77 percent of those in poverty, and half of the poverty population live in families headed by females with no husband present. The average female worker earns barely enough to keep a family of four above the poverty line. To do more than just escape from poverty a female must have a job substantially above the average.

The work situation of women does not merely affect the lower end of the income distribution. Women are increasingly influencing what a family must do if it wishes to have a middle-class standard of living. In 1984 the U.S. had 87 million households. Some 50 million of them were traditional husband-

Figure 3: **Family income has been changing in distribution quite significantly over the past decade. The four lower curves show the maximum income in the 20 percent of the population with the lowest income, the 20 percent with the second-lowest income, the middle-income group and the next-to-highest group. The curve represents families that are in the top 5 percent of income groupings. The data, encompassing 63.5 million families in 1985, are from the Bureau of the Census.**

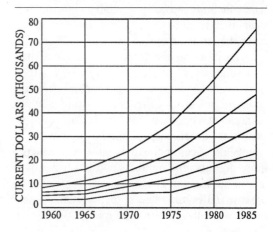

wife families, 40 million of which had earnings (most of the others consisted of retired couples). Of the 40 million, 28 million (70 percent) reported earnings by both husband and wife. These families had a median income of $31,000–$22,000 earned by the husband, $9,000 by the wife.

Among working men only 22 percent will earn $31,000 or more on their own, among working women only 3 percent. As a result few families can afford the $31,000 middle-class life unless both husband and wife have jobs. And although the dominant pattern today is a full-time male worker and a part-time female worker, the pattern is rapidly shifting toward a way of life in which both husband and wife work full time. In 1984, 11 million families had two full-time workers, and those families had a median income of $39,000–$24,000 earned by the husband and $15,000 by the wife. As an increasing number of families have two full-time workers, the households that do not will fall farther and farther behind economically.

Rising female participation in the labor market is also one of the factors leading the incomes of the highest-earning families to grow much faster than those of average families. If high-income males marry high-income females and low-income males marry low-income females (tendencies that are borne out by the available statistics), the net result is wider income gaps as potentially high-income women married to already high-income males enter the labor force.

To describe the trend toward inequality as a surge might imply a high rate of change. Such is not the case; like a glacier, this kind of economic trend in reality moves quite slowly. A national economy can easily adjust to a shift in the distribution of purchasing power. It simply produces more low- income products, more high-income products and fewer middle-income products. The discount (K Mart) and upscale (Bloomingdale's) department stores thrive while the stores in the middle (Gimbels)

go out of business.

The Great Society programs of the 1960's to alter the distribution of income grew out of the political unrest of the civil-rights movement. Black and Hispanic households still have incomes far below those of whites (respectively 59 and 70 percent of white incomes), but the majority no longer seem to care and the minorities, even if they are not happy, do not seem to be aggressively complaining.

The distribution of income in Japan is about half as unequal as that in the U.S. In West Germany, before taxes and transfers, 28 percent of the population have less than half the median income; in the U.S. the figure is 27 percent. After taxes and transfers, however, West Germany is left with only 6 percent of its population in that predicament, whereas the U.S. is left with 17 percent. But to say that the Japanese and the Germans have or want less inequality is not to say that Americans want less inequality.

At the beginning of the Reagan Administration, David A. Stockman, the director of the Office of Management and Budget, declared that the distribution of income was not an appropriate subject for public remediation. The Administration was overwhelmingly reelected and is still popular in the public-opinion polls. Such polls also find that most of the public are in general satisfied with their economic circumstances.

One answer may be that no one cares. If that is so, Americans have changed. The past 100 years of American economic history show government deliberately adopting policies to prevent the growing inequalities that all too often seemed to be arising. In the last half of the 19th century the Interstate Commerce Commission was established and the antitrust laws were enacted to stop a growing concentration of wealth and to prevent that wealth from being used exploitatively. The railroads were not to be allowed to exploit their economic advantage over farmers and the oil trust

Figure 4: **Net worth of families has been changing in distribution since 1970. Each narrow bar represents 1 percent of the families in the U.S. In 1970 some 38 percent of families had a net worth of less than $5,000, in 1983 some 33 percent. At the top levels (from $50,000 to more than $500,000) the percentages have been rising. Data are in constant 1983 dollars and exclude such durable items as automobiles and home furnishings.**

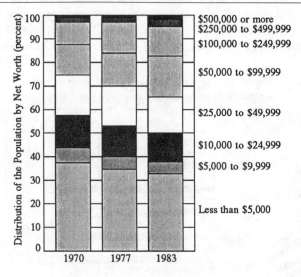

was not to be allowed to exploit the urban consumer. Compulsory education for all was established to create an egalitarian distribution of human capital and more marketable skills in order to prevent large inequalities in earnings.

In the 20th century inheritance taxes and progressive income taxes were adopted to lessen inequalities. The rising inequalities of the Great Depression brought Social Security, unemployment insurance and eventually medical insurance for the elderly and the poor to prevent people from falling out of the middle class when confronting unemployment, illness, old age and other harsh facts of life.

Whether one calls the increase in inequality modest or large depends on one's perspective. The bottom 20 percent of all families, who have seen their share of income decline

by 18 percent since 1969, would no doubt call it large. However it is described, the surge is still under way, and no one can predict when it will stop.

Once the income-distribution problem has become so acute that it actually creates social or political unrest, it will be very difficult to solve. Politically it is a lot easier to prevent an increase in the income share of a dominant group than it is to adopt policies designed to take income away from that group. In economic health care as in medical health care, prevention is always better than remediation but—it must be admitted—is just as seldom undertaken.

Prevention or remediation, whichever, will require a return to the structural policies of the 19th century rather than to the tax and transfer policies of the 20th century.

Regardless of what one thinks about the role of taxes and transfers in limiting inequality, they are clearly not the appropriate means for counteracting the current surge in inequality.

The heart of the solution will have to be found in a higher rate of growth of productivity and enhanced international competitiveness. Here the solution is not simply to lower the value of the dollar in order to regain a balance between exports and imports, although a dollar of lower value will have to be part of the cure until productivity growth can be

enhanced. A lowered dollar is simply a way to have a national "giveback" and lower everyone's wages and capital incomes in relation to those in the rest of the industrial world. The wisest policy would aim not to lower the U.S. standard of living but to raise productivity so that the nation can compete in world markets while its private sector pays good wages and receives acceptable profits.

Economically what has to be done is as clear as the politics of doing it are murky. To compete in industries that pay high wages

Figure 5: **Higher-paying jobs are mainly held by men; women predominate in jobs at low levels of pay and also in part-time work at the lower pay scales. The data are for 1985.**

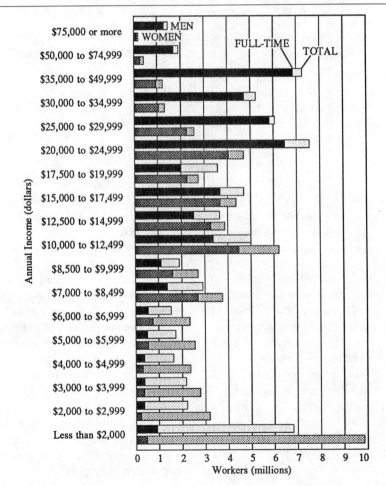

and make goods of high value a country must ensure that its labor force is as well educated and skilled as any in the world, must keep up with or ahead of competitors in investment in capital equipment and must make sure that the technologies being employed are the most effective. Comparisons with either Japan or Europe reveal that the U.S. is not world class in any of those areas. The problem is not that the U.S. is doing worse than it used to but that the rest of the world is doing much better.

Judged by educational attainments and working skills, the U.S. lags far behind. How could one expect American children to learn in a 180-day school year what Japanese children learn in a 240-day school year? Yet the political difficulties of extending the school year are formidable. Both West Germany, with elaborate apprenticeship programs, and Japan, with extensive company training programs, have well-developed systems for teaching technical skills to people who are not bound for college. Such people are the forgotten majority when it comes to training in the

Figure 6: **Feminization of poverty is evident in this depiction of the incomes of families in data for March, 1986. Families headed by women predominate at the lower levels.**

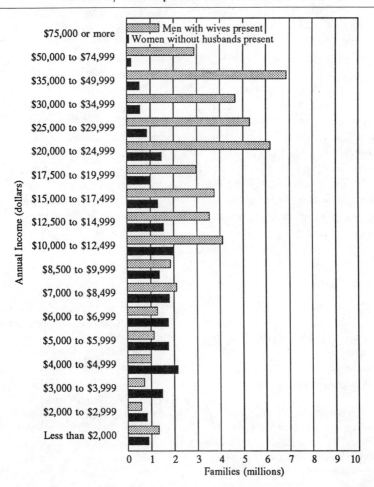

U.S. Yet the Administration gutted the training programs of the Department of Labor.

American companies invest only half as much as the Japanese and two-thirds as much as the Europeans. To invest more the American family must save more than 4 percent of its income. Eliminating consumer credit would go a long way toward raising the personal-savings rate, but what politician wants to advocate that?

Civilian spending on research and development as a fraction of the gross national product now lags behind that of Japan, West Germany and France. One way or another, however, governments pay for almost all R&D spending in every country. To spend more on R&D means higher government spending and more taxes. No one in the U.S. wants to pay more taxes. That is why the Federal deficit is more than $200 billion.

In short, the solutions to the problem of competitiveness are visible and at hand. To say that the nation knows how to solve its problems with competitiveness, however, is not to say that it will solve them.

Working women are a fact of life. If the U.S. wants to avoid increasing inequality and the feminization of the lower reaches of the income distribution, it will have to do something to raise the earning capacity of women. One can argue about whether the issue is one of comparable worth (female occupations that are simply paid less than male occupations because of habit, history and exploitation) or the relative skills of female workers. Probably both factors contribute to creating the problem. In any case, the society must do something to improve the earnings of women if current trends toward inequality are not to continue.

Families headed by women raise a variety of sociological, religious and ethical issues; they certainly create an economic problem. They are unlikely ever to be able to attain an economic standard of living anywhere near that enjoyed by intact two-earner families. Their problems can be lessened, however, by adopting efficient social policies that make fathers pay to support their children even if they do not live with them. Nature may make mothers but society can make financial fathers. There is an easy solution: if a court orders child-support payments, the Federal Government automatically sends the mother a monthly support check for that amount and collects the money from the father through the Internal Revenue Service — with the state guaranteeing a minimum level of support whatever the amount collected from the father may be.

If history is any guide, the current surge in inequality will sooner or later be met with a political countersurge to contain it. The nature of that countersurge, however, remains buried deep below the political ice.

# QUESTIONS

1. How have international competition and the movement of women into the labor force led to greater income inequality?

2. Thurow presents myriad statistical facts for his readers to ponder.

(a) The Federal Reserve includes capital gains and retained earnings as components of income, but the Census Bureau does not. If our definition of income is consumption plus any change in net wealth, which measure seems more appropriate?

(b) Look at the data behind Thurow's statement that 400,000 "middle-income male jobs" disappeared in the period 1976-1985. If women displaced men in some middle-income jobs, would Thurow's statistics count these as male jobs lost?

3. Thurow calls the increasing inequality in the income distribution "disturbing," linking it to a potential for social and political unrest. What, if any, causal link do you think there is between inequality (as opposed to poverty per se) and social-political unrest?

### Do welfare families migrate to high-welfare states?

Aid to Families with Dependent Children (AFDC) is the nation's principal welfare program. States with generous programs fear that their largesse will attract welfare families from neighboring states. The basis of this fear is easily seen: A family could increase its welfare payment by over 60 percent just by crossing the state line from Texas to Oklahoma, from Illinois to Wisconsin, from West Virginia to Pennsylvania, or from Nevada to California. (These calculations are based on S. Levitan, *Programs in Aid of the Poor*, fifth edition, p. 33.) This article examines the extent to which such welfare-based migration seems to occur.

# WELFARE PAYMENT LEVELS AND THE MIGRATION OF FEMALE-HEADED FAMILIES

*Rebecca M. Blank**

The program most frequently referred to as "welfare" in this country is Aid to Families with Dependent Children (AFDC), which is primarily available to low-income single-parent families. Although some of regulations governing the use of AFDC are established by the federal government, payment levels are set by states. The result is that AFDC benefits vary enormously between states, even after

*Assistant Professor of Economics and Public Affairs, Princeton University.

adjusting for regional differences in the cost of living. In 1986, a family of one adult and two children could receive a maximum AFDC payment of $120 per month if they lived in Mississippi, and $740 per month if they lived in Alaska. The median state's maximum payment level was $346 per month. [1]

These differential benefit levels have been criticized by many. For some, these criticisms are based on a concern that needy households in the United States should have similar help available to them, no matter where they live. However, outside of any concern with equity, many policy analysts worry about the incentives that the current system establishes for single-parent households to move to high benefit states. Officials within states that pay relatively high benefit levels often claim that high benefit levels increase the poor population in their state and thus increase the financial burden of welfare payments and other low-income support services. National policy analysts often cite this concern about migration as a primary reason why AFDC benefits levels should be at least partially regulated by the federal government.

Before developing a model to test the effect of AFDC on migration, it is important to understand how AFDC works and what effect higher AFDC benefits have on household utility and behavior.

## HOW DO AFDC BENEFIT LEVELS AFFECT HOUSEHOLD BEHAVIOR?

The amount of money a household receives from AFDC is determined by two parameters: the guarantee level (G) and the tax rate (t). As noted above, the guarantee level is set by the state. A household that has no other income receives the full guarantee. However, if the household head starts to work, the AFDC grant level is reduced as labor income rises. The rate at which AFDC payments fall is determined by the tax rate. The federal government mandates an AFDC tax rate of 67 percent for the first four months of participation in the program and 100 percent for all months thereafter. This means that for every dollar earned in the labor market, AFDC benefits are reduced by 67 cents for the first four months and by a full dollar in all following months. This can be expressed mathematically as

(1)        $AFDC Payment = G - t(wH)$

where $w$ is the wage earned by the worker and $H$ is the hours that she works. Clearly, as

labor market income rises, at some point the AFDC payment will reach zero. This occurs at the *breakeven income level (Y\*)*, which is the income level where

(2)     $0 = G - t(wH)$, *implying that* $Y^* = G/t$.[2]

The budget line available in the presence of the AFDC program is shown in Figure 1. The horizontal axis represents hours of work and the vertical axis represents total household income. A household with no other income receives $G$, the maximum grant level. As the household starts to work, the AFDC grant is reduced. For every hour worked the household earns the hourly wage, $w$, but their AFDC grant is cut by $tw$, so their net earnings are $(1-t)w$. This is the slope of the budget line as long as the household is participating in AFDC. However, at the breakeven level of earnings $(Y^*)$, the household is no longer eligible for AFDC, and the entire AFDC grant has disappeared. The household then earns $w$ for each hour of work, and the slope of the budget line increases to $w$.

The exact point at which a household will be located is determined by the location of the household's utility curves. Clearly, in trying to maximize utility, the household will choose to locate at the highest possible utility curve that is feasible given the budget constraint. This is typically the point where the utility curves are tangent to the budget set. Figure 2 depicts three possible choices. The household with utility curve A stays off the AFDC program entirely, maximizing its utility at $x$. The

Figure 1

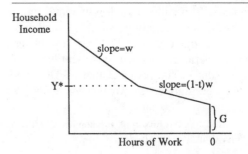

Figure 2

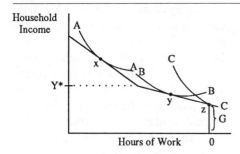

Figure 3

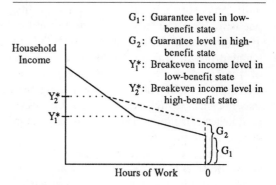

household with utility curve $B$ locates at $y$, both working and receiving AFDC benefits. A corner solution is also possible, as depicted by utility curve $C$, where the highest utility level is reached by not working at all, locating at $z$, and receiving the maximum AFDC grant.

Now, compare the budget lines available to an identical household in two states that have different AFDC benefits. Figure 3 graphs these on top of each other. It is clear that households who participate in the AFDC program in the low-benefit state will be uniformly better off in the high-benefit state; their income and their utility will rise, since they can move to a higher, parallel budget line. In addition, there may be a number of nonparticipants in the low-benefit state who would find it worthwhile to enter the AFDC program in the high-benefit state because it would allow them to reach a higher utility level. This is because the breakeven point of the budget line is higher in the high-benefit state, making it more likely that AFDC will be an attractive option. Finally, there will be some set of individuals who maximize their utility at a point that does not involve participation in the AFDC program, who would be unaffected by the higher benefit levels. These households will be off AFDC in either state and are unaffected by the difference in benefit levels.

In summary, the AFDC program is set up in such a way that a state that pays higher benefits may provide both higher utility levels and a greater probability of entering AFDC

for many households than a lower benefit state would provide.

## HOW ARE MIGRATION DECISIONS MADE?

A simple model of migration decisions assumes that individuals compare the costs and benefits of relocation with the benefits of remaining in their current location. Thus, any individual initially located in state $B$ presumably considers the potential advantage of relocating to any of the other 49 states. We will start by assuming that the household has complete information on the job opportunities and welfare benefits available in all other states. The individual household makes 49 comparisons between the utility available in its current location and the net utility available in all alternative state locations. Thus, for every possible alternative location, the household compares $U_B$, the utility in state $B$ (where members are currently living), with $U_C$, the utility in an alternative state $C$, minus the cost of moving from state $B$ to state $C$, $M_{BC}$. If

$$(3) \qquad U_B < U_C - M_{BC}$$

then the household should find moving to state $C$ an attractive option. But if

$$(4) \qquad U_B \geq U_C - M_{BC}$$

it will not move.

Ideally, an individual considering a move will look not only at her *current* utility, but will also consider future expected utility. Thus, $U_B$ and $U_C$ may actually reflect the discounted present value of utility over a period of future years. A houshold that does not expect to remain on AFDC for a long time may not find the high-AFDC state raises utility as much as an individual who has few future alternative options to AFDC.

Assume that the current location (state *B*) is a low-AFDC state, while the alternative (state *C*) is a high-AFDC state, but that in all other respects states *B* and *C* are identical, so that the wage and employment opportunities are the same. How will an individual decide whether or not to move? Those households who do not expect to participate in AFDC in either state will face identical income and utility levels in each state, since all non-AFDC earning opportunities are identical. Since there are always some expenses associated with a move, these households will never find moving attractive. However, two groups of individuals will indeed expect to receive higher utility in state *C*. Those households on welfare in state *B* will be able to raise their welfare level in state *C*, as discussed above. And those households that are not on AFDC in state *B* but would be if given the opportunity to live in state *C* will also clearly be at a higher utility level in the higher benefit state.

Of course, this does not mean that all these individuals will move. For many of them, the costs of moving may be quite large and more than outweigh the potential utility gain. One would expect that households that are further away from the high-benefit state will face higher moving costs and be less likely to move. Thus, poor households from neighboring states may be far more likely to move than poor households from faraway states. However, even short moves may involve expenses (such as paying a month's security deposit on a new apartment) that low-income households are unable to afford, since they are unlikely to have significant savings.

Note that the model in equations (3) and (4) measures moving costs not in dollars but in the same units as utility, so that both monetary and nonmonetary costs are accounted for. Thus, one would also expect that households who have many family and friends in their current location and who dislike the thought of putting down new roots will find moving far more expensive and be likely to stay where they are.

Until now we have assumed that households know exactly what to expect in other locations and make a choice based on full information about the job opportunities and AFDC benefits levels and moving costs that relocation will involve. In reality, households may be very unlikely to know a great deal about AFDC benefit levels in other states or about job opportunities and wage levels. To the extent that individuals have no information on alternative locations they are unlikely to consider them as migration possibilities. Thus, a state like Alaska can perhaps pay high AFDC benefits both because it is a far distance from other states, so monetary relocation costs are high, and also because individuals in the "lower 48" are unlikely to know anything about AFDC benefit levels in Alaska and thus do not consider a move.

We have assumed that the only difference between states *B* and *C* is their welfare benefit levels. Clearly, if other economic differentials occur in wages or employment opportunities, these will also affect the relative attractiveness of the two locations. As it happens, AFDC benefit levels and overall wage levels across states are positively correlated, implying that high-AFDC states are also likely to be high-wage states. Since higher wages also increase the expected income in a location (and thus raise the budget line and the expected utility level for a household), it is clearly not enough to simply look at migration between high- and low-AFDC states. Some of this migration might be induced by wage differentials rather than welfare differentials. One must control for the non-AFDC economic differences between states before drawing any conclusions about the effect of AFDC differentials.

In sum, AFDC differentials between states should create an incentive for low-income households to move to high-benefit states, given other economic opportunities are equivalent; however, the extent to which a significant number of households actually find it advantageous to move depends upon the size of the benefit differential, the extent to which non-AFDC economic opportunities also vary between the states, and the magnitude of moving costs. If few low-income households have information about alternative locations, or if they are severely income constrained and cannot afford to pay any moving expenses, then even large AFDC differentials may persist over long periods of time and result in very little migration of low-income households.

## WHAT DOES THE EVIDENCE SHOW?

One recent study attempts to measure the effect of AFDC differences between states, controlling for differences in wage levels and tax rates.[3] Using data on migration patterns for a random sample of female-headed households between 1975 and 1979, this study concludes that both wage levels and AFDC levels have significant effects on the migration probabilities of these households. The overall probability of a typical female-headed family leaving a typical high-welfare state is 8 percent over these four years and increases to 11 percent if welfare were cut by $100 per month. Conversely, the probability of leaving a typical low-welfare state is 15 percent and falls to 10 percent if welfare were raised $100 per month. The probability of this family leaving an area with both low welfare payments and low wages can be as much as 12 percentage points higher over a four year period than the probability of leaving a high-welfare, high-wage area. However, the impact of these economic variables, although significant, still accounts for very little movement within the population. (Only about 10 percent of all female-headed households moved across state lines over this time period.) Most of these households do not move, despite significant differences in potential income levels between different states. This seems to indicate that moving costs are quite high for this population.

Thus, while the empirical evidence supports the theoretical predictions, the amount of low-income migration induced by AFDC benefit differentials at any point in time appears to be relatively low. Of course, over the long run, even small effects can cumulate, and a study that investigated migration of poor households over several decades might find much stronger effects. In addition, states with high AFDC benefits that border states with low AFDC benefits might be quite concerned about high "cross-border" migration rates even in the short run. In this situation, economic opportunities might be quite similar on either side of the state border, individuals near the border might know a lot about AFDC benefit levels in the nearby state, and the cost of migration may be low since small distances are involved.[4] Thus, in particular situations the problem of cross-state migration of poor households could be quite acute.

# Notes

1. U.S. House of Representatives, Committee on Ways and Means (1986).

2. For simplicity, any non-AFDC, nonlabor market income (such as alimony or unemployment compensation) is ignored in this analysis. The first $30 per month of labor market income earned by an AFDC recipient is not taxed, and this effect is also ignored.

3. Blank (1987). For an alternative empirical discussion of this issue, see Gramlich and Laren (1984).

4. For an analysis of this problem on the Illinois-Wisconsin border, see Stumbras (1985).

# References

Blank, Rebecca M., "The Effect of Welfare and Wage Levels on the Location Decisions of Female-Headed Households," *Journal of Urban Economics,* forthcoming, 1987.

Gramlich, Edward M., and Deborah S. Laren, "Migration and Income Redistribution Possibilities," *Journal of Human Resources,* 19:4, 1984: pp. 485-511.

Stumbras, Bernard, "Migration as an Issue in the Wisconsin AFDC Program," Institute for Research on Poverty. Unpublished paper, December 1985.

U.S. House of Representatives, Committee on Ways and Means, *Background Material and Data on Programs within the Jurisdiction of the Committee on Ways and Means: 1986 Edition,* Washington D.C.: Government Printing Office, March 3, 1986: table 8., p. 373.

# QUESTIONS

1. Explain why someone not participating in AFDC in a low-benefit state might, other things equal, choose to migrate to a high-benefit state.

2. Prince Hamlet said we prefer to bear the ills we have rather than to fly to others we know not of. How would uncertainty affect a migration decision? Would aversion to risk be consistent with the evidence Blank finds on levels of migration?

3. One argument against mandating a national benefit level is that, in low-wage regions, welfare recipients might enjoy a living standard too close to that of the working poor.

(a.) Given that we have a nationally mandated minimum wage, do you expect the working poor to be much poorer in some regions than in others? What does your answer imply for evaluation of a proposal to link a national benefit schedule to the minimum wage?

(b.) Consider a proposal setting benefits equal to either a minimum acceptable level or a specified fraction of the median wage in a state, whichever is higher. Describe how proponents and opponents of such a measure might differ in their views of (i) the proper role of AFDC and (ii) an equitable income distribution.

## *Workfare.*

Our welfare system has been accused of contributing to the social and economic ills of the people it supports. We see a pattern of welfare families without fathers. Teenagers are having babies. Unemployment rates for single young men are appalling. In ill-conceived dense-pack public housing, a generation of welfare dependency has made the work-a-day world of labor force participation more remote than welfare offices and food stamps.

Would things be any better if welfare recipients worked for their checks? These are some of the potential benefits often touted by proponents of workfare:

☐ Since welfare would no longer be a "free ride," many people would find a job and get off the welfare roles. This would reduce the pervasiveness of the welfare culture and reduce the government's financial burden at the same time.

☐ Especially among young recipients, workfare could provide valuable habit formation for and education about the job market. Workfare, in essence, teaches punctuality and consistent performance. These skills will have long-term payoffs in the labor market.

☐ It would reinforce a general work ethic and assuage taxpayers who don't like to see people getting something for nothing.

☐ As welfare became less attractive, the financial advantages of two-parent households might reduce the number of female-headed households. Such a demographic change would almost certainly reduce the incidence of poverty.

Others are skeptical of workfare and suggest that most of these effects are likely to be small. Opponents of workfare call it demeaning and point to examples of "make-work" tasks. Some caution that jobs will be lost as workfare workers displace paid employees.

In this article, Levy and Michel address the likely effects of workfare on labor supply behavior and household formation.

# WORK FOR WELFARE: HOW MUCH GOOD WILL IT DO?[†]

*Frank S. Levy and Richard C. Michel**

It is an axiom of policy analysis that the good is in the particulars. The axiom is well-taken. When people discuss a new policy proposal in general terms, details are vague and the proposal can seem to serve a number of conflicting goals. It is only when we get down to details that the inherent conflicts and disappointments appear.

The axiom might usefully be applied to the increasingly frequent call for a tighter relationship between welfare and work. During the 1950's and 1960's, the idea was largely dormant. But over the last 15 years, it has gained wider acceptance for a number of different reasons. One is the feeling that requiring work of welfare recipients makes welfare more politically acceptable. A second is the sense that, contrary to social goals, welfare disconnected from work leads to a growing underclass within the poverty population (Charles Murray, 1984; Lawrence Mead, 1985).

More recently, a closer connection between work incentives and welfare has been implicitly advanced as the answer to a third problem: a looming budetary crisis which has led to challenges to the cost of the American welfare state. This third rationale is the subject of this paper.

## THE COMING CRISIS FOR THE WELFARE STATE

The emerging crisis for the welfare state in America begins with the changing nature of both poverty and the American income distribution.

Consider first the income distribution. From 1947 through the present, the bottom quintile of the income distribution has received a small and fairly steady share of all income— between 4.7 percent and 5.6 percent. But while the quintile shares of income have been relatively constant, the sources of this income

†Reprinted by Permission of *American Economic Review,* May 1986, pp. 399–404

*University of Maryland, The Urban Institute, respectively.

*decreasing*

have changed substantially. In 1959, the Census reported that about 70 percent of all income in the lowest quintile came from earnings. By 1969, the proportion had declined to 60 percent. And by 1983, earnings comprised only 42 percent of all income in the lowest quintile.[1] Government cash benefits have increased correspondingly with combined welfare and Social Security benefits approaching 45 percent of total income for this group.

The lowest quintile of the distribution and the poverty population are, of course, separate concepts: the first is relative while the second is absolute. But recent statistics on poverty show a comparable situation: in 1983, earnings comprised only 46 percent of the income of the poor and this occurred after a 2-year recession which had drawn many near (and presumably working) poor into the poverty population.

Government benefits thus now play a crucial role in shoring up the bottom of the income distribution. But it is precisely these benefits that are now called into question. The recently passed Gramm-Rudman legislation formalizes what most people long ago admitted: that the supply-side tax cuts of 1981 could never produce sufficient growth to become self-financing. They left a structural federal budget deficit that can only be closed by expenditure reductions or tax increases, and the reductions will apparently get first priority. For the moment, major income support programs such as Social Security and Aid to Families with Dependent Children are off limits in the sense that they are exempt from Gramm-Rudman's automatic reductions. But these automatic reductions are only a fail-safe strategy if Congress and the administration cannot agree on an alternate plan. In the initial phases of formulating such a plan, income support programs would surely be on the table, as they have been since 1981.

It seems then that the income distribution has evolved to the point where the goal of a balanced budget is on a collision course

with the goals of reducing poverty and income inequality. In this situation, it is natural enough to look for escape hatches and implementing work requirements in welfare programs appears to provide one exit. If welfare recipients could be put into jobs—if earnings could substitute for benefits in their incomes—the collision described above might be avoided.

How might this substitution be accomplished? If the object is to save public funds, a large-scale public jobs program such as that proposed by the Carter Administration is obviously not the answer. What is implied is a gradual reduction in the value of welfare compared to the value of work: a tightening of eligibility restrictions and a continued erosion of maximum benefit levels by inflation which reduces real outlays. If—as the story goes—the expansion of the benefits increases dependency, then the contraction of benefits should decrease dependency. Earnings per family will increase and neither equality nor poverty will suffer. And ultimately, government outlays would be reduced.

The argument is appealing because in a pure accounting sense, it is clear that government benefits substituted for declining earnings. But it is essential to understand the causes of this substitution in order to determine whether a stronger work-welfare policy will succeed in saving substantial public monies. Only if the rising importance of transfers *caused* the replacement of earnings will this be true.

It is important to first understand that the shift in income sources among low-income families was accompanied by (and perhaps in part caused by) the growing relative numbers of poor female-headed families in the 1960's and 1970's. Between 1959 and 1984, the number of female-headed families in poverty grew from 1.9 million, making up 23 percent of all poor families to 3.5 million, making up 46 percent of all poor families. A corresponding dramatic growth in the number of families

*res in poor female-headed families*

receiving welfare benefits in the late 1960's and early 1970's combined with the shift in the composition of the poor to make female-headed families the principal targets of government-initiated work incentive policies.

The question then remains as to what policies would reverse the processes by which female-headed families became poor in such large numbers and by which poor families came to rely less on earnings. The answer to this depends on what mechanisms led to these outcomes.

In practice, two such mechanisms are implicit in the literature. One is a labor supply effect in which transfers permit families to reduce work effort and earnings. The other is a demographic effect in which transfers induce the creation of female-headed families—families with traditionally weak earnings potential. One can make a theoretical case for either effect. But again the good is in the particulars and so it is necessary to assess how strong each effect is. In this paper, we review the evidence on each one: labor supply in Section III, family effects in Section IV, and in Section V, draw some brief conclusions.

## TRANSFERS AND LABOR SUPPLY

In the short run—that is, the horizon over which we hope to balance the budget—it is far easier to imagine reversing labor supply effects than demographic effects and so it is with labor supply that we begin.

The case for labor supply effects begins with the observation of Murray and others that during the 1970's, GNP per capita grew rapidly—more rapidly than in the 1950's—but the poverty rate remained constant. Therefore, Murray argues, welfare programs must have been luring people out of the labor force.[2] One might counter that this was really a demographic argument—that increasing benefits created more dependent households. But an overview of the postwar period suggests something more was going on. Let us define

"dependent" families as families headed by someone over 65, or a woman under 65. This is an admittedly simple definition but one which corresponds to historically accepted definitions of groups which, when they are poor, deserve society's support.

During the postwar period, the proportion of such dependent families has grown in both the poverty population and the bottom quintile of the income distribution. But in both cases, the proportion of families with no member in the labor force has grown much faster (Table 1).

A closer inspection of the data shows that to the extent that labor has been cut back, it is not on the part of female family heads. Among those females heading families in poverty, the proportion who worked at some time during the year has fallen only slightly over time: 43 percent in 1959 and 1969, 37 percent in 1975, 39 percent in 1981 and 38 percent in 1984. The proportion who worked year-round behaved in a similar fashion declining from 16 percent in 1959 to 13 percent in 1969, and then

Table 1

| A. Characteristics of the Lowest Quintile of the Family Income Distribution | 1949 | 1979 |
| --- | --- | --- |
| Proportion of families headed by a person over 65 or a woman under 65 | 50% | 59% |
| Proportion of all families with no earner | 21% | 40% |

| B. Selected Characteristics of the Poverty Population | 1959 | 1981 |
| --- | --- | --- |
| Proportion of families headed by a person over 65 or a woman under 65 | 41% | 57% |
| Proportion of all families with no earner | 24% | 39% |

*Sources:* Herman Miller (1966), Bureau of the Census *Current Population Reports,* Series P-60, No. 147, and our tabulations from Decennial Census files (1960, 1970).

dipping slightly in the 1970's only to return to 13 percent in 1984. The small magnitude of potential labor supply effects have been confirmed by a wealth of micro-level analysis as well. While the effect is almost always significant in a statistical sense, it rarely reaches proportions large enough to have more than nominal budgetary impacts (Levy, 1979, and Robert Moffitt, 1984.)

A further look at welfare benefits helps explain the stability in the proportion of workers. For many years, researchers argued that the work incentives of welfare were contained in its tax rates. In practice, however, this view overstated the case. Unlike a standard income tax, welfare has only a one-month accounting period. Over so short a period, there is little room to modulate labor supply, particulary for low-income workers who typically have no control over their hours of work for pay. Thus, an AFDC mother is generally faced with a decision to work full time for a period or not at all. And if she chooses to work full time, she is likely to be off the welfare roles altogether, if only for that month.

Given this kind of on-off behavior, one simple measure of welfare's work disincentives is the gap between welfare benefits and wages. Let us approximate the value of work by using the average wage paid in the retail trade industry.[3]

Looking at the value of the combined AFDC and food stamp benefits to an average AFDC family over time and comparing it to full-time work in the retail trade industry shows that while the relative generosity of benefits rose during the 1960's, it peaked in 1970, and by 1983 had returned to 1960 levels. In 1960, welfare benefits stood at 40 percent of wages. They rose to 57 percent by the early 1970's and declined to 40 percent in recent years (Table 2).

Throughout this period, the estimated participation rate in AFDC fluctuated. In the late 1960's, less than one-half of all eligible female-headed families participated in the AFDC program. This percent rose to 92 percent in the early 1970's, fell again in the mid-1970's, then reached a new peak of 97 percent in 1979. Recent calculations indicate that the rate has dropped steadily since 1979, reaching 78 percent in 1983 (Michel, 1980, unpublished data from the Urban Institute's TRIM2 simulation model).

Furthermore, during this same period, the labor force participation rates among all women (white, black, poor, and nonpoor) continued to rise. Between 1970 and 1983,

Table 2: **Comparison of Combined Welfare Benefits with Retail Trade Wages**

| Year | Average Annual AFDC plus Food Stamp Benefit | Full-time Annual Wages | Ratio of Welfare to Wages |
|------|------|------|------|
| 1960 | 1,269 | 3,162 | .401 |
| 1970 | 2,880 | 5,075 | .567 |
| 1975 | 3,315 | 6,989 | .474 |
| 1980 | 4,333 | 10,150 | .427 |
| 1983 | 4,741 | 11,939 | .397 |

*Sources:* We calculated welfare and food stamp benefits from program data. Food stamp benefits are those for a family with average AFDC income. Wages are from the *Economic Report of the President,* February, 1985, Table B-38, page 276.

labor force participation rate of white women rose from 43 percent to 53 percent, duplicating the percentage changes for all women. For black women, the participation rate rose from 50 to 54 percent and for poor female family heads from 47 to 54 percent.

If in fact a rise in welfare benfits causes a large reduction in labor effort among women, there is no evidence in either aggregate or micro data. Whether welfare benefits were rising or falling, whether participation rates in welfare increased or decreased, and whether poverty rates were growing or shrinking, the labor force participation rates of the largest group categorically eligible for welfare continued to rise over the period from the late 1960's to the early 1980's.

To the extent that the growth in aggregate government transfers had any important labor supply effects, it was of course among the elderly. Throughout the postwar period (and in fact much earlier), the labor force participation among elderly men (those 65 and older) has fallen steadily from about 50 percent at the end of World War II to less than 20 percent today. A principal reason for this may have been the maturation of the Social Security program which allowed many men to leave the labor force in their sixties and still have an adequate income. Reflective of this is the fact that in 1979, only 25 percent of all men over 65 reported any earnings and only 8 percent reported year-round full-time work. Not surprisingly then, 42 percent of all families headed by an elderly family were in the lowest quintile of the income distribution.

It seems to follow from the numbers above that if we seek to limit or reverse the growth of the postwar transfer system by curbing labor force effects of transfer programs, the place to concentrate is not among female-headed families but among the elderly. No one has seriously proposed workfare for the elderly (nor are we), but it is important to understand that in terms of pure work incentive effects, that is where the dollars are.

## DEMOGRAPHIC EFFECTS

If welfare payments do not have strong labor supply effects, what are their effects on family structure? The argument we advance is similar to the one advanced by black writers beginning with W. E. B. DuBois (1899) and Franklin Frazier (1939). It has most recently been articulately revived by William Julius Wilson (1978). If a man cannot find suitable work and has few prospects for finding work, then it is logical to ask what he can bring to a marriage and, in particular, if he brings more income to a marriage than available from welfare. Thus if welfare benefits are higher than the incomes of a significant portion of men, it may provide an incentive to create more female-headed families.

Evidence from Decennial Census data and the March Current Population Survey files is suggestive (though by no means conclusive). In 1960, the average welfare benefit for an AFDC family was $1,269. About 31 percent of black males aged 20-24 had incomes below this level. By 1970, the average combined AFDC and food stamp benefit was $2,880. According to the CPS, fully 46 percent of young black men aged 20-24 had incomes lower than that figure. Combined welfare benefits also exceeded the incomes reported by 17 percent of black men aged 25-34 (compared with 15 percent in 1960).

Earlier, we saw how the gap between welfare and wages reached a minimum in the early 1970's and increased thereafter. But, while welfare benefits declined, the bottom part of the distribution of black men's incomes declined as well. In 1983, the average combined welfare benefit was $4,741. This figure was higher than the incomes reported in that year for 62 percent of black men aged 20-24 and 29 percent of black men aged 25-34. Both figures represent dramatic increases from earlier periods.

The potential relationship of those figures to the family formation prospects of black males and females can be demonstrated by linking them to the cohort sizes of males and females of marriageable age. In 1960, for example, there were 1.1 million black men and 1.3 million black women aged 25-34, a ratio of 1.2 women for every man. The cohort size of both sex groups nearly doubled by 1983 and this ratio remained roughly the same. But, if we look at the ratio of black women in this age group to black men whose income was above average welfare benefits, the ratio rises from 1.3 in 1960 to 1.6 in 1983. Similar increases in the ratio were experienced for younger black men and women. These facts confirm the findings of Wilson, and suggest a situation in which there was a decreasing number of black men who could provide income significant enough to maintain a family at above welfare level.

In presenting these findings, we recognize the counterargument: if women did not have the welfare option, more husbands might be "acceptable" and, given the responsibility, husbands might indeed work more. This is certainly a possibility, but the logical policy alternative here is to eliminate welfare for single women altogether. In spite of the fact that some conservatives have suggested this, it is not a policy likely to be adopted if only because current average welfare benefits are about one-half the poverty line.

## CONCLUSION

In Section I, we showed that government transfers had replaced earnings as the most significant source of income for the poor in the last 15 years. It seems that this replacement has occurred through two different mechanisms. First, the elderly have reduced their labor supply participation substantially. Second, the growth of transfers combined with market conditions or behavioral changes of unknown origin has induced the formation of female-headed families by pricing potential husbands out of the family market.

Having made these assertions, it is not clear how these problems can be resolved given current budgetary pressures and the apparent disinclination of the public to expand programs for the poor. Workfare for the elderly is almost certainly a nonstarter politically. And while one might want to put welfare mothers to work, work requirements alone are unlikely to solve what appears to be a major source of the welfare problem: the financial barriers to the formation of two-parent families. Workfare for AFDC mothers may be good policy for other reasons, but most certainly it will not provide significant near-term budgetary savings, since it is not labor-leisure decisions but demographic ones that are acting to maintain the size of the eligible population. The thing to do may be to find a way to put young men to work, but most policy options are too expensive to be considered seriously in this decade.

We began this paper with one axiom of policy analysis that the good is in the particulars. The particulars in the case of welfare policy have in recent years led to a stalemate. Changing the system invariably would involve cutting it back to levels that appear to be socially unacceptable or expanding the system at costs which are currently unaffordable. And in recent years, humanitarian instincts have clashed with fiscal constraint to prevent us from moving in either direction.

# Notes

1. If we improved upon the Census definition of income to delete taxes and add the value of in-kind benefits such as food stamps, Medicaid, and Medicare, the proportion of this redefined income that came from earnings would undoubtedly fall still lower.

2. The argument itself is fallacious on a number of counts. First, per capita income was not a good measure of economic growth in the 1970's because it was largely a result of demographic

adjustments. Second, the link between poverty and welfare that Murray makes implies that leisure was so valuable to these families that they opted for the subpoverty benefits in AFDC over minimum wage jobs. But between 1967 and 1973, welfare roles (as measured by paticipation in the AFDC program) *grew* by 5.9 million persons while the number of persons below the poverty line *fell* by 4.8 million persons. For detailed arguments, see, among others, our paper (1985).

3. This industry generally includes checkout clerks in a variety of retail stores such as groceries and fast-food outlets and has historically had the lowest hourly wage of major nonagricultural industries. In 1984, retail trade wages were about two-thirds of manufacturing wages and less than one-half of construction wages.

# References

DuBois, W. E. B., *Philadelphia Negro* (1899), rev. ed., New York: Schoken Books, 1967.

Frazier, Franklin E., *The Negro Family in the United States,* Chicago: University of Chicago Press, 1939.

Levy, Frank S., "The Labor Supply of Female Household Heads, or AFDC Work Incentives Don't Work Too Well," *Journal of Human Resources,* Winter 1979, 4, 56-79.

Levy, Frank and Richard C. Michel, "Losing Perspective: The Recent Debate Over Welfare and Poverty," Working Paper 2081- 02, Urban Institute, June 1985.

Mead, Lawrence W., *Beyond Entitlement: The Social Oblications of Citizenship,* New York: Free Press, 1985.

Michel, Richard C., "Participation Rates in the Aid to Families with Dependent Children Program: National Trends From 1967 to 1977," Working Paper No. 1387-02, Urban Institute, December 1980.

Miller, Herman P., *Income Distribution in the United States,* Washington: USGPO, 1966.

Moffitt, Robert, "Assessing the Effects of the 1981 Federal AFDC Legislation on the Work Effort of Welfare Recipients." Discussion Paper 742-84, University of Wisconsin Institute for Research on Poverty, January 1984.

Murray, Charles, *Losing Ground: American Social Policy,* 1950-1980, New York: Basic Books, 1984.

Wilson, William J., *The Declining Significance of Race: Blacks and Changing American Institutions,* Chicago: University of Chicago Press, 1978.

U.S. Bureau of the Census, *Current Population Reports,* Series P-60, 1973-83.

U.S. Bureau of the Census, Decennial Census files, 1960, 1970.

U.S. Council of Economic Advisers, *Economic Report of the President,* Washington, 1985.

# QUESTIONS

1. Three decades ago, earnings represented a much greater share of income going to the poor. If welfare benefits are reduced, will earnings increase substantially?

2. Are the authors equating working for welfare and reduced welfare checks? Under what circumstances might such an equation make sense?

3. Many states now have welfare programs that allow two-parent households to qualify for AFDC (these are AFDC-UP, "unemployed parent" programs). If welfare is hindering the formation of families by dwarfing the earnings of potential of young men, what hypothesis can you form about differential rates of family formation across states with and without AFDC-UP? What other variables would you want to control for?

# Further Issues and Questions in Income Redistribution

## *Workfare as preparation for the job market.*

Levy and Michel do not address the arguments that workfare provides needed and helpful labor market experience. Much of the welfare population may be a more appropriate target for further education rather than immediate work experience, as this article suggests.

# STATE STUDY FINDS 57% ON WELFARE LACK BASIC SKILLS[†]

*Richard C. Paddock**

Examining the link between education and welfare dependency, a new state study has found evidence that more than half of California's aid recipients lack the basic skills that would enable them to find and keep a job.

The state, undertaking what is believed to be the nation's most extensive literacy testing of welfare recipients, found that 57% of those surveyed needed remedial education in reading, writing or math.

[†]*Los Angeles Times*, April 27, 1987. Copyright 1987, Los Angeles Times. Reprinted by permission.

*Times Staff Writer

"The welfare system is a holding area for people who did not get a good enough education," said Carl Williams, a Department of Social Services deputy director who heads the state's new Workfare program. "The message is pretty clear that we have one heck of a population out there that's in need of remediation."

The study, released last week, gives officials concrete evidence that the educational needs of welfare recipients are far greater than they had anticipated when the Workfare program began. It is also likely to focus attention on the shortcomings of the state's school system and make education a top priority in the effort to get recipients off public aid.

The study was conducted in conjunction with the Workfare program now in its first year. Known formally as Greater Avenues for Independence (GAIN), it is designed to replace welfare checks with paychecks by giving remedial education, job training, or work assignments to able-bodied welfare recipients with children over the age of 6.

As the first step in their enrollment in Workfare, more than 6,000 welfare applicants and recipients in nine counties were given standardized reading and math tests.

Of those who were tested, 36% scored so poorly they were referred to remedial education for six to 12 months before receiving training or work assignments, the study shows.

Nineteen percent who scored somewhat higher but showed a lack of basic knowledge in some areas were referred to remedial education for from one to 12 months to obtain the equivalent of a high school diploma.

In addition, 2% of those tested scored so low that officials have not been able to develop an educational program to help them, according to the study.

## FIRST REAL INSIGHT

"Because of GAIN, we are getting our first real insight into who these people really are," said Assemblyman Art Agnos (D-San Francisco), a key architect of the program. "These people simply are not ready for the fundamentals of work. They cannot read, write or count well enough to hold a job.

"Many people out there think that these are lazy, shiftless, unmotivated people. But these people simply missed the earlier opportunity in their lives to be educated, for whatever reason. We have to pick up where the other parts of our societal systems have failed, and that is education."

Agnos and other state officials had expected that only about half as many participants in the program would need remedial education before they began looking for work, receiving training or were assigned to public service jobs.

As a result, the Workfare program is off to a slower start than they had hoped and could end up costing more than the $300 million annually that they had forecast because it will take longer to get welfare recipients off the rolls.

## LARGEST STUDY SO FAR

Welfare experts at the New York-based Manpower Demonstration Research Corp. said the California survey constitutes the largest such literacy study so far attempted and is an important step in broadening the nation's understanding of welfare recipients.

More than half the states have adopted their own work programs for welfare recipients. The California program, with its education, job training, and mandatory work components, is the most complex and is increasingly viewed as a model for the rest of the country.

"There is a new seriousness in many states around the country to implement new-style workfare programs," said Richard Nathan, a professor at Princeton University and chairman of the research group. "California is leading the way."

Williams cautioned that the study does not provide a complete picture of welfare recipients statewide because the tests were conducted only in the nine counties that were the first to begin implementing the Workfare program.

In fact, he said, the percentage of welfare recipients who lack basic educational skills is probably higher than the study indicates because the tests were given primarily to applicants for welfare—not long-term recipients of aid who may have greater educational handicaps.

## DETAILED PROFILE EXPECTED

Eventually, most welfare recipients will be required to take the tests and the results are expected to provide the most detailed profile ever of the state's welfare population. This should enable welfare officials to design programs that best fit the needs of recipients with different levels of skills and education.

Of the first 6,000 people who took the literacy tests, 48.1% had completed the 12th grade or higher, including 2.1% who had obtained a degree from a four-year college.

In all, 56.4% had obtained at least the equivalent of a high school diploma, yet only 43% scored well enough to avoid referral to a remedial education program.

More than 87% of those tested said English was their native language, while 9.5% listed Spanish.

Females made up 57% of the study population; males 43%. Of those tested, 50% were between 25 and 34, 31% were over 34 and 19% were under 25.

In general, participants in the study did far better on the reading portion of the test than on the math section. Questions on the tests included such tasks as adding two four-digit numbers, figuring out how much it would cost to park in a lot with varying hourly rates and identifying the meaning of a sign reading "Authorized Personnel Only."

## CHANGE IN VIEWPOINT

Williams, a longtime advocate of mandatory work for welfare recipients who helped institute former Gov. Ronald Reagan's ill-fated workfare program in the early 1970s, said the results of the study have helped further a change in his own viewpoint about the problems-faced by welfare recipients.

"Back in the early '70s, when we started talking about workfare, we were very unsophisticated and naive about the conditions we were trying to deal with," he said. "I have to admit my views have changed considerably since then. For example, I was unaware how important basic education was, how essential child care was. For the first time, we are getting real information and we are getting away from the rhetorical debate on this subject."

Agnos, a liberal Democrat who once opposed the idea of mandatory work that has been incorporated in the state program, agreed: "We're finally doing the job right, instead of just with political rhetoric and sleight-of-hand programs.

"These are people who simply lack the tools that we are finally giving them. That's why they have been unable to find jobs all these years while politicians have been mired in a stalemate about what to do."

# QUESTIONS

1. The article suggests that the welfare population probably has lower skill levels than the group of typical welfare applicants studied here. Explain why the characteristics of a group moving onto welfare roles might be a biased measure of the characteristics of the welfare population. (HINT: Think about the characteristics of the people who get off the welfare roles.)

2. Two percent of this sample had college degrees. Should skilled welfare recipients be required to work at unskilled jobs in order to receive their welfare check?

3. In economic terms, how do you measure the costs and benefits of 12 months of remedial education that enables a welfare recipient to function in the job market?

### Experimental projects for Medicaid.

Demonstration projects have experimented with assigning specific health care providers to Medicaid recipients. As the following article shows, these projects are confronted with some thorny issues, such as appropriate pricing and quality control.

# AFTER FIVE YEARS, EXPERIMENTAL HEALTH PROJECT FOR MEDICAID RECIPIENTS SHOWS MIXED RESULTS[†]

*Clare Ansberry\**

In Jackson County, Mo., federal Medicaid recipients no longer rush to the hospital emergency room for treatment of common ailments ranging from a head cold to a rash. As a result of an experimental program, each recipient has been assigned a doctor or health clinic and can get medical help 24 hours a day. State officials figure they've saved $2.5 million since 1984 as a result of the program.

However, in Monterey County, Calif., a similar experiment failed miserably in 1985 after the program had millions of dollars of losses because of lax cost controls.

The widely disparate results of these federal projects—two of a half dozen initiated in 1982 and aimed at curbing exploding Medicaid costs while also improving medical care—underscore the difficulties in stemming sky-high health-care costs to the poor.

Since its inception two decades ago, the federal program providing health care to the

\*Staff Reporter of *The Wall Street Journal*

poor has been plagued by escalating costs, which now exceed $42 billion annually. A great deal of that Medicaid bill has reflected inappropriate use of hospitals. The poor, often turned away by doctors who consider Medicaid's reimbursement fees too low for the care they assumed the poor needed, are forced to rely on the nearest health facility. Typically, that's an inner-city hospital where costs are even higher than a doctor's office but where the much-needed continuity of care is lacking.

That situation stimulated the federal Health Care Financing Administration to fund the pilot programs in Missouri and California as well as New York, Minnesota, New Jersey and Florida.

Most of the half dozen experiments follow the Health Maintenance Organization concept, in which doctors, health groups, hospitals or HMOs are paid a fixed amount in advance of all treatment; patients are "locked" into one such medical care provider. Under Medicaid, doctors are paid a fee for each service. Furthermore, the states set their prepaid rate at 90% to 95% of the fee-for-service cost, thus guaranteeing a savings.

The demonstration projects are being watched closely since states increasingly are encouraged by Uncle Sam to use prepayments rather than the fee-for-service approach. Indeed, President Reagan's proposed federal 1988 budget seeks to give states a bonus if they pay standard amounts in advance for each Medicaid beneficiary.

But a chief concern about the pilot programs is the quality of care the poor receive. Both state and federal authorities acknowledge that the prepaid system can be abused by providers who collect regular rates but give only cursory care. They have cause for concern; a Rand Corp. study last year found that HMO-style programs "in general may be predisposed to underserve and the poor may be less likely to overcome this obstacle."

"We know there's a danger," says Ronald Deacon, an official of HCFA's demonstra-

tion division, explaining that's the reason the agency has monitoring programs. Among other things, officials of the demonstration projects keep tabs on whether the use of medical specialists for the poor seems unusually low and also attempt to assess whether doctors try to "dump" high risk poor patients on other health-care providers.

In Jackson County, which includes Kansas City, Medicaid recipients long knew only the hospital emergency room; most had no family doctor. Thus, for example, an asthmatic suffering frequent attacks might see one emergency-room physician one visit and another the next. "There was no way to keep track of what medications and treatments had been tried and what worked," says Ronald Meyer of Missouri's state Medicaid program.

## MEDICAL CARDS LIST

Under the pilot project, a Medicaid recipient's monthly medical cards list the name and telephone number of their doctor or health group. Besides the 24-hour care available, a doctor who can't provide the needed assistance gets authorization to refer the patient to a specialist or to hospitalize the patient. With ongoing care, patients don't get as sick, Mr. Meyer contends.

This feature has been especially beneficial to pregnant Medicaid recipients, many of whom under the traditional program wouldn't see a doctor until their eighth month of pregnancy. And by then, lack of a proper diet and medication might have made them high-risk patients and require "two weeks in the hospital at delivery instead of two days," says Mr. Meyer.

In Jackson County, most previous Medicaid providers opted to participate in the pilot project rather than lose a portion of their business. This required them, however, to change their billing and more closely monitor care since they weren't guaranteed payment for each service.

Some health care providers in the program found that some specialists were balking at accepting Medicaid patients referred to them by the providers. The solution to that problem has been quite simple. "You tell a radiologist that if he or she won't take your Medicaid patient, you won't send your cash-paying patients there either," says Starks Williams, a Jackson County physician and medical consultant.

As a result, health groups are beginning to market "extras" such as dental care and nutrition counseling to snare a greater share of Medicaid recipients.

The results in Jackson County are considered encouraging. For example, costly inpatient days for the Medicaid population in the program have dropped to 600 from 1,100 for every 1,000 recipients. The state has received permission to make the experiment an ongoing program.

A similarly structured pilot project in Santa Barbara County, Calif., also has proven successful and the state has asked to adopt its model as a continuing program.

## A $6 MILLION DEFICIT

However, the Monterey County, Calif., project was dismantled after less than two years because of a $6 million deficit. HFCA's Mr. Deacon blames the Monterey failure on the county's approach: Although Medicaid recipients were "locked" into one care giver, doctors still were paid a separate fee for each service as opposed to one lump sum in advance. In addition, physicians at one point received a monthly $3 case management fee for each Medicaid recipient.

"There was little incentive to control costs," says Mr. Deacon. Indeed, unlike Missouri and Santa Barbara, Monterey County's model didn't require doctors to get any formal authorization for referral care and nonemergency hospitalization. "In hindsight, the county didn't negotiate tough enough with physicians" Mr. Deacon contends.

In Florida, rate-setting was also a problem. In that state, only two of 12 HMOs agreed to participate in the project; the rest claimed rates were too low. As a result, the program has been downscaled to work with only the frail elderly and one hospital. In Monroe County, N.Y., providers also contend rates are too low and have threatened to pull out in July. The providers say that as a group, they had a loss of $2 million in 1986 after payments dropped 12%. There the problem seems to reflect the use of 1984-85 as a base year to set rates. That was a year in which medical costs were untypically low, says James Fatula of Medicap Inc., which administers the demonstration.

Still even in Monroe County, where the future of the program is tenuous at best, providers believe in the concept. "The idea of a prepaid system is much better for everyone," say Richard Greene, president of the Rochester Health Network. "That being the case, it's only a matter of time before everyone does it."

## QUESTIONS

1 What evidence is there in Jackson County that providers want more Medicaid patients? What evidence is there that Florida's providers did not want more Medicaid patients?

2. One factor in the profitability of prepaid care to Medicaid recipients is the type of patient. With prepayment set at 95 percent of fee-for-service costs, delivering care for a Medicaid pregnancy, for example, could be an attractive deal financially. Explain why this is so.

3. By assigning care providers available 24 hours a day, the program seeks to reduce cost by providing continuity in care as well as promoting preventative medicine and reducing emergency room use. What do the Monterey County, California results suggest about the relative importance of assigned providers and of prepayment as approaches to cost containment?

# PART IV

# Social Insurance Programs

### Proposals for Social Security reform.

Social Security's Old Age and Survivors Insurance (OASI) is the nation's largest entitlement program. It stands separate from the general budget, financed by its own tax. Since today's taxes are used to pay benefits to today's retirees, it does not accumulate a fund to make future payments. When the number of retirees to be supported increases relative to the number of workers paying payroll taxes to support them, it is easy to see how the system can get into financial trouble. One possible reform would be to move to a fully funded system.

Because a funded program would increase national savings and thereby affect the macroeconomy, some macroeconomists, such as James Tobin, have become interested in Social Security reform. The sections, from a longer paper on Social Security, reproduced here review the economic environment that has caused past problems for the system and propose reforms that include establishing Social Security as a funded pension program.

# THE FUTURE OF SOCIAL SECURITY:

## One Economist's Assessment[†]

James Tobin*

On its golden anniversary OASI is both successful, surely even beyond the dreams of its founders, and troubled. In the *1985 Economic Report of the President* his Council of Economic Advisers credits OASI for the remarkably healthy economic position of the elderly.

*Professor of Economics, Yale University and a recent Nobel Laureate in Economics.

†Theodore R. Marmor and Jerry L. Mashaw, eds., *Social Security in Contemporary American Politics*. To be published by Princeton University Press: excerpts from Chapter 2 reprinted with permission of Princeton University Press.

The other side of the same coin is the growth in the cost of the program, a source of considerable anxiety and alarm. Panic in 1981–1982 about the imminent "insolvency" of the trust fund was dissipated by legislation in 1983, a bipartisan compromise package of future payroll tax increases and benefit cuts projected to keep the fund in the black for several decades.

Nonetheless Social Security continues to be a candidate for federal budget makers seeking ways to cut deficits in the overall federal budget. Moreover, the 1983 package may not forestall another and more serious insolvency threat in the twenty-first century.

## HOW SOCIAL SECURITY GOT INTO TROUBLE

Why and how did so successful and popular a program run into financial difficulties and come to encounter distrust among its future beneficiaries? There are several reasons in recent history, some related to the general economic and political environment and some intrinsic to the OASI system.

### Stagflation

The American economy, along with the rest of the world, went sour beginning in 1970. The period since then has been an era of stagflation, OPEC shocks, four recessions, and low productivity growth. The most important symptom relevant to our topic is that real after-tax wage incomes, instead of rising at 2.5 to 3 percent per year as they had in the two previous decades, actually declined. A young man starting work in 1963 or 1973 has not experienced the progress toward the American dream that his father rightly took for granted a decade or two earlier. Indeed, from 1973 to 1983 his real wage income went down.[1] If young families nonetheless advanced their incomes during the 1970s, it was because both spouses worked and postponed or eschewed child-bearing. The commitment of today's young women to working careers in preference to motherhood also means that there will be few payroll taxpayers relative to OASI beneficiaries next century.

Meanwhile the living standards of the elderly not only were immune to the economy-wide setbacks but sharply improved. From 1970 to 1980, while average monthly real wages declined by 7.4 percent, average monthly OASI benefits rose in real terms by 37 percent. Generous improvements of benefits were enacted in the early 1970s, and were

protected by automatic adjustment of the Consumer Price Index beginning in 1973.[2]

### The Political Climate

The contrast of the stagnant 1970s with the prosperously growing 1960s was summarized by Lester Thurow in the term "zero-sum society," implying intensified conflict over the distribution of a national pie that was no longer growing. Redistributions of income of all kinds via taxes and governmental transfers waned in popularity. Tax revolts mushroomed in local, state, and national politics. General trust in government was eroded by Vietnam and Watergate. Conservative economics and ideology gained influence. The public was receptive to the conservative diagnosis of the 1970s, which attributed the disappointing economic performance to the size and growth of government—expenditures, taxes, regulations—rather than to OPEC and other external misfortunes. The last two, maybe even three, Presidential elections have been won on the slogan "government is not the solution, it is the problem."

### Demographic Trends

The age distribution has turned adverse to Social Security. Aged workers retire sooner and live longer. Births, low in the 1920s and 1930s, zoomed after the Second World War, began to decline in the 1960s, and now hardly suffice to replace parents. The trends are shown in Figure 1. The ratio of persons aged 20 to 64 to persons 65 and over is falling, and so, of course, is the number of workers per OASI beneficiary.

These clouds have some silver linings. Official projections have gone wrong in the past, and the current ones may be unduly pessimistic. Lower natural population and labor force growth may open the doors to more legal immigrants, mostly young workers who will be paying in to the trust fund. Greater

Figure 1. **Measures of available workers to "support" the elderly: the ratio of persons age 20 to 64 to persons age 65 and over and the ratio of covered workers to OASI beneficiaries, 1960–1980 and as projected 1985–2060.**

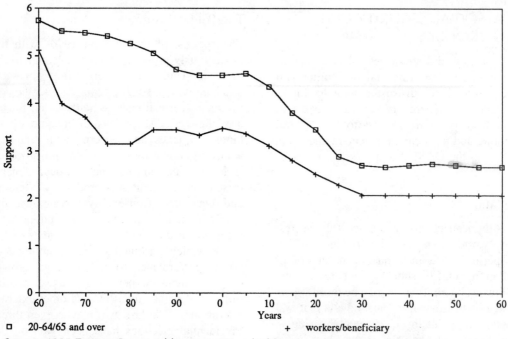

□   20-64/65 and over                                    +   workers/beneficiary

*Source: 1985 Trustees Report*, table A1, p. 77 and table 29, p. 65.

scarcity of labor might lead to faster growth of real wages—though given present uncertainties about capital formation and technological progress, this is by no means a sure thing. In any case, workers with fewer children will be able to afford either higher payroll taxes or additional saving on their own for retirement.

## The Maturing of the System

Some difficulties endemic to the OASI system became salient in the less benign environment after 1970, especially after 1973. Even though the climate is now improving, these problems once surfaced will not go away. They have roots in the history of OASI.

OASI took a long time to grow to maturity, and growing up was a lot easier than adulthood. The reach of the system, thus of the payroll tax, was gradually extended by legislation and by economic change (for example, migration from rural self-employment to nonfarm wage labor). Ratios of persons in covered employment any time during a year to average civilian employment for the year are indicative. They were .82 in 1950, 1.10 in 1960, 1.13 in 1984.[3] During this long period of expanding coverage, the number of contributing active workers was growing more rapidly than the labor force, and of course the covered percentage of retired workers was always lagging behind. By the 1970s we were coming to the end of this road. The few remaining pockets of exempt private employment were being absorbed. (State and local governments still have discretion and are likely to continue successfully their resistance to compulsory inclusion.)

Growth of coverage combined with growth of labor force and productivity to swell the proceeds of the payroll tax, faster than the benefit payments committed by previous legislation. The surpluses might have been allowed to pile up in the OASI trust fund, the way an insurance company channels current premiums into reserves against its liabilities to future beneficiaries. This was not done. Even so, the taxes and benefits set in the original Act in 1935 would have built a substantial fund, estimated at the time to reach in 1980 $47 billion (equivalent to about 300 billion actual 1980 dollars—compare 1980 benefit outlays of $105 billion). In the event, the trust fund was $23 billion in 1980. The 1939 Amendments deliberately scaled down the growth of the fund, aiming only at a modest contingency reserve. In addition, as surpluses loomed after 1950, Congress regularly increased the scope and size of benefits. The reforms were always very desirable improvements in the effectiveness and fairness of the system. Several generations of beneficiaries have, therefore, obtained excellent returns on their contributions, and I will too. But as the system approached maturity, these enlarged benefits could be continued only by successive increases in payroll taxes.

## Indexation

In 1972 another fateful decision was made: the automatic indexing of benefits. At the same time, benefits were scaled up by 20 percent. Indexation was well intended. Indeed, it was an act of political abnegation by Congress. The setting of benefits (including, but in practice not confined to, adjusting them for inflation) was taken off the regular political agenda. Moreover, there was every reason in past experience to believe that the move was financially prudent. OASI revenues would grow with wages, benefits with prices. Wages grow faster than prices; anyway they always had. Came the OPEC rise in oil prices and the van-

ishing of productivity growth and this relationship was reversed. In this way the stagflation of the 1970s hit OASI finances very directly. The blow was compounded by an inadvertent technical error in the 1972 legislation, which in the circumstances turned out to overindex benefits; this was corrected in 1977.

In retrospect it is easy to see that indexing by the CPI is not a good idea, even in economic times less turbulent than the 1970s. It is not a good idea for government-paid benefits, and it is not a good idea for wage contracts. Such indexing immunizes the favored individuals from losses the nation as a whole cannot escape—in 1973-1974 and 1979-1980 the big rises in the cost of imported oil—and throws their costs onto unprotected fellow citizens. Likewise, indexation in effect exempts its beneficiaries from paying increased taxes embodied in the prices that compose the index; others must bear the burdens of the public programs financed by those taxes. It would be both possible and desirable to construct an index purged of these unintended implications and to mandate its use, not only in Social Security but wherever indexed commitments are made, before we run again into stormy weather like the 1970s.[4]

## SOCIAL SECURITY AND NATIONAL SAVING

The issue of pay as you go versus funding is both more basic and more difficult than correcting for inflation. At the macroeconomic level the question is how OASI financing affects national saving and capital investment, and through them future productivity and standards of living. It is obviously related to the similar questions about overall federal fiscal policies.

Martin Feldstein has been the most prominent and insistent critic of pay-as-you-go financing. He argues that this system greatly diminishes aggregate national saving. Workers regard their payroll tax contributions as saving; the prospect of future OASI pensions spares them, at least in part, the need to provide for retirement on their own. But under pay as you go, the government treats receipts from those taxes like any other revenues and spends them. They are not channeled, directly or indirectly, through the capital markets into investment in productive capital assets whose yields could pay the future pensions. Feldstein estimated the national capital stock to be trillions of dollars smaller than it would have been with a funded system.

Feldstein's argument overstates the problem, both theoretically and empirically.[5] It probably is true that OASI taxes displace some voluntary saving. For example, some private pension plans, explicitly aiming at a target ratio of total retirement income to wage or salary, offset OASI improvements by lowering their own provisions. On the other hand, many workers are so constrained by their current liquid resources that they cannot offset OASI taxes by consuming more and saving less on their own. Moreover, many elderly pensioners do not consume all their pensions during retirement, as the Feldstein scenario assumes they do. Their benefits wind up, in part, in larger bequests to their children. Middle- and upper-income retired individuals typically save actuarially excessive amounts against the risk of prolonged high medical and custodial expenses, knowing that any unneeded amounts will end up in their estates.[6] Empirical studies provoked by Feldstein's work are inconclusive, but they indicate that the effects of unfunded OASI on voluntary private saving are at most much smaller than Feldstein asserted.

## OASI FINANCING AND FEDERAL FISCAL POLICY

The issue turns also on the effects of OASI financing on general federal fiscal policy, and of that policy on the economy and its rate of capital accumulation. Would the overall, "unified" budget deficit be smaller if, because of funding, OASI were in surplus? Or would the political and economic strategies that determine the budget offset the OASI surplus with a larger deficit in other transactions? A test may come in the 1990s and 2000s, when thanks to the 1983 legislation the OASI trust fund is projected to grow to 10 to 20 percent of GNP with annual surpluses of 2 to 2.5 percent of GNP.[7] Moreover, we are about to return to the pre-1968 practice of focusing official attention on the "administrative" budget and deficit, thus separating the trust funds from the budget that it is presumptively supposed to balance.

My guess is that in the past the federal government would have run larger administrative deficits had the trust funds been raking in surpluses. Indeed this often would have been good macroeconomic policy, because fiscal stimulus was needed to avoid or overcome recessions and keep the economy close to full employment. Fund surpluses, if not offset by administrative deficits or by aggressively stimulative monetary policy, would frequently have meant greater unemployment rather than more capital accumulation. If we were to assume that nowadays Federal Reserve monetary policy calls the macroeconomic tune, so that national output and employment are always what the "Fed" wants and will permit, irrespective of fiscal policy, the situation would correspond more closely to Feldstein's assumptions. Conditional on monetary policy, we would get more capital formation the lower the federal deficit. And funding, combined with segregated accounting, probably would lower the overall deficit, although by less than the OASI surplus.

A truly funded system could be expected to yield on average a higher rate of return on participants' contributions. A mature pay-as-you-go system cannot do better than the rate of growth of real payrolls—the sum of the rates of growth of employment and real wages. In the long run the growth of real wages is the growth of labor productivity. The formulas prescribed in 1972 and 1977 legislation pretty much guarantee that real benefits will grow along with real wages (i.e., with productivity). That is how earnings replacement rates are maintained. The formulas ignore trends in labor force and employment, which also determine the growth in real payrolls and thus in OASI contributions. As those growth trends decline, it will not be possible to pay the benefits the formulas generate without raising payroll tax rates. To make the same point another way, in those circumstances it will not be possible to hold tax rates constant without lowering earnings replacement rates.[8]

For the rest of the century, the growth of real payrolls looks to be about 3 percent per annum. Subsequently labor force growth will slow down. The baby-boomer bulge will subside, and the growth of the female labor force will decline as women's participation in the labor force approaches that of men. In official middle-range economic and demographic projections for the first half of the next century, real earnings per worker grow at about 1.8 percent per year and the covered labor force at a tenth of one percent, implying growth of taxable payrolls at well below 2 percent. The major uncertainty is productivity growth. The sources of its decline in the 1970s are still a mystery to students of the subject. Should labor productivity take off next century, the returns on the contributions of younger persons currently working or entering the labor force will be much better than they look now.

A funded system could in principle yield a rate of return equal to the economy's real interest rate, basically a reflection of the marginal productivity of capital. (Social Security trust funds, invested in federal securities, actually earn a bit less, because the federal government's borrowing rate is lower than rates on private securities. Those beneficiaries partially subject to income tax would earn still less, but this liability also reduces their return under pay as you go.) At present the pretax

real rate appears to be 4 to 5 percent, thus higher than the current 3 percent growth rate of real payrolls. Over a working career, this difference compounds to a 20 to 50 percent advantage in benefits.

An advantage of this kind is not, however, an opportunity available to OASI participants without a long transitional period of extra saving to do the funding, at the expense of the consumption of taxpayers and/or beneficiaries. Moreover, the differential in favor of funding may not last. In the past, real rates of interest in financial markets often have been lower than the growth of real payrolls.

## A POSSIBLE FUNDED SYSTEM

No radical change of OASI is likely in the near future. The Greenspan compromise has assured its "solvency" well into the next century. No crisis is likely to return OASI to the urgent agenda of politics for a couple of decades, although it may continue to be vulnerable to budget cutters who try to resolve general fiscal imbalances without raising taxes or cutting defense. The trust fund surpluses anticipated in the 1990s might tempt Congress to sweeten benefits or lower payroll taxes, although the deficits anticipated some decades later should be an inhibition. The Greenspan Commission left unresolved the financial crunch projected 50 to 60 years from now. The generations involved have the time and opportunity to choose among various ways of averting it. As a contribution to that debate, let me spell out what a funded system recast along purer insurance lines would look like. I shall draw in part on the proposals of Professors Boskin, Kotlikoff, and Shoven for "personal security accounts."[9]

1. Every individual participant would have a funded account, which would vest him or her with rights to pensions, and to ancillary insurance and benefits, from first cov-

ered job until actual retirement. The age of retirement (i.e., commencement of benefits) would be discretionary within a specified interval. Benefit claims would depend on the dates and amounts of contributions in the same way for all participants. The fund would grow during the participant's working career, not only by additional contributions but also by compound interest. The interest rate would vary with the government's borrowing rate, but would never be less than the rate of inflation of a suitable consumer price index (purged of the price effects of uninsurable shocks and indirect taxes).

2. At the time of retirement, this fund—less amounts charged to it for disability insurance, death benefits, and other ancillary items—will be converted actuarially into an indexed annuity, either for the life of the participant alone or with continuing payments to a surviving spouse, at the choice of the participant.

3. Contributions of married workers will be divided equally between the two spouses' accounts, as long as they are married. There will be no spousal benefits or benefits to a surviving spouse other than the optional survivor annuity mentioned above. But a married retired couple will receive all the benefits the two of them earned by working or by being married to a worker. Changes of this type are overdue. The present system does not do justice to working spouses or to divorcees.[10]

4. During periods of registered unemployment, a participant's compulsory payroll contributions to OASI in his previous job will be credited to his account without payments by the participant or his previous employer. The government could also credit extra contributions to participants who worked at low wages or were registered as unemployed for, say, at least 40 weeks of a year. These extra contributions could be proportional to the shortfall of earnings from, say, half the earnings cap for the year. Thus could some progressivity be built into the system.

5. The system will be funded in aggregate. The trust fund will receive the payroll contributions and credits, and disburse the annuities and other benefits. The Treasury will pay the trust fund interest on its balance at the designated rates. Since the scheme is essentially a "defined contribution" plan, its solvency will not be a problem unless real interest rates are chronically so low as to bring into force the guarantees of purchasing power.

6. Transition to such a funded system could take place slowly, as follows: Following its adoption, only new participants below age 35 would play by the new rules. Their aggregate contributions and credits would build up a new trust fund, Trust Fund II. Everyone else would play out the game by the old rules, via existing Trust Fund I. That fund would be deprived of receipts from the Fund II participants. The Treasury would "borrow" those receipts from Fund II and pay them out as necessary to Fund I beneficiaries. At the end of some 40 years of transition, Fund II would hold Treasury obligations equal in value to the accounts of its participants. From a macroeconomic standpoint, total receipts and payments throughout the transition would be virtually the same as if there were no new program. The difference would be simply that the government would now be acknowledging its liabilities to future beneficiaries, the Fund II participants. Present federal accounting does not reckon such liabilities as public debt, though they really are.

I do not want to be misunderstood. Accounting is not magic. It cannot produce the economic funding that Feldstein advocated unless the nation does some extra saving during the transition. This proposal does not assign that task to any particular generation, contributors or beneficiaries, but via the overall federal budget to the nation as a whole. Only if the gradual acknowledgment of the Treasury's debt to Fund II inspires Presidents and Congresses to lower their deficits on non-OASI transactions will the accounting reform have macroeconomic substance. At the end of the transition, OASI would be a funded system for its participants, but overall effects on national saving and capital formation would still depend on general fiscal and monetary policies.

The slow transition just outlined has the advantage of breaking the bad accounting news quite gradually. More important, it respects the legitimate expectations of everyone in the existing system. Faster transitions, under which many beneficiaries would receive benefits from both Funds I and II, would cause too many confusions, anomalies, and inequities.

The trade-off between workers' contribution rates and beneficiaries' earnings replacement rates is likely to be painful in the next century. (See Appendix A.) The generations concerned have time to work out a solution. The present system biases the result to maintaining the replacement rate and raising payroll taxes as necessary to pay the ever higher benefits. The proposed new system would be an opportunity to choose other options. One of them is to freeze the payroll tax and adjust future benefits accordingly; there are many options in between.

The new system would be much less vulnerable to economic and demographic shocks of the kind that spawned recent "crises." Blind adherence to pay as you go seems to result in raising taxes to cover previously committed benefits whenever adverse events threaten to deplete the fund. Even when the problems are foreseen, action is postponed so long that benefits cannot be touched without violating commitments to those retired or about to retire. At the same time, the new system would give participants a fair, clear, and continuously reported link between their individual contributions and their benefit rights. Although the system as outlined could accomplish some redistribution in favor of poorer participants, that burden is placed mainly on the general federal budget.

Proposals of this kind are worth considering in the next national debate about Social Security. The questions they raise are not in my view liberal/conservative or Democrat/Republican issues. They are issues of pragmatic management. Aging is a common human fate, irrespective of politics, ideologies, and generations. How people choose to trade consumption when they are young for consumption when they are old should not bring them to the barricades. It should bring them to face squarely economic and demographic realities. I hope the generations who will work out the structure of the system in the next century will do so in this spirit.

## APPENDIX A: THE SIMPLE ARITHMETIC OF OASI

The tradeoff between the contribution tax rate $c$ and the replacement rate $r$ under pay as you go is easy to see if it is assumed that every year benefits and contributions are strictly equal and that the trust fund is always zero. Such calculation also indicates starkly how the tradeoff worsens when, as will be happening next century, the number of contributing workers per contemporaneous retired beneficiary declines.

Let $x$ be worker-support, the number of workers per beneficiary; let $w$ be their real wage; and let $b$ be the real benefit. The replacement rate $r$ is by definition $b/w$. Pay as you go implies $b = cwx$, or $r = cx$. If $x$ is lower, it takes proportionately higher $c$ to keep $r$ constant, or proportionately lower $r$ to keep $c$ constant. This is the political-economic dilemma discussed in the text.

Table A.1

|                              | 1984 | 2004 | 2044b | 2044c |
|------------------------------|------|------|-------|-------|
| Worker–support, x            | 3.3  | 3.2  | 2.0   | 2.0   |
| Replacement ratio, r         | 0.38 | 0.41 | 0.40  | 0.25  |
| Tax rate, c                  | .114 | .124 | .20   | .124  |
| Real wage w (1984 = 100)     | 100  | 136  | 302   | 302   |
| Real benefit b = rw          | 38   | 56   | 121   | 75    |
| Real benefit b (1984 = 100)  | 100  | 147  | 318   | 197   |

Notes: Data from *Trustees Report*, projection II-A. Tax rates as now legislated in 2004. Two alternatives for 2044: 2044b holds replacement rate at present level, as will occur from automatic continuation of present benefit formulas. 2044c freezes tax rate at 12.4 percent; nevertheless real benefit is twice its 1984 amount. Under projection II-B, with less real wage growth, freezing the tax rate would bring a benefit in 2044 equal to 155 percent of that in 1984.

Table A.1 gives some illustrative numbers.

## Notes

1. Frank Levy and Robert Michel, "Are Yuppies Selfish?" *American Demographic Magazine*, April 1985.

2. *1985 Economic Report of the President*, Chapter 5.

3. Covered workers, *1985 Annual Report of the Board of Trustees of the Federal Old Age and Survivors Insurance and Disability Insurance Trust Funds*, Table 29, p. 65; civilian workers, *1985 Economic Report, op. cit.*, Table B-32, p. 270.

4. Indexation modified in the way described has been adopted in Austria and Sweden. For the United States, the appropriate index is conceptually a National Income and Product Accounts deflator for the personal consumption expenditures (PCE) component of Gross National *Income*. This is the deflator for the PCE component of gross national product modified to exclude changes in indirect taxes. It would measure changes in the dollar cost per unit of value added by payments of income to domestic factors of production in the making and delivery of consumption goods and services to domestic consumers. Increases and decreases in the dollar prices of imported consumption goods, or of imported materials used in mak-

ing domestic consumption goods, would not be counted. Neither would changes in indirect taxes— mainly sales, excise, and payroll taxes. Although the Department of Commerce PCE "deflator" is closest conceptually to the desired index, the Bureau of Labor Statistics Consumer Price Index could be modified to approximate these exclusions. Between 1971 and 1981, the period of import price shocks, the PCE deflator rose 10 percent less than the CPI; the difference would be somewhat greater if the deflator were purged of indirect taxes.

5. For review of the controversy see Henry Aaron, *The Economics of Social Security*, Washington: Brookings Institution, 1982.

6. Regarding the saving behavior of the elderly and its departure from Feldstein's assumptions, see S. Danziger, J. van der Gaag, E. Smolensky, and M. K. Taussig, "The life-cycle hypothesis and the consumption behavior of the elderly", *Journal of Post Keynesian Economics*, vol. V., Winter 1982–83, pp. 208–227.

7. On the fiscal issues posed by these projections see Alicia H. Munnell and Lynn E. Blais, "Do we want large Social Security surpluses?" *New England Economic Review*, September–October 1984, pp. 5–21.

8. In Appendix A the tradeoff between replacement rates and tax rates is explained with some simple algebra and arithmetic, and illustrated in relation to projections well into the next century.

9. Michael J. Boskin, Laurence J. Kotlikoff, and John B. Shoven, "Personal Security Accounts:

A Proposal for Fundamental Social Security Reform," presented to the National Commission on Social Security Reform, August 1982, unpublished. Revised version, unpublished, September 1985.

10. On this complex subject see Richard Burkhauser and Karen Holden, editors, *A Challenge to Social Security,* New York: Academic Press 1982.

## QUESTIONS

1. If real interest rates are generally higher than real payrolls growth, which system brings in more revenue for a given generation's benefits, a pay-as-you-go system or a funded one?

2. Tobin objects to indexation based on the Consumers Price Index. Would a wage index overcome his objections? If payroll taxes for Social Security are rising dramatically, does your answer depend on the incidence of the payroll tax?

3. How does Tobin propose the system move to a funded basis? Give two plausible scenarios illustrating how the burden of reduced consumption (in order to accumulate a trust fund) might be allocated, given Tobin's general framework.

### Proposals for Medicare Reform.

The federal government provides medical insurance for most of the nation's elderly through the Medicare program. Medicare's role in providing care is that of a third-party—neither patient nor doctor—insurer. This is a position from which it is very hard to control costs. Doctors advise their patients and prescribe treatments; when an outside party bears most of the costs, there is little incentive for either doctor or patient to limit the scope of treatment.

If the government could devise a way to fund most medical treatment for Medicare patients without bearing the costs of patients' marginal additions to care, costs might be lower. If patients or doctors (or doctors' employers) bear marginal costs, prescribed care is more likely to approach the level at which marginal costs approximate marginal benefits. One reform proposal for Medicare is the adoption of a prepayment structure that incorporates this kind of incentive structure.

# CONTROLLING MEDICARE OUTLAYS:

# Will Prepaid Health Plans Work?

*Stephen Zuckerman**

The Medicare program has, historically, paid for health care services provided to its beneficiaries on a fee-for-service or cost basis. These payment approaches, combined with an expanding elderly population with little or no incentive to seek out the most efficient means of treatment, have led to rapidly escalating program outlays. Medicare payments for personal health care rose by over 15 percent annually between 1970 and 1985 (Waldo, Levit, and Lazenby, 1985), while the number of enrollees was growing by only about 2 percent per year (Health Care Financing Administration, 1984). The serious fiscal consequences associated with this rate of expenditure growth

*Senior Research Associate, Health Policy Center, The Urban Institute.

are forcing policymakers to look for alternative payment policies that can create incentives to control both quantities and prices in Medicare's health care market.

A policy option that has the potential to meet this objective is to have Medicare move away from paying for individual services and pay for all of the elderly's health care through a capitated arrangement. Under capitation, a health care provider is prepaid a fixed amount for each enrollee in exchange for covering all medical services over a specified period of time. The capitated payment is, in effect, a health insurance premium. However, capitation differs from traditional health insurance in that the insurer (normally a third-party to the provision of care) is also the producer of medical services. One way to implement Medicare capitation would be to encourage beneficiaries to enroll in health maintenance organizations (HMOs) or other competitive medical plans that are willing to accept the capitated payment in exchange for incurring the costs of all necessary care that the program covers.

Traditional health insurance plans subsidize the patient's purchase of medical services by keeping the patient's marginal costs well below society's marginal costs of production. Since the insurer exerts little influence over individual medical choices, these subsidies result in the actual decision makers— patients and providers—choosing a quantity of services in excess of the one that equates social costs with the patient's benefits at the margin. For example, under present arrangements, physicians prescribe services whose benefits are below their full marginal costs so long as their benefits are greater than private marginal costs. These services may do little to improve the quality of treatment; they certainly cause a reduction in the insurer's profit margin. By combining the financial incentives of the insurer with those of the physician, capitation increases the probability that a lower volume of medical services will be consumed. In a real sense, the insurer is no longer a third party in the medical care transaction.

HMOs primarily succeed in reducing the overall volume of care relative to fee-for-service providers by hospitalizing their patients to a lesser degree.

Although capitated plans will result in the consumption of fewer medical services than an overproducing fee-for-service marketplace with traditional insurance, they may not produce the efficient quantity of care. Providers can influence the patient's perception of the marginal benefits of a particular test or course of treatment with the advice they offer. Since capitation allows providers to profit by providing fewer services, it gives them the incentive to undervalue the benefits of some medical services relative to the fee-for-service setting. (Of course, fee-for-service providers may overvalue these benefits.) Whereas society stands to have its resources used inefficiently under fee-for-service medicine, patients are at risk of being denied necessary care under capitation. Of course, patients can be protected from this phenomenon to the extent that the threat of malpractice suits or other damage to their reputations force capitated providers to deliver an acceptable quality of care.

## DRGs AND OTHER PRICE CONTROLS

The attention now being paid to capitation (for example, see Abramowitz, 1987) is in part a response to a major new policy initiative in the area of hospital reimbursement. In 1983, Medicare moved from a system that paid the costs of individual hospital services to one that paid hospitals a predetermined flat rate for each Medicare patient admitted within a particular diagnosis-related group (DRG), independent of the volume of services provided. If the total treatment costs were less than this rate, the hospital could retain all of the profits. Conversely, hospitals would have to absorb most costs in excess of the flat rate. This new approach gave hospitals the incentive to provide less costly care, whenever possible, and to shorten hospital stays. Evidence suggests that hospitals have responded accordingly (Feder, Hadley, and Zuckerman, 1986; Guterman and Dobson, 1986).

This cost-containment policy can be undermined if some of the services traditionally delivered during a hospitalization can be provided at other times. For example, some diagnostic testing that was previously performed after a patient was admitted might now be done in a physician's office or hospital outpatient department, with Medicare paying for this outside of the DRG system. Similarly, if an early discharge results in a patient needing skilled nursing home or visiting nurse care, the program will incur these costs in addition to the hospital payments. As long as Medicare pays for different types of care through different payment mechanisms, any efforts to contain overall costs are susceptible to this type of "unbundling." The ultimate cost of unbundling and similar changes in the volume of specific services in response to limited price controls will depend on the elasticities of substitution between the various services used in the production of health care and on the elasticity of program outlays with respect to these services.

## CAPITATION GRANTS

Whether or not HMOs will be successful with Medicare beneficiaries, in the long run, is an open question. In 1982, 26 demonstration projects were established to test various forms of a Medicare capitation policy. These demonstrations were used to evaluate alternative payment methodologies (including varying the degree of financial risk the HMO is exposed to by limiting the total per-patient losses an HMO might incur) and benefit packages as well as to explore providers' reactions to Medicare and beneficiaries' acceptance of HMOs. Capitation became a regular part of the Medicare program in 1985, but fee-for-service policies were allowed to coexist. However, only 2.2 percent of the Medicare

population is presently enrolled in a prepaid plan with a risk-based contract (Langwell and Hadley, 1986). While this represents a dramatic increase since the late 1970s, it clearly shows that Medicare is far from being able to rely on capitation to generate major savings. Two major roadblocks Medicare is likely to face in expanding capitation are beneficiary reluctance to enroll in a capitated plan, especially if this means changing their primary physician, and limits on the available number of plans willing to accept capitated payments, especially if payment amounts are not realistically tied to expected costs. This latter issue has become central to the debate over the future success of capitation and will be discussed below.

Many health care analysts argue that capitation will foster competition that can ultimately contain program costs. In fact, advocates of the policy see it as one in which beneficiaries, providers, and the program will all gain relative to current payment approaches. If an HMO believes it can earn profits by enrolling Medicare patients, it will offer incentives to join its plan. Presumably, given the same capitated payment amount, more efficient plans will be able to offer a greater array of supplemental benefits or subsidies as enrollment incentives. This occurred in many of the demonstration projects. Other things equal, this would make beneficiaries who enroll in these plans better off than they are under current fee-for-service arrangements. Enrollees who choose less efficient plans sacrifice these potential additional benefits and, implicitly, share in the higher costs of less efficient plans. This cost sharing would take the form of foregone coverage, an opportunity cost, and gradually should shift enrollees toward more efficient providers.

Making any capitated arrangement work in Medicare will not be easy.[1] A number of practical implementation issues must be addressed to the satisfaction of the program, beneficiaries, and providers before capitation can really be viewed as a long-term cost control mechanism. These include (1) setting the "correct" capitated payment amount and avoiding adverse selection, (2) regulating plans to ensure minimum benefit packages and quality, and (3) educating consumers with respect to their options. Adverse selection is the process through which individuals who consume more medical care—that is, the sicker people—gravitate toward certain plans or insurers. This leads to cost differences across plans that reflect differences in patient mix and not just differences in production efficiency. To the extent that the mechanism used to determine payment amounts does not fully reflect variation in expected use patterns, plans experiencing adverse selection will suffer financially. In the long run, this process may lead to the sickest beneficiaries being denied access to most plans and suggests that Medicare will need to retain its current insurance package as a default option.

## Payment Amounts and Adverse Selection

The Medicare program has three basic options available to determine capitated payment amounts. First, it could accept the rate the HMOs or insurers would charge to private patients, that is, a market approach. This would certainly assure access to providers for beneficiaries but might not be the most effective cost-containment policy. The reason for this is that Medicare currently is able to exercise some monopsony power to extract discounts and pay less than private insurers for most services.

A second approach would be to have the program set the capitated payment amount through some type of regulatory mechanism. While administered pricing is more consistent with present payment approaches, if the rates set are not actuarially correct for all beneficiaries, barriers to access might be created. Medicare's current mechanism for setting capitated rates exemplifies potential problems with

administered pricing. At present, an HMO is paid a rate based on a comparison of its estimate of the costs of providing the basic Medicare package of services and the adjusted average per capita cost (AAPCC) as computed by the program.

The AAPCC represents what the federal government would have paid for a comparable beneficiary if they had received care through the fee-for-service system in the plan's county. The ceiling for payments is 95 percent of the AAPCC per beneficiary. However, if more efficient plans have estimated costs that are below the AAPCC, the HMO must offer an enhanced benefit package or receive a payment rate below the ceiling.

The AAPCC assigned to each potential enrollee takes into account variation in expected health care outlays associated with age, sex, Medicaid eligibility, and nursing home residence. However, if capitated plans have access to a better set of these adjusters to explain expected variation in health service use across beneficiaries, they will have an incentive to identify potentially high-cost patients and avoid enrolling them. Something as simple as putting the enrollment area on the second floor of a nonelevator building might screen out Medicare's sickest beneficiaries. Alternatively, if plans are legislatively forced to accept all interested beneficiaries, then an inaccurate AAPCC may result in an inequitable distribution of financial hardships or windfalls across plans.

Patient responses to the additional benefits generated by efficiency may itself result in a type of adverse selection. If inherently more efficient plans offer a generous benefit package to attract enrollees, they may end up being more attractive to sicker patients. These people will place a higher expected value on the extra benefits than will the healthier segments of the population. Since research has shown that the AAPCC does not adequately predict the expected costs of different Medicare beneficiaries (see Eggers, 1980 and Eggers and

Prihoda, 1982), selection may lead to excessive financial risk for plans that try to pass efficiencies on to enrollees in the form of extra acute-care benefits. Of course, HMOs may seek some other mechanism (for example, providing additional preventive care rather than acute-care benefits) that would be less likely to attract Medicare's highest cost beneficiaries. Therefore, using the AAPCC to capitate payment amounts might leave the sickest people with access to plans that provide only a minimal benefit package. In this case, an imprecise AAPCC would deny extensive coverage to those people who would get the greatest marginal benefit from its use, placing the burden of AAPCC "errors" on those whom society might most want to insure.

Adverse selection can also affect the concept of capitation as a means of controlling program costs when the enrollment choice is voluntary. Since AAPCC rates are based on the average experience of the fee-for-service sector, the program might not save money if capitated plans attracted below-average users of Medicare services. Patients with ongoing physician relationships are less likely to enroll in a capitated system, leaving the fee-for-service default option (if it is permanently retained) with these above-average-cost beneficiaries. Under this scenario, program costs could actually rise in the short run by paying more for patients in capitated plans than would have been paid under fee for service. In the longer run, this adverse selection problem would get worse since the AAPCC rate, based on the average costs for the remaining fee-for-service beneficiaries, would rise as a result of a deterioration in the average health status of the fee-for-service group.

A third approach to setting payment levels, and one that would avoid problems associated with administratively setting the wrong prices, is to require plans to submit competitive bids for a predetermined set of program benefits. Within this system, plans could establish as many rates for different types of patients as they feel adequate.

This would remove the complaint that the AAPCC approach does not adequately distinguish among patients with different expected costs of care. However, since plans are not likely to reveal their lowest price unless they are at risk of being excluded from the treatment of Medicare patients, successful bidding will work only if there is a credible threat of excluding some plans from the Medicare system. While this is not likely to be a popular option anywhere, it will be a particularly difficult threat to enforce in areas with a limited number of health care providers. In any case, collusion among health plans might restrict the potential effectiveness of bidding as a means of setting capitated rates in areas with few providers. Negotiated rates might be a viable middle ground between pure bidding and administered rates, but, once again, some threat of exclusion may be necessary.

## Regulating Benefit Packages and Quality

One of the risks of encouraging a highly competitive system based on capitated rates is the potential for plans to reduce service provision to the point that beneficiaries receive inadequate treatment. While there is little evidence to suggest that HMOs have produced a low quality of care to date, experiences with the care of the elderly under capitation are limited. Small compromises in quality may be more problematic with respect to the care of the more seriously ill aged population than they would be to a younger group. Since patients are often incapable of evaluating the quality of care they receive, some regulatory oversight might be required despite the desire to stimulate competition.

## Consumer Education

Expansion of Medicare's HMO program will require consumers to make potentially important choices about the type of planning in which they would like to enroll. In order for these choices to be informed, the elderly will require a great deal of information to allow for accurate comparisons among plans. The Medicare program, in all likelihood, will have to screen the type of information provided to ensure that consumers are protected from misleading sales pitches. Performing this function will not be simple. For example, plans that cover the same medically necessary services may differ with respect to their determination of necessity. The problem is further complicated if plans provide financial incentives to encourage patients to use providers that tend to have lower costs. In this case, the actuarial value of the insurance varies with patient decisions that are made after the plan is joined. Unless Medicare can convince beneficiaries that it can perform this education function or, at least, insure people against legitimate mistakes (for example, when they make no choice if they are satisfied with the status quo) without incurring excessive administrative costs, capitation could fail on this implementation issue alone.

## SUMMARY

This review of capitation policy covers some of the basic issues that must be addressed before the policy, in any form, can become a major part of the Medicare program. With fewer than 5 percent of beneficiaries currently receiving care through capitated plans and with so many potential implementation problems, one has to question whether or not capitation will be a viable tool to deal with Medicare's impending fiscal problems. Recent simulations suggest that program outlays will exceed projected tax revenues (at current rates) by 30 percent in the year 2000, with the shortfall increasing dramatically in the years immediately following (Holahan and Palmer, 1987). While all potential solutions deserve attention, it appears that modifications to current payment methods with more direct utilization control policies might prove to be easier to implement and, therefore, more likely to succeed than capitation.

## Notes

1. While this article focuses on capitation through HMOs, another way to capitate program payments would be to issue vouchers that would be good for the purchase of any health care coverage—provided by Blue Cross plans, HMOs, or others. This approach could retain vestiges of traditional health insurance, something that may be desirable to many elderly beneficiaries. A voucher system can be thought of as capitation in which payments are made to beneficiaries rather than health care plans. This approach forces beneficiaries to make direct choices about individual coverage requirements. For example, the elderly might have to decide if expanded coverage for nursing home care was more or less valuable as a benefit than comprehensive coverage for preventive care. In all likelihood, however, current entitlements would have to be retained as a default option. While these sorts of decisions would be difficult, there is no reason to believe that currently mandated benefits are necessarily superior from a welfare standpoint to those that would be chosen by individuals.

A major drawback to a voucher-style form of capitation is that, by making individuals the purchasers of health care coverage, Medicare would be forfeiting some of its present monopsony power to drive its prices below those of other payers. Providers might feel little pressure to continue current Medicare rates. This would probably force the program to set voucher amounts above current costs to maintain access with the hope that competitive forces would ultimately drive down required outlays. An approach that did not compensate for this cut in monopsony influence might save the program money but could shift substantial burden to beneficiaries and, as such, might be politically untenable. For further discussion of the pros and cons of Medicare vouchers, see Friedman, LaTour, and Hughes (1984) and Luft (1984).

## References

Abramowitz, M. "Putting Medicare in Private Hands." *The Washington Post,* March 15, 1987, p. H1.

Eggers, P. "Risk Differentials Between Medicare Beneficiaries Enrolled and Not Enrolled in an HMO." *Health Care Financing Review,* 1(3) (Winter 1980): 91-99.

Eggers, P. and R. Prihoda. "Pre-enrollment Reimbursement Patterns of Medicare Beneficiaries Enrolled in 'At-Risk' HMOs." *Health Care Financing Review,* 4(1) (September 1982): 55-73.

Feder, J., J. Hadley, and S. Zuckerman. "How Did Medicare's Prospective Payment System Affect Hospitals?" Urban Institute Working Paper 3429-02. Washington, D.C.: The Urban Institute, November 1986.

Friedman, B., S. LaTour, and E. Hughes. "A Medicare Voucher System: What Can It Offer?" in U.S. Congress, *Proceedings of the Conference on the Future of Medicare, February 1, 1984.*

Guterman, S. and A. Dobson "Impact of the Medicare Prospective Payment System for Hospitals." *Health Care Financing Review* 7(3) 1986: 97-114.

Health Care Financing Administration. "Health Care Financing Trends." *Health Care Financing Review* 5(4) Summer 1984: 75-80.

Holahan, J. and J. Palmer. "Medicare's Fiscal Problems: An Imperative for Reform." Changing Domestic Priorities Discussion Paper. Washington, D.C.: The Urban Institute, February 1987.

Langwell, K. and J. Hadley. "Capitation and the Medicare Program: History, Issues, and Evidence." *Health Care Financing Review,* Annual Supplement, 1986, pp. 9-20.

Luft, H. "On the Use of Vouchers for Medicare." *Milbank Memorial Fund Quarterly* 62(2) Spring 1984: 237-250.

U.S. Congress, House of Representatives, Committee on Ways and Means, Subcommittee on Health. *Proceedings of the Conference on the Future of Medicare, February 1, 1984.* Washington, D.C.: U.S. Government Printing Office, 1984.

Waldo, D., K. Levit, and H. Lazenby. "National Health Expenditures, 1985." *Health Care Financing Review* 8(1) Fall 1986: 1-22.

## QUESTIONS

1. What is meant by the statement, "Capitation would move Medicare out of its current role as a third-party insurer"? Why might this lead to a reduction in Medicare costs?

2. Nursing home care is a big-ticket item not currently covered by Medicare. In a capitated system, do you think competition among health care providers will bring some nursing home coverage into the care plans being offered?

3. In many states, auto insurance companies are required to accept a share of the high-risk drivers who otherwise would not find insurance at affordable prices. Would you recommend such an "assigned risk" policy as part of a capitated Medicare program? How might this affect prices and the availability of services to other Medicare patients? What alternatives can you think of for getting care to high-cost Medicare enrollees?

4. Some of the arguments supporting capitation rely on competition among health care providers leading to efficiently designed programs. In rural areas, there is likely to be little competition. Of course, rural hospitals currently treat Medicare patients, without facing much competition. What arguments for capitation are relevant outside large urban areas?

*Equity in social insurance programs: Why do private insurance programs look at gender while social insurance programs do not?*

Unlike social insurance programs, such as Medicare and Social Security, private insurance rarely ignores gender in setting premiums and benefit amounts. Is this one more case of the government sacrificing efficiency for equity, or is something else going on? The reasons for this difference should become clear after reading this article. The special features of insurance markets, such as adverse selection and statistical discrimination, are important concepts for evaluating some of the reforms suggested for Medicare and Social Security.

# UNISEX INSURANCE

*Edward Golding and Nadja Zalokar\**

## I. GENDER DIFFERENCES IN INSURANCE MARKETS

Men are almost twice as likely as women to be involved in an automobile accident in a year (see Table 1). Should men pay the same premium for automobile insurance as women? Or should they pay a higher premium than women? Men at age 65 can expect to live 14 years, and women at age 65 can expect to live 18 years.[1] Should men and women receive the same monthly pensions from their employers even though this implies that women would receive a larger total lifetime payment? Or should women receive smaller monthly pensions so that the total lifetime payments are on average equal for men and women? Gender is currently used in determining individual premiums in many insurance markets. Should insurance companies be banned from using gender in setting rates? Both the courts and legislatures are grappling with numerous proposals for mandatory "sex-blind" or "unisex" insurance.

We begin our discussion of unisex insurance by explaining why insurance companies currently use gender in setting rates. We use the example of the automobile insurance market, but the argument carries over to other insurance markets. In order to simplify our discussion, we consider a hypothetical com-

*Special Assistant in Economics to the Federal Home Loan Bank Board and staff economist at the U.S. Commission on Civil Rights, respectively.

Table 1: **1982 Accident Rates by Sex**

|                                          | Men    | Women  |
| ---------------------------------------- | ------ | ------ |
| Accidents per driver                     | .26    | .14    |
| Accidents per 1,000,000,000 miles driven: |        |        |
| All accidents                            | 19,800 | 18,600 |
| Fatal accidents                          | 47     | 27     |

Source: National Safety Council, *Accident Facts*, 1983 Edition, p. 54.

petitive market where all drivers buy insurance, either because they are sufficiently risk averse or because they are required by law to do so.

Let us assume that there are two types of drivers, reckless drivers and careful drivers. These differences arise either because of differences in tastes (reckless drivers enjoy the thrill of dangerous driving more than careful drivers do) or because of differences in innate ability (reckless drivers do not have as good eye-hand coordination as careful drivers). Reckless drivers have a higher accident rate than careful drivers. If an insurance company insures a reckless driver, it can expect to incur $1000 a year in costs. This figure includes the average claim paid to reckless drivers and the "load," the cost of writing and administering the insurance policy. If the insurance company insures a careful driver, it can expect to incur costs of $200 a year.

If insurance companies could perfectly distinguish between reckless and careful drivers, the competitive premium for reckless drivers would be $1000 per year; for careful drivers it would be $200 per year. Insurance companies would earn zero economic profits. The premium each driver, male or female, would pay would depend only on whether the driver was reckless or careful. If relatively more men than women are reckless drivers, men's insurance premiums would be higher than women's on average even though the insurance is "sex-blind."

## II. ADVERSE SELECTION

Unfortunately, it is difficult for insurance companies to distinguish reckless drivers from careful ones. Insurance companies cannot simply ask this information on insurance applications, because all drivers have an incentive to say that they are careful in order to get the lower premium. Enterprising insurance companies thus seek ways of cheaply distinguishing between the two types of drivers. What indicators can insurance companies use to determine whether drivers are likely to be reckless or careful? One obvious indicator is the driver's accident history. Drivers who have had more accidents are more likely to be reckless than those who have had fewer accidents. Another easily observed indicator is the driver's gender, because men are more likely than women to be reckless.

To see how gender acts as an indicator of risk, suppose that 1/4 of men and 1/10 of women are reckless drivers. We can calculate the expected cost for an insurance company of insuring a male driver ($C_m$) as the proportion of men who are reckless (1/4) times the cost of insuring a reckless driver ($1000) plus the proportion of men who are careful (3/4) times the cost of insuring a careful driver ($200).

$$C_m = (1/4)\,\$1000 + (3/4)\,\$200 = \$400$$

Similarly the expected cost of insuring a female driver ($C_w$) can be calculated as:

$$C_w = (1/10)\,\$1000 + (9/10)\,\$200 = \$280$$

Since men are on average more costly to insure than women, insurance companies in a competitive market are forced to take gender into account in setting premiums for individual drivers. To see this, assume for the moment that company A decides not to use gender in setting rates, but instead to charge everyone the same premium. If there are equal numbers of male and female drivers, company A's average cost is then $(1/2)C_m + (1/2)C_w = \$340$, and thus it must charge $340 to break even. Another insurance company, company B, can underprice company A's policy for women (for instance, charge women $300). Company B attracts women away from company A and earns a profit (since its average cost is $280). Only male drivers continue to buy company A's policy. If it continues to charge $340, it will lose money because its average cost is now $400.

This is an example of what is known as the adverse selection problem. In general, the adverse selection problem occurs for insurance markets when buyers know their own risk, or likelihood of collecting on the policy, better than insurance companies do. When this is the case, if insurance companies charge a price chosen so that the company would break even if their policy is purchased by a representative sample of the population, they will lose money. Some low-risk individuals will find the insurance relatively expensive and will choose not to purchase the policy. High-risk individuals will find the insurance relatively cheap and will choose to purchase the policy. The individuals actually purchasing the policy will not be a representative sample of the population: They will be higher risk than average. Thus, the individuals purchasing the insurance are "adversely selected" from the point of view of the insurance company. In our example above, the adverse selection problem affects company A. By ignoring drivers' genders, the company puts itself at a competitive disadvantage relative to other insurance companies. The price it charges for insurance,

$340, would break even if it attracted a representative sample of the population. However, the people attracted to the policy will be men, who are higher risk than average, and company A loses money.

## III.  STATISTICAL DISCRIMINATION

The adverse selection problem forces insurance companies in competitive markets to use gender in setting rates. In our example, all men are charged a premium of $400 and all women are charged $280. Insurance companies are charging a higher premium for men than for women based on their different statistical probabilities of being reckless drivers. This behavior on the part of insurance companies is called "statistical discrimination," because the premium charged an individual driver is based on the statistical proportion of reckless to careful drivers for that driver's sex. Insurance companies are thus treating drivers as members of a group rather than as individuals.

When drivers are treated as members of groups, careful men are charged more than reckless women. It is this seeming inequity that causes many people to object to allowing statistical discrimination. It is argued that it is unfair to penalize careful men just because some men are reckless. Whether to allow statistical discrimination is a normative issue over which there is often considerable disagreement.

In addition to the automobile insurance market, there are numerous other markets where statistical discrimination based on gender is present. One example is the market for life insurance. Life insurance premiums are higher for men than for women, because men as a group have a higher death rate than women as a group (see Table 2). Again, some men are being "penalized" because they are members of a high-risk group.

An important example of statistical discrimination based on gender is the provision of pensions and annuities. Many firms provide retiring workers with pensions in the form of annuities: These are monthly payments of a fixed size made to the worker for as long as he or she lives. Annuities can be thought of as providing insurance against running out of money if the worker lives longer than expected. Since women have higher life expectancies at retirement than men, annuities paid to women often have smaller monthly payments than annuities paid to men. The amounts of the monthly payments to men and women are determined based on life tables so as to equalize expected total lifetime payments for men and women (appropriately discounted). Women who die young are "penalized" for being members of a long-lived group. In this example it is women who are hurt by statistical discrimination.

Those who judge statistical discrimination to be unfair have proposed banning the use of gender in insurance markets. Under these proposals, insurance companies would no longer be able to charge men and women different premiums. The movement to implement "unisex" insurance has pressed the issue in three forums. Legislation has been proposed both at the federal and state level. Court challenges to statistical discrimination have been mounted. Citizens' groups, such

Table 2: **Proportion Who Die within Five Years by Age, Race, and Sex**

| Age | White Men | White Women | Black Men | Black Women |
|-----|-----------|-------------|-----------|-------------|
| 20 | .0079 | .0026 | .0109 | .0039 |
| 30 | .0080 | .0033 | .0194 | .0078 |
| 40 | .0144 | .0078 | .0359 | .0181 |
| 50 | .0383 | .0211 | .0729 | .0388 |
| 60 | .0954 | .0517 | .1488 | .0861 |
| 70 | .2111 | .1195 | .2619 | .1672 |
| 80 | .4260 | .2946 | .4596 | .3534 |

*Source:* U.S. Department of Health and Human Services, National Center for Health Statistics, *Vital Statistics of the United States, 1984, Life Tables* Vol. II, Section 6, pp. 9-10.

as the Women's Equity Action League and other women's groups, have lobbied insurance providers to persuade them to eliminate the use of statistical discrimination.

To date, the movement for unisex insurance has had only limited success in pressing its cause. The most notable success so far has been the 1983 Norris decision. In this decision the Supreme Court ruled that Title VII of the 1964 Civil Rights Act, which forbids sex discrimination in employment, makes it illegal for employer-sponsored pension plans to pay lower monthly sums to women than to men based on women's statistical probability of living longer. Since Title VII pertains only to employment, the Supreme Court ruling in the Norris case does not apply to annuities not sponsored by employers or to other insurance markets. More sweeping legislative initiatives, such as the Packwood-Dingell bills proposed in Congress in 1983, which would have banned statistical discrimination based on gender in all insurance markets, have met with much opposition on the part of insurance companies and have not progressed through Congress. Some insurance plans have voluntarily adopted unisex rates, perhaps as the result of political pressure from within their constituencies. For example, TIAA-CREF, an organization that provides annuities and life insurance for college professors, voluntarily switched to providing unisex life insurance at the time the Norris decision required it to provide unisex annuities.

We argued above that companies cannot unilaterally adopt unisex insurance in competitive markets, because adverse selection would lead to losses. How then could some companies have voluntarily adopted unisex insurance? There are two factors that mitigate the adverse selection problem in many insurance markets. First, if a company has some monopoly power, then adopting unisex rates lowers its profits but does not necessarily force the company out of business. Second, if the insurance company provides group insurance, adverse selection is less of a problem as long as purchasing the insurance is compulsory for all members of the group. Adverse selection occurs when high-risk individuals buy more insurance and low-risk individuals opt out of the insurance plan. When all members of a group are required to purchase a single insurance plan, then high-risk individuals cannot purchase more insurance, and low-risk individuals can only opt out of the plan by leaving the group. For example, when the group is all people working for a particular firm, opting out entails looking for a new job. If the costs of searching for new jobs are high, low-risk individuals may not find it worthwhile to opt out of the insurance plan by leaving their jobs. Thus, it is possible for group insurance plans to introduce unisex insurance without facing much of an adverse selection problem. An extreme example of group insurance with unisex rates is the Social Security System. Almost all American workers are required to participate in the plan, and payments are sex-blind.

## IV. MANDATING UNISEX INSURANCE

Most of the insurance plans that are currently sex-blind are group insurance plans. The Norris decision, since it covers employer-provided pensions, applies to group insurance plans. Because of the severe adverse selection problem faced by insurance plans not tied to group membership, the only way that unisex insurance is likely to be introduced for insurance plans purchased by individuals is for the government to require sex-blind insurance. If the government requires sex-blind rates, then members of the lower risk gender can no longer opt out of the unisex insurance plan by switching to a competing company without such a plan, and the adverse selection problem is greatly mitigated.

What will happen if new court decisions or legislative initiatives extend mandatory unisex insurance to areas where insurance is generally provided on an individual basis, such as automobile insurance? In general, there will be three separate effects of mandatory unisex insurance. First, there will be transfers from some population groups to others. Second, there will be a change in deadweight loss as individuals alter their activity levels. Third, there will be a change in deadweight loss because insurance companies will redesign their rating systems. We discuss each of these effects in turn.

### Transfers

Let us consider first the case of automobile insurance. Men currently pay higher premiums for automobile insurance than women. (In our hypothetical example, men pay $400 and women pay $280). Suppose that sex-blind premiums are mandated for automobile insurance. The new premium charged members of both sexes is an average of the men's old premium and the women's old premium. (In our example the new premium will be $340.) As a result of mandatory unisex insurance, women pay more and men pay less than before. Thus, there has been an implicit transfer of income from women to men. (The transfer is $60 per individual in our example.) Men are better off, and women are worse off. Since one group is better off and the other is worse off, it is not possible to use the Pareto criterion to evaluate the change.

Although men would benefit from unisex automobile insurance, in other insurance markets women would benefit from unisex rates. Because of the number of markets involved, it would be a mammoth task to determine whether men or women would benefit more overall if unisex insurance were imposed universally. The calculations would be further complicated by the potential difficulty of determining the incidence of transfers under unisex insurance. For example, it is unclear whether the lower rates paid by men for unisex life insurance benefit the men themselves or, instead, the beneficiaries of their life insurance policies, often their wives.

## Loss from Individuals Changing Their Activity Levels

The adoption of unisex insurance alters the price individuals pay for automobile insurance and hence alters the price of driving. When the price of driving changes, the number of individuals who drive can be expected to change unless the demand for driving is perfectly inelastic. Does the change in the price of driving increase or decrease efficiency? A market is "efficient" if price is equal to (social) marginal cost. Notice that the unregulated competitive automobile insurance market described above is inefficient, because no driver pays a price equal to the cost of his or her insurance. Reckless men and reckless women are charged prices ($400 and $280 respectively) that are less than the cost of their insurance ($1000), and careful men and careful women are charged prices (again $400 and $280) that are higher than the cost of their insurance ($200). Therefore, since the competitive market does not lead to efficient pricing, we cannot conclude that altering the competitive prices is necessarily harmful. This is an example of what is known as the "second best" problem. Because of the lack of information necessary to identify reckless and careful drivers, prices are already distorted in the competitive market, and additional distortions in prices may prove either beneficial or harmful.

A price change that increases the divergence between price and (marginal) cost increases deadweight loss, and a price change

that decreases the divergence between price and marginal cost decreases deadweight loss. (If price is greater than marginal cost, too few individuals drive; if price is less than marginal cost, too many individuals drive.) To see whether the adoption of unisex insurance increases or decreases deadweight loss, we must determine whether the price of unisex insurance moves closer to or further from marginal cost for each of the four groups of drivers (careful men, reckless men, careful women, and reckless women). Table 3 summarizes the changes for each group.

Notice (see column e) that for careful men and reckless women there is a decrease in deadweight loss because the prices under unisex insurance are now closer to the cost of their insurance. For reckless men and careful women the opposite is true. Column (e) shows only whether the change in the deadweight loss is positive or negative. The magnitude of the changes for each group depends on their elasticity of demand for driving. The more inelastic the demand for driving, the smaller the change in the deadweight loss.

What can we predict about the aggregate effect? There are more reckless men than reckless women and more careful women than careful men.

Thus, there are more individuals in the groups where deadweight loss is increasing. Therefore, if we assume that all four groups have the same elasticity of demand for driving, we can conclude that unisex insurance leads to an increase in deadweight loss, that is, more

Table 3: **Efficiency Effects of Unisex Insurance, Automobile Insurance Example**

|  | (a) Cost | (b) Priced without Unisex | (c) Priced with Unisex | (d) Change in Divergence $\lvert c-a \rvert - \lvert b-a \rvert$ | (e) Change in Deadweight Loss |
|---|---|---|---|---|---|
| Reckless men | $1000 | $400 | $340 | +$60 | + |
| Careful men | $ 200 | $400 | $340 | −$60 | − |
| Reckless women | $1000 | $280 | $340 | −$60 | − |
| Careful women | $ 200 | $280 | $340 | +$60 | + |

people making the inefficient choice over whether or not to drive. How much the deadweight loss increases depends on the elasticity of demand for driving. If the demand for driving is inelastic (as we might expect since few people gave up driving when the price of gasoline increased in the 1970s) the efficiency loss from unisex insurance is likely to be small.

The deadweight loss from mandating unisex insurance for group insurance plans is also likely to be small. In the case of group insurance, the relevant elasticity of demand is that for group membership. If demand for group membership is inelastic, unisex insurance will have little effect on behavior. Thus, for Social Security, the relevant elasticity is the elasticity of demand for working (the elasticity of lifetime labor supply).

## Loss from Insurance Companies' Altering Their Rating Systems

Even if statistical discrimination based on gender is made illegal, insurance companies will still be allowed to use indicators other than gender in rating drivers. Insurance companies will have the incentive both to rely more heavily on indicators already in use and to find new indicators. When insurance companies alter their rating systems, there are likely to be efficiency losses.

If insurance companies are banned from using gender in rating drivers, they may rely more heavily on other indicators of risk that they are already using. For example, one indicator currently used to determine risk is the driver's past driving record. Drivers who have had more accidents generally pay higher premiums. If insurance companies can no longer use gender, they may charge even higher premiums to drivers who have had more accidents, because an accident now provides them with more information about risk.[2] Raising a driver's premium whenever he or she is involved in an accident imposes a cost on the driver. In effect, the driver now must bear some of the accident risk, because the driver

pays a higher premium in the event of an accident. Since risk averse drivers buy insurance to avoid risk, mandating unisex insurance in the automobile insurance market reduces the effective amount of insurance available in the market and therefore causes an efficiency loss.

In addition to relying more heavily on indicators already in use, insurance companies may turn to new indicators of risk. One new indicator they might use is the driver's performance on a driver's test. Requiring insured drivers to take a driver's test could help firms to distinguish between reckless and careful drivers since more careful drivers are more likely to pass the test. However, these driver's tests would involve a substantial resource cost, which would be passed on to drivers in a competitive market. New indicators of risk turned to by insurance companies will generally be more costly to use than gender, for if they were as cheap as gender they would already be used in the nonregulated insurance market.

One possibility is that insurance companies may attempt to use new indicators that are not directly related to a driver's risk but rather merely indicate the driver's gender. This possibility increases the cost of enforcing unisex insurance laws. One such potential indicator is height. Men are more likely than women to be tall, and they are also more likely to be reckless drivers. Therefore, tall people are more likely than short people to be reckless drivers. However, charging tall people more for automobile insurance would seem to violate the intent of any unisex insurance law. A regulatory body or the courts would have to rule on whether various indicators could be used in determining insurance rates. The enforcement and administrative costs involved with this type of regulation are likely to be substantial.

The above arguments all point out potential costs of imposing unisex insurance. These potential costs may well be outweighed by equity considerations. It is illegal to use race or religion in setting insurance rates even if they can be shown to be reliable indicators of risk. Why should gender be treated any differently? On the other hand, age is routinely used in determining insurance rates without much public uproar.

Can we distinguish any patterns for when indicators are allowed and when they are not? Two patterns are discernable. First, if no one is unduly penalized by the use of the indicator, then the indicator is usually allowed. Statistical discrimination based on age hurts younger drivers and helps older drivers. Since most people are both young and old in their lifetime, these effects tend to balance out. On net, few people can expect to be harmed by the use of age as an indicator of risk. The same could have been said about statistical discrimination based on gender when the traditional family unit was more the norm. The effects of gender-based insurance tend to balance out within the traditional family. Perhaps it is not surprising that the movement towards unisex insurance has emerged now that the traditional family is less common.

Second, society's acceptance of statistical discrimination seems to depend on whether or not individuals can affect the indicator. Smokers pay higher prices for life insurance even though not all smokers will die early. No one has advocated eliminating using smoking as a risk factor in setting life insurance rates. One reason it does not seem unfair to charge smokers higher rates is that smokers have the option of quitting and having their insurance rates lowered. In contrast, men cannot readily change their gender in order to lower their life insurance premiums or their automobile insurance premiums. Therefore, it seems somewhat unfair to charge men higher rates than women. Similarly, one reason statistical discrimination based on race is not allowed may be that individuals cannot change their race. In general, when individuals can voluntarily place themselves in or out of the high-risk group, society seems to allow statistical discrimination.

Adopting unisex insurance would likely create distortions in insurance markets, more in some markets than in others, and effect transfers between men and women. Some may view the imposition of unisex insurance as unwarranted government intervention into markets; others may feel that more equal treatment of men and women is worth the cost. The question of whether or not to adopt unisex insurance remains a normative one.

## Notes

1. U.S. Department of Health and Human Resources, National Center for Health Statistics, *Vital Statistics of the United States, 1984, Life Tables,* Vol. II, Section 6, p. 2.

2. To understand why insurance companies might rely more heavily on a driver's record if not allowed to use gender in setting premiums, imagine that gender were a perfect indicator for risk. If so, if insurance companies are allowed to observe a driver's gender, they would already know precisely which drivers are reckless and which are careful. There would be no need to look at a driver's record, because it would provide them with no new information. On the other hand, if insurance companies are not allowed to observe a driver's gender, a driver's record can provide them with a great deal of information. The more accidents the driver has had, the more likely he or she is to be a reckless driver. This line of reasoning carries over even if gender is not a perfect indicator of risk.

## Suggested Further Reading

Crocker, K. and A. Snow, "The Efficiency Effects of Categorical Discrimination in the Insurance Industry," *Journal of Political Economy,* vol. 94, no. 2, (April 1986): 321–344.

Dahlby, B. G. "Adverse Selection and Statistical Discrimination: An Analysis of Canadian Automobile Insurance," *Journal of Public Economics* 20(1983): 121–137.

Hoy, M. "Categorizing Risks in the Insurance Industry," *Quarterly Journal of Economics* 97(May 1982): 321–336.

## QUESTIONS

1. Why is it that most sex-blind insurance plans are group insurance?

2. The structure of Social Security makes it a much worse deal financially for some people (high-wage, never-married men, for example, pay lots in taxes, get a low fraction of wages back in benefits, receive no dependent spouse benefits, and die relatively young) than for others. One policy response to this inequity has been to suggest making Social Security a voluntary program. What do you predict would happen if people could choose whether or not to participate in Social Security?

3. Consider the hypothetical example in the article. If women as a group have more elastic demand for driving than men do, does this difference increase or decrease the deadweight loss (sometimes called excess burden or welfare loss) associated with a switch to unisex insurance?

4. Women are more likely than men to get pregnant. Men are more likely than women to contract AIDS. In each case, do our general standards for allowing statistical discrimination apply?

# Further Issues and Questions in Social Insurance

### *Extending the scope of Medicare benefits*

Congress has been urged to expand Medicare benefits in three areas: limiting out-of-pocket expenses of medications, covering nursing home care, and providing catastrophic health insurance.

A. Would you expect prepaid Medicare and Medicaid programs to address any of these concerns?

### *Monitoring HMO performance*

Since February 1985, Medicare patients have been allowed to enroll in prepaid health maintenance organizations. The Medicare-HMO program cost $1 billion in 1985, and yet fewer than 35 employees are monitoring the HMO's performance. Some participating HMOs have declared bankruptcy; others have been indicted on criminal charges by federal grand juries.

A. How would you determine the optimal level of expenditures on supervision of participating HMOs?

### *Personal habits and insurance costs*

Life insurance programs can afford to charge lower-than-average premiums to members of groups (for example, nonsmokers) whose lifestyles increase their life expectancy. The opposite is true, however, for pension plans, since long-lived participants are the more expensive ones. Shoven, Sundberg, and Bunker ("The Social Security Cost of Smoking," National Bureau of Economic Research working paper #2234) estimate that a middle-income male smoker saves Social Security about $20,000 by reducing his life expectancy;

a female with median female earnings saves Social Security about $10,000 if she smokes.

A. Should Social Security reward smokers with increased monthly benefits? Try to answer this question from two perspectives.

1. Assume that smokers are fully informed, rational actors and that the Social Security system is simply pursuing economic efficiency.
2. Modify your answer with any further considerations you think are relevant.

## Trade-offs involving human life.

Life is precious, but not infinitely so. We all make choices in our personal lives that to greater or lesser extents jeopardize our health and safety: We drive on freeways, drink coffee and exercise too little, and work and party too hard. No society has ever been rich enough to give every citizen unlimited medical care; in contemporary America, with our expanding arsenal of expensive high-tech medical options, many choices must be made about who is to receive how much care.

These decisions will not be made purely on economic grounds. But spelling out clearly the opportunity costs of pursuing certain medical programs at the expense of others can help to bring into focus the consequences of the choices we make.

## VALUING HUMAN LIFE

Economics assigns people two basic roles. As a productive asset, the value of a life is its value as human capital. This is measured as the present value of expected economic output. From this perspective, young lives are more valuable than old, men more valuable than women, workers more valuable than members of the leisure class. In wrongful death lawsuits, this measure of the value of life is often used to calculate the loss suffered by a family bereft of a breadwinner. It is not often used to represent society's valuation of life, however, since it counts as valueless retired and severely handicapped people who will not be producing. This approach to valuing life would, for example, allocate few resources to fighting cancer (a disease of the elderly) or to developing prosthetic aids for the handicapped; it would not invest in medical techniques to alleviate the pain associated with terminal conditions.

The second economic role people play is that of consumer. We can value life as a consumption good based on what people are willing to pay for it. While we do not in everyday situations pay to save lives directly, we do spend or forego money in order to reduce risk. We can look, for example, at labor markets to see how much more people must be paid to induce them to take risky jobs. If equally able people are paid $2000 a year more to be firefighters than to perform a perfectly safe job, and if the annual on-the-job mortality rate for firefighters is one in three thousand, then the one lost life is offset by $6 million in wage payments; this number can be thought of as a market value of life. Similarly, we can look at private expenditures on safety devices (for example, smoke detectors or safety belts) or at public expenditures on safety (for example, guard rails on highways). If the least usefully placed guard rails installed (that is, the marginal ones) each have an annualized cost of $20,000 and are expected to save one life every 20 years, then 20 such guard rails cost $400,000 and save one life yearly; this is the value of life revealed by our willingness to pay for guard rails. The numbers in these examples are hypothetical, but they give an idea of the frustratingly large range of values calculated under this method. Guidelines in federal agencies range from $400,000 to $7.5 million.

One important problem in which lives must be valued, implicitly or explicitly, is how to allocate medical resources. Economic efficiency dictates that we assess the average value of lives saved by various medical techniques and budget funds so that the marginal benefit of an additional dollar is equated across procedures. One suspects this is not exactly how the medical world works. It is interesting to see how the rationing of medical care conforms to narrowly conceived economic guidelines. In *The Painful Prescription: Rationing Hospital Care*, Aaron and Schwartz examine this question in the budget-conscious British health service. Excerpts from their 1984 book form this article.

# THE PAINFUL PRESCRIPTION:

## Rationing Hospital Care[†]

*Henry Aaron and William Schwartz\**

With some important exceptions, the norm for hospital care in the United States approximates the maxim "if it will help, do it." The system of third-party payment that dominates hospital reimbursement in the United States encourages the provision to most patients of all care that promises to yield benefits, regardless of cost. Most American patients are insulated from the financial consequences of most hospital episodes. Most American physicians gain financially from providing additional care, and medical ethics preclude only the delivery of care that will do harm, not of care that is unreasonably expensive. Hospital administrators seek facilities of high enough quality to satisfy the professional goals of their staffs. Thus care in the United States is usually close to what would be provided if cost were no object and benefit to patients were the sole concern.

## RATIONING CARE IN BRITAIN

At least seven features of the British health care system have facilitated the imposition of budget limits and made them stick. First, the National Health Service is organized within a parliamentary democracy marked by party discipline; the House of Commons does not usually reverse policies set by the cabinet. Second, the principle of public ownership and management of important sectors of the British economy is widely accepted, particularly for health care services. Third, a reservoir of goodwill exists for the NHS because of its origins in wartime adversity and its assurance of care to even the poorest people. Fourth, sequential referral of patients—from general practitioner to consultant—creates a mecha-

*Senior Research Fellow in Economic Studies, the Brookings Institution; Professor of Medicine, Tufts University, respectively.

†Reprinted by permission from the Brookings Institution.

nism not present in the United States, which allows the trusted family doctor to screen out cases not deemed medically suitable for complex care. Fifth, the residue of class structure in Britain increases the ability of physicians to persuade patients that aggressive treatment is inappropriate and increases the willingness of patients to accept such bleak news. Sixth, the British are less driven than Americans by the "don't just stand there, do something" attitude toward disease. Finally, hospital governance by salaried consultants provides a notably effective instrument for encouraging the quiet enforcement of budget limits.

## PRELIMINARY HYPOTHESES

As we began our examination of responses to budget limits, we held certain hypotheses about the kind of trade-offs that budget limits would have forced the British to make. We anticipated that treatment for the elderly would be curtailed more than treatment for the young. We predicted that lifesaving treatments would be curtailed less than those that improve the quality of life. Because of the relative ease of deciding not to buy new equipment, as opposed to directly refusing care to a sick patient, we expected that treatments dependent on costly equipment would be reduced more than those dependent only on staff time and ordinary supplies. The special terror that cancer seems to arouse led us to speculate that its treatment would be curtailed relatively little. We expected that new treatments would be provided in relatively smaller amounts than old ones, because new treatments would have to compete with established services for available resources. We expected diagnostic procedures about which patients were likely to know little to be supplied in smaller amounts than procedures about which the public was better informed. In general, we expected the degree to which a service is curtailed to depend on the height and shape of the "social benefit" curve per dollar of expenditure.

We found that most of our hypotheses seemed to be consistent with observed British behavior. On the other hand, we also realize that we have more plausible explanations for the observed patterns than we could test with the number of alternative medical procedures we examined. For this reason, we cannot claim to have tested in a statistically rigorous way our explanations for why the British limit different forms of care in such different degrees. Readers will have to decide whether we tell a plausible story about why the British have limited care as they have.

## Acute, Life-Threatening Illness

One class of conditions—acute, life-threatening illnesses—is largely exempt from the rationing process in Britain. Successful treatment of a brief but life-threatening illness yields a large payoff and thus encourages generous investment. Moreover, the way in which people with an acute illness usually enter the system facilitates their getting the most favorable treatment. Patients who arrive in an emergency room suffering from such acute conditions as diabetic coma, myocardial infarction, or trauma are promptly admitted to the hospital and given all available care. Once that step is taken, no effort is spared as long as there is even a remote chance of restoring normal or near normal health.

To test this perception, we asked several British physicians how they would handle an accident victim whose injuries we described. We based our query on a real case admitted to a large U.S. teaching hospital. Included in the case history was the estimate that the patient had one chance in a hundred of surviving and that the cost of his care could be expected to exceed $100,000. Confronted with one hundred similar cases, one would expect to save one life and to spend $10 million. Despite the limitations they face, the British physicians unanimously stated that they would have used all available resources just as their American counterparts had done. The same approach, we were told, is apparently not followed consistently with the elderly.

## CHRONIC DIALYSIS

As we have pointed out, the restriction of chronic dialysis in Britain causes many people to die earlier than they would if treatment were fully available to them. Many influences seem to contribute to this decision.

First, a commitment to treat all cases of chronic kidney failure would be extremely costly. If Britain dialyzed at the same rate as the United States, it would have to increase its total health expenditures by over 1 percent. But this increment equals the real growth in all health expenditures planned for the next two years, according to Prime Minister Margaret Thatcher's budget request for 1983-84. Given this constraint, full-service dialysis could be provided only if large sacrifices were made in other areas of health care.

Second, hospital dialysis facilities can be limited in a fairly centralized way by controlling capital expenditure on equipment and by limiting numbers of qualified nurses and technicians. Thus doctors and patients alike perceive the limitation as an external constraint rather than as a personal choice.

Third, the general practitioner seldom has to face the constraint on dialysis. Given the rates at which kidney failure occurs, the typical family doctor may see only one case every two or three years. Consultants see many more cases, of course, but their burden is lightened because general practitioners try not to refer patients who, their experience has taught them, are unlikely to be treated.

Finally, renal failure, which is usually manifested by weakness, nausea, and drowsiness, is neither a highly visible nor a dread disease. Furthermore, it is often accompanied by other diseases, such as long-standing diabetes, which can be used to rationalize the refusal of care.

## HEMOPHILIA

Whatever can be said about chronic renal failure should be reversed for hemophilia, a disease that is treated as often and almost as intensively in Britain as in the United States. The illness is highly visible, and its symptoms alarm any observer. Treatment is conspicuously successful in the short run because patients feel almost entirely well between episodes. Capital investment required for treatment is minimal, and the total cost of treating all hemophiliacs, $30 million to $40 million a year, is one-tenth the potential cost of offering dialysis to all patients in chronic renal failure. Moreover, full treatment of hemophilia has the further benefit that it largely eliminates the potentially costly disabilities that result without it. Dialysis, on the other hand, may be perceived as a form of disability itself, because treatment immobilizes the patient several times a week and is accompanied by complications and discomforts of its own.

## HIP REPLACEMENT

Hip replacement is rationed in Britain, and the waiting lists are notoriously long, but in reality the British insert about 75 to 80 percent as many artificial hips per capita as Americans do. The total cost of this program is relatively high—about $100 million to $150 million a year.

Why is so much spent on hip replacement to reduce pain and improve mobility of the elderly, but so little on dialysis to save lives? First, hip replacement helps many people and at less total cost than dialysis. The typical dialysis patient is treated for several years or longer at an average cost of about $15,000 a year, whereas patients requiring hip replacement are treated once at a cost of only about $6,000. Moreover, those who undergo successful hip surgery enjoy a life of good quality, whereas dialysis is beset by complications and does not restore normal quality of life.

Finally, restoring mobility for the large number of patients with hip disease who otherwise would require extensive nursing care, either at home or in a public institution, avoids large indirect costs. By contrast, little would be saved by eliminating the modest expense of supporting the elderly, undialyzed renal failure patient during his brief terminal illness.

## CORONARY ARTERY SURGERY

The low rate of coronary artery surgery in Britain—10 percent of that in the United States—calls out for an explanation. Even if the American rate is too high, as seems likely, experts we have consulted believe that the British might do perhaps seven times as many cases a year with considerable medical profit.

Age hardly seems to be a factor. Hip surgery is provided to the same age group far more generously than is coronary artery surgery. Hip replacement, it is true, costs only one-half to two-thirds as much as a coronary bypass procedure, but this difference in cost does not seem to explain the large disparity in numbers of procedures performed. In 1977 some 27,000 hip replacements were performed on an estimated pool of 34,000 candidates, as contrasted with 3,000 bypass grafts for 20,000 highly suitable candidates for the surgery.

Two factors may account for this seeming anomaly. First, hip disease is more obvious than coronary artery disease. One can more easily apprehend the anguish of an elderly woman, bedridden or barely able to walk, than that of a middle-aged man who must walk slowly to avoid discomfort. Bypass surgery may also command fewer resources because the untreated patient with angina does not place the same burden on society's resources as do those with untreated hip disease. With medication alone, angina patients can usually look after their personal needs and remain mobile enough not to require nursing or other supportive care. Severe hip disease creates far greater demands.

## RADIOTHERAPY

The quantity and quality of megavoltage radiotherapy in Britain and the United States are similar. Expenditures on radiotherapy in Britain are probably somewhat more than $100 million a year (based on an estimate of $500 million in the United States), a substantial sum in Britain's $13 billion hospital budget for 1980. Radiotherapy is the one expensive technology provided to the elderly for which demand is fully satisfied. Only hip replacement comes close.

Radiotherapy seems to enjoy a favored position for several reasons. One of them is historical. As one of the earliest of the expensive technologies, it came into use when resources were still relatively plentiful and thus was fully funded—an unlikely outcome today. Perhaps equally important, cancer is a dread disease. The special position of cancer in the public mind probably assures generous support for radiotherapy. This special concern is also seen in the large sums raised by such patient organizations as the Imperial Cancer Fund, which establishes professorships of oncology and supports other work on cancer.

## CANCER CHEMOTHERAPY

Cancer chemotherapy is administered to patients with potentially curable metastatic tumors at the same rate in Britain as in the United States. Here, age of the victims is an obvious reason; many of the potentially curable malignancies occur in relatively young people. A few thousand dollars may yield many years of life. Moreover, the total cost of the program is modest.

On the other hand, the British are much more conservative than Americans in their approach to tumors that respond poorly to chemotherapy, such as carcinomas of the pancreas or stomach. British oncologists say that in such cases the decision not to treat is made not on financial grounds but to spare their patients pointless suffering.

We could predict, however, that resource constraints would loom large if an expensive but effective form of chemotherapy could be developed for one or another of the common cancers. Tens of thousands of patients would be candidates, and the total cost would become large.

When asked what would happen under these circumstances, a leading British oncologist responded, "It is something I wake up screaming about. I suspect that not everybody who might benefit from [chemotherapy] would get it in practice. If you could cure every patient who has carcinoma of the colon, most of whom are going to be over sixty-five, over fifty-five anyway, I think we might find ourselves making value judgments about which to treat and which not to." As the case of chronic dialysis shows, even decisions to fund lifesaving care may become sensitive to the total cost of rendering such care.

## BONE MARROW TRANSPLANTATION

Bone marrow transplantation is provided in Britain as frequently, per capita, as in the United States. Here the youth of the recipients and the often lifesaving nature of the treatment are important factors. Moreover, the diseases that are treated—chiefly leukemia and aplastic anemia—are visibly devastating. The aggregate cost is also relatively low because no more than a few hundred patients a year are suitable candidates for treatment. These influences work together to encourage full funding.

## CT SCANNERS

On its face, the relative lack of CT scanners in Britain is hard to explain. The technology is now recognized as a powerful, indeed revolutionary, diagnostic tool in many clinical situations. Nevertheless, the British spend only $20 million a year on CT scanning and have the capacity to perform only a fifth as many scans per capita as do Americans. Most hospitals, including many major centers, do not have a machine, and their patients do not have ready access to a CT facility located elsewhere.

To reach a capacity comparable with that in the United States, Britain would have to spend only another $80 million. But the funds would have to come out of the limited resources available for capital expenditures on equipment and for the creation of staff positions. In other words, hospital physicians cannot simply commandeer a larger share of drugs, clinical space, or beds from the pool of general hospital space as with coronary bypass grafts or hip replacement. Obtaining new funds is also made more difficult by the absence of a constituency with a disease that depends on the machine. Most people do not know the circumstances under which a scan would benefit them and are unaware that they are being denied valuable care.

Nevertheless, the donation of scanners shows an increasing popular recognition of the shortage. Unless operating funds are also donated, the recipient hospital is forced to assume the ongoing costs of the machine, including its staffing.

## INTENSIVE CARE BEDS

With only one-tenth to one-fifth the number of intensive care beds available per capita as in the United States, British physicians acknowledged that they could use more to medical advantage. But planners and physicians alike perceive the overall cost to be excessive. To reach parity with the United States, Britain would have to increase its total health care budget some 10 percent. One director of an intensive care unit in a teaching hospital said, "Such a move would be inappropriate given the enormous negative impact on other services that would have funds withdrawn from them. This [our unit] is about right and appropriate. It balances with the rest of what goes on around here. It would be crazy [to have more beds], you see, because it would be out of proportion to what we offer in the renal unit and what we offer anywhere else."

## TERMINAL ILLNESS

We were told repeatedly that British physicians discontinue aggressive therapy for the terminally ill earlier than their American counterparts do. They also, and just as repeatedly, assert that they would elect to stop treatment earlier than Americans do, even if their resources were not constrained. We have no reason to dispute this claim, which undoubtedly reflects cultural traditions and ethical views.

On the other hand, the limitation on intensive care beds, the relative lack of facilities for chronic dialysis, and other constraints force British physicians to practice triage. They cannot routinely place a seventy-five-year-old patient with advanced metastatic cancer in an intensive care unit without an awareness that the bed is likely to be needed by a twenty-five-year-old accident victim. In the United States a physician who might explicitly agree with values expressed by his British colleague may nevertheless be allowed to avoid a hard decision by the sheer availability of the bed.

## FACTORS THAT SEEM TO INFLUENCE RESOURCE ALLOCATION

A set of general principles can be extracted from the representative technologies we have examined. Some reflect the influence of administrative arrangements on the allocation process. Others are an expression of society's value judgments or of attempts to make the most efficient use of resources.

### Age

If all other factors were held constant, we would expect less rationing of health care for children than for adults. Aggregate data support this prediction. Health expenditures per child in Britain are 119 percent of expenditures per prime age adult, whereas in the United States they are only 37 percent as much.

These results are hardly surprising. Adults respond to sick children with strong emotions. Furthermore, care that saves a child's life or improves its quality yields benefits much longer than those same resources used on an older person.

The responsibilities of prime age adults as parents and earners sometimes override these considerations, but such offsetting factors seldom apply to the elderly. The low incidence of chronic dialysis among the elderly with renal failure dramatizes such discrimination. The limitation of resources allocated to the treatment of terminal illness is another expression of this bias.

### Dread Disease

Some diseases, depending on the culture and the historical moment, inspire more fear than others. Currently, the prime example is cancer. One might expect that such diseases would receive a disproportionate share of the available resources.

Such appears to be the case. Megavoltage radiotherapy is made available to all who can benefit from it, even if the expectation is palliation rather than cure. Moreover, cancer chemotherapy is provided to all in whom there is hope of prolonging life by as much as several years or an expectation of significant palliation of symptoms.

### Visibility of Illness

People do not like visible misery. They are made uncomfortable if they must watch severe and untreated suffering. The bleeding joints, swelling, and disabilities of hemophilia are likely to stir more feeling in bystanders than the silent pain of angina pectoris. It is thus not surprising that more support is allocated to clotting factors for hemophiliacs than to bypass surgery for angina patients, as is indeed the case in Britain.

## Advocacy

Organized advocates can try to use political pressure, publicity, or charity to obtain facilities and personnel for a particular service. Oddly enough, we found little evidence that advocacy plays an important role in shaping allocation decisions in Britain. Other than bone marrow transplantation, we have found no service significantly increased by the efforts of pressure groups. We suspect that in this regard the United States will prove to be quite different.

## Aggregate Cost

A service that is costly relative to the benefit it yields may still be provided if the total cost for all patients is fairly small. It may simply not be seen as worthwhile to enforce the general principles of rationing when the total cost of a program seems negligible. The full-scale treatment of hemophilia in Britain may be an example. Only about seventy-five new cases of hemophilia are diagnosed each year in Britain. At an annual cost of $10,000 to $20,000 each, this small number of patients appears to be exempted from rationing. It seems less likely that the same would be true if there were 25,000 new patients every year.

## Need for Capital Funds

The use of new technology can be controlled much more easily if it requires a large capital outlay than if it depends only on funds from the hospital's operating budget. A vivid contrast is provided by outlays on CT scanners as opposed to expenditure for total parenteral nutrition. Only about $10 million a year is committed to CT scanners, which have been installed in only a few hospitals, even though they could make an important contribution in any facility with more than 200 beds. By contrast, the benefit of total parenteral nutrition to most of the patients receiving it has not been well documented. But Britain spends as much on this service as on CT scanning. At least part of the reason, we surmise, is that total parenteral nutrition requires no appreciable capital outlay and can be allocated, case by case, at the discretion of individual physicians.

## Costs of Alternative Modes of Care

Our observations support the notion that a given therapy will be provided in larger quantity if the costs of not treating the patient exceed the costs of active intervention. This thesis gains compelling support from a comparison of coronary bypass surgery with hip replacement. The costs of each operation are similar, as are the ages of the patients, but hip replacements are done with far greater frequency. As we noted earlier, the much higher cost of caring for disabled patients with hip disease than for that for patients with angina seems likely to be the main determinant of the difference.

# QUALITY VERSUS QUANTITY

Resources could be saved by reducing quality as well as quantity. Would it not therefore be sensible to dilute the quality of care in order to extend the quantity? In most instances the answer is no, and British decisions on resource allocation appear to reflect this judgment.

The British, as far as we could tell, and in the opinion of experts, maintain virtually the same standards of quality for CT scanning, coronary bypass surgery, hip replacement, cancer chemotherapy, and other such technologies as do Americans. In each of these instances, cutting corners would exact a heavy toll of bad outcomes and therefore make little sense. Instead, dollars are saved by reducing quantity.

In the few instances in which quality can be reduced without substantial harm, the British indeed have made the cuts. In diagnostic radiology, for example, the British use half as many films per examination as American radiologists. They also have older and much less sophisticated equipment and a less than optimal number of radiologists. The economies achieved in this way reduce the quality of information to some degree, but the dollars saved almost certainly can be applied to greater advantage elsewhere in the health care system.

Cost-saving is also achieved in radiotherapy by less than optimal staffing patterns. In radiotherapy, as in diagnostic radiology, such economies make sense because their effect on quality is viewed by experts as marginal.

A reduction in quality is also seen in hospital structure. Even though the United Kingdom has only slightly fewer beds per capita than the United States, it spends, on average, only $12 per capita annually on the construction of medical facilities, while the United States spends $25. Most hospitals in Britain were built before World War II and many before World War I. These older hospitals obviously do not offer the same amenities or the same efficiency in providing patient care as do new facilities. Given competing demands, however, the cost of replacing them would be excessive.

## QUESTIONS

1. In their statement of preliminary hypotheses, the authors outline half a dozen specific principles they expect will guide resource allocation in a regime of rationed care. Of these six principles, which ones are directly consistent with cost-benefit principles? Which ones are more related to the objective of cutting costs in ways that raise little public outcry? Do any of them focus on the intangible "insurance" benefit of treating dread diseases that many people fear they might contract?

2. From a cost-benefit perspective, name a treatment you think is underprovided in the British system. Name one that is overprovided, relative to other medical treatment. State your reasons briefly.

3. Using the principles that seem to guide the allocation of resources in the British system, how do you predict the system will respond to AIDS victims? At the time of this writing, there is no known cure for AIDS, and the costs of minimal treatment are (in very rough terms) comparable to those for chronic kidney dialysis, with full-blown costs much higher.

# Further Issues and Questions in Cost-Benefit Analysis

### *The costs and benefits of AIDS testing.*

One of the most emotional public debates of the mid 1980s is whether Americans should be routinely tested for AIDS. While cost-benefit principles cannot resolve the question of AIDS testing, a careful statement of the costs and benefits involved can help to clarify the debate. For example, do the opposing parties differ in points of "fact," say, in their evaluation of the epidemiological benefits of testing? Do they put different weights on intangibles like "privacy"? A point-by-point comparison can focus the debate and perhaps relieve some hysteria by showing how reasonable people might come to disagree with one another. The *Wall Street Journal* published a pair of articles debating the testing issue, along with some background material on how AIDS testing works. These articles reveal two thoughtful analyses leading to opposite conclusions.

# DEBATE RAGES OVER AIDS-TEST POLICY†

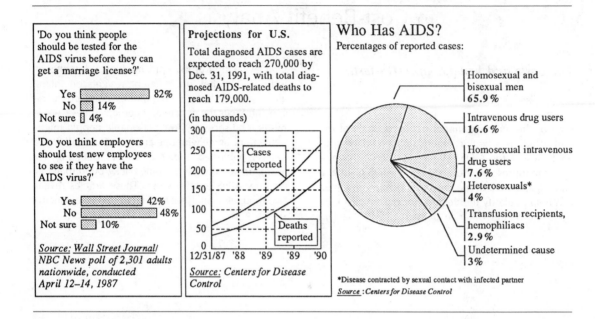

'Do you think people should be tested for the AIDS virus before they can get a marriage license?'

Yes 82%
No 14%
Not sure 4%

'Do you think employers should test new employees to see if they have the AIDS virus?'

Yes 42%
No 48%
Not sure 10%

*Source: Wall Street Journal/ NBC News poll of 2,301 adults nationwide, conducted April 12–14, 1987*

**Projections for U.S.**

Total diagnosed AIDS cases are expected to reach 270,000 by Dec. 31, 1991, with total diagnosed AIDS-related deaths to reach 179,000.

(in thousands)

Cases reported

Deaths reported

12/31/87  '88  '89  '89  '90

*Source: Centers for Disease Control*

## Who Has AIDS?

Percentages of reported cases:

Homosexual and bisexual men
65.9%

Intravenous drug users
16.6%

Homosexual intravenous drug users
7.6%

Heterosexuals*
4%

Transfusion recipients, hemophiliacs
2.9%

Undetermined cause
3%

*Disease contracted by sexual contact with infected partner

*Source: Centers for Disease Control*

## HOW TESTING WORKS

AIDS testing is designed to spot the antibodies developing in persons infected with the human immunodeficiency viruses that cause acquired immune deficiency syndrome. The antibodies show that a person has been infected even though he or she doesn't display symptoms of the disease itself.

As many as four tests may be required on each individual to obtain results with a high degree of certainty. An initial screening is performed with a test known as Elisa (for enzyme-linked immunosorbent assay), which is suited for relatively cheap, large-scale use. A negative response on the first try usually means no further testing. But because the test tends to err on the side of false positives, a positive result is normally followed by a second or even third Elisa.

If the result is again positive on one of the follow-up tests, a final test—the Western blot—is given, using a very different immunology. Only if that, too, shows positive is a person regarded as infected.

Medical researchers say that the latest studies indicate that nearly 80% of those infected with the viruses will develop symptoms of the disease itself within seven years. Infection lasts for life, and anyone infected is capable of transmitting the disease to others.

†Reprinted with permission. *The Wall Street Journal*, June 18, 1987, p. 29. Copyright © 1987 by Dow Jones & Company, Inc. All Rights Reserved.

# ADVOCATES SEE NEED TO TRACK DISEASE'S SPREAD[†]

*Gerald F. Seib*[*]

WASHINGTON—As Gary Bauer sees it from his office deep in the west wing of the White House, the case for broader AIDS testing is a powerful one.

In the eyes of this soft-spoken presidential assistant, history, protection of the healthy, cost-effectiveness and the need for nationwide vigilance all argue for greatly expanded testing. "The burden is on those who don't want to use such time-honored procedures in this case," he says.

The pro-testing argument has the Reagan administration as its chief proponent. President Reagan recently launched a policy that expands mandatory testing—which already applied to military recruits and many foreign-service officers—to include federal prisoners and immigrants as well. And some advisers want him to begin requiring tests for those entering Veterans Administra-

*Staff reporter of *The Wall Street Journal*
†Reprinted with permission. *The Wall Street Journal,* June 18, 1987, p. 29. Copyright © 1987 by Dow Jones & Company, Inc. All Rights Reserved.

tion hospitals. More broadly, the policy aims to create an atmosphere in which AIDS testing becomes "routine" for Americans in certain situations, such as when seeking a marriage license or getting a medical checkup.

The administration and its conservative allies aren't alone in supporting wider testing for the viruses that cause AIDS, or acquired immune deficiency syndrome. An eclectic group of liberals and medical professionals also backs the idea, although individuals might not agree with all details of the administration's policy.

## A HISTORICAL PRECEDENT

For starters, proponents argue that history is on their side. "When faced with other epidemics we've used testing," says Mr. Bauer, who cites earlier national decisions to test for tuberculosis and syphilis. Moreover, the testing for TB and syphilis began before there were cures for those diseases, as is the case with AIDS testing, notes Robert Redfield, a physician at Walter Reed Army Medical Center who helped launch an Army AIDS-testing program.

More important, advocates assert, is that wider testing is the only reliable way to see how AIDS is spreading beyond the groups hit hardest so far: homosexual and bisexual males and intravenous drug users. Proponents point out that the AIDS-causing viruses can incubate in a body for nearly 10 years before developing into a full-blown case of the disease.

"We have to change our focus in this country from AIDS to the virus," says Dr. Redfield. By concentrating on the disease rather than testing for its cause, he contends, the country is dealing with infections that began years ago instead of trying to prevent cases that could erupt in the decade to come.

Thus, proponents argue, it is wise to test such seemingly low-risk groups as marriage-license applicants. Dr. Redfield says that in the only study of marriage-license applicants so far, undertaken last year in Oakland, Calif., eight of every 1,000 subjects were found to be carrying the AIDS virus.

Similarly, Dr. Redfield asserts that the military's testing program—the biggest case study to date—suggests that the disease can hit married people almost as hard as it does single people. The armed forces, which have tested some 2.5 million military personnel and recruits, have found AIDS-causing viruses in roughly 1.5 of every thousand people tested. Dr. Redfield says that a surprising 40% of those who tested positive in the Army program were married.  •

Though there isn't a cure for AIDS, proponents argue that those who test positive can be offered treatments to prolong their lives. For instance, they can take medication to prevent catching the kind of pneumonia that most commonly leads to the death of AIDS sufferers. And those who have not yet developed AIDS can take steps to guard against other diseases, such as herpes and hepatitis, that are believed to accelerate its onset.

## A DESIRE TO KNOW

"I'd want to know" if infected with the virus, says Robert C. Gallo, chief of the laboratory of tumor-cell biology at the National Cancer Institute. "I'd want a chance of not passing it to my wife. I'd want to be near a good doctor, and I'd want AZT," or azidothymidine, an experimental antiviral drug that prolongs the survival of many AIDS patients but can produce severe side effects.

Testing advocates contend that identifying carriers now is also important so that when an anti-AIDS drug is developed, it can be distributed to as many infected people as possible. (A test of AZT is now under way involving people who are infected with an AIDS virus but haven't yet developed symptoms.)

Perhaps most important to many testing advocates is that most people who test positive for an AIDS-causing virus are likely to take precautions against spreading the disease to others. Even the spouse or lover of a carrier can be saved from infection if a test discloses the presence of the virus soon enough. Dr. Redfield, for instance, says that among the married AIDS patients he has treated in the military program, only about half had already infected their spouses.

At a minimum, testing advocates assert, the spouses or lovers of virus carriers have the right to know that their partners are infected. And Mr. Bauer contends that medical professionals who treat virus carriers have the right to know as well, which is why he favors testing in VA hospitals. Mr. Bauer argues, too, that it would be "extremely helpful" if people infected with the AIDS-producing virus carried identification cards—like those carried by people with other medical conditions—so that doctors and nurses would know when treating them in emergencies.

If nothing else, proponents say, testing should become common enough to stop the spread of AIDS to its most innocent victims: unborn infants who get the disease from their mothers' blood.

Expanding AIDS testing along the proposed lines would be relatively cheap now and clearly cost-effective in the long run if it does nothing more than slow the spread of the disease, advocates say. According to government officials, the initial screening test costs just a few dollars. A subsequent test used to confirm the presence of the virus is more expensive, but that test isn't required in most cases and is dropping in price as testing expertise grows.

The military, for example, has found that the cost of the follow-up test has dropped from as high as $300 to about $75, a Pentagon spokesman says. Overall, Dr. Redfield adds, the cost of the military program is less than $5 per person tested. This estimate is lower than that cited by some testing critics because it is for a large-scale program and doesn't include the follow-up counselling or overhead costs that might be incurred in other programs.

In any event, Mr. Bauer asserts, it is far cheaper to use tests to check the spread of AIDS in such places as federal prisons and hospitals than to pay the estimated $75,000 to $100,000 it costs annually to treat each victim of the disease.

Testing proponents argue that AIDS-test results can be kept confidential in the same way the medical community has always kept other medical information secret. In some cases—when it comes to informing spouses or the nurses and doctors who must treat infected patients, for example—the results of a test shouldn't remain confidential, they contend.

Nor will there be a stigma attached to those who undergo AIDS tests if the government succeeds in making testing a truly routine practice, administration aides insist. "If everyone's being tested," says Dinesh D'Souza, a White House policy analyst, "you don't have a funny feeling about standing in line."

# OPPONENTS CITE PRIVACY, COSTS, TESTING ERRORS[†]

*Alan L. Otten\**

WASHINGTON—Sure it's vital to protect the country against the further spread of AIDS, says Harvey Fineberg, dean of the Harvard School of Public Health. It's just that mandatory testing is the least effective way to do the job.

"The very people you need most to counsel and test are scared away," he explains. "They feel in jeopardy. They fear job discrimination, housing discrimination, insurance discrimination, social ostracism."

Public-health officials, civil libertarians, gay-rights organizations, and others concerned with the problem have from the very start urged the widest possible voluntary AIDS testing. But the Reagan administration's policy of broader mandatory testing, coupled with its recommendation of "routine" testing in several areas, is causing alarm.

Opponents stress not only the danger of loose record-keeping and subsequent disclo-

sure and discrimination in a mandatory-testing program, but also a likely increase in false results and the inefficient use of funds. Their major argument, however, is that mandatory testing is likely to scare off such high-risk groups as homosexuals and intravenous drug users, who must change their sex and drug habits if the epidemic is to be slowed.

"The administration doesn't seem to understand that, unlike other tests where you can treat people and cure them, there is no treatment for AIDS yet," declares Ronald Bayer, an associate at the Hastings Center, a bioethical think tank north of New York City. "The critical thing here is to get people to change their behavior to minimize the risk to themselves and others. And for that you need cooperation."

Officially, where the administration is calling for "routine" testing, people have the right to refuse. But opponents say that as a practical matter, with the suspicion that would automatically attach to a refusal to take the test, "routine" is in fact "mandatory." (Some administration officials admit that this is what they really have in mind.)

*Staff reporter of *The Wall Street Journal*

†Reprinted with permission. *The Wall Street Journal,* June 18, 1987, p. 29. Copyright © 1987 by Dow Jones & Company, Inc. All Rights Reserved.

And there are critics who worry that many influential testing advocates actually favor some sort of quarantine for AIDS carriers. On a television panel show last Sunday, Secretary of Education William Bennett suggested that some AIDS-infected prisoners might have to be kept confined even after they finish serving their prison terms. "Somewhere along the line," added Sen. Jesse Helms (R., N.C.), "we are going to have to quarantine if we are really going to contain this disease."

Moreover, the opponents say, the administration and others proposing stiff testing haven't thought through all the implications of their plans: What will be done with the information collected? What efforts will be made to notify former sex partners of infected men and women—and, realistically, how successfully can this be done? How will prison officials go about isolating AIDS-infected prisoners?

"That may be all right for a state with four or five AIDS cases in its prisons," says Mr. Bayer. "But states like New York and California would have to create two parallel prison systems."

AIDS testing for marriage-license applicants is likely to involve high expenditures on a very low-risk population, opponents say. "The highest-risk groups aren't the most likely to be coming forward to be married," observes Katherine McCarter, associate executive director of the American Public Health Association.

## ASSESSING THE COST

Palmer Jones, executive vice president of the New Hampshire Medical Society, estimates that of the 22,000 marriage-license applicants in his state each year, 220 would test positive on the initial screening, based on estimates of local infection rates. But follow-up testing, he says, would show that only two of those were true positives.

The governor of New Hampshire has proposed covering the cost of such testing by charging each applicant a fee of $8 to $10. Given the total paid by the 22,000 applicants, that would work out to a cost of anywhere from $88,000 to $110,000 to detect each of the two AIDS carriers—and some state officials think that even the governor's fee scale won't cover testing costs.

A hypothetical study by the federal Centers for Disease Control put the cost of finding AIDS carriers in screening 10,000 low-risk individuals at a lower but still significant $18,197 per carrier. Figures like these, the critics claim, prove that wide-spread testing will cost far more than its advocates admit.

Those who oppose mandatory testing also contend that money used to fund such programs would be better spent to expand voluntary testing and counseling at present AIDS-testing sites, drug and venereal-disease clinics and family-planning clinics. They point out that in many cities there are waiting times of three to six weeks or more for testing at these places, and that many family-planning clinics don't have the AIDS test available at all. (The family-planning clinics are particularly important as a way to reach infected women, or women at risk of infection, before they become pregnant and pass the disease on to their children.)

"We need to put our time and effort into providing for those willing to be tested," says Ms. McCarter.

Opponents worry deeply about the lack of confidentiality likely in marriage-license bureaus and other places where mandatory-testing programs would be inaugurated. "The administration hasn't coupled its calls for more testing with calls for stricter legislation to protect confidentiality and prohibit discrimination," notes Nan Hunter, head of the AIDS project at the American Civil Liberties Union.

Many critics of mandatory testing consider counseling and confidentiality all the more important because as testing is expanded, the number of false positives and false negatives will inevitably increase. Both outcomes are worrisome.

## NO ROOM FOR ERROR

A person testing falsely positive not only goes through needless anxiety and family strain but could face job loss and all the other forms of discrimination confronting those truly infected. And persons testing falsely negative may display what Ms. Hunter calls the "disinhibition factor"—a feeling they can afford to continue risky sexual or drug behavior.

This is especially dangerous because some false negatives may be due to the fact that while antibodies usually show up in six to eight weeks, they can take as long as six months. Thus, someone tested soon after exposure may show negative but then develop an infection. (This raises the possibility that repeated testing at six-month intervals may ultimately be proposed.)

Critics of mandatory testing concede the need to get far more information on the spread of AIDS, but they see no reason why researchers and public-health officials can't get the data they require from anonymous testing. Some of this is already being done, in fact. The CDC, for example, has several hospitals routinely testing blood samples collected anonymously from patients as part of regular diagnostic testing, and it is slowly expanding this network.

If AZT proves successful in its current tests on healthy but infected gay men, or if some other form of effective early-stage treatment is found, the balance of self-interest could tip toward testing. A number of other developments might also make routine testing more attractive, some critics concede: tight supervision of new laboratories, tougher confidentiality laws, and anti-discrimination legislation. "But at the present time," Dr. Fineberg says, "given where all these things are, mandatory testing is quite wrong-minded."

## QUESTIONS

1. Construct an outline of the perceived costs and benefits. For each cost or benefit item, determine whether it can be quantified.

2. Put unmeasurable items in a separate list of "intangibles." Do intangibles play a large role in the AIDS debate?

## *What cost extinction?*

In 1977, scientists discovered a rare blue butterfly that fed on locoweed. According to the *Los Angeles Times* ("Peninsula City Charged with Killing Butterfly," April 3, 1987), the city of Rancho Palos Verdes apparently drove the butterfly to extinction when it built a baseball field on a vacant lot where locoweed had grown. The city faces a fine of up to $20,000 if convicted of violating the Endangered Species Act.

The city is protesting. It seems the U.S. Fish and Wildlife service never notified them of the habitat's boundaries, fearing an influx of butterfly collectors. Other locoweed patches had succumbed to steady development over a period of years, and the Wildlife Service hadn't intervened. It was the Wildlife Service's legal duty to protect the butterfly.

## QUESTIONS

1. How could you measure people's willingness to pay to save a butterfly from extinction? Does this seem to be the appropriate measure of the benefits of saving the butterfly?

2. If a butterfly feeds in several locations, how would you decide which ones should be developed and which ones left alone?

## PART VI

# Taxation: Incidence, Efficiency, and Equity

### *Are lifetime measures of tax incidence very different from annual measures?*

A progressive tax system tries to take from the rich to give to the poor. But we are all richer at some ages and poorer at others, and a system that simply returns to each of us when we are poorer what it took when we were richer is not really redistributing wealth from one person to another. To separate such life-cycle transfers from bona fide intragenerational redistribution, we need a measure of the lifetime incidence of government policies. This article is excerpted from a longer paper that estimates lifetime tax incidence and compares it with annual incidence estimates which, since they are calculated at a single point in time, do not separate out life-cycle effects.

# SOME CALCULATIONS OF LIFETIME TAX INCIDENCE[†]

*James Davies, France St-Hilaire, and John Whalley\**

This paper reports a set of lifetime tax incidence calculations using a life-cycle simulation model for Canada due to Davies (1979a, 1982). A repeatedly stated qualification to annual calculations in the empirical tax inci

*Department of Economics, University of Western Ontario, London, Canada, N6A 5C2. We thank participants in workshops at McMaster University and the University of Western Ontario, as well as an anonymous referee, for useful comments. St-Hilaire and Whalley gratefully acknowledge financial support from the Social Sciences and Humanities Research Council of Canada.

†Reprinted with permission. *The American Economic Review*, September 1984.

dence literature is that it would be more satisfactory to make calculations on a lifetime basis. Even though it is acknowledged that lifetime tax incidence could well differ from annual, it is widely believed that data and other difficulties make such calculations next to impossible. Indeed, the wide-spread acceptance of the data problems of lifetime calculations seems also to have inhibited speculation about how lifetime tax incidence might differ from annual. As a result, redistributive tax policy judgments continue to be based on annual incidence calculations in spite of the reservations many have about their usefulness. Our paper is intended to reorient discussion towards lifetime tax incidence by providing some initial null hypotheses about the shape of lifetime tax profiles.

Our main finding is that under the standard competitive assumptions common in the incidence literature, lifetime and annual incidence calculations both produce mild progression in tax rates across household deciles (ignoring the bottom decile in the annual calculation). While the income tax is less progressive in lifetime than in annual calculations, other taxes are for the most part less regressive. Also, lifetime incidence calculations are much more robust to alternative shifting assumptions than annual calculations. In the lifetime context, key distributions such as earnings, transfer payments, and consumption are less heavily concentrated in particular percentiles of the population than is true in annual data. As a result, changing the allocative series for any particular tax does not have the large effect on incidence results found in annual calculations.[1]

In both lifetime and annual calculations, we allocate five groups of taxes among households using distributive series which come partly from the 1971 Statistics Canada Survey of Consumer Finances (*SCF*) and partly from the life cycle simulation model. The *SCF* data are used to construct synthetic longitudinal lifetime profiles of earnings and transfer payments for a sample of 500 households. The latter are assigned inheritances by simulating patterns of mortality and bequest. These data are then used in the life-cycle model to generate lifetime consumption profiles and bequests. The earnings, transfer, and inheritance data, plus the model output provide the distributive series on which alternative incidence calculations are based.

While the incidence calculations presented in this paper use Canadian data, results would likely be similar for the United States as is true of annual calculations (see St-Hilaire and Whalley, 1982). Relative to overall tax revenue, personal and corporate income taxes

are of roughly the same importance in the two countries. The personal income tax in Canada has a flatter rate profile, less significant exemptions and deductions, and more extensive tax shelters than its U.S. counterpart (for example, mortgage interest is not deductible, but there are larger shelters for savings for retirement). Taxes levied by the provinces are relatively more important than those at state level in the United States. Finally, sales and excise taxes are higher than in the United States, but social security taxes are considerably lower. This latter feature produces an offsetting effect in standard incidence calculations where both taxes are largely regressive.

## I. ANNUAL INCIDENCE CALCULATIONS AND LIFETIME ISSUES

### A. Annual Incidence Studies

Tax incidence calculations which use annual data typically focus on five key taxes or tax groups: income, corporate, sales and excise, property, and social security. Each tax is treated as having sources (income) side and/or uses (expenditure) side effects for each group of households who, in turn, are usually stratified by income. Incidence calculations for whole tax systems use a separate tax burden calculation for each tax by income range. The overall redistributive effect of the tax system is usually evaluated by examining the pattern of combined average tax rates across income ranges.

Three main income sources—capital, labor, and transfer income—can bear the burden of taxes either singly or jointly. In annual data, transfers are heavily concentrated in the lower tail of the income distribution. Capital income is a relatively high proportion of total income in the upper tail, but also in the lower tail due to the presence of retirees. Labor income increases sharply as a fraction of total income for the bottom few deciles, but is approximately proportional to income for about 70 percent of the population. Thus, on the sources side, widely varying patterns of progressivity or regressivity can result depending upon whether a tax is allocated to capital, labor, or transfer income, or to income in general.

On the uses side, the strongest effects occur through differences in household saving rates. This is because a tax assumed to be forward shifted in higher prices is treated as borne by households out of consumption. In annual data, saving rates differ sharply by income range, with around 70 to 80 percent of household saving commonly concentrated in the top 10 percent of the income distribution. Forward-shifted taxes allocated to consumption are therefore regressive.

One of the most widely cited annual incidence studies is Pechman and Okner, which uses detailed merged data involving approximately 87,000 1966 U.S. income tax returns and 30,000 households appearing in a Survey of Economic Opportunity data file. Alternative incidence calculations are made using different shifting assumptions as to the burden of certain taxes. Their main conclusion is that "regardless of the incidence assumptions, the tax system is virtually proportional for the vast majority of families in the United States" (p. 64). This, however, omits the bottom 10 and top 3 percent of the population (see Pechman and Okner, pp. 5-6), which has an effect on the conclusions. In their most progressive variant, for example, where corporate and property taxes are borne by capital, the total effective tax rate for the bottom 10 percent is much lower than for other deciles and that for the top 3 percent far above average (see Tables 4.4 and 4.9 on pp. 51 and 61, respectively).

This "proportionality" view of overall tax incidence has been questioned in recent work by Browning (1978) and Browning and Johnson (1979). The main difference concerns the treatment of sales and excise taxes which are regressive in Pechman-Okner and progressive

in Browning-Johnson. Browning and Johnson argue that uses side effects of sales and excise taxes due to different saving rates by income range are insignificant when consumption out of normal or permanent income is considered. They therefore only consider the sources side effects of sales and excise taxes, pointing out that since transfers are largely indexed for price level changes, only factor incomes can bear the burden of taxes. The concentration of transfers in the lower tail of the income distribution, and saving in the upper tail means that sales and excise taxes which appear as strongly regressive in Pechman-Okner are strongly progressive in Browning-Johnson.

The incidence assumptions used in this literature are crucial to the extent of progressivity in results. The income tax is universally treated as paid by income recipients and is progressive. However, widely varying assumptions for other taxes are examined in the literature. Social security is treated either exclusively or predominantly as a payroll tax on labor and (outside of the lower tail of income distribution) is regressive due to ceilings on contributions. Corporate and property taxes are regressive if treated as shifted forward onto consumption, but mainly progressive if assumed shifted backwards onto capital income. Finally, sales and excise taxes are regressive if borne by consumers, and progressive if treated as borne by recipients of factor incomes. Depending on the combination of shifting assumptions the tax system can be made to appear regressive or progressive in annual calculations. (See St-Hilaire and Whalley, 1982.)

## B. Lifetime Incidence—Expected Contrasts with Annual Calculations

Despite the extensive literature reporting annual incidence calculations, it is widely acknowledged that lifetime calculations would be preferable. Data limitations are usually cited as precluding such an approach. (See, for example, Browning and Johnson, p. 81.) The lack of incidence calculations on a lifetime basis is especially unfortunate, since on a priori grounds there are several reasons to believe there may be significant differences between annual and lifetime incidence results. First, much of the observed inequality in earnings and transfer payments disappears when we examine lifetime rather than annual distributions. According to the estimates of Jacob Mincer (1974), Lee Lillard (1977), and Nils Blomqvist (1981), about one-half of annual earnings inequality (according to conventional measures) disappears when one looks at lifetime earnings. Social security and other income support payments, in particular, are much more equally distributed when examined on a lifetime rather than an annual basis. Lifetime transfers are therefore not concentrated chiefly in the hands of the poor as is true in annual data. These differences imply less progressivity of personal income taxes in the lifetime context. Also, with transfers less important and earnings more important in the bottom tail the significance of the indexation issue stressed by Browning and Johnson is weakened.

A second issue relevant to lifetime calculations is the treatment of capital income. This important element in annual incidence calculations is not part of a household's discounted lifetime income. It therefore cannot bear the burden of taxes on the sources side in the same way as in annual calculations since it is not part of the income base. As a result, a fundamentally different treatment of taxes thought to be borne by capital (for example, corporate, property) is required.

A third important difference between annual and lifetime calculations arises from the differing time profiles of taxes over the life cycle. Taxes on labor income, for example, are paid until retirement, but those on consumption are paid until death. Hence the relative lifetime importance of various taxes may differ significantly from their relative annual importance, due to the effect of discounting.

Finally, the profile of consumption as a proportion of income will differ considerably between annual and lifetime data. While there is reason to expect higher income groups to save a larger proportion of their lifetime resources for bequests, the lifetime profile of savings rates by income range ought to be much flatter than the annual. Therefore sales and excise taxes treated as borne by consumers should appear less regressive in the lifetime calculations. Also, switching the incidence assumption for corporate or property taxes from full burden on capital income to partial forward shifting should produce a less dramatic shift towards regressivity.

## II. A LIFE CYCLE APPROACH TO INCIDENCE ANALYSIS

Later in the paper we report tax incidence calculations based on lifetime rather than annual data. Our approach is similar to that used in annual calculations in that we adopt alternative distributive series for the allocation of various taxes between household groups. The main differences are that distributive series are generated using lifetime rather than annual data, households are grouped by lifetime income, and taxes paid over the lifetime rather than in a single year are allocated.

Our distributive series rely on the data used in, and the output from, a microsimulation model of life cycle saving and bequest behavior of Canadian households reported in Davies (1982). In Davies' model, each household includes a husband and wife who start economic life together at age 20 and die together at age 75. Households are assigned realistic (exogenous) streams of earnings, transfer payments, and inheritances over the lifetime, as described below. The simulation generates lifetime paths of consumption and investment income which along with the lifetime income data provide the distributive series for our incidence calculations.

## A. The Behavioral Model

Each household receives an exogenously determined stream of earnings. $E_t$ , and government transfers, $G_t$ (depending on age, $t$) over its lifetime. We refer to the sum of earnings and transfers as noninvestment income, $N_t$. Real interest before tax on wealth, $W_t$, is received at a constant rate, $r$, giving rise to investment income, $M_t = rW_t$. Annual income gross of (direct) tax, $Y_t$, is thus given by

$$(1) \qquad Y_t = E_t + G_t + M_t = N_t + M_t.$$

This income is divided between consumption, $C_t$ (gross of indirect taxes); direct taxes, $T_t$, and saving, $S_t$.[2] The annual budget constraint is thus:

$$(2) \qquad Y_t = C_t + S_t + T_t.$$

Over the lifetime, resources are augmented by an exogenous stream of capital transfers, $I_t$, which we refer to as inheritances. Denoting discounted present values over the lifetime by dropping the $t$ subscript, lifetime income or lifetime resources, $L$, is given by

$$(3) \qquad L = E + G + I = N + I,$$

where discounting occurs at a family's after-tax discount rate, $r^*$.

Like annual income $Y_t$, lifetime resources $L$ are gross of direct tax. However, because lifetime investment income $M$ is not included in $L$, direct taxes on investment income are not included in the lifetime measure of direct taxes on $L(\tilde{T})$ as they are in the annual measure of direct taxes on $Y_t(T_t)$. The $\tilde{T}$ represents direct taxes on $E$ and $G$ ($I$ is net of estate taxes). With this definition, and denoting the discounted value of bequests as $B$, we have the lifetime budget constraint:

$$(4) \qquad L = C + B + \tilde{T}.$$

Households generate a time path of $C_t$ and a value of $B$ by maximizing an intertemporal utility function defined over consumption and bequests, subject to (4). The utility function is of the familiar additive iso-elastic form (see, for example, Alan Blinder, 1974) but with parents' consumption and children's expected lifetime income (which depends partly on parents' bequests) as arguments. Bequests have a compensatory element since they are directly related to parents' income, but inversely related to children's anticipated earnings. Because the later regress to the mean, on average, bequests rise as a proportion of parents' income. Lifetime consumption $\tilde{C}$ therefore declines as a proportion of $L$, although to a much smaller extent than does annual consumption as a fraction of annual income.

## B. The Simulation

The simulation model assumes that Canada is in balanced growth with labor force growth in efficiency units of 2 percent. Per capita earnings, transfer payments, taxes, and other flows all grow at the same rate, and successive cohorts are identical except for a proportional increase in their resources and expenditures. The balanced growth assumption makes it possible to infer time paths of the distributions of all the annual flows ($E_t$, $G_t$, $Y_t$, etc.) for each cohort from the observed values of a representative cross section at a point in time. The before-tax interest rate $r$ is set at 6 percent.

Lifetime paths of $E_t$, $G_t$, $T_t$, and $\tilde{T}_t$ are generated for each cohort by taking random samples of 500 households for each of 11 different age groups (20–24, 25–29, . . . , 70–74) from the 1971 Statistics Canada Survey of Consumer Finances (*SCF*). The data are adjusted to a 1970 basis, correcting for inflation and growth, to make them consistent with the rest of the model data base. Households are ranked according to total reported income in each age group. They are then linked across age groups in order to construct 500 life histories for $E_t$ and $G_t$. The linking procedure contains a random element, whose strength may be varied to produce more or less earnings mobility. We parameterize this process to reproduce the degree of earnings mobility implicit in Lillard's study of the relationship between annual and lifetime earnings in the United States. Sensitivity of the incidence results to the assumed degree of earnings mobility is checked by repeating our calculations assuming zero and free (random) mobility.

The simulation assigns each household a constant marginal tax rate, $u$, on investment income over its lifetime. Hence, the after-tax rate of interest, $r^* = (1 - u)r$. The rate $u$ is calculated by examining each household's reported income tax payment when aged 45–49 in the 1971 *SCF* data. The 1971 tax tables indicate the corresponding marginal tax rate. Since taxable investment income is affected by various exclusions (for example, non-taxation of imputed rent and capital gains on owner-occupied houses, and one-half of all other capital gains), and the lack of accounting for inflation, this legal rate does not correspond to the effective tax rate on true investment income. Legal rates are transformed into effective marginal tax rates as follows. Comparison of aggregate taxable, and simulated total, investment income for 1970 shows that the former was approximately 15 percent of the latter. We make the strong assumption that this ratio is the same for all households. The effective tax rate on broadly defined investment income is therefore set at 15 percent of the legal rate for each household.

## III. IMPLEMENTING INCIDENCE CALCULATIONS IN THE LIFE-CYCLE FRAMEWORK

Our life-cycle incidence calculations use the data and the output from the model described above in a procedure commonly used in annual incidence calculations. As a central case we use a set of standard competitive incidence assumptions adapted to the lifetime context and employ alternative lifetime distributive series for the five major tax groups listed earlier.

In contrast to the annual calculations where investment income $N_t$ is an important distributive series, and inheritances, $I_t$ do not appear, the key distributive series on the sources side in the lifetime calculations are discounted lifetime earnings, $E$; inheritances, $I$; and transfers, $G$. These series sum to the gross of tax lifetime income base, $L$. On the uses side, two rather than the one key series in the annual calculations ($C_t$) are used: lifetime investment income $M$, and lifetime consumption $C$.

### A. Obtaining Comparable Annual Results

We not only generate lifetime incidence calculations but also annual estimates. A natural method of generating comparable annual incidence calculations is to use annual cross sections from the life cycle simulation to produce distributive series. However, in the simulation model, households are free from liquidity constraints and dissave rapidly when transitory income is negative. The consumption pattern across annual income deciles is therefore more extreme than in actual annual data. Thus while the simulation provides useful information on patterns of saving over the lifetime, it is not as reliable a guide to patterns of saving on an annual basis.

In order to obtain annual tax incidence results we have used the same primary data source (the 1971 *SCF*) as far as possible to produce the distributive series for allocating taxes. The only series that cannot be obtained in this way is consumption, which we generate by simulation. We have found that when zero earnings mobility is assumed — greatly reducing the importance of transitory income — the simulated annual consumption profile becomes reasonably similar to that reported in other data sources. The annual consumption profile obtained in the zero mobility simulation run was therefore used in the annual incidence calculations reported below.

## B. Lifetime vs. Annual Distributive Series

Table 1 shows the main features of both the lifetime and annual data used in the incidence calculations reported in the next section. The following contrasts between the annual and lifetime data should be highlighted:

1. There is less inequality in the distribution of lifetime income $L$, than in that of annual income $Y$. (Both distributions are gross of direct taxes.) It is therefore not surprising that the lifetime data show a lower variance of personal income tax rates over households ranked by income than the annual data.

2. Over the lifetime, transfers are less heavily concentrated in the bottom two deciles of the population than in the annual data. The decline in the relative importance of transfers as income rises is also less marked. This tends to reduce the quantitative importance of Browning and Johnson's argument regarding the impact of indexed transfers in a lifetime calculation.

3. Variation in consumption to income ratios is smaller in lifetime than in annual data. This reduces the regressivity of taxes assumed to be borne out of consumption, such as sales and excise.

4. There is less variation in the relative importance of earnings as we move up the income scale in lifetime data as against annual data. This is partly associated with the more even distribution of government transfers in the lifetime data. A consequence is that the progressivity of social security taxes over the low deciles in annual data is replaced by rough proportionality in the lifetime calculations. (In addition, regressivity over the upper deciles is reduced.) Also, the flatter earnings series again means that the Browning and

Johnson procedure of allocating sales and excise taxes to factor incomes has less tendency to produce progressivity for these taxes.

5. Overall, lifetime earnings are larger in relation to lifetime consumption than are annual earnings compared with annual consumption. This reflects the fact that, on average, earnings occur earlier in the lifetime and are less heavily discounted. We see in the next section that this factor tends to make overall lifetime incidence slightly more progressive than annual, since the relative importance of taxes falling on consumption is smaller and that of taxes on earnings is increased.

## C. Central Case Lifetime Incidence Assumptions

The lifetime distributive series can be used in alternative ways to allocate the various taxes across deciles. Our central case uses standard competitive assumptions: the income tax is assumed to be borne by income recipients; corporate and property taxes by recipients of investment income; social security taxes by earnings recipients; and sales and excise taxes in proportion to consumption.

While for the most part it is clear from the central case incidence assumptions which distributive series should be used for which taxes, this is not true for taxes borne by capital in the lifetime context. In lifetime incidence, taxes on capital income have both sources and uses side effects rather than just a source side impact as assumed in annual calculations.[3] By reducing the rate of interest they increase the relative lifetime incomes of those whose receipts occur later in life (via the discounting effect)—a sources side effect. In addition, they reduce the relative real incomes of persons who consume more later in the lifetime by increasing the price of future consumption—a uses side effect. While the sources and uses side effects of taxes borne by capital could be accounted for separately in the lifetime inci-

Table 1: **Basic Data in Lifetime and Annual Incidence Calculations**[a]

| Decile | Share of Total L | Composition of L | | | Uses of L | | | |
|---|---|---|---|---|---|---|---|---|
| | | $E/L$ | $G/L$ | $I/L$ | $C/L$ | $B/L$ | $\tilde{T}/L$ | $M/L$ |
| **A. Lifetime** | | | | | | | | |
| 1 | 4.2 | 81.2 | 15.3 | 3.5 | 86.7 | 4.4 | 8.9 | 9.4 |
| 2 | 6.2 | 86.8 | 10.4 | 2.8 | 82.3 | 5.2 | 12.5 | 12.2 |
| 3 | 7.3 | 89.2 | 7.9 | 2.8 | 81.5 | 4.7 | 13.8 | 10.9 |
| 4 | 8.3 | 91.2 | 6.6 | 2.2 | 80.4 | 5.0 | 14.6 | 12.8 |
| 5 | 9.1 | 90.3 | 6.2 | 3.5 | 79.4 | 5.2 | 15.4 | 12.4 |
| 6 | 9.7 | 92.7 | 4.5 | 2.8 | 77.9 | 6.0 | 16.1 | 14.1 |
| 7 | 10.7 | 91.6 | 4.7 | 3.7 | 78.4 | 5.1 | 16.5 | 14.0 |
| 8 | 12.0 | 92.5 | 3.3 | 4.3 | 76.7 | 6.1 | 17.1 | 17.5 |
| 9 | 14.0 | 91.3 | 3.0 | 5.7 | 76.2 | 5.6 | 18.2 | 14.2 |
| 10 | 18.4 | 88.3 | 2.3 | 9.4 | 71.7 | 8.6 | 19.7 | 21.8 |
| All | 100.0 | 90.1 | 5.2 | 4.7 | 77.7 | 6.0 | 16.4 | 15.1 |

| Decile[b] | Share of Total $Y_t$ | Composition of $Y_t$ | | | Uses of $Y_t$ | | |
|---|---|---|---|---|---|---|---|
| | | $E_t/Y_t$ | $G_t/Y_t$ | $M_t/Y_t$ | $C_t/Y_t$ | $S_t/Y_t$ | $T_t/Y_t$ |
| **B. Annual** | | | | | | | |
| 1 | 1.0 | 44.2 | 51.5 | 4.3 | 157.2 | −62.4 | 5.2 |
| 2 | 3.1 | 50.1 | 44.2 | 5.7 | 117.0 | −21.1 | 4.1 |
| 3 | 4.8 | 77.2 | 15.8 | 7.0 | 91.4 | −0.3 | 8.9 |
| 4 | 6.4 | 85.6 | 7.7 | 6.7 | 84.2 | −4.0 | 11.9 |
| 5 | 7.7 | 90.0 | 5.1 | 5.0 | 80.9 | 5.1 | 14.0 |
| 6 | 9.0 | 89.8 | 4.3 | 5.9 | 77.6 | 7.1 | 15.4 |
| 7 | 10.4 | 91.3 | 3.4 | 5.3 | 77.9 | 6.4 | 15.7 |
| 8 | 12.1 | 90.2 | 2.6 | 7.2 | 76.3 | 7.2 | 16.5 |
| 9 | 14.9 | 86.6 | 2.1 | 11.3 | 73.8 | 9.3 | 16.9 |
| 10 | 30.6 | 57.5 | 1.2 | 41.4 | 49.2 | 34.4 | 16.4 |
| All | 100.0 | 77.1 | 5.3 | 17.7 | 71.6 | 13.5 | 15.0 |

*Sources:* $E_t$, $G_t$, $T_t$, $E$, $G$, and $\tilde{T}$ are based on data from the 1971 Statistics Canada Survey of Consumer Finances (*SCF*), as described in the text. All other variables are from the authors' simulations.

*Notes:* Part A: Gini coefficient of $L$ = .218 ; Part B: Gini coefficient of $Y_t$, = .410. Part A: $L$, $E$, $G$, $I$, $C$, $B$, $\tilde{T}$ and $M$ are all present discounted lifetime values; $L$ = lifetime resources, $E$ = earnings, $G$ = transfers, $I$ = inheritances, $C$ = consumption, $B$ = bequest, $T$ = direct taxes on $L$, and $M$ = investment income.

Part B: $Y_t$, $E_t$, $G_t$, $M_t$, $C_t$, $S_t$, and $T_t$ are all annual flows; $Y_t$ = income, $E_t$ = earnings, $G_t$ = transfers, $M_t$ = investment income, $C_t$ = consumption, $S_t$ = saving, and $T_t$ = direct taxes on $Y_t$.

[a]Shown in percent.

[b]Deciles are sorted by annual income as reported in the 1971 Statistics Canada *SCF*.

dence calculations, it is simpler to net them out. This can be seen in the case of a family which consumes its total income in each year and is unaffected by taxes borne by capital, since it never saves and therefore feels no effect of a reduced interest rate. In contrast, a family which saves suffers from the reduced reward for abstinence.

Thus, taxes borne by capital reduce the welfare of families which defer consumption. In any year, in the absence of taxes borne by capital, a family which accumulated savings could consume more than with those same taxes present. The amount of additional consumption would equal the reduction in current investment income due to the taxes borne by capital. The appropriate distributive series for taxes borne by capital in lifetime incidence calculations is therefore the discounted value of all investment income received over the lifetime, $M$.

## D. Computing Tax Burdens

As mentioned earlier, personal income tax payments are taken directly from the primary data source—the 1971 *SCF*. Social security tax payments are imputed using the applicable rates and ceilings under both the Canada Pension Plan (*CPP*) and Unemployment Insurance (*UI*) programs to determine employer and employee contributions on the basis of earnings reported in the 1971 *SCF* by simulation households. Other taxes must be imputed by establishing an overall tax rate and applying this to the appropriate distributive series.

For corporate and property taxes, rates are determined using 1970 tax collections and an estimate of total 1970 household investment income. We estimate the sales and excise tax rate by comparing actual 1970 tax collections with observed aggregate consumption. Lifetime capital and sales and excise tax burdens are calculated by applying these tax rates to discounted lifetime investment income $M$, and consumption $C$, respectively, for each simulation household.

## IV. LIFETIME TAX INCIDENCE RESULTS

Our central case lifetime tax incidence results are displayed in Table 2, Part A, with comparable annual tax incidence calculations reported in Part B. Several interesting points emerge from a comparison of these results.

First, the overall tax system appears mildly progressive in both the annual and lifetime calculations. While in the annual results there is regressivity from the bottom to the second decile, from the second to the ninth deciles rates increase slowly, and in the top decile a significant increase occurs. In the lifetime data there is progressivity throughout—with moderate increases in overall rates from the first to the fourth deciles, a slow rise from the fourth to the ninth deciles, and once more a larger increase for the top decile. While the regressivity at the bottom end in the annual run is an important feature, we conclude that both profiles show mild progression overall across the income ranges.

An alternative method of summarizing differences in tax profiles is to examine the proportional impact on a summary measure of income inequality. Following the suggestion of Musgrave and Tun Thin (1948), this is often done using the Gini coefficient. The pre-tax Gini of .218 in the lifetime run is reduced to .184 by the tax system; in contrast, the annual Gini falls only 10 percent—from .410 to .370. On this basis it might be claimed that the lifetime tax structure is significantly more progressive than the annual.

A second interesting point evident from Table 2 is that there is considerably less variation in incidence patterns across taxes in the lifetime calculation. Lifetime income taxes while progressive are less so than in the annual case: sales and excise are less regressive; social security is initially less progressive and subsequently less regressive by income range, and corporate and property taxes are less progressive (especially at the top end). This reflects a greater flatness of the underly-

Table 2: **Average Tax Rates of Canadian Households by Decile, Central Case Assumptions**

| | 1 | 2 | 3 | 4 | 5 | 6 | 7 | 8 | 9 | 10 | All Deciles |
|---|---|---|---|---|---|---|---|---|---|---|---|
| *A. Lifetime Incidence (Deciles Ranked by Lifetime Resources (L))* | | | | | | | | | | | |
| Corporate income tax | 2.2 | 2.9 | 2.6 | 3.0 | 2.9 | 3.3 | 3.3 | 4.1 | 3.4 | 5.1 | 3.6 |
| Property tax | 2.4 | 3.1 | 2.8 | 3.3 | 3.2 | 3.6 | 3.6 | 4.5 | 3.7 | 5.6 | 3.9 |
| Sales and excises | 15.0 | 14.3 | 14.1 | 13.9 | 13.8 | 13.5 | 13.6 | 13.3 | 13.2 | 12.4 | 13.5 |
| Social Security | 3.9 | 4.0 | 3.9 | 4.0 | 3.8 | 3.8 | 3.6 | 3.6 | 3.4 | 2.8 | 3.6 |
| Personal income tax | 7.3 | 11.3 | 12.5 | 13.5 | 14.5 | 15.1 | 15.7 | 16.7 | 17.7 | 20.5 | 15.8 |
| All taxes | 30.9 | 35.5 | 35.9 | 37.7 | 38.1 | 39.3 | 39.8 | 42.2 | 41.3 | 46.5 | 40.2 |
| *B. Annual Incidence (Deciles Ranked by Annual Income (Y$_p$))* | | | | | | | | | | | |
| Corporate income tax | 1.0 | 1.3 | 1.6 | 1.6 | 1.2 | 1.4 | 1.2 | 1.7 | 2.7 | 9.8 | 4.2 |
| Property tax | 1.1 | 1.5 | 1.8 | 1.7 | 1.3 | 1.5 | 1.3 | 1.9 | 2.9 | 10.6 | 4.5 |
| Sales and excises | 27.2 | 20.3 | 15.8 | 14.6 | 14.0 | 13.4 | 13.5 | 13.2 | 12.8 | 8.5 | 12.4 |
| Social Security | 1.7 | 2.5 | 4.1 | 4.3 | 4.2 | 3.9 | 3.8 | 3.4 | 3.0 | 1.4 | 2.9 |
| Personal income tax | 4.3 | 2.8 | 6.8 | 9.7 | 11.9 | 13.4 | 13.8 | 14.8 | 15.4 | 15.7 | 13.5 |
| All taxes | 35.4 | 28.4 | 30.1 | 31.9 | 32.6 | 33.6 | 33.7 | 35.0 | 36.8 | 46.0 | 37.5 |

*Source:* Computations performed by the authors. See text.

124

ing lifetime distributive series and means that changes in incidence assumptions have less impact on lifetime than on annual incidence results.

## V. CONCLUSION

In this paper we report a set of lifetime tax incidence calculations which combine the data and output from a life-cycle, microsimulation model for Canada due to Davies (1979, 1982) with incidence assumptions comparable to those used in previous annual incidence studies. While incidence calculations have several limitations, previous annual calculations have received so much attention in policy debate that it is important to analyze to what extent they correspond to the more interesting case of lifetime tax incidence.

We offer two main findings. The first is that using standard "competitive" shifting assumptions, lifetime and annual incidence patterns both display mild progression of overall tax rates across income ranges (ignoring the bottom decile in the annual calculation). While the personal income tax becomes less progressive in a lifetime context, offsetting changes occur in the incidence of other taxes. Sales and excise taxes, for example, become less regressive since the fraction of income saved rises less sharply with income. The regressivity often found at the bottom end of the income scale in annual calculations is not present in the lifetime calculations. This is largely the result of the reduced regressivity of sales and excise taxes.

Our second finding is that lifetime incidence results are far more robust to alternative incidence assumptions than is true of annual results. The principal distributive series in the lifetime context—transfers, earnings, and consumption, as a fraction of lifetime income— are all closer to uniform across income ranges than corresponding annual series. As a result, changes in incidence assumptions such as the

indexing of transfers (suggested by Browning and Johnson), or the forward shifting of capital taxes have much less impact on the overall progressivity of the tax system than in annual calculations. Our results thus indicate that we can perhaps be more confident than on the basis of annual incidence calculations alone that the incidence of the overall tax system is mildly progressive.

## Notes

1. See St-Hilaire and Whalley (1982) for an investigation of the impact of changing incidence assumptions in annual tax incidence calculations. We note that several of the issues raised by St-Hilaire and Whalley, including the implications of the open economy and the treatment of human capital for tax incidence calculations, are not taken up in this paper. Lifetime calculations may well be sensitive to the way these are treated, and this should be explored in future work.

2. Direct taxes, $T_t$, include employees' share of Social Security premiums (imputed on the basis of reported $E_t$ and the statutory rate schedule) and personal income taxes.

3. The nature of the uses side effect over the lifetime was pointed out by Browning and Johnson: ". . . corporation income taxes and property taxes reduce the net interest rate that savers receive. Consequently, these taxes harm savers and benefit consumers on the uses side. . . " (p.27).

## References

Atkinson, Anthony B. and Stiglitz, Joseph E., *Lectures in Public Economics*, London: McGraw-Hill, 1980.

Blinder, Alan S., *Toward an Economic Theory of Income Distribution*, Cambridge: MIT Press, 1974.

Blomqvist, Nils S., "A Comparison of Distributions of Annual and Lifetime Income: Sweden

Around 1970," *Review of Income and Wealth*, September 1981, *27*, 243–264.

Browning, Edgar K., "The Burden of Taxation," *Journal of Political Economy*, August 1978, *86*, 649–671.

———. and Johnson, William R., *The Distribution of the Tax Burden*, Washington: American Enterprise Institute, 1979.

Davies, David G., "An Empirical Test of Sales-Tax Regressivity," *Journal of Political Economy*, February 1959, *67*, 72–78.

Davies, James B., (1979a) "Life-Cycle Savings, Inheritance, and the Distribution of Personal Income and Wealth in Canada," unpublished doctoral dissertation, London School of Economics, 1979.

———, (1979b) "On the Size Distribution of Wealth in Canada," *Review of Income and Wealth*, September 1979, *25*, 237–259.

———, "The Relative Impact of Inheritance and Other Factors on Economic Inequality," *Quarterly Journal of Economics*, August 1982, *97*, 471–498.

Gillespie, W. Irwin, "On the Redistribution of Income in Canada," *Canadian Tax Journal*, July-August 1976, *24*, 419–450.

———, *The Redistribution of Income in Canada*, Ottawa: Gage Publishing, Ltd., 1980.

Kakwani, Nanak C., "Measurement of Tax Progressivity: An International Comparison," *Economic Journal*, March 1976, *87*, 71–80.

Kotlikoff, Laurence J. and Summers, Lawrence H., "The Role of Intergenerational Transfers in Aggregate Capital Accumulation," *Journal of Political Economy*, August 1981, *89*, 706–723.

Lillard, Lee A., "Inequality: Earnings vs. Human Wealth," *American Economic Review*, March 1977, *67*, 42–53.

Liu, Pak-Wai, "Lorenz Domination and Global Tax Progressivity," *Canadian Journal of Economics*, forthcoming.

Mincer, Jacob, *Schooling, Experience and Earnings*, New York: Columbia University Press, 1974.

Musgrave, Richard A. and Musgrave, Peggy B., *Public Finance in Theory and Practice*, New York: McGraw–Hill, 1980.

———, Case, Karl E. and Leonard, Herman B., "The Distribution of Fiscal Burdens and Benefits," *Public Finance Quarterly*, July 1974, *2*, 259–311.

——— and Thin, Tun, "Income Tax Progression, 1929–48," *Journal of Political Economy*, December 1948, *56*, 498–514.

Pechman, Joseph A. and Okner, Benjamin A., *Who Bears the Tax Burden?*, Washington: The Brookings Institution, 1974.

St-Hilaire, France and Whalley, John, "What Have We Learned from Tax Incidence Calculations?" mimeo., University of Western Ontario, 1982.

——— and ———, "A Microconsistent Equilibrium Data Set for Canada for Use in Tax Policy Analysis," *Review of Income and Wealth*, June 1983, *29*, 1975–204.

Suits, Daniel B., "Measurement of Tax Progressivity," *American Economic Review*, September 1977, *67*, 747–752.

Statistics Canada Survey of Consumer Finances (*SCF*), 1971 *Income Distribution by Size in Canada*, Publication No. 13-207, Ottawa: Ministry of Supply and Services, 1973.

# QUESTIONS

1. Use the receipt of Social Security benefits to illustrate how annual and lifetime incidence (by income class) may differ markedly from one another.

2. Table 2 shows that from an annual perspective the poorest decile faces a combined sales and excise tax rate of 27 percent, while the rate in lifetime calculation is only 15 percent. Explain why the rate is lower in the lifetime case.

3. Try to think of an important policy arena in which the annual incidence of government activity is more important than lifetime incidence. When is lifetime incidence the more appropriate measure?

### Efficiency and the personal income tax.

The 1986 tax reform cut the number of marginal tax brackets down to three. It also broadened the tax base. Each of these changes improved economic efficiency. The excess burden of a tax increases with the square of its tax rate, so a broader base allows lower rates and less welfare loss. A broad base also prevents inefficient substitution of tax-favored income sources for highly taxed income.

In his article, Penchman shows how far short we fall of achieving a comprehensive tax base. The Brownings, in this article, argue that pushing reform all the way to a comprehensive base *and* a single tax rate would have wrought huge efficiency gains.

# WHY NOT A TRUE FLAT RATE TAX?[†]

*Edgar K. Browning and Jacquelene M. Browning**

A true flat rate tax on income has two characteristics: first, the tax base is a comprehensive measure of income with no preferential treatment given to specific sources or uses of income, and second, a single tax rate is applied to that base. In short, a flat rate tax is a proportional tax on total income. By contrast, all of the proposals for reform of the federal individual income tax that have received serious attention are so-called modified flat tax proposals. They differ from a true flat rate tax by using a less comprehensive definition of taxable income (though often more comprehensive than under current tax law) and by applying a small number of graduated tax rates to that base. Since any of the modified flat tax proposals are more complex, more inefficient, and more horizontally inequitable[1] than a true flat rate tax, why are modified flat rate tax proposals considered the only serious contenders in the tax reform sweepstakes?

There is, of course, a simple answer to that question, an answer that seems to be

[†]*Cato Journal*, Vol. 5, No. 2 (Fall 1985). Copyright © Cato Institute. All rights reserved.

*Edgar K. Browning is Professor of Economics and Jacquelene M. Browning is Visiting Associate Professor of Economics at Texas A&M University.

almost universally accepted. In the words of the recent Treasury Department study on tax reform options (Treasury I 1984, pp. 21-23):

> These important advantages [of the flat rate tax] must be compared to the troublesome distributional implications of a pure flat rate tax. A single, totally flat rate, whether imposed on income or on consumption, would involve a substantial shift of tax burden from those in the highest income brackets to low- or middle-income taxpayers. . . . Because of the massive redistribution of tax burdens a pure flat tax would produce, the Treasury Department recommends against its enactment.

Put differently, a true flat rate tax is thought to harm low-and middle-income taxpayers, a politically unacceptable consequence. Although there may be other disadvantages to the flat rate tax, this is the only one the Treasury Department mentions, and we suspect it is the principal objection most people have to the idea of a true flat rate tax.

The primary purpose of this paper is to examine carefully this objection to true flat rate tax. Basically, we show that a flat rate tax will harm lower income households to a much smaller degree than is generally believed or estimated, and may even benefit them over the long run. Our conclusions follow from an analysis that incorporates the efficiency gains from the tax reform as offsets to the direct effects of changing tax liabilities.

## THE ECONOMIC EFFECTS OF FLAT RATE TAXATION

In examining the effects of a flat rate tax, we assume that a flat rate tax is substituted for the present federal individual income tax and that the single tax rate is set so that government revenues remain unchanged. In this framework, it is reasonable to suppose that government expenditure policies do not change, so we can concentrate on the consequences brought about by the change in the tax policy alone. As will become clear, most of the

advantages expected from this change in tax policy are really the alleviation of the disadvantages of the current income tax.

Once of the most important advantages of the flat rate tax is that it will improve incentives to produce by reducing the marginal tax rates of most or all taxpayers. It is important to recognize that the marginal tax rate that applies to the earnings of productive resources is what produces adverse effects on resource supplies. If the marginal tax rate is 40 percent, for instance, a person who has an opportunity to earn an extra $100 will decide whether it is worth the effort based on the $60 in after-tax income that he gets to keep. The higher the marginal tax rate, the lower is the net rate of remuneration received and the more adversely resource supply is likely to be affected. Currently, marginal tax rates under the federal income tax range from 11 percent to 50 percent. In 1979, 35 percent of taxpayers filing joint returns faced marginal rate brackets of 28 percent or higher, and 13 percent were in marginal rate brackets of 37 percent or higher.

Under a flat rate tax using a comprehensive definition of income, the single marginal rate used could be as low as 10 to 12 percent. Thus, most or all taxpayers would confront a substantially lower marginal tax rate, and this in turn means the after-tax reward for earning more income would be increased. Although the magnitude of response to the higher after-tax returns is disputable, recent empirical research as well as common sense suggest that people will choose to make greater efforts to earn income when the returns are higher. These efforts could take the form of increased labor supply or increased saving and investment (or both).

Two further advantages can be expected from the use of a comprehensive measure of income coupled with a low marginal rate. Currently, taxable income is only about half of total personal income—which accounts in part for the high marginal rates that must be used today. When high marginal tax rates are applied to an emasculated definition of income, taxpayers are encouraged to channel part of their incomes into untaxed forms. This change in the composition or use of income reflects a loss in economic productivity as taxpayers devote resources to lower-valued uses simply because they are untaxed. Consider a person in a 50 marginal percent tax bracket. An additional $100 in taxable income is only worth $50 to him since the government collects $50 in taxes. If the taxpayers can transfer the $100 in taxable income to a nontaxed form, he will be better off even if the nontaxed use of $100 produces benefits worth only $51. In this case, the taxpayer benefits by $1 while the government loses $50 in revenue; $49 is effectively lost because the $100 in resources is devoted to a lower-valued use.

This type of waste, or efficiency loss, reflects a misallocation of resources caused by the existence of many untaxed sources and uses of income. A flat rate tax with a comprehensive measure of income would avoid this problem. In addition, even if some items continue to be given preferential treatment, the incentive for taxpayers to utilize these tax "loopholes" would be reduced due to the lower tax rate of the flat rate tax, so the efficiency losses of any remaining tax preference would be lower.

Another benefit from the use of a more comprehensive tax base is that it would produce a fairer distribution of taxes among those with equal real incomes. Currently, taxpayers who are able to shift large portions of their incomes into untaxed forms pay less in taxes than those with equal incomes who are unable or unwilling to make as much use of tax preferences. The result is a wide dispersion in tax burdens among those who are equally well off. A flat rate tax with a broad measure of income would come closer to the ideal that "equals should be treated equally."

A final advantage that can be claimed for the flat rate tax is that it would be simpler. No one needs to be told that the present tax law is highly complex. Tax returns require a good deal of time to fill out correctly, and additional time is required to keep the necessary records. The time required to comply with the tax laws is a (socially) unproductive use of resources: if a taxpayer could pay the same final tax without spending 30 hours locating records and filling out forms, he would be better off and the government would receive the same tax payment. In the same sense, payments for professional tax assistance represent an efficiency loss. Today, nearly half of all taxpayers use professional tax preparers, up from 10 to 15 percent 30 years ago.

Complexity exacts another cost in addition to these outright resource costs: it makes the consequences of the income tax more difficult for the public to understand. Consider, for instance, the widely held view that wealthy taxpayers largely avoid paying taxes through ingenious and excessive use of tax loopholes, perhaps even to the extent of paying a smaller share of their incomes in taxes than middle income taxpayers. While the evidence shows this view to be untrue for the average high income person—only a tiny percentage of wealthy taxpayers accomplish this feat—it requires a fairly sophisticated knowledge of the present complex system to recognize how tax burdens are really distributed among income classes. A flat rate tax would not only be simpler to comply with, it would also be easier to understand the broader social consequences it produces.

These general advantages of a true flat rate tax are widely recognized, but against them must be balanced one overriding disadvantage: the distributional effects of the tax. To examine that aspect of the issue, we will rely on data from the Joint Committee on Taxation. In 1982 the Joint Committee on Taxation estimated that a flat rate tax of 11.8 percent would raise the same amount of revenue in 1984 as the present tax (assuming income levels were the same in 1984 as in 1981) if the tax base were expanded by eliminating all exemptions, deductions, and tax credits and all capital gains were taxed. While it would be possible to define an even more comprehensive tax base, we will examine this specific flat rate tax because of the availability of data concerning how it would affect various income classes.

Table 1 shows how the Joint Economic Committee estimates the distribution of tax burdens would be affected by substituting a flat rate tax of 11.8 percent for the federal income tax in 1984. (Incomes are expressed at 1981 levels; although incomes and tax revenues would be higher at today's price and income levels, the general pattern of effects should be about the same.) Note that tax liabilities rise at expanded (that is, more comprehensively measured) income levels below $30,000 and fall at higher income levels.[2] In total, the 77 percent of taxpaying units with incomes below $30,000 are estimated to pay $31 billion more in taxes under the flat rate tax, while higher income taxpayers pay this

much less. In 1981, $31 billion was about 1 percent of GNP and about 14 percent of income tax revenue. So the substitution of a flat rate tax for the present federal income tax can be expected to redistribute about 14 percent of the income tax burden from upper- to lower-income classes, a redistribution of about 1 percent of GNP.

The redistributional consequences of a flat rate tax have led to its summary dismissal as a serious candidate for tax reform. Yet calculations of the sort appearing in Table 1 overstate the extent to which a flat rate tax would harm persons in lower income classes. These calculations are based on the assumption that each taxpaying unit's earnings would be the same under the flat rate tax as under the current tax, and therefore take no account of the beneficial effects of improved productive incentives of the flat rate tax. They also ignore the benefits of simplification and the broadened tax base. In short, Table 1 ignores all of the efficiency gains that are expected to result

Table 1: **Distribution of Tax Liabilities: Flat Rate Tax versus 1984 Tax Law (1981 income levels)**

| Expanded Income[a] | Number of Taxable Returns[b] | Tax Liability[c] | | Change in Tax[d] |
|---|---|---|---|---|
| | | 1984 Law | Flat Rate Tax | |
| 0–5 | 6.48 | 0.40 | 5.48 | +783 |
| 5–10 | 15.06 | 5.77 | 14.28 | +565 |
| 10–15 | 13.09 | 12.53 | 19.70 | +548 |
| 15–20 | 10.74 | 17.46 | 22.50 | +469 |
| 20–30 | 16.80 | 44.08 | 49.70 | +335 |
| 30–50 | 13.57 | 63.83 | 60.58 | −240 |
| 50–100 | 3.58 | 38.69 | 27.39 | −3,156 |
| 100–200 | 0.63 | 18.66 | 9.87 | −13,921 |
| 200 and up | 0.16 | 16.39 | 7.68 | −53,107 |
| Total | 80.11 | 217.80 | 217.17 | −8[e] |

[a]Thousands of dollars.

[b]In millions.

[c]In billions of dollars.

[d]Dollars per return.

[e]Average tax change.

*Source:* Congressional Budget Office (1983, Table 7).

from a flat rate tax. Some of these gains will accrue to lower income classes, making the cost they bear less than is indicated in Table 1. Of course, the efficiency gains may offset only a trivial part of the cost on lower income classes. However, the analysis in the next two sections suggests that the efficiency gains of a flat rate tax significantly modify the picture of the distributional consequences suggested by Table 1.

## EFFICIENCY GAINS: LABOR SUPPLY, SIMPLIFICATION, BROADER BASE

In this section, we will develop an estimate of the magnitude of the efficiency gain from a flat rate tax due to improved labor supply incentives, reduced compliance costs, and improved resource allocation from a more comprehensive tax base. In addition, we will allocate this aggregate gain among income classes. Making these estimates will require some heroic assumptions, but the economics literature does provide some guidance concerning the magnitudes we need to use. We caution, however, that this exercise does not purport to provide definitive conclusions; instead it is intended only to indicate the likely orders of magnitude involved.

We begin by considering the gains from increased labor supply under the flat rate tax. Two pieces of information are required to estimate how much labor supply will increase. First, we need to know how much marginal tax rates will fall under the flat rate tax since this determines how much after-tax rates of pay will rise. Second, we need to know how responsive workers are to an increase in the after-tax rate of pay. Our conclusion is that a flat rate tax will increase aggregate labor supply by about 5 percent. The reasoning that leads to this conclusion is fairly involved and occupies us for the next five paragraphs. For those readers willing to accept 5 percent as a reasonable figure, the next five paragraphs

may be skipped. We should note at the outset that our estimate falls far short of the supply-side effects assumed by disciples of the Laffer curve. However, we believe it is a plausible estimate of the labor supply response to a flat rate tax that substantially reduces marginal tax rates.

In evaluating the effect on labor supply, it is important to distinguish between effective and statutory marginal tax rates. The statutory rates are simply those nominal rates in the law that identify the marginal rate that applies to changes in taxable earnings. The effective marginal tax rate measures the marginal tax relative to changes in total earnings, comprehensively measured. Changes in effective marginal tax rates are what affect labor supply, but unfortunately these changes are not easily measured.

To see the significance of the distinction between statutory and effective marginal tax rates, consider how a hypothetical taxpayer now in a 30 percent statutory marginal tax bracket is affected when his gross earnings rise by $100. Part of the $100 increase is likely to be received in nontaxable forms, such as fringe benefits, and part is likely to be devoted to outlays that are deductible, such as charitable contributions. Thus, taxable income may rise by only $70, and the 30 percent rate applied to this sum results in $21 in additional taxes. Relative to total incremental earnings, the effective marginal tax rate is only 21 percent, and we argue that it is the effective marginal rate that acts as an impediment to work incentives, not statutory rates. To see this, suppose that the statutory marginal rate is reduced to 21 percent at the same time that the tax base is broadened so that the entire incremental $100 is taxable. Nothing will have changed: if $100 more is earned, $21 in taxes will be paid and $79 retained. Although the statutory rate is lower, the *effective* rate is not, and there is no reason to expect work incentives to be improved. Only reductions in effective marginal tax rates will improve work incentives. While a flat rate tax will reduce effective marginal tax rates, it will reduce them less than the change in statutory rates suggests.

It is also important to recognize that it is the reduction in the combined effective marginal tax rate from all taxes affecting labor earnings, including the federal and state income taxes, social security, and sales and excise taxes, that is significant. Moreover, this rate varies among households. Ideally, we should consider the change for each household separately, but the detailed information necessary to do this is lacking. Instead, we will consider how the weighted average for the combined effective marginal tax rate of households will be affected. Based on other research, it is reasonable to take 44 percent as an economywide average value for the combined effective marginal tax rate.[3] According to a study by Barro and Sahasakul (1983), the weighted average marginal tax rate for the individual income tax alone was 29 percent in 1979 (which should be similar to 1984 levels). This may seem to suggest that a flat rate tax of 11.8 percent would reduce marginal rates on average by 17.2 percentage points. However, this estimate is larger than the reduction in the effective marginal rate: the Barro-Sahasakul estimate is for the average statutory marginal rate under current law, but the 11.8 percent rate would apply to a broader measure of earnings. So instead of assuming a 17.2 percentage point drop in the effective marginal tax rate, we assume the 11.8 percent rate only represents a reduction. of 8 percentage points in the effective marginal tax rate. Although the precise value is largely conjecture on our part, we believe it is more accurate than simply assuming that the statutory reduction of 17.2 percentage points produces an identical reduction in effective marginal tax rates.

Thus, we assume that a flat rate tax of 11.8 percent applied to a comprehensive base will reduce the effective marginal tax rate from 44 percent to 36 percent on average. This assumption in turn implies that the after-

tax rate of pay will rise from 56 percent of the before-tax rate of pay to 64 percent, a 14.3 percent rise. Next, we need to consider how much labor supply will increase as a result. The size of the adjustment in labor supply depends on how responsive workers are to changes in net wage rates at the margin. Labor supply elasticities which estimate the percentage change in labor supply resulting from a given percentage change in the wage rate, have been studied extensively. Based on available evidence, an economywide average value for the labor supply elasticity of 0.3 seems reasonable.[4] This implies that labor supply would rise by 4.3 percent, a result that does not seem excessive given a 14.3 percent increase in the net rate of pay.

This calculation, however, understates the effect of the flat rate tax. Recall that the 11.8 percent rate is estimated to raise the same amount of revenue if actual incomes remain unchanged; if incomes rise, as we have argued they would, a lower rate could be used and still raise the same revenue. Based on the assumptions described above, we estimate that a 10.0 percent tax rate would raise the same total revenue as an 11.8 tax rate with no increase in work effort.[5] Making these adjustments, the effective marginal tax rate would fall from 44 percent to 34.2 percent, and the after-tax rate of pay would rise by 17.5 percent. With a labor supply elasticity of 0.3, this implies labor supply would rise by 5.25 percent. This is our estimate of how much labor supply would rise under a flat rate tax applied to a comprehensive measure of income.

With such an increase in labor supply, labor earnings would rise by about $105 billion (at the 1981 levels used in Table 1). This increase does not represent a net gain to taxpayers, however, since they would be working more (consuming less leisure) to produce the additional $105 billion. The net gain is the extra earnings less the value of leisure given up. By using the after-tax rate of pay to value leisure, we estimate that the cost (in sacrificed leisure) of producing the extra $105 billion is

$64 billion.[6] Therefore, we arrive at a net gain to taxpayers as a group of $41 billion from the improved work incentives of the flat rate tax.

There are two other efficiency gains that we can roughly estimate. First, there is the gain from tax simplification. Taxpayer compliance cost and the cost of collecting taxes would be lower under the flat rate tax. Slemrod and Sorum (1984) have recently estimated that the time cost of taxpayers complying with the current tax has a value of about 5 percent of tax revenue. In addition, the costs firms bear in administering withholding, costs of professional assistance, and collection costs of the Internal Revenue Service can conservatively be estimated at 2 percent of revenue. Therefore, total compliance and collection costs are probably about 7 percent of revenue, or $15 billion. We assume that the simpler flat rate tax would reduce these costs by one-third, or by $5 billion.

Second, there is the gain from the use of a more comprehensive tax base, which avoids the uneconomic shifting of resources to lower-valued uses because of tax advantages. The efficiency cost of these distortions under the present tax has been estimated to be about 7 percent of revenue (J. Browning 1979), or a total of $15 billion at 1981 levels. Since no feasible tax base is likely to eliminate all these distortions, we assume that a flat rate tax will result in a gain of $10 billion through improved resource allocation due to base-broadening.

Combining these three efficiency gains yields a total annual net gain of $56 billion. Again, we emphasize that this is only a rough estimate, but the assumptions on which it is based are entirely reasonable given the available evidence. This gain means that shifting to a flat rate tax of equal yield will increase the real income of the nation by $56 billion annually (at 1981 levels). Stated differently, the real burden of a flat rate tax that raises the same revenue as the present income tax would be about 20 percent less.

Recognizing these efficiency gains does not mean that everyone would benefit from the flat rate tax. The question of who would receive these gains is therefore of interest. We start with the changes in tax liabilities by income classes implied by the data in Table 1; the changes in tax liabilities are shown explicitly in the first column of Table 2. Recall that these changes are based on the assumption of an 11.8 percent tax rate applied to an unchanged level of earnings.

Because of the increase in earnings under the flat rate tax, we have seen that a 10 percent tax rate can be used. Thus, even though all households may not increase labor supply to the same degree, all will benefit from the efficiency gain which permits use of a 10 percent rate rather than an 11.8 percent rate. (Note that a household whose income does not rise at all will benefit because its tax burden would be nearly 20 percent lower than estimated in Table 1.) Since all households benefit from a lower tax rate, we can allocate the efficiency gain from increased labor supply in proportion to tax liabilities calculated from the flat rate tax when no change in earnings is assumed. Column 2 in Table 2 shows the size of this efficiency gain when apportioned among income classes in this way.

The gains from improved simplicity and a broader tax base are allocated in a different way. These gains will likely accrue primarily to those who pay taxes under the present system, and are probably greater the more taxes currently paid. Therefore, the $15 billion efficiency gain from these sources is allocated in proportion to tax liabilities under the present income tax. The distribution of these gains by income class is shown in column 3 of Table 2.

The change in real net income for each income class is given by combining the change in tax liability as originally calculated in column 1 with the efficiency gains in columns 2 and 3; the results are displayed in column 4. Recall that Table 1 suggested that the lowest five income classes would suffer a loss of $31 billion from the substitution of the flat rate tax for the present income tax. The estimates

Table 2: **Distributional Effect Incorporating Some Efficiency Gains**

| Expanded Income[a] | Change in Tax Liability[b] | Efficiency Gains[b] | | Change in Real Incomes[b] |
|---|---|---|---|---|
| | | From Increased Labor Supply | From Simplicfication and Broader Base | |
| 0–5 | +5.08 | 1.03 | 0.03 | −4.02 |
| 5–10 | +8.51 | 2.70 | 0.40 | −5.41 |
| 10–15 | +7.17 | 3.72 | 0.86 | −2.59 |
| 15–20 | +5.03 | 4.25 | 1.20 | .42 |
| 20–30 | +5.62 | 9.38 | 3.04 | 6.80 |
| 30–50 | −3.25 | 11.44 | 4.40 | 19.09 |
| 50–100 | −11.30 | 5.17 | 2.66 | 19.13 |
| 100–200 | −8.78 | 1.86 | 1.29 | 11.93 |
| 200 and up | −8.71 | 1.45 | 1.13 | 11.29 |
| Total | −0.63 | 41.0 | 15.01 | 56.6 |

[a] In thousands of dollars.

[b] In billions of dollars.

*Source:* Table 1 and calculations explained in text

in Table 2, however, imply that the combined loss of the lowest three income classes (the only ones that lose) is only $12 billion. Families with incomes above $15,000 are estimated to gain a total of $68 billion. Tax reform is not a zero sum game; the gains to those who are benefited are more than five times as large as the losses to those who are harmed.

This exercise shows that the adverse distributional consequences of a flat rate tax are likely to be substantially smaller than common estimates that ignore efficiency gains would imply. Moreover, there is one significant efficiency gain that we have not yet considered, namely, the gain from the increase in saving that a flat rate tax would produce.

## THE EFFICIENCY GAIN FROM INCREASED SAVING

There are several reasons why the introduction of a flat rate tax can be expected to increase private saving. First, the redistribution of the

tax burden in favor of upper income classes will increase total saving if upper income households tend to save more out of disposable income at the margin than lower income households. Second, lower effective marginal tax rates will tend to increase the after-tax return from saving, and more saving may be forthcoming when the return on saving increases. It is important, however, not to overstate the extent to which the after-tax rate of return will increase. Since much saving is already preferentially treated under the present income tax, moving to a flat rate tax might not increase after-tax returns for many taxpayers. Third, some portion of the increase in labor earnings that results from the improved work incentives will be saved.

In order to estimate the gain from increased saving, we require an estimate of how much saving will rise. Because saving is already preferentially treated and we do not know how much (if any) after-tax rates of return will increase under a flat rate tax, our estimate is based exclusively on the third source of increased saving mentioned above, that is, increases in saving resulting from increased labor earnings. In the last section, we estimated that disposable incomes would rise by $105 billion as a result of increased labor supply. Now we further assume that the marginal propensity to save is 0.15; thus, we estimate that saving will rise by $15.75 billion. This figure would represent about a 4 percent increase in the level of annual saving.

Why is an increase in saving a source of an efficiency gain? Under certain circumstances, it would be irrelevant to our analysis whether people spent or saved their increments in labor earnings. Specifically, if taxes on labor earnings are the only distortions in an otherwise competitive economy, there would be no efficiency gain. In this case, a person who saves an additional dollar receives the entire gain associated with providing funds that finance capital formation. If the real rate of interest is 5 percent, for example, an additional dollar saved would finance capital that (net of depreciation) will augment future production at an annual return of 5 percent. The saver, then would receive the full increment in production that his saving makes possible. In this situation, if an increase in work effort raises income and leads to a dollar increase in saving, only the saver receives any benefit, and that benefit is correctly measured as one dollar.

The situation is different, however, when the government levies taxes on capital income. In the United States, several taxes fall on the return to capital, notably state and federal corporation income taxes, property taxes, and state and federal income taxes. The combined effect of these taxes is to make the rate of return received by the saver less than the rate of return actually generated when that saving finances capital investments. In a recent study, it was estimated that the before-tax real return to capital investments in the corporate sector was about 10 percent, but after taxes savers receive a real rate of return of about 3 per-

cent (Feldstein, Poterba, and Dicks-Mireaux 1981). In other words, the effective tax rate on corporate capital is about 70 percent.

Consider what happens when a person saves an additional dollar, and the return on that dollar is taxed at a rate of 70 percent. To make matters simple, assume that the person will maintain the principal intact in the future and only consume the net return it provides. The saver then receives a stream of annual returns of 3 cents per year from a one dollar investment; that part of the gain from increased saving is received by the saver himself. At the same time, however, there is another gain that is not received by the saver, namely, the stream of annual capital tax payments of 7 cents per year that is also produced by one dollar in savings. People other than the saver himself will benefit because the increased future tax collections that his saving generates can finance lower tax rates and/or higher public expenditures. This part of the gain from increased saving was not taken into account in our previous estimates, and it represents a further increase in real incomes that result from the tax reform.

Now we turn to the estimation of the magnitude of the efficiency gain from increased saving. While the proper way to do this is a complex theoretical issue, we can easily explain why this gain is likely to be substantial by continuing with our previous example. The after-tax rate of return of 3 percent can be taken as a measure of how much people discount benefits received in the future: a benefit of $1.03 one year in the future has a present value of $1.00. When saving rises by one dollar, society in total receives a stream of annual benefits of $0.10 ($0.07 of which will go to the government and $0.03 of which goes to the saver). The present value of an infinite stream of annual benefits of $0.10, when the discount rate is 3 percent, is equal to $3.33 ($0.10/.03). Thus, when saving rises by $1, the present value of the future benefits is $3.33; one dollar of this is the present value of the benefit received by the saver and the remaining $2.33 is the present value of the future tax payments that the saving will generate.

What we have just illustrated with a simplified example is the calculation of what economists call the shadow price of capital. The shadow price of capital is intended to measure the present value of the future benefits that flow from an additional dollar of saving (and hence capital formation). Calculating a value for the shadow price of capital is more involved than in our example since the future effects of present saving also depend on how long the principal is held intact, the extent to which some of the annual net returns may themselves be saved, and other factors. In a recent survey related to these matters, Lind (1982) concludes that 3.80 is a reasonable estimate of the magnitude of the shadow price of capital. We will rely on his estimate and hope that our example makes the size of this figure plausible.

Coupled with our estimate that a flat rate tax will increase saving by $15.75 billion, a shadow price of capital of 3.80 implies that the present value of future benefits from that saving is $59.85 billion. (Note that this is the present value of benefits from one year's increase in savings.) Of this gain, savers themselves receive $15.75 billion—the present value of the after-tax returns received— and that amount is already included in our previous analysis as part of the increase in labor earnings. The remaining $44.1 billion represents an efficiency gain from the increased saving.

For our purposes, we also need to know how this gain will be distributed among income classes. It is not clear how best to proceed in this case, and we propose two alternatives. First, since the gain takes the form of higher future capital tax revenues, it would be possible to reduce the flat rate tax in future years and still generate the same tax revenue. This suggests allocating the gain in proportion to tax liabilities under the flat rate tax. Alternatively, the government might spend this additional revenue rather than reducing tax rates. Based on other research, it seems reasonable to assume that benefits from government spending are distributed equally among taxpaying units.[7]

Table 3 uses both approaches to allocate the efficiency gain from increased saving. The first column gives our previous estimates of the changes in real incomes by income classes (from Table 2). Columns 2 and 3 show the additional efficiency gains accruing to each income class when the aggregate gain is allocated in proportion to tax liabilities under the flat rate tax (column 2) and alternatively when it is allocated in proportion to the number of taxpaying units (column 3). The last two columns give the two alternative estimates of the total change in real income for each income class. These represent our final estimates of the distributional effects of substituting a flat rate tax for the present federal income tax. The results are striking. Instead of an aggregate loss of $31 billion to lower income classes, the lowest two income classes (the only two estimated to be harmed) lose only $5.4 billion when the gain from saving is allocated in proportion to taxes, while the higher income classes gain about $106 billion. When the gain from increased saving is allocated to taxpaying units, all income classes are estimated to benefit from the tax reform. In both cases, the aggregate efficiency gain is estimated to be in excess of $100 billion.

## EVALUATION OF DISTRIBUTIONAL EFFECTS

Our analysis has been based on the fact that if a flat rate tax leads to increased labor supply and/or saving, then lower income classes will receive some benefit even if their own labor supply and saving does not change. The reason, often overlooked, is that increases in earnings will generate additional tax revenue

Table 3: **Distributional Effect Incorporating All Efficiency Gains**

| Expanded Income[a] | Changes in Real Income Excluding Saving[b] | Efficiency Gains from Increased Saving Allocated to: | | Change in Real Income Including Saving Allocated to: | |
| --- | --- | --- | --- | --- | --- |
| | | Tax Liabilities[b] | Taxpaying Units[b] | Tax Liabilities[b] | Taxpaying Units[b] |
| 0–5 | −4.02 | 1.11 | 6.60 | −2.91 | 2.58 |
| 5–10 | −5.41 | 2.90 | 7.67 | −2.51 | 2.28 |
| 10–15 | −2.59 | 4.00 | 6.67 | 1.41 | 4.08 |
| 15–20 | 0.42 | 4.57 | 5.47 | 4.99 | 5.89 |
| 20–30 | 6.80 | 10.09 | 8.56 | 16.89 | 15.36 |
| 30–50 | 19.09 | 12.30 | 6.91 | 31.89 | 26.00 |
| 50–100 | 19.13 | 5.56 | 1.82 | 24.69 | 20.59 |
| 100–200 | 11.93 | 2.00 | 0.32 | 13.93 | 12.25 |
| 200 and up | 11.29 | 1.56 | 0.08 | 12.85 | 11.37 |
| Total | 56.6 | 44.1 | 44.1 | 100.7 | 100.7 |

[a]In thousands of dollars.

[b]In billions of dollars.

*Source:* Table 2 and calculations explained in text

and permit either a tax rate reduction or an expenditure increase (or both), and in this way the efficiency gains from tax reform tend to be spread more widely through the income distribution. Our major finding is that the harm done to lower income households is substantially less than commonly supposed; indeed, they could actually benefit. While the exact values of our estimates should be viewed as merely suggestive, we believe they are based on plausible economic assumptions.

Before considering the significance of this finding, there are several additional aspects to the distributional issue that should be discussed. The first concerns the mobility of households within the income distribution. Figures like those in our three tables are based on the incomes households have in a single year. Often, however, a single year's income is not an accurate indication of the household's average economic position over a longer period of time. For example, suppose that a household in the lowest income class is there because of a temporary illness of the

household head, and that in all other years that family has a higher income. In this situation, what really matters to the family's well-being is how the tax reform affects real tax burdens at the family's normal, higher income level. Calculations of the sort shown in our tables, which indicate how much taxes increase for the lowest income class, can be very misleading in situations like this.

From an equity standpoint, it is important to consider how the tax system affects households for longer than a single year. Unfortunately, what the distribution of income looks like over extended periods of time is not known exactly, but some recent estimates demonstrate that people shift around in the income distribution to a dramatic extent. For example, the Panel Study on Income Dynamics found that nearly half of families whose incomes placed them in the bottom 20 percent of the income distribution in 1971 were in higher income classes only seven years later (Lilla 1984, p. 70). The same study also found that only one-third of those counted as poor in a given year were poor in eight or more years out of a ten-year period. Even more interesting are the results of a computer simulation study of lifetime tax incidence in Canada by Davis, St.-Hilaire, and Whalley (1984, pp. 663-49). The Canadian study found that the poorest decile of households received only 1 percent of total national income in the annual data, but the lowest decile received 4 percent of total income when lifetime incomes were compared. To find that the lowest income class could have an average income over its lifetime that is four times as high as its income in each year's annual data is quite remarkable.

What data of this sort suggest is that it may be largely irrelevant how the tax system is estimated to affect people in the lowest one or two income classes shown in our tables: there may be very few households that remain in these classes when a longer-run viewpoint is adopted. Taking account of mobility, therefore, serves to strengthen our contention that low income groups will not be harmed as much as conventional analysis of annual data imply. Moreover, families that are not upwardly mobile can be helped with income transfers, as we will discuss below.

A second factor related to the significance of our estimates is the timing of the labor supply and saving consequences we have estimated. In our calculations, it was assumed that people would respond immediately to the lower marginal tax rate of the flat rate tax. In effect, we estimated the permanent, long-run effects of the tax reform. It takes time, however, for people to fully adjust to a major change in the tax structure, and the immediate, or short-run, effects will be quite different. For instance, two studies have estimated that it takes from two to four years for half the eventual change in labor supply to be realized. Moreover, the full effects of the increase in saving will be even more delayed; although we have expressed the benefits in present value terms, the effect of increased saving on augmenting capital income tax revenues would

be quite small in the beginning and perhaps take 20 to 25 years to grow to its full magnitude.

In the short run, that is, the period immediately following the tax reform, labor supply and saving would probably not increase significantly. Consequently, the short-run, albeit temporary, effect of the tax reform on the distribution of income might look more like Table 1 than the other tables. In other words, the immediate consequences would involve substantial costs on low income households. Although these costs would diminish over time and for many households actually become benefits after a few years, there is no avoiding the fact that present costs must be borne for a time before future benefits will be realized.

Because the short-run effects of a movement to a flat rate tax differ in this way from its long-run effects, tax reform of this nature is likely to be difficult. Politicians are widely thought to take a short-run viewpoint in evaluating public policies, and that viewpoint naturally leads to an emphasis on the "massive redistribution" of tax burdens that a flat rate tax would produce. It would be unfortunate if such a perspective is the basis for rejecting a tax reform that holds out the promise of benefiting most people. Such an outcome is, however, understandable.

It is probably true that a concern for the well-being of low income households accounts for the lack of serious attention given a true flat rate tax. It is simply taken for granted that the income tax must exempt the neediest households from taxation. There are other ways, however, to assist the needy that should also be considered. For example, government transfer programs can also serve this function. In fact, transfer programs are far more important to the well-being of low income households than is the federal income tax. Even if a flat rate tax were used, government transfers to the poorest 20 percent of households would still be three times as great as the total (federal, state, and local) tax burden on these households. What this fact should make clear is that our redistributional goals are now being served primarily through our system of transfers instead of by the progressive nature of the income tax. Moreover, this is as it should be. Through transfer programs, we can better target assistance on the neediest households than we can by manipulating the tax law. (Cutting taxes for low-income people and raising taxes for high income people, for example, does little to help the neediest families if they have little or no taxable income. Increasing transfer payments, however, can help.)

What is not adequately appreciated is that the existence of a well-developed (if not well-designed) system of transfers greatly reduces our need to rely on the income tax as a redistributive device. It is simply not necessary for every government policy to serve a redistributive goal since transfers can be adjusted so that the net effect of the system as a whole is to help the poor. For example, it would be possible to couple enactment of a flat rate tax with a moderate (and perhaps temporary) increase in transfers to the poor, thereby mitigating or avoiding harming the truly needy while at the same time realizing the efficiency advantages of the flat rate tax. While we do not necessarily advocate this approach (since it could easily be abused), we only suggest it to show that the cost the tax reform considered by itself would impose on the poor is not a sufficient reason to dismiss it.

## MODIFIED FLAT TAX PROPOSALS

All of the proposals for tax reform that are receiving serious attention are modified flat tax proposals. These proposals are quite different from what we have described as a true flat rate tax. Specifically, there are two important differences. First, the tax base is defined in a way that continues to exempt large amounts of income so that taxable income continues to fall far short of the total income of taxpayers.

Second, instead of a single rate applied to this base, a set of graduated rates is used. Generally, however, the number of separate marginal rate brackets is lower than under the present tax.

Perhaps the most important of the tax proposals are the Bradley-Gephardt bill, the Kemp-Kasten bill, and the recent Treasury Department proposal (Treasury I). All three of the proposals would selectively eliminate certain tax preferences, although there are differences in exactly which preferences would be abolished. All three would increase personal exemptions, thereby expanding one important tax preference, and all three would reduce the number of separate marginal rate brackets effectively to three. Under Bradley-Gephardt, the marginal brackets are 14 percent, 26 percent, and 30 percent; under Kemp-Kasten, they are 20 percent, 28 percent, and 25 percent[8]; under Treasury I, they are 15 percent, 25 percent, and 35 percent.

We have argued that the efficiency gains of a true flat rate would probably be substantial. The natural question to consider now is how the modified flat tax proposals compare to the true flat rate tax in this regard. Supporters of these measures claim that their lower marginal rates—although not as low as could be achieved under a true flat rate tax—would increase incentives to work, save, and invest. However, we contend that none of these proposals would lead to any significant improvement in productive incentives.

To demonstrate this, it is not necessary to engage in any sophisticated theorizing. Instead, we need only accept the claims of the sponsors of these proposals that they would not effect any significant change in tax liabilities by income class. If the actual degree of progressivity of the present tax system is retained, it immediately implies that effective marginal tax rates have not been reduced at all. This is simply a matter of arithmetic. If the present and new tax liability is $3,000 at an income of $30,000, for example, and both taxes impose a liability of $5,000 at an income of $40,000 (the assumed unchanged degree of progressivity), then the effective marginal tax rate applied when income increases from $30,000 to $40,000 must be 20 percent under both taxes since the additional tax liability is $2,000. Similar reasoning applies for other income classes. It makes no difference whether the statutory marginal tax rates are lower; if they are applied to a broadened measure of income at the margin, as they must be if actual tax liabilities are to remain unchanged, then the effective marginal tax rates will not be any lower. And incentives will improve only if effective marginal tax rates are reduced.

We are not arguing that these proposals will not improve any single person's incentive to earn, but just that on average there will be no improvement. Some people may face lower effective marginal tax rates, but others in the same tax brackets must be facing higher effective marginal rates if the tax liabilities by income class really do remain largely unaffected. For example, last year *Newsweek* (1984) published a comparison of average tax liabilities by income class under Bradley-Gephardt and the present tax. There was, in fact, very little difference in the average tax liabilities for each income class; Bradley-Gephardt produced slightly lower taxes on households with incomes under $25,000 and slightly higher taxes on those with higher incomes. This implies that the additional taxes paid if a taxpayer moves from a lower to a higher bracket will be greater under Bradley-Gephardt: how could this possibly give one more incentive to earn more under Bradley-Gephardt?

What the modified flat tax proposals do is to produce lower statutory marginal tax brackets by broadening the tax base in a way that does not produce the lower effective marginal tax rates on which incentive effects depend. An example may help to make this clear. Suppose a person is now in a 40 percent tax

bracket; then the marginal tax is reduced to 36 percent at the same time the tax base is broadened by disallowing the deduction of state income taxes. Does this person have any greater incentive to earn income? If he is in a 10 percent state tax bracket, the answer is no. Suppose the person under current law earns $100 more. Ten dollars is paid to the state and 40 percent of the $90 taxable income under the federal tax ($100 less the $10 deduction), or $36, is paid to the federal government. He keeps $54 out of the $100; his effective marginal tax rate is 46 percent. Under the alternative tax, the $10 deduction is not allowed, and the lower statutory rate of 36 percent applies to the full $100, so the federal tax liability is still $36 and the state liability is still $10. He still gets to keep only $54 out of the extra $100 earned; his effective marginal tax rate is still 46 percent even though the statutory rate of the federal tax has been reduced from 40 percent to 36 percent.

Insofar as these modified flat tax proposals really do not significantly change actual tax liabilities at each income level, they must do so in a way analogous to the example above. They produce illusory lower marginal tax rates by applying these rates to a larger part of each additional dollar of earnings than the present law. Consequently, it is difficult to see how they can be expected to improve incentives to earn income.

The modified flat tax proposals, therefore, cannot be expected to produce the increases in labor supply and saving that a true flat rate tax can. This is not the same as saying that they are undesirable, but only that the efficiency gains will be less than under the tax reform we evaluated earlier in this paper. To indicate the significance of this, we estimated a total efficiency gain for a flat rate tax of $100 billion annually, of which $41 billion was due to increased labor supply and $44 billion to increased saving; a modified flat tax would realize none of these gains because saving and work effort would be unaffected. The remaining $15 billion gain we estimated for a true flat rate tax was due to improved resource allocation from a broadened tax base and to the greater simplicity of the tax. Since the modified flat tax proposals broaden the tax base by less than a true flat rate tax and simplify the tax less, they will produce only a fraction of the $15 billion in efficiency gains. Overall, the efficiency advantages of the modified flat tax proposals can realistically be expected to be only a small fraction of the gains that could be expected from a true flat rate tax.

Modified flat tax proposals are predicated on the assumption that it is politically infeasible, or for some other reason undesirable, to substantially change the distribution of tax burdens by income class. Accepting that as a constraint, however, is equivalent to forgoing much of the sizable efficiency gain that is possible from a true flat rate tax.

## CONCLUSION

Why not a true flat rate tax on total earnings in place of the present complex, inequitable, and inefficient income tax? As we have seen, the advantages are substantial. The major objection that has forestalled debate on this type of tax reform has been that it will impose huge costs on middle- and low-income households. We have argued that the efficiency gains are sizable enough to offset a large part of these costs. Moreover, once it is recognized that transfer programs are a better way to insure adequate income for the truly impoverished, the possibility of a meaningful improvement in our tax system becomes real. We can have a simpler, more easily understood, more equitable, and more efficient tax system.

# Notes

1. Horizontal inequity refers to the imposing of different tax burdens on people with equal ability to pay taxes. In other words, two people with the same incomes may pay different taxes because one makes greater use of tax preferences.

2. We are puzzled by the large increase in taxes per return shown for the under $5,000 class. If every family had income at the top of that class ($5,000), its total tax from an 11.8 percent levy would be $590, but the table shows an increase of $783.07. We suspect that this is due to the number of taxable returns in the table counting only those that are taxable under current law, while the number would be much larger under the flat rate tax. If so, the increase in tax liability per family would be less than shown for the lower income classes which contain significant numbers of nontaxable returns under current law.

3. Browning and Johnson (1984, Table 3) have developed estimates of weighted average marginal tax rates for each quintile of households in 1976. By weighting each of these rates by the share of labor earnings of each quintile we get an overall rate of 43 percent. Since both social security and income taxes are higher today, we think 44 percent is a reasonable figure to use, though it could easily be off by a few percentage points.

4. We interpret the 0.3 figure as a compensated labor supply elasticity. Since the tax reform in question does not change the amount of tax revenue collected, there is no income effect for the community as a whole, and the compensated change in labor supply should equal the actual change. For references to the econometric literature dealing with labor supply elasticities, see Browning and Johnson (1984) and Stuart (1984).

5. This 10.0 percent tax does not yield the same revenue as the present income tax. With additional labor earnings, tax revenues under social security, state income, and sales and excise taxes will rise, so an unchanged total government revenue implies less revenue from the income tax considered by itself. From a welfare standpoint, it is total revenue and not its distribution among separate taxes that is important.

6. The after-tax rate of pay is initially 56 percent of the market rate and rises to 65.8 percent under the flat rate tax, so the average value of the after-tax rate of pay over the change in earnings is 60.9 percent. Multiplying this by the increase in earnings gives the value of leisure given up in earning the extra $105 billion.

7. In Browning and Johnson (1984), it is estimated that government transfers per household for each quintile in 1976 were $2,874, $3,317, $2,441, $2,117, and $2,485. These figures suggest to us that allocating the benefits of government spending to taxpaying units is not likely to be too far off.

8. The Kemp-Kasten plan has a nominal marginal tax rate of 25 percent that applies to all taxable income. However, it also utilizes an earned income exclusion of 20 percent of earnings that applies up to $40,000, and that makes the net marginal tax rate equal to 10 percent up to that level of income. The exclusion is gradually phased out at earnings between $40,000 and $100,000 in a way that makes the net marginal tax rate 28 percent over this range. For incomes over $100,000, only the 25 percent rate applies.

# References

Barro, Robert J., and Sahasakul, Chaipat. "Average Marginal Tax Rates from Social Security and the Individual Income Tax." NBER Working Paper No. 1214. Cambridge, Mass: National Bureau of Economic Research, October 1983.

Browning, Edgar K., and Johnson, William R. "The Trade-Off between Equality and Efficiency." *Journal of Political Economy* 92 (April 1984): 175–203.

Browning, Jacquelene M. "Estimating the Welfare Cost of Tax Preferences." *Public Finance Quarterly* 7 (April 1979): 199–219.

Congressional Budget Office. *Revising the Individual Income Tax*. Washington, D.C.: CBO, July 1983.

Davies, James; St.-Hilaire, France; and Whalley, John. "Some Calculations of Lifetime Tax Incidence." *American Economic Review* 74 (September 1984): 663–649.

Feldstein, Martin; Poterba, James; and Dicks-Mireaux, Louis. "The Effective Tax Rate and Pretax Rate of Return." NBER Working Paper No. 740. Cambridge, Mass.: National Bureau of Economic Research, August 1981.

Lilla, Mark. "Why the 'Income Distribution' is So Misleading." *The Public Interest* 77 (Fall 1984): 62–76.

Lind, Robert C. "A Primer on the Major Issues Relating to the Discount Rate for Evaluating National Energy Options." In *Discounting for Time and Risk in Energy Policy*, pp. 443–457. Edited by Robert C. Lind et al. Washington, D.C.: Resources for the Future, 1982.

Slemrod, Joel, and Sorum, Nikki. "The Compliance Cost of the U.S. Individual Income Tax System." *National Tax Journal* 37 (December 1984): 461–474.

Stuart, Charles. "Welfare Costs per Dollar of Additional Tax Revenue in the United States." *American Economic Review* 74 (June 1984): 352–362.

"The Tax Maze: Time to Start Over?" *Newsweek* (16 April 1984): 67.

[Treasury I]. U.S. Department of Treasury. *Tax Reform for Fairness, Simplicity, and Economic Growth*. Vol. 1, *An Overview*. Washington, D.C.: Government Printing Office, November 1984.

# QUESTIONS

1. Browning and Browning estimate that a broad-based flat tax of 10 percent could raise as much revenue as the current system.
(a) Explain the role played by estimates of labor supply elasticity in arriving at this tax rate.
(b) Explain how increased labor supply leads to an estimated efficiency gain of $41 billion.

2. In Table 3, Browning and Browning present estimates of the distributional consequences of a flat tax that also stimulates savings. Increased savings matter because they are invested in taxed capital that yields both a competitive return to the investor and a future stream of tax payments. To see who benefits, the authors consider two cases. If the tax rate falls so that total revenue is held constant, they get the numbers in the "tax liabilities" column. If the tax rate

is held constant and spending increases, the benefits are distributed roughly equally among households, giving the "taxpaying units" column.

A third option that is especially relevant in the 1980s is that the extra tax revenue be used to reduce the federal deficit, holding both tax rates and expenditure levels constant. How do we distribute the benefits from a reduced deficit? One point of view suggests that benefits go to future generations, whose tax burdens will be lower. If this is the right story, two facts concern us: first, lower-income households (within a given generation) have more children than higher-income households, but, second, if their children are more likely to be low-income adults, their children's individual tax liabilities will on average be lower.

Other economists view a deficit as similar to a tax. Since current generations realize their children will bear a burden from the deficit, they transfer extra resources to their children, thus sharing the burden. If this were the whole story, the distribu-

tional gains from deficit reduction would be proportional to tax liabilities.

If these effects are roughly offsetting, then the benefits from reduced deficit are distributed roughly equally across taxpaying units.

(a) Which view of the burden of deficit finance leads to a more optimistic view of the impact of a flat tax on low-income households?

(b) An increase in potential tax revenue would probably be split among these uses: reduced tax rates, higher spending, and lower deficits. If the result is a distribution halfway between those found by allocating benefits by tax liability and by taxpaying unit (see Table 3), calculate the change in real income for each income group when a flat tax has savings effects.

3. In the long run, expenditure programs can also be modified. Once a society decides on a certain level of desired redistribution, how should it divide progressivity between its tax system and its expenditure programs?

## *Is the tax code fair in its distinctions between married and unmarried persons?*

The family is generally regarded as a natural economic unit. Its members' activities are coordinated with one another, and each member's needs are considered when the family budget is planned. Major federal programs, in particular Social Security and the personal income tax, are designed to take marital status into account, recognizing that marriage joins individuals into a single economic unit. In both of these programs, however, troublesome questions of efficiency and equity arise from the special treatment awarded married couples.

## WHY NOT VIEW THE INDIVIDUAL AS THE ECONOMIC UNIT?

In asking whether it is fair to treat households (or married couples) as the economic unit, we apply the concept of "horizontal equity": people in similar circumstances should be treated similarly by government tax and transfer programs. In what way does formation of a joint household make the circumstances of a married couple dissimilar to their circumstances when living separately? Two possibilities come to mind. First, there are economies of scale in joint living: a couple needs only one kitchen, for example. These economies might suggest that persons in otherwise similar circumstances have a greater ability to pay taxes when they are living jointly rather than as separate individuals. Horizontal equity could plausibly be interpreted to imply that single individuals should pay less (per person) in taxes than married persons in otherwise similar circumstances. A second economic consequence of household formation is joint resource allocation. A two-adult household, for example, might allow one member to go to school full time while the other works full time, whereas full-time schooling might not be affordable in a one- member household. This full-time worker is less able to pay taxes than one who is not supporting a full-time student. Applying horizontal equity, a worker with a dependent spouse should pay less in taxes than an identical worker with no dependents.

Fairness is not the only issue that arises. Because household formation allows joint resource allocation, there are also efficiency implications of the ways in which household status is accommodated in federal programs. For example, labor supply elasticities are higher for married women than for single women; a tax code that, all else equal and taking labor force participation of husbands as given, offers higher marginal tax rates to married women than single women is going to be inefficient.

So far, this discussion has used marriage and household formation interchangeably. But is the legal distinction of marital status the best available measure of economic household formation? It has become increasingly common for unmarried persons to share joint responsibility for a common household. The recent emergence of "palimony" payments upon dissolution of such households has given increased legal stature to extramarital partnerships. And marital status is an especially unfair measure of household formation when some households do not have legal marriage as an option. Homosexual partnerships are the most prominent example; others are constrained by religious restrictions on divorce and remarriage.

In short, even when it makes sense to distinguish between individuals according to household status, marital status is an imperfect proxy. An alternative variable might be self-declaration of household formation by persons living at the same address. No simple rule will be without error, but one must wonder whether marital status is still the most useful rule in contemporary America.

Fair or not, how much does marital status actually matter for federal income taxes? This article shows that, for many couples, tax liabilities change by hundreds and even thousands of dollars a year, depending on marital status.

# THE MARRIAGE TAX IS DOWN BUT NOT OUT[†]

*Harvey S. Rosen**[‡]*

## I. INTRODUCTION

The Tax Reform Act of 1986 (TRA86) will lead to large changes in the after-tax returns associated with various personal and business activities. The magnitudes and consequences of these changes were vigorously debated when TRA86 was under legislative consideration, and they continue to receive a lot of attention from the popular press as well as academic economists. One topic that has received scant coverage is how TRA86 affects the tax consequences of being married.[1] In contrast, the public discussion preceding the important 1981 tax reform was replete with references to the fact that people's tax liabilities depended on their marital status. In particular, there was much concern that income tax liabilities

*Professor of Economics, Princeton University

†*National Tax Journal,* forthcoming December, 1987. Reprinted by permission.

‡I am grateful to Lawrence Lindsey, Andrew Mitrusi and James Poterba for helpful suggestions. Mitrusi provided superb assistance with the computations. This work was supported by the National Bureau of Economic Research's Project on Taxation, and by a grant from the Olin Foundation to Princeton University.

often increased when a couple married—the so-called "marriage tax"—, although it was also possible for couples in some situations to receive implicit subsidies for being married.

Public concern over possible non-neutralities in the tax treatment of married couples has dissipated. This appears to be due to the perception that TRA86 has lowered marginal tax rates to such an extent that the magnitudes of marriage taxes and subsidies are inconsequential. In this paper we show that to the contrary, the new law creates large taxes on being married for some couples, and large subsidies for others. Non-neutralities with respect to marital decisions remain an important part of the tax code.

In order to put the marriage tax consequences of TRA86 in perspective, Section II briefly recounts the history of the tax treatment of the family under the personal income tax. Section III discusses the relevant portions of TRA86, and provides examples of how it will affect the tax consequences of marriage for various kinds of couples. In Section IV, data from a sample of actual tax returns are used to compute estimates of the marriage tax by income class for the year 1988. It is shown that

40 percent of American couples will pay an annual average marriage tax of about $1100, and 53 percent will receive an average subsidy of about $600. Section V concludes with a summary and a discussion of some implications of the findings.

## II. BACKGROUND

Prior to 1948, individuals' tax liabilities under the U.S. personal income tax were independent of their marital status. There was one rate schedule that applied to each person's income, regardless of whether he or she was married. In 1948 income splitting was introduced.[2] Under this regime, when a man and woman married, their joint tax liability was computed as twice the tax liability on half their joint income. In the presence of a tax schedule with increasing marginal rates, this meant that joint tax liabilities for couples fell when they got married, *ceteris paribus*. The tax system, in effect, subsidized marriage.

By 1969, it was possible for a single person's tax liability to be 40 percent higher than that of a married couple with the same income. This was perceived as a major inequity, and in 1969 Congress created a new tax schedule for unmarried people. Under this schedule, a single person's tax liability could never be more than 20 percent higher than the tax liability of a married couple with the same taxable income. A side effect of the new tax schedule was that it became possible for persons' tax liabilities to increase when they married, i.e., when they filed a joint return instead of two single returns. This situation was particularly likely to emerge when both husband and wife had earned income. Thus, the marriage tax was born. It is important to note that the law did not *force* married couple to file joint returns. Married persons could file "single returns," but they were treated differently from the "single returns" filed by the unmarried. In particular, the rate schedule for separate returns was higher than that on the other schedules.

As noted in Section I, by the late 1970s, the fact that the tax code imposed a penalty on some couples for being married became a hot political issue. President Carter, for example, disapprovingly noted that the system seemed to be encouraging people to live in sin. A response finally came in 1981 in the form of the "two-earner deduction." The two-earner deduction allowed joint filers to deduct from Adjusted Gross Income an amount equal to 10 percent of the earnings of the spouse with the lower earnings, up to a maximum of $3000. As Feenberg (1983) showed, while the two-earner deduction did not eliminate the marriage tax, it did reduce its magnitude. In any case, since 1981 the marriage tax has not been a major public issue.

The Tax Reform Act of 1986 repealed the two-earner deduction. The Joint Committee on Taxation (1986, p. 3) noted, "Adjustments made in the standard deduction for married individuals filing jointly and in the relationship of the rate schedules for unmarried individuals and married individuals filing joint returns are intended to compensate for the repeal of this provision." The next section examines more carefully the "adjustments" embodied in TRA86 to see whether or not they do indeed "compensate" for the repeal of the two-earner deduction.

## III. RELEVANT ASPECTS OF THE LAW

This section outlines the provisions of TRA86 that are most relevant to the calculation of marriage taxes and subsidies, and then provides some preliminary calculations of their significance.

### A. Rate Schedules

TRA86 maintains the practice of mandating different rate schedules depending upon marital status. The top of Table 1 shows for 1988 the correspondence between marginal tax rates

Table 1: **Rate Schedules and Standard Deductions for 1988 Under TRA 86**

| | Rate Schedules | | | |
|---|---|---|---|---|
| | Taxable Income | | | |
| Marginal Tax Rate | Joint | Separate | Single | Head of Household |
| 15% | $ 0– 29,750 | $ 0– 14,875 | $ 0– 17,850 | $ 0– 23,900 |
| 20% | $ 29,750– 71,900 | $ 14,875– 35,950 | $ 17,850– 43,150 | $ 23,900– 61,650 |
| 33%* | $ 71,900–171,090 | $ 35,950–124,220 | $ 43,150–100,480 | $ 61,650–145,630 |
| 28% | $171,090– | $124,220– | $100,480– | $145,630– |

| Standard Deductions | |
|---|---|
| Type of Return | Standard Deduction |
| Joint | $5,000 |
| Separate | $2,500 |
| Single | $3,000 |
| Head of Household | $4,400 |

*The top of the 33 percent bracket depends upon the number of exemptions. The schedules for joint and head of household returns are based on the assumption of two exemptions; those for separate and single returns assume one exemption. For each additional exemption, the 33 percent bracket is increased by $10,920.

and taxable income for married couples filing joint returns, married couples filing separate returns, singles, and heads of households.[3] (A head of household is an unmarried individual who maintains a household which includes as a member a son, daughter, or any other person eligible to be claimed as a dependent.) Note that the "separate" schedule is set so that it is generally disadvantageous to use.[4] The breakpoints for the first two brackets on the separate return are exactly half those of their counterparts on the joint return. This means that in these brackets, a couple could at best come out just even by filing separate returns. To make things worse, the breakpoint for the top of the 33 percent bracket on the separate return is more than half its counterpart on the joint return.

The schedules in Table 1 demonstrate that just as under the old law, it is possible for marriage to lower a couple's joint tax liability. If $A$ has a taxable income of $29,000 and $B$ has no income, then if they marry, all of $A$'s income is taxed at a 15 percent rate, while before marriage, some would also be taxed at a 28 percent rate. But the possibility of tax liabilities increasing with marriage is also present. If $C$ and $D$ each have taxable incomes of $17,000 and file as singles, then all of their income is taxed at a rate of 15 percent. But if they marry, then part of their income is taxed at a 28 percent rate. Hence, their joint tax liability increases with marriage.

These comparisons are somewhat misleading because they fail to take into account that couples and singles with the same AGI have different taxable incomes due to differences in the standard deductions they are allowed to take. The calculations done at the end of this section incorporate this information, and the qualitative result that emerges is similar—spouses with roughly equal incomes tend to pay a marriage tax, while spouses with unequal incomes tend to receive a marriage subsidy.

An important aspect of the tax schedule facing low income households is not reflected in Table 1. This is the earned income credit

(EIC), under which households with at least one child receive a 14 percent tax credit on earnings under $5714. Thus, 800 dollars (.14 × $5714) can be subtracted from the individual's tax liability on other income; if this tax liability is less than $800, the difference is refunded. Starting at $9,000 of earnings, the credit is reduced by 10 cents for each dollar earned; hence, at $17,000 of earnings, no credit is received. The key point in the current context is that on a joint return, eligibility for the EIC is based on the couple's joint earnings. Hence, an unmarried individual with a child may lose part or all of the credit upon marriage. As we shall see, this can impose a relatively high burden when both spouses have low earnings.

## B. Standard Deduction

The standard deduction allowed on each type of return is recorded in the bottom of Table 1. Note that the standard deduction associated with two single returns is $6,000 (= 2 × $3,000); this exceeds the standard deduction on a joint return by $1,000. This difference will tend to create a penalty for marrying, *ceteris paribus*. The penalty is even more severe when two heads of households marry; in this case, the loss of deductions amounts to $3800 (= 2 × $4,400 − $5,000).

## C. Some Examples

This section illustrates how the provisions in Table 1 determine the tax consequences of marriage. These illustrations assume that all income is from earnings and every return uses the standard deduction. The only other subtraction from AGI to obtain taxable income is the personal exemption of $1950 times the number of people on the return. (The exemption is constant regardless of filing status.) For the sake of comparison, we also compute what the marriage tax would have been under the old law.[5]

The results are reported in Table 2. The table shows marriage taxes and subsidies for couples with various incomes under the old and new laws. Results for childless couples and couples with two children are reported separately. Negative numbers indicate that tax liabilities go down with marriage. Thus, for example, if the primary earner has an income of $10,000 and the secondary earner has zero income, then if the couple is childless, under the new law the couple receives an annual marriage subsidy of $592. However, when both spouses earn $10,000, the couple's joint tax liability increases by $150 with marriage.

Taken together, the figures for childless couples suggest the following observations:

a. For low income couples (i.e., wages of primary earner are $10,000), the general tendency is for the absolute values of marriage penalties and subsidies to be greater under TRA86 than the old law, *ceteris paribus*. Hence, for these couples, TRA86 is less neutral with respect to marriage decisions than its predecessor.

b. The new tax law can provide a substantial "dowry" for an individual who marries someone with no income. Suppose, for example, that E, who has an AGI of $50,000 is living with F, who has no income. According to the table, if they marry, *E's* tax liability decreases by about $2700. One spouse having zero income is not a necessary condition for a dowry, however. The figures indicate that marriage is subsidized as long as the spouses' incomes are sufficiently far apart.

c. Conversely, TRA86 penalizes marriage for couples whose incomes are relatively close. Suppose G and H both have $25,000 incomes. According to the table, if they marry, their joint tax burden increases by about $1,000.

d. On the basis of these examples, it is hard to say much in general with respect to whether marriage taxes are greater or less under

TRA86 than the old law. As already noted, for many of our hypothetical low income couples, marriage taxes are higher under TRA86. But there are also many cases in which marriage penalties fall with TRA86. For example, consider a childless couple whose members have incomes of $50,000 and $30,000. According to Table 1, their marriage tax is more than $1200 lower under TRA86 than under the old law.

We next consider couples with two children. Thus, if the couple is married, four exemptions can be claimed on their joint return. It is assumed that for unmarried couples, the individual with the higher earnings claims the two children as dependents and files as a head of household, while the other parent files as a single.[6]

The results are reported in the right-hand portion of Table 2. Perhaps the most dramatic result that emerges is the relatively large marriage tax borne by some couples whose members both have low earnings. For example, individuals with earnings of $10,000 and $6,000 face a tax increase of more than $1400 when they marry, about 9 percent of their joint gross wages. The increase is partly due to the fact that the standard deduction on a joint return is $2,400 less than the sum of the deductions on head of household and single returns. In addition, the spouse who was taking the earned income credit finds the amount of the credit reduced, perhaps to zero. In short, the new tax law appears to be quite "anti-family" for low income workers with children.

Taken together, the results in Table 2 suggest that TRA86 is far from marriage

Table 2: **Marriage Taxes and Subsidies for Hypothetical Couples\***

| Primary Earner's Wages | Secondary Earner's Wages | Childless | | Two Children | |
|---|---|---|---|---|---|
| | | Old Law | New Law | Old Law | New Law |
| $ 10,000 | $      0 | $−392 | $−592 | $−486 | $−465 |
| 10,000 | 2,000 | −162 | −293 | −  80 | 15 |
| 10,000 | 4,000 | 71 | 8 | 339 | 675 |
| 10,000 | 6,000 | 94 | 150 | 580 | 1,415 |
| 10,000 | 8,000 | 93 | 150 | 333 | 1,650 |
| 10,000 | 10,000 | 88 | 150 | 64 | 1,550 |
| 25,000 | 0 | −1,123 | −879 | −1,239 | −918 |
| 25,000 | 5,000 | −292 | −136 | 127 | 532 |
| 25,000 | 10,000 | 106 | −136 | 1 | 817 |
| 25,000 | 15,000 | 459 | 40 | 345 | 317 |
| 25,000 | 20,000 | 699 | 690 | 618 | 436 |
| 25,000 | 25,000 | 944 | 1,054 | 782 | 1,054 |
| 50,000 | 0 | −2,726 | −2,748 | −3,023 | −3,199 |
| 50,000 | 10,000 | −394 | −705 | −633 | −164 |
| 50,000 | 20,000 | 1,189 | 595 | 1,043 | 436 |
| 50,000 | 30,000 | 2,217 | 959 | 2,059 | 1,054 |
| 50,000 | 40,000 | 3,200 | 1,419 | 3,089 | 1,319 |
| 50,000 | 50,000 | 3,600 | 1,824 | 3,564 | 1,819 |

\*Positive numbers are taxes; negative numbers are subsidies.

neutral. Some couples will experience substantial tax increases upon marriage, others substantial tax reductions. The discussion surrounding the table also indicates that the marriage tax faced by a couple depends crucially on the incomes of each of its members and on their number of dependents, *inter alia*. Hence, in order to say anything about the overall magnitude of the marriage tax, we require data on the joint distribution of these variables in the population. Such a data set is analyzed in the next section.

## IV. TAX SIMULATION RESULTS

In this section we use information from a sample of actual U.S. tax returns to calculate marriage taxes under TRA86, and compare their magnitudes to those under the old law. The figures are generated by the Tax Simulation Model (TAXSIM) maintained by the National Bureau of Economic Research.[7] TAXSIM contains a stratified random sample of 30,723 tax returns filed in 1983. To obtain estimates for years subsequent to 1983, the data are "aged"—raised in proportion to the growth of population and income as measured in the national income and product accounts. The adjustments used to make projections from 1986 to 1988 assume 7 percent income growth and 3.5 percent inflation over that period, as predicted by the U.S. Office of Management of Budget. A computerized representation of the tax code is used to estimate the tax liability of each return. Unlike the simple examples of the previous section, the tax computation allows for different tax rates on different sources of income, itemized deductions, etc. Sample weights are applied to the results on each return to obtain totals for the population as a whole.

The sample used in this study consists of all joint returns. Tax liabilities on these joint returns are calculated under both the old law (as it would have looked in 1988) and

TRA86. Then, the joint tax liability of each couple is computed under the assumption that a divorce occurs. Members of childless couples are assumed to file as singles; if there are itemized deductions on the return, they are allocated to the spouse with higher earnings. For couples with children, we assume that exemptions are allocated such that the joint tax liability is minimized. Spouses who end up not claiming a child file as singles; otherwise they file as heads of households. Of course, one can imagine other reasonable algorithms for allocating exemptions and deductions among the spouses. We experimented with several others (e.g., allocating all itemized deductions in proportion to spouse's earnings), and found that the results were not materially affected.[8]

Column (1) in Table 3 shows the average marriage tax under the new law by adjusted gross income class. The figures in square brackets show the comparable figures for the old law. The general tendency is for the marriage tax to be negative for couples with relatively low AGIs. However, once AGI exceeds $30,000 the average marriage tax is generally positive. For example, in the $50-75,000 range, the annual tax cost of being married is about $750. The figures near the bottom of the column indicate that under TRA86, the average marriage tax per return will be $119, and its aggregate value about $6.4 billion.

Compared to the old law, TRA86 appears more favorable to marriage. On average, TRA86 provides a larger marriage subsidy or a smaller marriage tax in each AGI class. Indeed, under the old law the average marriage tax would have been more than four times its value under TRA86—about $529 per couple or $28 billion in aggregate.

Of course, the averages in column (1) are over both positive and negative values of the marriage tax. As we saw in the last section, however, it is possible for couples with about the same AGI to have marriage taxes of opposite signs; the answer depends upon the relative incomes of the spouses, *inter alia*. This

Table 3: **The Marriage Tax by Income Class (1988) [Figures in brackets are for the old law.]**

| AGI Class | (1) Average Marriage Tax | (2) % Positive Tax | (3) Average Positive Tax | (4) % Negative Tax | (5) Average Negative Tax | (6) S.D of Marriage Tax |
|---|---|---|---|---|---|---|
| $ 10,000< | 135.4 | 1.5% | 135.8 | 37% | −367.1 | 293 |
| | [−42.06] | [3.2%] | [119.8] | [32%] | [−142.6] | [87.2] |
| $ 10– 20,000 | −215.3 | 20% | 559.8 | 74% | −447.4 | 494 |
| | [−60.90] | [25%] | [377.8] | [69%] | [−226.7] | [305] |
| $ 20– 30,000 | −61.11 | 35% | 611.1 | 64% | −430.6 | 602 |
| | [114.8] | [39%] | [620.2] | [59%] | [−223.7] | [467] |
| $ 30– 40,000 | 98.13 | 49% | 620.4 | 50% | −414.3 | 618 |
| | [442.0] | [54%] | [986.5] | [45%] | [−205.5] | [678] |
| $ 40– 50,000 | 200.0 | 57% | 844.3 | 42% | −656.8 | 844 |
| | [801.3] | [62%] | [1435.] | [38%] | [−246.0] | [945] |
| $ 50– 75,000 | 758.7 | 64% | 1765. | 35% | −1051. | 1551 |
| | [1517] | [70%] | [2289] | [29%] | [−301.7] | [1470] |
| $ 75– 100,000 | 573.6 | 51% | 2748. | 47% | −1777. | 2570 |
| | [1871.] | [59%] | [3558] | [39%] | [−613.7] | [2590] |
| $ 100–200,000 | −134.6 | 34% | 3225. | 66% | −1882. | 2853 |
| | [1431.] | [42%] | [4366] | [54%] | [−755.5] | [3352] |
| >200,000 | 973.2 | 72% | 2132. | 25% | −2332. | 4688 |
| | [484.2] | [33%] | [4922] | [58%] | [−1977] | [4398] |
| Grand mean | 119.0 | 40% | 1091. | 53% | −608.8 | — |
| | [528.6] | [45%] | [1463.] | [47%] | [−269.0] | — |
| Total | 6.41b | — | 23.79b | — | −17.38b | 1164* |
| | [28.49b] | — | [35.37b] | — | [−6.88b] | [1269]* |

*These are standard deviations for the sample as a whole, *not* the average of the standard deviations for each income group.

suggests that a low marriage tax on average does not necessarily imply that the system is marriage neutral. It can just as well mean that some families have very high marriage taxes while others have very high marriage subsidies.

To investigate this possibility, we divided the sample into couples who pay a positive marriage tax and those who receive a marriage subsidy, and calculated the average tax/subsidy for each group. Column (2) of Table 3 shows the proportion of couples in each AGI group who pay a positive marriage tax, and column (3) shows the average tax paid by members of that group. Similarly, column (4) shows the proportion who receive a marriage subsidy in each AGI group, and column (5) the average subsidy received. (In any given AGI group, the percentages in columns (2) and (4) may not add to 100 percent because the tax liabilities of some couples are approximately unchanged by marriage.)

The results in column (2) suggest that relatively few people in lower income brackets are penalized by marriage. But in the upper income brackets the percentage is quite substantial; in the $50-75,000 range, 64 percent of the couples pay a positive marriage tax.

Moreover, the column (4) results suggest that the size of this tax can be quite substantial. The average value in the $50-75,000 range is $1765; in the $75-100,000 range it is $2748. The figures near the bottom of columns (2) and (3) indicate that 40 percent of all couples will pay a positive marriage tax under TRA86, and its average will be about $1100. This is still less severe than under the old law, under which 45 percent of the couples paid an average marriage tax of $1463. But the percentage reduction in the marriage tax under TRA86 will be less impressive than one would gather from the figures in column (1).

The figures in columns (4) and (5) indicate that under TRA86 about 53 percent of the couples will receive a marriage subsidy, and the average value of this subsidy will be about $609. This is more than the average subsidy of $269 received under the old law. In addition, under the old law, only 47 percent of the couples received the subsidy.

A thought suggested by our discussion of columns (2) through (5) is that under both the old and new laws the dispersion of the marriage tax is large, and that TRA86 may have increased the dispersion even while lowering its mean. To get a handle on this issue, we computed the standard deviation of the marriage tax for all returns within each AGI bracket. The results are reported in column (6) of Table 3. The first thing to note about these numbers is that they are large relative to the size of the average marriage tax. For example, for the sample as a whole, the standard deviation of $1164 is almost 10 times the average value of $119. Second, within some income brackets (particularly in the middle and the bottom of the income distribution), TRA86 increases the standard deviation of the marriage tax over its value under the old law. Nevertheless, for the sample as a whole, the standard deviation of the marriage tax will be somewhat lower under TRA86 than its predecessor—$1164 rather than $1269. In short,

TRA86 has reduced the dispersion of taxes and subsidies on marriage, but not by very much.

## V. CONCLUSION

Despite the fact that TRA86 eliminated the two-earner deduction, both the percentage of families paying a positive marriage tax and its size will be lower than under the old law. Indeed, on average the marriage tax under TRA86 will be quite modest—$119 per couple. However, this figure conceals the fact that some families will be paying substantial penalties for being married. In 1988, about 40 percent of U.S. families will pay an average marriage tax of $1100. This corresponds to a total of about $24 billion. At the same time, about 53 percent of the families will receive a marriage subsidy averaging $609 per family; the aggregate amount will be $17.4 billion. TRA86 is far from neutral with respect to marriage decisions.

Are the transfers implicit in this arrangement desirable? To think about this question, recall that the source of the marriage distortion is the fact that married and single people have different tax schedules. A separate schedule for married couples guarantees that families with the same joint incomes have the same tax burdens, *ceteris paribus*. Hence, what the marriage distortion "buys" is horizontal equity among married couples. However, given the fact that in today's society there are many arrangements for living together outside of marriage, it is not obvious why the existence of a marriage license *per se* should have such a large impact on the design of the tax system.[9] Perhaps this issue will be more prominent in the next round of tax reform.

# Notes

1. For example, recent evaluations of the new law by Aaron (1987), and Hausman and Poterba

(1987) do not deal with this topic, although Pechman (1986) does mention it.

2. Prior to 1948, citizens of community property states were effectively already allowed the benefits of income splitting. Congress introduced universal income splitting in order to correct this inequity. See Brazer (1980) for further details on the history of the tax treatment of the family.

3. Some taxpayers will face higher marginal tax rates than those in Table 1 due to provisions such as the phaseout for deducibility of Individual Retirement Accounts. See Hausman and Poterba (1987).

4. Exceptions can occur when one spouse has deductions which can only be taken in excess of some percentage of Adjusted Gross Income. An example is the deduction for medical expenses.

5. Specifically, this is the 1986 law as it would have looked in 1988 after the bracket widths and personal exemptions were indexed for inflation in the intervening years.

6. An alternative procedure is to assume that the dependents are allocated so as to minimize joint tax liability. This assumption would tend to increase the marriage tax relative to the amounts in Table 2.

7. See Lindsey (1986) for a detailed discussion of TAXSIM.

8. We also implicitly assume that the (positive or negative) changes in tax burdens associated with marriage do not affect before-tax earnings. Feenberg's (1983) discussion of the marriage tax suggests that allowing for an endogenous labor supply response for females does not have a major impact on estimates of the marriage tax.

9. See Brazer (1980) and Munnell (1980) for further arguments along these lines. Rosen (1977) discusses the implications of the marriage tax for labor supply decisions of secondary earners.

# References

Aaron, Henry J., "The Impossible Dream Comes True: The New Tax Reform Act," *The Brookings Review,* Winter 1987, 3-10.

Brazer, Harvey E., "Income Tax Treatment of the Family," in Aaron, Henry J. and Michael J. Boskin (eds.), *The Economics of Taxation,* The Brookings Institution: Washington, D. C. 1980, 223-246.

Feenberg, Daniel, "The Tax Treatment of Married Couples and the 1981 Tax Law," in Penner, Rudolf (ed.), *Taxing the Family,* American Enterprise Institute: Washington, D.C. 1983, 32-63.

Hausman, Jerry A. and James M. Poterba, "Household Behavior and the Tax Reform Act of 1986," *Journal of Economic Perspectives,* Vol. 1 no. 1 (Summer 1987), 101-119.

Joint Committee on Taxation, *Summary of Conference Agreement on HR 3838 (Tax Reform Act of 1986)* (JCS-16-86), August 29, 1986.

Lindsey, Lawrence B., "Individual Taxpayer Response to Tax Cuts 1982-1984, With Implications for the Revenue Maximizing Tax Rate," National Bureau of Economic Research, Working Paper No. 2069, December 1986.

Munnell, Alicia H., "The Couple vs. the Individual Under the Federal Personal Income Tax," in Aaron, Henry J. and Michael J. Boskin (eds.), *The Economics of Taxation,* The Brookings Institution: Washington, D.C. 1980, 247-278.

Pechman, Joseph A., "Tax Reform: Theory and Practice," Brookings Discussion Papers in Economics, October 1986.

Rosen, Harvey S., "Is It Time to Abandon Joint Filing?" *National Tax Journal,* 30, December 1977, 423-428.

# QUESTIONS

1. The welfare system (AFDC) has been widely credited with breaking up families by making eligibility depend on the absence in the household

of a potential breadwinner. Rosen finds that low income couples (for example, those with earnings of $10,000 and $7500) with children face substantial tax gains (for example, $1500 for this couple with two children) if they are unmarried, thanks to the generous tax schedule for (single) heads of household. Since such couples could increase their after-tax income by well over 10 percent without the welfare-story inconvenience of living apart, do you predict that low-wage working couples with children will be induced to divorce or never marry? Why or why not?

2. Refer to the tax rate schedules in Rosen's first table. We can think of the marriage tax as having two components, a marginal and an inframarginal one. If an extra dollar to either half of a couple is taxed at a different rate depending on the couple's marital status, there is a marginal marriage tax (or subsidy). Because the tax law now has wide ranges of income taxed at the same rate, tax reform has decreased the likelihood of a couple facing a marginal tax liability difference.

The other component of a marriage tax (subsidy) is inframarginal. The incomes at which married versus unmarried couples are kicked into higher brackets differ. This means there is a marital-status-dependent advantage from lower inframarginal tax rates. Of course, these inframarginal advantages are taxed away in the 33 percent bracket.

(a) For each pair of individuals described below, do marginal tax rates depend on marital status? (Compare "single" and "joint" rates.)

(i) Each earns $30,000 of taxable income.

(ii) One earns $30,000, the other $40,000.

(iii) One earns $10,000, the other $20,000.

(iv) Each earns $50,000.

(b) For the couple in part (i) above, how much of their income is taxed at the low inframarginal rate of 15 percent if they are single? If they are married and file jointly? Compute the marriage tax for this couple.

# Further Issues and Questions in Incidence, Efficiency, and Equity

## Exporting taxes

The U.S. highway system is dotted with small towns that seem to raise most of their revenue by giving speeding tickets with stiff fines to motorists passing through. Since few of the fines are paid by the residents who benefit from the revenue, the incidence of this method of revenue collection is on outsiders, and we say the burden has been "exported."

A. Many major cities have hotel room taxes. Several have special entertainment taxes on, for example, tickets to professional sporting events.
1. In each case, do you think a lot of the tax is exported?

2. What elasticities do you have to take into account in answering the question?

## Legal incidence versus economic incidence.

This item appeared in the *Wall Street Journal*'s Tax Report column.

The X-FLIX TAX came from box-office bux, South Carolina's top court says.

In 1984, the state Supreme Court declared that South Carolina's 20% admissions tax on X-rated and unrated movies was unconstitutional. Multi-Cinema Ltd., a theater chain, sought a refund, which was denied by the state tax commission. The state said the tax was paid by theater-goers and only they could seek refunds. The theater chain appealed to a court and won, so the state appealed to the state Supreme Court.

The Supreme Court said the state law imposing a general tax on movie admissions specifies that it shall be paid by the person paying for admission. Yet the overturned law providing for "a license tax . . . on admissions" to X-rated films contained no such language. Because that specific provision was missing, Chief Judge Ness and two other judges concluded that legislators meant the tax to be paid by theaters. They upheld a refund to Multi-Cinema.

*But dissenting Judge Gregory said that "perverts" legislative intent.* *

A. What lesson from tax incidence theory might be relevant to this case?
B. If you were arguing in court, what economic information would you use to recommend the proportion of tax payments that should be refunded to theater owners?

### Marginal excess burden.

If the government increased tax rates enough to raise another dollar in revenue and then threw that dollar away, how much worse off would society be? If behavior is affected as people try to avoid extra taxation, the welfare loss is greater than the dollar of revenue, and this excess loss is one measure of the marginal excess burden of the tax system. Attempts to measure this loss are understandably sensitive to assumptions made about the incidence of the taxes examined and to the behavioral elasticities involved. Ballard, Shoven, and Whalley ("General Equilibrium Computations of the Marginal Welfare Costs of Taxes in the United States," *American Economic Review,* March 1985) estimate this marginal excess burden to

be at least 17 cents and perhaps as much as 56 cents. Edgar Browning ("On the Marginal Welfare Cost of Taxation," *American Economic Review,* March 1987) obtains similar results for intermediate values of the marginal tax rate (43 percent on labor income) using a partial equilibrium framework.

A. Consider a potential government project that, properly discounted, can earn $1.10 for every dollar invested. Based on the estimates given for marginal excess burden, should taxes be raised to finance the project?
B. If new research shows that people have grown more elastic in their labor supply behavior, perhaps because fewer are the sole breadwinner for a large family, would this increase or decrease marginal excess burden?

### Marital status and returns from Social Security.

The Social Security (Old Age and Survivors Insurance) program is funded by a payroll tax that ignores martial status. It is the benefit structure of Social Security that introduces substantial differences in the return workers get on their tax dollars. These returns can vary markedly, depending on marital status.

Spouses of Social Security recipients are eligible for a payment equal to half their partner's benefit level. Spouses who are also eligible for benefits based on their own work history may choose whichever benefit is higher, the amount corresponding to their past tax payments or half the spouse's amount. Similarly, surviving spouses of Social Security recipients are eligible for survivor's benefits. For those married women who work but do not earn enough to make it worthwhile to collect benefits based on their own earnings, there is no return on the payroll taxes paid to Social Security. In 1982, only two-fifths of women ever married received benefits based on their own work histories (Boskin and Puffert, "Social Security and the American Family" NBER working paper 2117, January 1987).

In a world where only one member of a couple is working, the notion of equity behind this benefit structure is clear: A retired worker with a dependent spouse needs more money to maintain a given standard of living than does a single worker. Married couples with one earner get an especially good deal from the system. But when both members of a couple work, the present structure violates another very plausible interpretation of horizontal equity: Households required to pay the same taxes for Social Security should receive the same levels of benefits from Social Security. Since most married couples receive exactly the benefits they would have even if the wife had paid no taxes at all, the payment of dependent's and survivors' benefits conflicts with this notion of equity.

Boskin and Puffert (1987) calculate the marriage subsidy or penalty for couples who differ in their earnings levels and in whether the lower-wage spouse (in their example taken to be the wife) continues to work after

marriage. Their calculations are presented in Table 1. The present value of the extra taxes minus the extra benefits a couple gets when the wife continues to work amounts to a penalty of roughly $9000. If a woman with annual earnings of $15,000 to $20,000 marries and quits work, the net transfer to the couple increases by about $50,000, a not insubstantial amount.

Besides its inequitable treatment of one- and two-earner couples, the dependents' benefits obviously make Social Security a better deal for one-earner couples than for single workers. These comparisons, also from Boskin and Puffert, are shown in Table 2.

A. Would removing the dependent spouse benefit from Social Security be sufficient to remove the effect of marital status on people's returns from Social Security?

B. Should the dependent spouse's benefit be removed from Social Security? If it is justified by arguments that a retired couple needs more to live on than a single person, it is primarily a poorly targeted welfare program. Do you think the payroll tax is the appropriate financing tool for its payment? Why or why not?

Table 1: **Comparison Among Single-Earner Couples, Single Males, and Single Females of 1945 Cohort, Various Earnings Levels (1985 dollars discounted at rate 3% to 1985)**

| Family Type | Earnings Level (at 1985 wage index) | | |
|---|---|---|---|
| | 10,000 | 30,000 | 50,000 |
| **Single-earner Couple*** | | | |
| Benefits | 62,679 | 109,128 | 100,503 |
| Taxes | 48,951 | 136,498 | 140,253 |
| Transfer | 13,727 | −27,370 | −39,750 |
| Rate of return | 3.74% | 2.30% | 1.95% |
| | | | |
| **Single Male*** | | | |
| Benefits | 29,913 | 52,282 | 48,532 |
| Taxes | 48,951 | 136,498 | 140,253 |
| Transfer | −19,038 | −84,216 | −91,721 |
| Rate of return | 1.42% | −0.25% | −0.60% |
| | | | |
| **Single Female*** | | | |
| Benefits | 40,306 | 71,715 | 69,590 |
| Taxes | 46,901 | 130,802 | 144,723 |
| Transfer | −6,595 | −59,087 | −75,133 |
| Rate of return | 2.55% | 1.13% | 0.68% |

Source: Michael Boskin and Douglas Puffert, "Social Security and the American Family," NBER Working Paper 2117, January 1987.

*All benefits, taxes and transfers are present value.

Table 2: **Marriage Subsidy or Penalty (1945 cohort; 1985 dollars discounted at 3 percent to 1985**

| Husband's Earnings Level | Wife's Earnings Level | Wife Keeps Working (Change in Benefits minus Change in Net Transfer) | Wife Stops Working | | |
|---|---|---|---|---|---|
| | | | Change in Benefits | Change in Taxes | Change in Transfer |
| $40,000 | $40,000 | −8,749 | −25,814 | −117,089 | 91,275 |
| | 20,000 | −4,471 | −14,568 | −69,496 | 54,928 |
| | 0 | 54,388 | — | — | — |
| $30,000 | 30,000 | −9,551 | −25,305 | −103,170 | 77,865 |
| | 15,000 | 3,214 | −2,051 | −52,122 | 50,071 |
| | 0 | 56,846 | — | — | — |
| $20,000 | 20,000 | −4,656 | −18,672 | −69,514 | 50,842 |
| | 10,000 | 9,422 | 6,584 | −34,748 | 41,332 |
| | 0 | 47,050 | — | — | — |

Source: Michael Boskin and Douglas Puffert, "Social Security and the American Family," NBER Working Paper 2117, January 1987.

## PART VII

# Federal Taxation

**Issue:** *Allocating resources through tax shelters and tax preferences.*

*"Housing the Poor: Shelter by Tax Shelter"* James P. Luckett

**Issue:** *Did Individual Retirement Accounts increase personal saving?*

*"Did IRAs Stimulate Personal Saving?"*

**Issue:** *From a historical perspective, was the Tax Reform Act of 1986 really so radical?*

*"Tax Reform: Theory and Practice"* Joseph A. Pechman

**Issue:** *Do tax incentives stimulate corporate investment?*

*"The Shaky Case for Aiding Investment"* Marc Levinson

*"A Fair Tax Act That's Bad for Business"* Lawrence H. Summers

*Further Issues and Questions in Federal Taxation*

> **Issue:** *Sin taxes.*

> *"White House Study Says Sin-Tax Boost May Be Justified by Health-Care Costs"* Paul Blustein

**Issue:** *Itemized deductions and tax progressivity.*

**Issue:** *Asset markets and the changing treatment of capital gains.*

## *Allocating resources through tax shelters and tax preferences*

The market for low-income housing is similar to the market for cheap cars. Anybody with $2000 to purchase a car will have to look in the used-car segment of the auto market. Cars are too expensive for producers to build new cars for consumers in this price range. Availability of cheap cars depends on the "trickle down" of old cars that have depreciated enough to fall into a modest price bracket.

Low-income housing is also provided through a "trickle down" market. A house is far more expensive than a car, however, so the low-income housing market tends to be a rental market. This means someone has to be interested in low-income rental housing as an investment if the free market is going to provide low-income housing. For there to be an adequate low-income housing stock, enough units have to depreciate to affordable prices without being allowed to depreciate beyond acceptable quality standards.

A recent study by Neighborhood Reinvestment Corporation concludes that the market mechanism is not working well. Between now and 2003, the demand for low-income housing is estimated to increase 44 percent, while the supply, already inadequate, is expected to increase 27 percent. The projected housing shortfall is 7.8 million units, representing housing for between 18 and 19 million people. The study defines low-income households as those with incomes less than 50 percent of the national median and low-income housing as units renting for no more than $325 a month. These projections can be compared to an estimated 3.5 million low-income people currently unable to find low-income housing.

When private markets fail to meet social objectives such as "decent and affordable housing," the government may intervene directly, say, by building new housing and renting it cheap to low-income families. It may also choose indirect action, such as altering the incentives facing private actors in the housing market. While the 1986 tax reform dramatically limited tax breaks for most real estate, low-income housing still provides a fascinating example of our penchant for subsidies through the tax code.

# HOUSING THE POOR: SHELTER BY TAX SHELTER

*James P. Luckett**

The 1986 push to close tax loopholes exploited by the rich posed a grave threat to poor Americans in need of better housing. In the end, disaster (for the poor) was averted and the final outcome was merely outrageously inefficient.

Congress was focused on the ways in which tax treatment of rental real estate provides tax shelter for other kinds of income received by wealthy real estate investors. The politicians decided to cut tax rates and make up the lost revenue by eliminating many tax shelter opportunities. As a perhaps unintended byproduct of this "reform," however, the incentive to produce rental housing was severely reduced.

Here is how real estate tax shelters used to work: The typical real estate investment broke even or made money in the sense that cash revenue exceeded cash expenses. However, taxable income was usually negative because of large write-offs for depreciation of the buildings. Depreciation was a "cost" for tax purposes, but it was not a bill you actually had to pay. Instead, you paid mainte-

*Managing Director, Boston Housing Partnership, Inc.

nance expenses to keep your property from depreciating and you deducted that as well. Thus, there were "paper losses" that reduced the investor's taxable income but not his or her cash income. With the majority of capital costs covered by mortgage debt on the real estate, the present value of these losses was typically several times larger than the amount of equity invested. Often, investors could make a profit on the tax savings alone, without any cash return from operations. Every dollar of loss allowed the investor to shelter a dollar of unrelated income from the IRS. For investors in the 50 percent tax bracket, a dollar of paper loss was therefore worth 50 cents in avoided taxes. In this upside-down world, losses were valuable and investors paid millions to get more millions in losses so they wouldn't have to pay taxes on millions in other income.

Real estate developers typically generated far more paper losses than they could utilize themselves—once you have reduced your taxable income to zero, further paper losses are worthless unless you can transfer them to another taxpayer. Therefore, a large market grew up for the buying and selling of interests in real estate projects ("syndication") in which the main positive attribute of the investments was their tax-shelter value. Investors who had absolutely nothing to do with managing the properties invested in projects in order to shelter income generated by other activities.

Congress has now severely limited the ability of individual taxpayers to do this. Corporate taxpayers are subject to far less restrictive rules, but the tax shelter value of most real estate is nevertheless far reduced from its pre-1986-tax-act level, because the allowable losses are smaller and tax rates are lower. Who benefitted and who was hurt by this aspect of tax reform? The primary effect was to end a subsidy to the rental real estate industry, thereby reducing the supply of rental real estate and raising rents (relative to what they would have been had the tax law remained unchanged). Thus, those in the construction industry, real estate developers, syndicators, and some investors in old deals were clearly hurt. Those in need of rental housing also were and will be hurt.

(What about the wealthy individuals who would have bought this type of investment in the future, had the tax law not been changed? The effect on them is slight: First, their tax rates have been cut, offsetting the loss of opportunity to shelter taxable income. More importantly, we must recognize that their assets are mobile; they will simply stop investing in rental property and start investing in something else that pays almost as good a return. The return of the new investment is more likely to be in the form of additional dollars earned instead of tax dollars avoided, but the taxpayer really does not care.)

Fortunately, the story does not end here. Advocates of low-income housing were able to persuade Congress to give them a new tax provision that would provide a subsidy through the tax code for the production and rehabilitation of rental housing occupied by low-income persons. Congress enacted, as part of the 1986 tax bill, the Low Income Housing Credit (LIHC), a novel new chapter in the long history

of writing tax law to create incentives for private actors to accomplish public purposes.

The LIHC is a direct reduction in tax liability for those who develop low-income housing. The value of the credit can be as high as 9 percent of total development cost per year for ten years—a 90 percent rebate of costs (70 percent on a present-value basis) through reduction of taxes owed the federal government. If tax-exempt debt financing is used in the project, then the maximum value of the LIHC is 4 percent per year for ten years. That the LIHC is novel is beyond dispute. It should also be beyond dispute that some form of capital subsidy to low-income housing is needed. But whether the LIHC is sensible, efficient, or effective is very questionable, however.

Consider this stark fact: Less than half the money lost to the federal treasury due to LIHC will actually go into the production of rental housing. The rest will get eaten up in transactions costs, return to investors, and other "nonproductive" uses resulting from the convoluted nature of the tax law. This is appalling at any time; it is all the more so in this era of diminishing government assistance to the poor and soaring housing costs. The one positive thing that can be said for the LIHC is that it is more sharply targeted to low-income households than the previous tax subsidy of rental housing.

To understand the inefficiency of the LIHC, one has to wade into a mass of detail concerning the tax law and the economics of producing low-income housing. Perhaps the best way to do this is by means of an example, abstracted from an actual project now being developed.

## LOW-INCOME HOUSING UNDER THE 1986 TAX ACT: AN EXAMPLE

The project involves the rehabilitation of about 1000 apartments in a major urban center by a coalition of nonprofit groups experienced in housing development. Acquisition cost is nil because the federal government is donating the buildings. It acquired them recently through foreclosure of federally-insured mortgages that financed acquisition and renovation by a for-profit company about 15 years ago. The previous owner cashed in on the syndication and then defaulted on the mortgage, a familiar pattern.

Construction cost will be $44,000 per apartment. In addition, there are professional fees (architects, engineers, and so on), $5000; tenant relocation, $2000; contingency reserves, $4000; financing costs (including debt service during the construction period), $9000; and miscellaneous, $2000. Total capital costs will therefore be $66,000 per apartment.

Why does it cost so much? One reason is labor costs: Under federal and state law skilled construction workers on government-assisted projects must be paid about $25 per hour (about $50,000 per year). The open-market nonunion wage is about 20 to 25 percent lower. Another reason is the difficulty of working in occupied buidings. A third is the cost of extraordinary items like removing lead paint and asbestos and correcting structural defects. High as these costs are, they reflect only a moderately extensive renovation, with many building elements retained. A complete "gut job" would run about $75,000 per unit in construction costs. (New construction would be at least that much or a little more.) Furthermore, if the buildings were acquired on the open market it would add about another $40,000 per unit in acquisition cost, even in their present deteriorated state. So, more typical development costs would be in excess of $100,000 per unit, for basic, unfancy housing.

If the entire project were financed with debt, say a 9.5 percent mortgage with a 30-year term, the monthly mortgage payment would be $555 per unit per month. (The 9.5 percent rate is based on a May 1987 AAA tax-exempt bond rate of 8.2 percent, plus 0.8 percent in "overrides" charged by various govern-

ment agencies involved in issuing and guaranteeing the bonds, plus 0.5 percent for the mortgage insurance premium). In addition, lenders require the project to show projected net income equal to 10 percent of the debt service ("debt-service coverage") or $56 per month.

Once completed, operating cost per apartment will be (in 1989) about $388 per month, not including mortgage payments. This breaks down into $104 for utilities, $83 for managerial salaries, $129 for maintenance, $18 for replacement reserve (funds accumulated for major repairs, appliance replacement, and so on), $29 for insurance, and $25 for taxes. Again, shockingly high numbers, but they are realistic for well-run inner-city housing in 1989 dollars in a high-cost-of-living locale.

Adding $555 for the mortgage, $56 for debt-service coverage, and $388 for monthly operating costs yields a total revenue requirement of $999 per month per apartment. Allowing 5 percent for vacancy and bad debt losses, we arrive at a required rent level of $1,052 per month. Assuming the typical tenant household in the buildings earns about $1,200 per month before taxes and can afford 30 percent of gross income for rent, we cannot charge more than $360. The need for substantial subsidy should now be apparent.

Enter the tax law. The buildings will produce a stream of paper losses due mostly to the depreciation write-off, even as they break even (with substantial subsidy of the rents) on a cash basis. Individuals can no longer make very much use of these losses, but corporations can. In addition, there is the LIHC, also more useable by corporate investors than individuals. The nuances are many and varied, but the bottom line is a stream of tax-shelter benefits with a net present value of about $20 million (at a 7.5 percent discount rate).

Unfortunately, the $20 million cannot simply be converted to $20,000 per unit spendable cash and applied against the $66,000 per unit of development cost. The first problem encountered is that the losses and the credits have to accrue to an entity with tax liability or else they have no value.

The organizations that will actually do the developing, being non profit charitable corporations, are tax-exempt. Tax shelter has no value to them unless it can be sold. Even if they were not tax exempt, they would have to be huge to utilize all of the tax shelter internally. So the tax shelter must be sold, and the only way to do that is to form partnerships. The buyers— corporations with an appetite for tax shelter—must become partners in an entity formed to hold title to the project. The particular type of partnership utilized will be a "limited partnership," meaning the liability of the investor partners is limited to their capital contribution. (If, for example, the local telephone company buys a $1 million interest in the deal, that is the most it can lose if the project fails. Creditors of the project cannot go after the other assets of the telephone company.) In addition, limited partners are prohibited by law from taking an active role in the management of the partnership.

How much can we expect the limited partners to pay for their $20 million in future tax savings? Perhaps $13 million. The $7 million (net present value) of "profit" to the investor is the minimum necessary to get them to bear the risk, the illiquidity, and the transactions costs of the investment and to forego the return available on alternative uses of their capital. Given the timing of investor payments and projected benefits, the internal rate of return on the investor's money works out to 15 percent per year. That may sound astronomical for an after-tax return, but our experience in the market is that we will be lucky to find takers for all of our shares. The market test says the return is not excessive.

Why is such a fat return necessary to attract investors?

1. Risk: If the project goes under, investors can lose some of their projected tax benefits. If bankruptcy occurs early in the life of the project, nearly all the benefits

would be lost. There is the additional risk that the tax code may change in an unfavorable way. Also, the investor may not be able to use its benefits in some future years because of the "alternative minimum tax," a provision that limits the degree to which taxpayers (including corporations) may reduce their taxes. Or, some of the tax shelter may prove unuseable because the investor has no profits in the future or already has an adequate tax shelter generated by some other activity.

2. Illiquidity: The limited-partner interests are extremely hard to resell. Basically, it is a 15-year, irrevocable commitment, unlike a stock or a bond that can be bought one day and sold the next.

3. Transactions Costs: This is an extremely odd, complex investment that cannot be evaluated without careful study of the tax code, which is complicated and hard to understand, and careful study of the project financing. Furthermore, once you have bought into the deal, it will complicate your future tax calculations and accounting and add an additional consideration to management planning. A decision to go into the leasing business, for example, could obliterate the value of the LIHC to a corporate investor, due to the provisions of the alternative minimum tax, the reason being that leasing generates a lot of tax shelter itself.

So, one-third of the $20 million dollars lost to the federal treasury goes to the investors to induce them to participate. Next, we have expenses for putting together the deal and making sure it works within the law: $1.5 million. The documents are inches thick and must be written, reviewed, and blessed by big-name law firms and accounting firms. The art of designing the financing to maximize the tax shelter produced is arcane and mysterious, and consultants must be hired to calculate all the angles and engineer all the gimmicks. Also in this category of expense is the cost of "investor servicing and regulatory compliance" for the next 15 years, that is, producing financial forecasts and reports and answering investor questions. The social product from all of these activities may be nil, but the private return is in the millions. So we pay a million and a half in syndication costs and now we are down to $11.5 million, or 58 cents net for each dollar of tax subsidy. But we're not done yet.

Next, we must deduct for the "net worth requirement." This is not really a cost, but you cannot spend the money so it is the next worst thing. Here is how it goes: A limited partnership must have at least one general partner with unlimited liability, or else the IRS will treat it as a corporation. If that happens, then the investors cannot use the credits and paper losses, because corporate losses and tax credits stay within the corporation that generates them and do not flow out to the shareholders. In this project, the general partners are subsidiaries of nonprofit charitable corporations. Since corporate liability is limited to assets of the corporation, the IRS requires that a general partner that is a corporation must have substantial net worth other than its interest in the partnership. The IRS wants to see that the general partner has something to lose in addi-

Table 1: **Summary of Syndication Sources and Uses**

| Sources | | |
|---|---|---|
| 20,000,000 | Present Value of Tax Shelter (Lihc Plus Losses) | |
| Uses | | |
| 7,000,000 | Profit to investors | |
| 1,500,000 | Transactions costs | |
| 3,250,000 | Net worth set-aside | |
| 11,750,000 | Subtotal | |
| 8,250,000 | Available to pay project costs | |
| 20,000,000 | Total | |

Available to projects = 41 percent of total sources

tion to its share of the project if the partnership fails financially, in other words.

The minimum net worth the IRS wants to see is 15 percent of the gross payments of the investors—$1.95 million on a $13 million deal. In this particular deal, for very good reasons that are too complicated to go into (having to do with this being a two-tiered partnership structure so that a single syndication can cover several projects), the legal structure is such that the IRS requires a total of 25 percent in net worth – $3.25 million. So now we are down to $8.25 million available for bricks and mortar out of the $20 million lost to the Treasury. That's 41 cents on the dollar!

The 25 percent net-worth requirement is 10 percentage points higher than is typical, but then there is no brokerage commission in this deal—we are marketing the investment ourselves—and that saves an equivalent amount. These two atypical features are exactly offsetting, in other words.

Why doesn't the government just make direct grants to projects and have 100 cents on the dollar go for project costs? The usual rationales for tax incentives, rather than direct grants, are: (1) It is easier for Congress to approve a tax break than a dollar expenditure of equivalent size. (The dollars they implicitly spend through tax breaks are less painful to politicians than the dollars they explicitly spend through grants.) (2) Tax incentives are largely self-administered, through the taxpayer's own calculation of his/her/its own tax return, eliminating the costly bureaucracy needed to administer grant programs. (3) Tax incentives harness the private profit motive and impersonal market mechanisms to the production of socially desired outcomes, eliminating the need for government employees to evaluate the myriad different project opportunities and choose among them, thereby also eliminating all the inefficiency and risk of improper influence that government allocation implies.

Rationale number (1) is not worthy of serious consideration from a social efficiency standpoint, whatever its value may be as pragmatic political wisdom. Rationales (2) and (3) simply do not hold for the LIHC. Unlike almost all other provisions of the tax code, the LIHC is not freely available to some objectively defined class of taxpayers. The LIHC has an expressly limited total value, allocated by statute among the 50 states. Developers wishing to utilize the LIHC must apply for an allocation of credit authority, and the government employees in each state must pass on each application. Thus, in the LIHC, Congress has created a new animal that combines the worst features of the grant and the tax break: It has the bureaucratic overhead and potential for political abuse of a grants program, plus the complexity and high private transactions cost of a tax shelter.

If, for political or other reasons, the subsidy must come through the tax code instead of the expenditure side of the budget, the inefficiency could be mitigated by dropping the restriction that the taxpayer who ultimately uses the tax benefit must have a direct ownership interest in the project. Let the tax credits be freely saleable, in other words, so that the transactions costs of forming limited partnerships can be eliminated and the risk and illiquidity, and therefore the return, to investors can be reduced.

Here is how this reform could work. A developer gets an allocation of credit authority and builds a project. It then receives a tax credit "ticket" from the state allocating authority, which can be used by any taxpayer in lieu of money to pay tax obligations to the federal government. The developer then sells the ticket to the highest bidder, presumably for about 99 cents on the dollar, it being almost free of risk and transactions costs. Done.

Since the marketability of the tax ticket would be assured and the right to receive it secured in advance through the allocation of credit authority, the developer could use the allocation as security to borrow capital funds to build the project or count on it as an oper-

ating subsidy to run the project after it was built.

There is precedent for this. The investment tax credit (ITC) was made transferable so that temporarily unprofitable corporations would not face an effectively higher cost of capital than profitable taxpaying ones. Thus, a struggling, money-losing Chrysler was able to modernize its plants and still cash in on the ITC by selling its ITC benefits to another corporation that was operating in the black.

Now, to finish up, let us return to our example. We have netted $8.25 million from sale of limited-partner interests, which reduces the mortgage we have to carry from $66,000 per apartment to $57,750. This reduces the mortgage payment by $69 and therefore the rent required by $81, leaving us with a required rent level of $971, still hardly affordable to a low-income family. So, just to complete this absurd circle, we turn back to the federal government and get a "Section 8" rent subsidy for about $611 per month, leaving $360 for the tenant to pay. (The tenant share is fixed at 30 percent of income, and the federal government pays the balance.)

The rent subsidy raises other efficiency questions, not the least of which is, "Why subsidize a capital project with a cash flow (rent subsidy), which then has to be capitalized in private capital markets when the federal government can borrow money more cheaply if it does so directly in its own name?" In other words, why are we using rent from the Treasury to borrow capital at 9.5 percent (AAA tax-exempt rate, including overrides and mortgage insurance fee) when the Treasury could borrow for us at 8.5 percent (taxable), pocket the immediate cash-flow saving, and, in addition, get back 28 percent of its interest cost in income taxes on the bond holders?

## REFORMING FEDERAL SUBSIDIES

This leads us to this revolutionary alternative: Suppose the federal government covered all of our capital costs with a grant and we promised not to syndicate the deal (no LIHC). The grant would only have to be $61,000 per unit, because we would save $5000 per unit in financing fees and construction- period interest (subtracting all the fees and some of the interest, because the federal government borrows at a lower effective interest rate). At 8.5 percent over 30 years, debt service cost to the Treasury on $61,000 is $469, of which $131 comes back as income tax paid by the bond holders on their interest income. With no mortgage payment, the cost of running the project is just the $388 per month in operating costs, which, with 5 percent vacancy requires rental income of $408. If the average tenant can pay $360, the federal government has to pay only $48 in rent subsidy.

Not doing any syndiciation allows the Treasury to collect more taxes. The LIHC, at 4 percent of $66,000, is worth $220 per month for ten years, plus there is the write-off for the losses. For simplicity, let us take the present value of the whole syndication package (credits plus shelter minus value of losses), $20,000 per unit, and estimate its monthly cost as being the debt service on this amount at current Treasury bond rates. This should be roughly a steady-state equivalent of the syndication's contribution to raising debt service on the national debt. Thus, it translates into a cost of $154 per month in debt service on the national debt, of which $43 would have come back in income tax payments by Treasury bond holders.

These calculations are summarized in Table 2. The grant-with-no-syndication-and-no-mortgage method of financing the project (column B) is roughly half as costly as the present method (column A) of rent subsidy, private tax-exempt mortgage, and syndication. Conclusion: With the grant method we could build and operate almost twice as much low-

Table 2: **Implicit Cost to Federal Treasury of Alternative Methods of Financing One Unit of Low-Income Housing**

|  | (A) Present Method | (B) Grant Method |
|---|---|---|
| Debt service on cap cost | 154[a] | 469[b] |
| Income tax on interest income | (43) | (131) |
| Rent subsidy | 611 | 48 |
| Total Monthly cost | 722 | 386 |

[a]$20,000 present value of tax credit at 8.5 percent, 30-year term.

[b]$61,000 in capital grant financed at 8.5 percent 30-year term.

income housing at no increase in cost to the federal treasury.

Why has our government designed such an inefficient method of financing housing? The fundamental problem, I believe, is an urge on the part of policymakers to try to make the legal and financial structure of low-income housing look like that of market-rate housing, with a for-profit, private landlord, a mortgage that covers most of the capital costs and a rent stream that pays the mortgage and operating costs. It is a bad model. Poor people cannot afford to pay any more than a tiny fraction of what it really costs to house them, so they have to be very heavily subsidized. The attempt to create free-market mechanisms to funnel this heavy subsidy into affordable housing for the poor has led to outrageous inefficiency in the use of public funds. The government would be well-advised to just accept the fact that housing the poor is a public-sector responsibility and do it the most efficient way possible — direct, outright grants for capital costs plus an operating subsidy, with the housing owned by not-for-profit entities.

# QUESTIONS

1. Explain how low-income housing is subsidized by (a) The Low Income Housing Credit (LIHC), (b) mortgage interest and depreciation cost deductibility, and (c) "Section 8" rent subsidies.

2. Luckett suggests that eliminating tax shelters from low-income housing is likely to hurt the poor while having little effect on the rich. What does this imply about the elasticities of (a) the supply of

funds for providing low-income housing and (b) the supply of investment opportunities?

3. Economists often abstract from a world in which transactions are costly. Are transactions costs important in the provision of subsidized low-income housing? How would freely saleable tax credits reduce transactions costs?

4. Luckett argues that decent low-income housing cannot be provided by the free market; rather, the public and not-for-profit sectors should jointly supply this market. Evaluate this perspective.

### Did Individual Retirement Accounts increase personal saving?

The tax code is frequently used to encourage specific kinds of behavior, from conserving energy to giving money to charity. Concerned that the national savings rate was too low, the tax code in the early 1980s offered incentives for workers to save part of their earnings.

# DID IRAs STIMULATE PERSONAL SAVING?

From 1982 through 1986, Americans could avoid paying taxes on up to $2000 of earnings by putting the money into an individual retirement account (IRA). Any interest earned in these accounts accumulated there tax free. IRAs proved to be a very popular savings vehicle, with contributions of about $45 billion in 1986. The 1986 tax law, however, now phases out the tax deductibility of contributions for individuals earning more than $25,000 and for families earning more than $40,000.

Did IRAs increase saving, or did they just substitute for other savings? Economic theory cannot resolve this question. Raising the after-tax rate of return to saving (by making it tax deferred) has both a substitution effect (the higher after-tax return makes saving relatively attractive) and an income effect (the higher return increases lifetime purchasing power, making increased current consumption—less saving—attractive). Which one dominates is an empirical question.

In spite of conflicting income and substitution effects, there were reasons to be skeptical about IRAs really increasing savings. First, lots of households weren't saving at all, and it wasn't clear that a more attractive savings vehicle would compete with the demands of current consumption. Second, many savers saved more than the $2000 annual limit on IRAs. These households, face no substitution effect, since their marginal dollar of savings can't go into an IRA. Since the income effect tends to reduce saving, theory predicts that these households would substitute IRAs for other investments but would not increase their overall savings.

It comes as something of a surprise, then, that some careful research is finding that a large fraction of IRA contributions seems to represent new net savings rather than substitution for other financial assets. Steven F. Venti and David A. Wise, in their paper, "Have IRAs increased U.S. saving? Evidence from Consumer Expenditure Surveys" (National Bureau of Economic Research working paper no. 2217), find that IRAs are funded almost entirely by new savings. They point out that this may be because IRAs are special in more ways than just their tax advantages. IRAs were widely advertised and were easily available through most banks. Unlike other savings accounts available at banks, IRAs have annual deadlines that force people to either make their contributions or lose an opportunity forever. Also, IRAs have penalties for money withdrawn early; while economists see this as an extra risk associated with IRAs, some people may see it as rein-

forcing their willpower to leave their savings alone.

Venti and Wise use a statistical model that allows consumers to respond to both rate of return and other differences between IRAs and non-IRA savings opportunities. Based on data from the second year that IRAs were generally available, they estimate that on average households would contribute almost 25 cents of an extra dollar of after-tax income to an IRA, saving only 1.5 cents in other financial assets. IRAs are obviously a preferred savings vehicle.

But is IRA savings just substituted from other assets? The authors look at households who save more than the IRA limit. They estimate that before the IRA limit is reached, each extra dollar of income leads to 3.3 cents in non-IRA saving. After the IRA limit is reached, this increases to 4.6 cents of non-IRA savings for every dollar of income. We can view this extra 1.3 cents as saving that, up to the IRA limit, was substituted into IRAs from other saving. These households' marginal propensity to contribute to IRAs is 33.3 cents, implying that only 4 percent of IRA saving was substituted from other assets.

## QUESTIONS

1. Theoretically, how might IRAs actually reduce saving?

2. In general, the families saving more than the IRA limit are high-income families. For such households, IRA contributions are no longer tax deductible, although interest still compounds tax-free and the other features of IRAs (advertising, deadlines, and so on) are unchanged. Based on the estimates reported above, what is the largest decline

in marginal saving rates that could result from the 1986 changes in the tax law? Why might the actual decline be smaller?

3. The Social Security retirement program was reformed in 1983 after a lot of public attention to its financial woes. Might this adverse publicity have helped the popularity of IRAs? In an ideal data set, could you use the fact that federal employees are not part of the Social Security system to test whether increasing worries about Social Security led to larger IRA contributions?

***From a historical perspective, was the Tax Reform Act of 1986 really so radical?***

The theory of public choice tells us how powerful special interest groups can be. When tax reform includes moving to a broader tax base, this implies that somebody is losing a special tax preference. Tax reform that takes away many special privileges is not to be taken for granted, then, since there is likely to be lots of lobbying against it. In these excerpts from a longer address, Pechman reflects on the alliances that led to tax reform and points out how far from comprehensive that reform was.

# TAX REFORM:

## Theory and Practice[†‡]

*Joseph A. Pechman**

The Tax Reform Act of 1986 is the most significant piece of tax legislation enacted since the income tax was converted to a mass tax during World War II. After decades of erosion, the individual and corporate income tax bases were broadened and the revenues were used to reduce tax rates. Loopholes and preferences that were formerly considered sacrosanct were eliminated or moderated despite the determined opposition of powerful pressure groups. Comprehensive income taxation, which had earlier been regarded as an impossible dream, carried the day with strong bipartisan support. I will trace the origins of the tax reform movement and speculate about why it was successful in 1986 after repeated failures

*Senior Economist, The Brookings Institution, and a long-time advocate of comprehensive tax reform.

†This paper was delivered as the 1986 Distinguished Lecture on Economics in Government, Joint Session of the American Economic Association and the Society of Government Economists, New Orleans, December 29, 1986. I am grateful to Henry J. Aaron, Edward F. Denison, Harvey Galper, Richard Goode, and Charles E. McLure, Jr. for helpful comments and suggestions, and to Charles R. Byce and Rob E. Luginbuhl for programming assistance.

‡Reprinted with permission of *Journal of Economic Perspectives*, Vol. 1, no. 1, Summer 1987.

in earlier years. I also explain what the 1986 act accomplished and what more needs to be done to achieve the objectives of comprehensive income taxation.

## THE SHRINKING OF THE TAX BASE

Despite the efforts of the tax reformers, the trend of U.S. tax policy since the end of World War II had been to expand old preferences and to introduce new ones to achieve various economic and social objectives. The list is long. It includes provisions that were intended to promote investment in general— accelerated depreciation and the investment tax credit—as well as tax favors to particular industries and firms, such as the extension of percentage depletion to sand, gravel, oyster shells, and salt, taxation at preferential capital gains rates of livestock held for more than six months, unharvested crops sold along with land, and coal royalties, and extension of immediate expensing of development and exploration costs to minerals as well as oil and gas. Many of these provisions, combined with the deduction for interest expense, permitted wealthy people and large corporations to avoid payment of any tax.

Some relief provisions were even tailored to fit specific individuals, the most famous of which was the "Mayer amendment," enacted in 1951. This amendment provided capital gains treatment for a lump sum distribution to Louis B. Mayer on his retirement from the movie industry. To avoid identifying him by name, the amendment was worded to apply to a movie executive who (1) had been employed for more than 20 years, (2) had held his rights to future profits for 12 years, and (3) had the right to receive a percentage of profits for life or for a period of at least five years after the termination of his employment.

The situation became so bad that in 1976 the House approved an amendment submitted by Congressman James Burke of Massachu-

setts, perhaps tongue-in-cheek, to provide a 7 percent tax credit for the purchase of garden tools "to encourage the private production of food." Sanity prevailed, however, and the amendment was removed by the Senate and not restored in conference. Louis Mayer and garden tools are only two examples. There were others.

The proliferation of tax preferences was interrupted in 1969, partly in response to the revelation by Treasury Secretary Joseph A. Barr of the outgoing Johnson administration that 154 persons with adjusted gross incomes of more than $200,000 had not paid tax in 1966. The reform spirit lasted until 1975, when percentage depletion was denied to large corporations. Congress then reverted to its old habits in 1978, when the exclusion for long-term capital gains was raised from 50 percent to 60 percent, homeowners over 55 years of age were given a lifetime exemption of $100,000 for capital gains realized on the sale of a principal residence, the limits on tax-exempt industrial development bonds were liberalized, and the investment tax credit was extended to outlays for rehabilitation of old buildings. In 1981, President Reagan easily persuaded Congress to enact his across-the-board individual income tax rate reductions and the excessively generous accelerated cost recovery system (ACRS) for depreciation, which were major features of his election campaign platform in the previous year. Congress got into the spirit of the occasion by adding to the bill a raft of unnecessary and costly deductions of its own, including an annual deduction of up to $2,000 for amounts set aside in individual retirement accounts (even by employees already covered by private pension plans), an exclusion of $750 ($1,500 on joint returns) for reinvested dividends paid by public utilities from 1982 through 1985, an exclusion of $1,000 ($2,000 on joint returns) for interest on savings certificates purchased in 1981 and 1982 (to help bail out the savings and loan industry), an increase to $125,000 in the lifetime capital gain exemption for homeowners, and a new deduction for charitable contributions of nonitemizers.[1] In the same bill, Congress gutted the estate and gift taxes by tripling the exemption and lowering the top rate from 75 percent to 50 percent.

## GATHERING THE FORCES FOR REFORM

In the light of this dismal history, particularly of the last seven years, the passage of the Tax Reform Act of 1986 is indeed a remarkable event. Political scientists will be trying for years to come to explain why it happened in 1986. I offer the following observations in full recognition of my amateur status as a political analyst.

First, the large tax cuts and new preferences enacted in recent years undermined the confidence of the people in the tax system. The growing use of tax shelters by wealthy people to reduce or eliminate their tax liabilities was well-known. So were the names of giant corporations (General Dynamics, General Electric, etc.) which had not been paying any taxes. Low- and middle-income taxpayers resented paying higher effective tax rates on their incomes than many wealthy individuals and large profitable corporations. Furthermore, the tax system has become so complicated that millions of people were paying someone else to prepare their returns. Tax reformers were promising greater equity, efficiency, and simplicity in taxation and this message struck a responsive chord.

Second, the old tax reformers were joined by the new breed of supply-siders in promoting lower tax rates (for example, see Meyer, 1981). The original idea of comprehensive reform was to maintain a system of graduated rates, but at a reduced level. The supply-siders added a new wrinkle: instead of a multiple-rate system, they proposed the use of a single flat rate, and were willing to sacrifice many tax preferences to get it. The flat tax movement collapsed when it was shown

in congressional hearings that a flat rate meant that people with very high incomes (those with incomes of about $50,000) would pay lower taxes, while those with lower incomes would pay higher taxes. But to their credit, many of the flat taxers continued to support tax reform at mildly graduated rates, but a low top rate. As it turned out, the coalition of liberals and conservatives favoring comprehensive reform and rate reduction prevailed in Congress.

Third, the Treasury and its supporters stressed the importance of allocating resources on the basis of economic, rather than tax, considerations from the very beginning. Although businessmen were split on the merits of tax reform, many influential corporate executives found the idea of a "level playing field" appealing and threw their support behind the tax bill. Even the financial community, which traditionally fought any increase in the capital gains tax, muted its opposition this time because of the attractiveness of the low top rate on other income.

Fourth, the support for tax reform by the President of the United States was crucial in the legislative history of the bill. Like other supply-siders, he was interested mainly in reducing tax rates and was willing to accept a considerable amount of base broadening to achieve them. He had earlier said that he opposed the corporate income tax, yet he accepted a large increase in corporate tax liabilities, which was needed to provide a cut in effective individual income tax rates at all income levels. At one stage in the legislative process, he persuaded the Republican minority in the House of Representatives to support a rule to permit debate on the bill to proceed. He also supported a radically altered version of the administration's plan in the Senate, and later in conference, in the interest of expediting passage of a bill. Without his support at these stages, the bill would never have emerged from Congress.

Fifth, influential members of the House and Senate from both political parties supported the ideas of broadening the tax base and reducing rates. Senator Bill Bradley was an early advocate of tax reform; his persistence in urging a comprehensive approach is widely acknowledged to have been a major contributing factor to its success. The bill he and Congressman Richard Gephardt introduced in 1983 became a model for responsible discussion of tax reform in recent years.[2] A somewhat similar bill followed from Congressman Jack Kemp and Senator Bob Kasten.[3] Other members of Congress followed suit, recognizing that Bradley-Gephardt and Kemp-Kasten has stolen a march on them.[4] Like the president, many of these legislators were more interested in rate reduction than in base-broadening, but they were willing to join forces with the tax reformers to achieve their objective. The bipartisan support for base-broadening kept the bill from foundering as it made its way through the legislative process.

Credit should also be given to the chairmen of the two tax-writing committees, who guided the tax bill through their committees and the two houses of Congress. Ways and Means Committee Chairman Dan Rostenkowski was particularly skillful in judging how far he could push his colleagues without losing their support. After a false start, Senator Bob Packwood was able to persuade the Senate Finance Committee, which he chairs, and the Senate to pass a real tax reform.

Finally, members of the staffs of the Treasury Department, the Joint Committee on Taxation, the Ways and Means and Finance Committees were strong supporters of tax reform and seemed always to be prepared with modifications to satisfy political realities without fatally weakening the bill. When the Senate Finance Committee had emasculated the bill and practically everybody was predicting its demise, William M. Diefenderfer, Chief of the Finance Committee staff, and David H. Brockway, Chief of the Joint Taxation Committee staff, persuaded Senator Packwood that it would be possible to reduce the maximum individual income tax rate to as low as 25 percent with sufficient broadening of the tax

base and higher corporate taxes. That rate was increased almost immediately to 27 percent to retain the homeowner preferences, but the principle that significant rate reduction could be achieved was established. At that rate, the objections of the opponents of tax reform faded and the bill ultimately sailed through Congress with a top effective rate of 28 percent.

## WHAT THE REFORM ACCOMPLISHED

The Tax Reform Act of 1986 is a major step toward comprehensive tax reform. I believe it will greatly improve the fairness of the tax system and remove major distortions from the economy. The many more improvements remaining to be made in the tax system do not detract from what has been achieved. The major accomplishments of the act are as follows:

1. By doubling the personal exemptions and increasing the standard deduction, the act removes 4,800,000 poor people from the tax rolls.[5] This step restores the principle (abandoned by Congress in 1978) that people who are officially defined as "poor" should not be required to pay income tax. The principle will be perpetuated by the resumption in 1989 of the automatic annual adjustment for inflation of the personal exemptions.

2. Significant increases were made in the earned income credit for wage earners with families.[6] These increases eliminated almost the entire Social Security tax (including the employer's share) for those eligible for the full credit and reduced the tax burden for many other low income workers, thus increasing the progressivity of the tax system.

3. Two rate rates—15 percent and 28 percent—were substituted for the earlier 14 rates, which rose to a maximum of 50 per-

cent. However, counting the 33 percent rate created by phasing out the lowest tax rate and personal exemptions for higher income taxpayers, the new rate structure will have four brackets, with rates of 15, 28, 33, and 28 percent. These lower marginal rates will reduce the attractiveness of tax shelters and the return to tax cheating and increase work and saving incentives. Some estimates of the supply response to changes in tax rates have been excessive, but the more responsible estimates suggest that there will be a modest improvement in work effort; the saving response is unclear (Bosworth, 1984, chapters 3 and 5; Hausman and Poterba, 1987).

4. The taxation of realized capital gains as ordinary income—the keystone of comprehensive tax reform—has finally been realized. This change will reduce the incentive to disguise ordinary income as capital gains, and thus make the tax code less complicated and simplify financial planning. Without this change, the act would have cut the taxes of the wealthy by large amounts and would have been grossly unfair. However, the continued exemption from the regular tax of accrued capital gains on assets transferred by gift or at death will increase the incentive of taxpayers to defer realizing gains until the assets are transferred to their heirs.

5. A good start was made on reversing the erosion of the individual income tax base. Unemployment benefits, which were previously taxable only if a married taxpayer's income exceeded $18,000 ($12,000 for single people), were made taxable regardless of the size of income. Deductions for state and local sales taxes and consumer interest were eliminated. Deductions for unreimbursed business expenses, costs incurred in earning investment income, and other miscellaneous costs were allowed only to the extent that they exceed a floor of two percent of income. The floor for the deduction

of medical expenses was raised from 5 percent to 7.5 percent of income. The exclusions for prizes or awards for scientific and other achievements and for scholarships and fellowships exceeding university tuition, books, and supplies, were eliminated. Perhaps most important, the deduction for investment interest of noncorporate taxpayers was limited to investment income. These changes and others will enlarge the tax base, reduce horizontal inequities, and simplify compliance by reducing the number of people who itemize their deductions.

6. The act makes a frontal assault on major loopholes and special benefits. Many tax shelters will no longer be profitable because of a new limitation on the deductibility of losses from passive investments,[7] tax subsidies for borrowing (other than for mortgages) will be eliminated by the limitation on the deduction for investment interest expense, the deduction for contributions to individual retirement accounts by persons already covered by private pension plans will be allowed only for taxpayers with incomes below $50,000 if married and $35,000 if single,[8] deductible business expense accounts for meals, travel, and entertainment will be limited to 80 percent of outlays, tax preferences benefiting defense contractors, banks, and other industries will be eliminated or narrowed,[9] and the minimum tax for both individuals and businesses will be strengthened.

7. Contrary to Henry Simons' views about the corporate tax, the U.S. Congress believes that a separate, unintegrated corporate tax is essential for effective income taxation. A separate corporate tax prevents individuals from avoiding income tax by accumulating earnings in corporations, although some might question whether it is appropriate to tax corporations at a higher tax rate than the top bracket individual rate. Simons disregarded the tremendous value

of tax deferral, which is possible when capital gains are taxed only when realized. The 1986 act reduced the general corporate tax rate from 46 percent to 34 percent, thus reducing the maximum tax on dividends at the margin by over a quarter (from 73 percent to 52.5 percent) in the top brackets. Nevertheless, the reform act increased corporate tax liabilities about 20 percent overall by eliminating the investment credit, reducing depreciation allowances for structures, and eliminating loopholes.

## HOW THE NEW TAX BURDEN IS DISTRIBUTED

The distributional effect of the act is distinctly progressive, especially if the increases in corporate income tax liabilities are taken into account. I have calculated the change in average effective tax rates on the basis of the most recent distribution of tax burdens estimated from the Brookings MERGE file (Table 1). The combined federal corporation and individual income tax burden is increased for the top 10 percent of the income distribution, but reduced for the lower 90 percent. Total federal tax burdens also decline in the lower nine deciles and then rise in the top decile. The tax reductions in the lower deciles are the result of the increases in the personal exemptions, standard deduction, and earned income credit under the individual income tax. The increases at the top reflect the increase in corporation tax liabilities, which are assumed to fall on owners of capital in these calculations.

The major complaint against the reform is that corporations will be paying higher taxes than before, which will increase the cost of capital and reduce investment. The fact is that the corporate rate reductions will be almost as large as the revenues raised by the elimination of the investment credit, reductions in depreciation allowances, and other changes in the capital cost allowances. Practically all the *additional* tax to be paid by corpora-

tions will come from eliminating loopholes and other structural changes. These reforms will increase average, but not marginal, tax rates and are less likely to affect investment incentives.

Critics of the increase in corporate tax liabilities neglect to mention that many corporations will actually be paying lower taxes than before. These are the corporation which have been paying taxes on most of their economic income. By eliminating preferences, the act will improve the allocation of investment and increase economic efficiency. Higher taxes will be paid by capital-intensive firms such as steel, aluminum, and utility companies, but they are the nation's sluggish industries. The less capital-intensive but more innovative industries—computers, electronics, biomedicine, and so on—will pay lower taxes

Table 1: **Change in Individual and Corporation Income Tax Liabilities Under the Tax Reform Act of 1986, by Income Decile**

| Income Decile[a] | Percent Change in | |
|---|---|---|
| | Federal Individual and Corporate Income taxes[b] | Total Federal Taxes |
| Lowest | −44 | −16 |
| Second | −32 | −11 |
| Third | −24 | −10 |
| Fourth | −16 | −7 |
| Fifth | −12 | −6 |
| Sixth | −8 | −4 |
| Seventh | −7 | −4 |
| Eighth | −6 | −3 |
| Ninth | −6 | −4 |
| Highest | +3 | +2 |
| Top 5% | +4 | +3 |
| Top 1% | +5 | +5 |

*Source:* Author's estimates based on the 1985 Brookings MERGE file

[a]The classification is by a comprehensive definition of income, including imputed rent and corporate earnings allocated to stockholders, whether distributed or not.

[b]Assumes the corporate tax is a tax on capital in general.

and will have higher after-tax profits to invest. This redistribution of the corporate tax burden should have a favorable effect on growth.[10]

## MISTAKES AND MISSED OPPORTUNITIES

Notwithstanding the accomplishments just enumerated, much remains to be done to reach the comprehensive reform target. In legislation as far-reaching and as complicated as the Tax Reform Act of 1986, some mistakes were inevitable and some real opportunities for improvement in the tax structure were ignored. Moreover, the bill contains the earmarks of numerous political bargains and compromises that make little economic or administrative sense.

Perhaps the most unsatisfactory feature of the act is the way it handles owner-occupied housing. Since the tax advantages of homeowners are regarded by politicians as untouchable, the act kept intact the exclusion of the rental value of owned homes from income, the deduction for interest on home mortgages, and the deduction for property taxes. At the same time, the deduction for consumer interest was eliminated and the deduction for investment interest was limited to the amount of reported net investment income. The public is already being bombarded by newspaper and magazine articles by so-called experts who advise taxpayers to increase their home mortgages as a device to generate deductible interest payments. The tax bill limits the extent to which this can be done, but the efforts to circumvent the law will be difficult to police.[11]

Even if the exemption of imputed rent and a deduction for mortgage interest are sacrosanct, it is possible to limit the borrowing subsidy without encouraging rearrangements of debt for tax purposes. The solution was first proposed by my colleague, Richard Goode, more than twenty years ago and the new law applies it to investment interest (Goode,

1976, p.152). The idea is to allow deductions for interest payments up to the amount of investment income reported on an individual's return. To accommodate the political requirement that mortgage interest be deductible, the limit can be raised to new investment income plus an arbitrary amount, say $10,000 or $15,000. At a 10 percent interest rate, such generous limits would permit deductions for interest on mortgages of up to $100,000 or $150,000—more than enough to take care of the vast majority of home owners. The limits would also remove the discrimination against borrowing for other purposes and the temptation to refinance home mortgages for the purpose of financing other consumption or investments.

A second unsatisfactory feature of the new law is the treatment of deductions other than interest. I interpret the Simons definition of income to include all sources of income, without any deductions for the uses of that income. For equity reasons, I believe it is appropriate to permit a deduction for unusual expenses that reduce the taxpayer's ability to pay, but they should be kept to a minimum. The law already contains deductions for unusual medical expenses, which are defined as medical payments in excess of 7.5 percent of income (up from 5 percent under the old law), and casualty losses, which are allowable to the extent they exceed 10 percent of income. The remaining deductions for state and local taxes and charitable contributions subsidize public services provided by state and local governments and provide an incentive for private charitable giving.

The Treasury I plan in 1984 recommended the complete elimination of the state-local tax deduction and the restriction of the charitable contribution deduction to amounts in excess of two percent of income. Congress retained the deduction for charitable contributions and eliminated the deduction for state and local sales taxes, but retained the deduction for income and property taxes. I do not believe that our federal system of government depends on the deductibility of state and local taxes, as some allege, and I agree with the Treasury that charitable giving would not be impaired if the deduction were limited to amounts given above a small floor. The revenue gained from restructuring all deductions as the Treasury proposed would be large (on the order of $40 billion in 1988) and could be used to finance further reductions in marginal tax rates or to reduce the federal deficit. In addition, further pruning of the personal deductions would reduce the record-keeping needed to prepare tax returns and simplify tax compliance and administration.

I find another feature of the new tax law bizarre. This is the telescoping of the schedule of fourteen rates into two, while concealing two additional brackets. The reduction in the number of rates is a response to the flat tax proposals which were being promoted when the tax reform bill began its journey through Congress. The simplifications from a single or double rate system are negligible, but the allure of the flat rate survived the legislative process, even though it was necessary to conceal two brackets to moderate the loss of revenue.

More important, I have serious reservations about the elimination of graduation at the top of the income scale. Surely there is a difference in ability to pay out of a marginal dollar at $30,000 than at $300,000 of taxable income, yet the 1986 act makes no distinction between the rates at these levels. Moreover, the 5 percent marginal rate increase in the phase-out range is an anachronism that should not be allowed to survive. I do not recommend going back to fourteen brackets, but I certainly believe that there is room for graduation beyond 4 brackets, especially when one of the brackets introduces an unsightly bulge into the rate structure.

The four-bracket structure led to two additional changes that I find objectionable. The first is the elimination of the deduction for two-earner couples and the second is the elimination of the privilege of averaging. Since graduation was reduced, Congress felt the remaining penalties on marriage and on fluctuating incomes were tolerable. These penalties were reduced, but they were not eliminated entirely. The annual marriage penalty can be as large as 13 percent and the penalty on fluctuating income can be as high as 40 percent over a period of five years. Moreover, omitting these provisions will act as a deterrent to the introduction of more graduation. Consequently, I hope that the two-earner deduction and averaging will be restored.

Another major neglected problem was the erosion of the tax base from the exclusion of employee fringe benefits. Congress has treated fringe benefits leniently because they benefit workers with moderate income, but in fact the largest per capita subsidy goes to the highest paid employees because of graduated tax rates. Moreover, loopholes for moderate income recipients are no more defensible than those for the rich. The Reagan administration proposed to limit the exclusion from the tax base for health insurance premiums paid by employers to a rather generous amount, but even this proposal was rejected by the Congress. The so-called "cafeteria plans," which give employees a choice between taking cash compensation or nontaxable benefits (for such things as medical and dental expenses, accident and health insurance, group term life insurance, and child care), were left untouched. The revenue leakage from these provisions has been growing rapidly and it is time to stop it.

Finally, the act continued the earlier practice of adjusting the personal exemptions, standard deduction, and rate bracket limits for inflation, but avoided adjusting the value of taxable assets. Economists agree that, of the two types of adjustment, the adjustment of asset values is by far the more important. Perhaps the major reason why the tax system was in such disrepute a few years ago was the discrimination against capital incomes inherent in a nominal tax system. Now that capital gains will be subject to full taxation and depreciation has been put on a more realistic basis, an inflation adjustment of the purchase price of assets to compute real gains and losses and real depreciation allowances is essential to avoid pressure to reinstate the ad hoc adjustments that did so much damage to the tax system.

The major inhibition against indexing the base is the difficulty of adjusting interest receipts and expenses for inflation. In 1984, the Treasury I report proposed an approximate plan. It assumed (incorrectly) that the inflation element in all interest payments was the same. Furthermore, the plan was defective when applied to banks and other financial institutions. The Treasury avoided calling for direct adjustments for inflation in each transaction for fear that many taxpayers would not be able to cope. I am not persuaded, however, that the problem is insuperable. Most interest payments are made by financial institutions, which can easily calculate the necessary inflation adjustments. Individual and small businesses might have a difficult problem in adjusting their interest payments, but it would be better to address these problems directly than to refrain from indexing altogether.

## Notes

1. The deduction was phased in from 25 percent of the first $100 of annual contributions in 1982 and 1983 to 100 percent of contributions in 1986.

2. S. 1472 and H.R. 3271, 98th Congress.

3. S. 2600 and H.R. 5533, 98th Congress.

4. Some examples are S. 557 introduced by Senator Dennis DeConcini, S. 1040 introduced by Senator Dan Quayle, H.R. 5432 introduced by Representative Mark Siljander, and H.R. 5811 introduced by Representative Cecil Heftel, all in the 98th Congress.

5. The personal exemption is increased from $1,080 in 1986 to $1,900 in 1987, to $1,950 in 1988, and $2,000 beginning in 1989. For married couples, the standard deduction is increased from $3,670 in 1986 to $3,760 in 1987 and $5,000 beginning in 1988; for single persons, it is increased from $2,480 in 1986 to $2,540 in 1987 and $3,000 beginning in 1988.

6. The earned income credit is increased from 11 percent to 14 percent of earnings, the maximum credit is raised from $550 to $800, and the phase-out range is lifted from $6,500-$11,000 to $9,000-$17,000. The maximum credit and the phaseout starting point will be adjusted for inflation.

7. Losses from passive activities will be deducted only against passive income. A passive activity is a trade or business in which the taxpayer (or spouse) does not materially participate. All rental activities are regarded as passive.

8. The IRA deduction is phased out between $40,000 and $50,000 of adjusted gross income for married couples and between $25,000 and $35,000 for single people.

9. For example, defense contractors are required to pay tax on at least 40 percent of income from long-term contracts, banks will be required to deduct actual losses on loans rather than set up loss reserves and will not be allowed to deduct interest incurred to purchase tax-exempt securities, and oil and mining firms will be required to amortize 30 percent of intangible drilling costs and exploration and development outlays (instead of 20 percent under the old law).

10. For an evaluation of the economic effects of the 1986 tax reform, see Pechman, ed. (1987).

11. Mortgage interest is deductible only on first and second homes and is limited to interest on mortgages up to the purchase price of the property plus the cost of any improvements and loans to pay educational or medical expenses.

## References

Aaron, Henry J., and Harvey Galper, *Assessing Tax Reform.* Washington: The Brookings Institution, 1985.

Andrews, William D., "A Consumption-Type or Cash Flow Personal Income Tax," *Harvard Law Review*, April 1984, 87, 1113–88.

Barr, Joseph A., *Statement before the Joint Economic Committee.* U.S. Congress, January 17, 1969.

Bittker, Boris I., Charles O. Galvin, R. A. Musgrave, and Joseph A. Pechman, *A Comprehensive Income Tax Base? A Debate.* Branford, Connecticut: Federal Tax Press, Inc., 1968. Much of this volume was originally published in the *Harvard Law Review*, 1967 and 1968, 80 and 81.

Blum Walter J., "Federal Income Tax Reform— Twenty Questions," *Taxes*, November 1963, 41, 672–691.

Boskin, Michael J., "The Choice of Tax Base: Consumption versus Income Taxation." In Boskin, Michael J., ed., *Federal Tax Reform: Myths and Realities.* San Francisco: Institute for Contemporary Studies, 1978, ch. 2.

Bosworth, Barry P., *Tax Incentives and Economic Growth.* Washington: The Brookings Institution, 1984.

Bradford, David F., "The Case for a Personal Consumption Tax." In Joseph A. Pechman, ed., *What Should Be Taxed: Income or Expenditure.* Washington: The Brookings Institution, 1980, 75-113.

Bradley, Bill *The Fair Tax.* New York: Pocket Books, 1984.

Committee for Economic Development, *A Post-war Federal Tax Plan for High Employment.* New York, 1944.

Douglas, Paul H., "The Problem of Tax Loopholes," *The American Scholar*, Winter 1967-1968, 37, 21-43.

Feldstein, Martin S., "The Welfare Cost of Capital Income Taxation," *Journal of Political Economy*, April 1978, 86, 529-551.

Fisher, Irving, "Income in Theory and Income Taxation in Practice," *Econometrica*, January 1937, 5, 1-55.

Goode, Richard, *The Individual Income Tax.* Rev. ed. Washington: The Brookings Institution, 1976.

Haig, Robert Murray, "The Concept of Income-Economic and Legal Aspects." In Haig, Robert Murray, ed.., *Federal Income Tax.* New York: Columbia University Press, 1921, pp. 1-28. Reprinted in Richard A. Musgrave anad Carl S. Shoup, eds., *Readings in the Economics of Taxation.* New York: Irwin, 1959, pp. 54-76.

Hall, Robert E., and Alvin Rabushka, *Low Tax, Simple Tax, Flat Tax.* New York: McGraw-Hill, 1983.

Hausman, J., and J. Poterba, "Household Behavior and the Tax Reform Act of 1986," *Journal of Economic Perspectives*, vol. 1, no. 1 (Summer 1987), 101-119.

Heller, Walter W., "Practical Limitations on the Federal Net Income Tax," *Journal of Finance*, May 1952, VII, 185-202.

Hobbes, Thomas, *Leviathan.* Westport, CT: Greenwood Press, 1977.

Humphrey, Hubert H., *Tax Loopholes.* Washington: The Public Affairs Institute, 1952.

Kaldor, Nicholas, *An Expenditure Tax.* London: George Allen and Unwin, Ltd., 1955.

Kay, John A., and Mervyn A. King, *The British Tax System.* Oxford: Oxford University Press, 1978.

Lodin, Sven-Olof, *Progressive Expenditure Tax— An Alternative. A Report of the 1972 Government Commission on Taxation.* Stockholm: Liber Förlag, 1978.

McDaniel, Paul R., and Stanley S. Surrey, *International Aspects of Tax Expenditures: A Comparitive Study.* Deventer, The Netherlands: Kluwer Law and Taxation Publishers, 1985.

Meyer, Lawrence H., ed., *The Supply-Side Effects of Economic Policy.* St. Louis: Center for the Study of American Business and the Federal Reserve Bank of St. Louis, 1981.

Mieszkowski, Peter, "The Advisability and Feasibility of an Expenditure Tax System." In Henry J. Aaron, and Michael J. Boskin, eds., *The Economics of Taxation.* Washington: The Brookings Institution, 1980, pp. 179-201.

Mill, John Stuart, *Principles of Policy Economy.* W. J. Ashley, ed. London: Longmans Green, 1929. Bk. 2, Ch. 2, sec. 4.

Musgrave, Richard A., *The Theory of Public Finance*. New York: McGraw-Hill, 1959, Ch. 8.

Organisation for Economic Co-operation and Development, *Tax Expenditures: A Review of the Issues and Country Practices*. Paris: OECD, 1984.

Paul, Randolph, "Erosion of the Tax Base and Rate Structure." In U.S. Congress. Joint Committee on the Economy Report, *Federal Tax Policy for Economic Growth and Stability*. Washington: U.S. G.P.O., 1955, pp. 297-312.

Pechman, Joseph A., "The Individual Income Tax Base," *Proceedings of the Forty-Eighth Annual Conference in Taxation Sponsored by The National Tax Association*, 1955, 1- 11.

Pechman, Joseph A., ed., *Tax Reform and the U.S. Economy*. Washington: The Brookings Institution, 1987.

Pechman, Joseph A. and Benjamin A. Okner, "Individual Income Tax Erosion by Income Classes," *The Economics of Federal Subsidy Programs, A Compendium of Papers Submitted to the Joint Economic Committee*. Part 1, *General Study Papers*, 92 Cong., 2nd session, 1972, 13-40.

Pechman, Joseph A. and John Karl Scholz, "Comprehensive Income Taxation and Rate Reduction," *Tax Notes*, October 11, 1982, 17, 83-93.

Simons, Henry C., *Federal Tax Reform*. Chicago: The University of Chicago Press, 1950.

Simons, Henry C., *Personal Income Taxation*. Chicago: The University of Chicago Press, 1938.

Surrey, Stanley S., "The Federal Income Tax Base for Individuals," *Tax Revision Compendium*, U.S. House of Representatives, Committee on Ways and Means, 1959, 1, 1-17.

Surrey, Stanley S., *Pathways to Tax Reform*. Cambridge, MA: Harvard University Press, 1973.

Surrey, Stanley S., and Paul R. McDaniel, *Tax Expenditures*. Cambridge, MA: Harvard University Press, 1975.

Surrey, Stanley S., Paul R. McDaniel, and Joseph A. Pechman, *Federal Tax Reform for 1976, A Compendium*. Washington: Fund for Public Policy Research, 1976.

U.S. Department of the Treasury, *Blueprints for Basic Tax Reform, 1977*. Reprinted by Tax Notes, Arlington, VA, 1984.

U.S. Department of the Treasury, *The President's 1978 Tax Program*. 1978.

U.S. Department of the Treasury, *Tax Reform for Simplicity, Fairness, and Economic Growth*. 3 vols., 1984.

U.S. House of Representatives, Committee on Ways and Means, *Tax Revision Compendium, Compendium of Papers on Broadening the Tax Base*. 2 vols. Washington: U.S. G.P.O., 1959.

Vickrey, William, *Agenda for Progressive Taxation*. New York: The Ronald Press, 1947.

von Schanz, Georg, "Der Einkommensbegriff und die Einkommensteuergesetze," *Finanz Archiv*, 1896, 13, 1- 87.

# QUESTIONS

1. Although TRA86 broadened the tax base, it fell short of a comprehensive definition of income. What are some of the major omissions?

2. Here are two political stereotypes: Liberals want to close tax loopholes exploited by the rich. Conservatives want to reduce taxes for the rich. Are these stereotypes helpful in explaining the political support behind the tax reform act of 1986?

3. Pechman is dissatisfied with several aspects of TRA86. Pick any two of these and consider whether his preferred reform differs from TRA86 because of:
(a) political compromises necessary to pass TRA86,
(b) political differences of opinion between Pechman and the Congress, or
(c) differences in opinion over the economic consequences of the provision.

4. In the complete address excerpted above, Pechman goes on to contrast TRA86 with a more compre-

hensive income tax. In the following passage he describes his tax base. His tax rates are given in Table 3.

(a) Does the average effective tax rate fall much when the tax base is expanded?

(b) Pechman stops short of a thoroughly comprehensive tax base. What seems to be the motive (fairness? progressivity? behavioral incentives?) behind each omission?

## TAX REFORM: THEORY AND PRACTICE (CONTINUED)

In addition to the items now taxed, adjusted gross income would include accrued capital gains on gifts transferred at death, interest on life insurance savings, employer contributions to health and life insurance plans, interest on newly issued state and local government securities, workers' compensation, and veterans' benefits. Half of all Social Security retirement and disability benefits would be included in the taxable income of all taxpayers rather than only those with other incomes of $32,000 if married and $25,000 if single. Deductions for IRAs would be available only to those not covered by private pension plans. Deductions for all state and local taxes would be eliminated, and there would be floors on all the remaining deductions (10 percent for medical expenses and casualty losses and 2 percent for charitable contributions and miscellaneous expenses). The personal exemption would be raised from $1950 to $2000 in 1988 rather than waiting until 1989, the standard deduction would be set at a uniform $4,000 for all taxpayers, and the special $600 standard deduction for the elderly and the blind and the child care credit would be eliminated. To avoid a marriage penalty, the deduction for two-earner couples (10 percent of the earnings of the spouse with the lower earnings up to $30,000) would be restored. As Table 2 shows, at 1988 income levels, this tax base would be 14 percent larger than the base under the 1986 act and thus permit further reductions in tax rates. [See Table 3.]

Table 2: **Adjusted Gross Income and Taxable Income Under the Tax Reform Act of 1986 and Under a Comprehesive Income Tax, 1988**

| | Billions of Dollars | |
|---|---|---|
| Item | Adjusted Gross Income | Taxable Income |
| Tax Reform Act of 1986 | 2,941 | 1,973 |
| Plus | | |
| Personal exemptions[a] | — | −8 |
| Personal deductions[b] | — | 101 |
| Transfer payments[c] | 80 | 75 |
| Fringe benefits[d] | 129 | 118 |
| Two-earner deduction[e] | −40 | −40 |
| Other[f] | 6 | 40 |
| Equals: Comprehensive Tax | 3,171 | 2,259 |

*Source:* Brookings 1983 tax file projected to 1988.

[a]Exemption increased from $1,950 to $2,000.

[b]Includes flat standard deduction of 4,000; investment interest limited to net investment income; no deduction for state-local taxes; 10% floor on deductions for medical expenses and casualty losses; 2% floors on deductions for charitable contributions and miscellaneous expenses, and no standard deduction for the elderly and the blind.

[c]Includes half of social security retirement and disability benefits for all taxpayers, workers' compensation, and veterans' benefits.

[d]Includes premiums paid by employers for health and life insurance; interest on life insurance policies; and IRAs of persons covered by employer pension plans.

[e]10 percent of earnings of spouses with lower earnings up to a maximum of $3,000.

[f]Including unrealized capital gains transferred by gift or death, interest on newly-issued state and local securities, and all perference items now subject to the minimum tax. Eliminates the child care credit.

Table 3: **Comparison of Tax Rates Under the Tax Reform Act of 1986 and Under a Comprehensive Income Tax, 1988**

| Tax Reform Act of 1986[a] | | Comprehensive Income Tax[b] | |
|---|---|---|---|
| Taxable Income | Rate (percent) | Taxable Income | Rate (percent) |
| $0–$29,750 | 15 | $0–$5,000 | 6 |
| 29,750– 71,900 | 28 | 5,000–10,000 | 12 |
| 71,900–192,930[c] | 33 | 10,000–20,000 | 17 |
| 192,930 and over | 28 | 20,000–50,000 | 21 |
| | | 50,000–70,000 | 24 |
| | | 70,000 and over | 26 |

[a]For a married couple with two dependents. Separate rate schedules apply to single persons and heads of household.

[b]Applies to all taxpayers, regardless of marital and family status.

[c]Range within which the 13-percentage point reduction in the first bracket and the personal exemptions are phased out. Top limit of the range increases or decreases by $10,920 for each exemption.

Table 4 compares the average effective rates under this tax and the law that will apply to incomes in 1988 (when the 1986 act becomes fully effective) for various income classes. The average effective rates, which are fairly close in both cases, rise to about 24.5 percent for persons with incomes of $1,000,000 or more, a modest degree of progression by any standard.

Table 4: **Effective Individual Income Tax Rates Under Current Law and a Comprehensive Tax, Both Measured at 1988 Income Levels**

| Adjusted Gross Income[a] | Percent Current Law | Comprehensive Tax |
|---|---|---|
| 0–5,000 | −1.0 | −0.9 |
| 5,000–10,000 | 0.4 | 0.3 |
| 10,000–15,000 | 3.5 | 2.8 |
| 15,000–20,000 | 6.1 | 4.9 |
| 20,000–25,000 | 7.7 | 7.0 |
| 25,000–35,000 | 9.1 | 9.1 |
| 35,000–50,000 | 10.9 | 11.9 |
| 50,000–100,000 | 14.9 | 15.0 |
| 100,000–500,000 | 21.6 | 20.2 |
| 500,000–1,000,000 | 23.6 | 23.7 |
| 1,000,000 and over | 24.5 | 24.7 |
| Total[b] | 12.0 | 12.0 |

Source: Brookings 1983 tax file projected to 1988.

[a]Under the comprehensive tax defined in tables 3 and 4.

[b]Includes negative incomes not shown separately.

### Do tax incentives stimulate corporate investment?

There are some important issues on which economists have not reached a consensus. One of these issues is whether tax breaks have encouraged firms to increase their levels of investment in productive capital to an extent sufficient to justify the loss of tax revenue. Each side of the debate is represented in the pair of articles below.

These articles were written for the popular press. Their authors, therefore, are not writing for academic audiences with an appetite for detailed analysis leading carefully from model to hypotheses to evidence. It befalls the careful reader, then, to keep in mind the logical constructs behind the arguments presented. A mental checklist should include, among others, the following items:

☐ What implicit assumptions, especially about behavioral elasticities, lie behind the argument?

☐ What would be the ideal test of the hypothesis made? Are the data presented the ones you would most like to see?

☐ Are parts of the story being omitted? What else do you wish the author would tell you?

# THE SHAKY CASE FOR AIDING INVESTMENT[†]

*Marc Levinson**

Incentives for business investment, widely heralded by Republicans and Democrats alike when they were enacted in 1981, are on the

*former Senior Editor, *Business Month*.

†Reprinted with permission, *Business Month* magazine, March 1986. Copyright 1986 by Business Magazine Corporation, 38 Commercial Wharf, Boston, Massachusetts, 02110.

line in Washington. The tax bill passed by the House would sweep away $140 billion of these incentives between now and 1990 to pay for lower corporate and individual rates. President Reagan backs the basic thrust of the House measure and the issue is now before the Senate, where capital-intensive companies are making a last-ditch stand to preserve business tax breaks. Repeal, they warn, would decrease capital spending and reduce economic growth.

But Congress has good reason to be skeptical about the 1981 investment package. It was no bargain for the taxpayers. Allen Sinai, chief economist for Shearson Lehman Brothers, estimates that each dollar of tax revenue lost due to accelerated depreciation and investment tax credits from 1981 to 1984 generated only 51 cents worth of investment. Adds Philip Webre, an analyst with the Congressional Budget Office: "The empirical evidence just isn't there that these things have done that much good."

The 1981 Economic Recovery Tax Act, the centerpiece of the Reagan Administration's "supply-side" economic program, sought to hike investment by allowing companies to depreciate assets more quickly. The investment tax credit for plant and equipment was increased, and easier rules governing leasing encouraged money-losing companies to sell their tax benefits to profitable firms seeking shelters. A 25% tax credit was allowed for research and development costs. The changes lowered the average tax that companies paid on their profits from 42.6% in 1981 to 36.5% in 1982. A 1982 revision cut back on some breaks, but left the basic law intact.

Studies of capital investment since 1981, however, reveal no clear-cut proof that the incentives worked. Many economists argue that the growth in investment since 1981 has been due more to economic expansion than to the incentives. And the new tax breaks may not have stimulated the kind of investment and innovation Congress had in mind. Moreover, many of the arguments advanced in Congress for retaining these investment incentives are on shaky economic ground.

The strong recovery of 1983–84, which would have caused investment to soar even without tax incentives, makes it difficult to tie capital spending in the early 1980s to the tax breaks. Filtering out normal capital spending in an expansion, studies for the Federal Reserve Bank of New York, the U.S. Chamber of Commerce, and the American Enterprise Institute estimate that the business tax cuts accounted for less than one-fifth of the increase in investment from 1981–82 to 1983–84. If those estimates are correct, the tax provisions increased nonresidential fixed investment by about $14.4 billion in 1984, at a cost of as much as $23 billion in tax revenues. Says Emil M. Sunley, director of tax analysis for Deloitte Haskins & Sells: "Clearly, investment as a percentage of GNP has not followed the path that the Administration expected it to follow in 1981."

Brookings Institution economist Barry Bosworth argues that much of the increased investment that did occur was unrelated to accelerated depreciation and higher investment tax credits. He notes that office equipment and automobiles accounted for almost all of the increase in spending on producers' durable equipment between 1979 and 1984, but the 1981 tax bill did not favor investments in autos and actually reduced benefits for computers.

The reason the investment increase occurred in unintended ways, Bosworth maintains, is that no one knows exactly what types of investments the tax code favors. "It's too damn complicated to take all the provisions, net them against one another and find out what they're doing," he contends. For example, machinery receives fast write-offs and investment tax credits, while buildings get slower write-offs and no credits. But machinery is often purchased with cash, whereas buildings are financed with mortgages. Since mortgage interest is tax-deductible, the net effect may favor buildings rather than machinery.

The highly touted research and development credit did not stimulate much R&D or innovation. After surveying 110 U.S. companies, University of Pennsylvania economist Edwin Mansfield estimates the credit has increased research outlays by no more than 2%, and has generated only about 30 cents in new research for each dollar of lost tax revenue. The main reason the credit failed to boost R&D is that research costs are only a small fraction of the total expenditures for a new product. In addition, many firms that invest heavily in research have no taxable income to shelter.

One rationale for the Reagan tax program was that investment in plant and equipment was declining relative to GNP. In particular, many economists, such as Harvard University's Martin Feldstein, contended that the escalating costs of new equipment far outstripped the amount companies were allowed to deduct and therefore rapid inflation was penalizing capital investment.

This view of the effects of inflation on investment is being challenged. Studies by Robert Chirinko of the University of Chicago and Stephen King of Stanford University indicate that it had little effect on investment in the 1970s. Alan Auerbach of the University of Pennsylvania contends the investment slowdown was due largely to a lackluster economy, not to inflation.

The performance of investment in the wake of the 1981 tax cuts is not the sole basis for skepticism about the efficacy of incentives. Many academics question whether incentives promote economic efficiency in the long run.

The economic case for investment incentives begins with the argument that corporate taxes artificially depress the return to investors and therefore discourage investment. For example, a new factory may earn 13% of its investment cost annually, but an investor might clear only 8% after taxes. If subsidies— either cash payments or tax breaks—reduce the gap between the investor's return and the return to society, a more "correct" amount of investment will occur. That's why many economists of all political stripes favor replacing the corporate income tax with a consumption levy, such as a Value-Added Tax, which would eliminate this difference between the individual's return and that to society.

The conventional wisdom—at least outside the economics profession—has it that government should encourage as much capital formation as possible. But that thinking does not take into account the fact that the nation pays for capital formation by reducing current living standards. "Capital does not have any desirable properties of its own," says Harvard University economist Dale Jorgenson. "The purpose of capital formation is to make it possible to have a higher consumption path." Capital formation requires a trade-off between today's living standards and tomorrow's. The most desirable trade-off is a matter of personal preference and is beyond the realm of economic science.

Many economists and lobbyists try to avoid that issue altogether by arguing that the United States should invest the same proportion of GNP as Japan or Germany. Although this argument carries weight in Washington, there is no economic reason that the United States would necessarily be better off if it invested in the same proportion as other countries.

In fact, most of the political arguments for promoting capital formation do not stand up to rigorous economic analysis. For example, many proponents of tax breaks promise higher levels of employment. But, as Dale Jorgenson notes, most job creation is due to development of new technologies. "It seems to take place in entities that at their inception are not capital intensive and are not very much affected by tax incentives," he says.

Similarly, lobbyists cite the need to improve the international competitiveness of American firms. But if investment incentives do indeed work, they actually make the competitiveness problem worse—unless savings go up as well. By encouraging foreigners to invest their capital in the United States, investment tax breaks raise the value of the dollar in terms of marks and yen, making it harder for U.S. firms to compete with imports.

With imports at 9 percent of GNP, and foreigners having more than $175 billion invested in the United States, many of the gains from investment incentives don't go to Americans. Since so much of the capital goods industry is now located abroad, many of the new capital equipment orders go overseas. And the growing participation of foreigners in the U.S. securities markets means that if investment incentives increase corporate earnings, much of that money will flow abroad in the form of interest and dividend payments. Notes economist John Makin of the American Enterprise Institute: "If you promote investment without promoting savings, you import the savings and the fruits of the investment are earmarked for foreigners."

The need to increase productivity is still another argument put forth to justify the incentives. Much investment does increase productivity, but by no means all. For example, a company's "investment" in a car for an executive does no more for productivity than a car bought by the executive with his own money, although the latter expenditure is labelled "consumption" rather than "investment." Investments induced by tax breaks, contends Northwestern University economist Robert Eisner, will necessarily be less productive than investments undertaken without them. The latter, obviously, make economic sense in and of themselves. An investment decision that is tipped by a tax break often involves a project that is marginal.

The other major benefit attributed to investment is faster economic growth. However, pushing growth above all else means postponing consumption. In Japan, for example, the high growth rate has been accompanied by relatively modest living standards compared with those in the United States. Moreover, economists are not even certain that high investment produces high growth rates. Observes John Makin: "High rates of capital formation are not the magic elixir for higher rates of growth. Rather, the way we use capital and—something that's hard to measure— the training of human capital are more important to growth."

Some economists, notably Alan Auerbach, contend that investment incentives actually reduce economic welfare by distorting decision making. Economic efficiency is promoted by an investment that makes sense on its merits rather than one that is stimulated by a higher after-tax return. Auerbach is correct—if investors respond to incentives. But even that is a matter of dispute. "I don't see any evidence for those responses being large," says Chicago's Robert Chirinko.

The Senate is now considering the tax bill passed by the House, which lengthens depreciation periods, eliminates the investment credit and slaps a minimum tax on corporate income. It also taxes retroactively some depreciation deductions taken in the past. The measure continues to subsidize R&D for three more years, but reduces the credit to 20% from 25%.

Although lobbyists for capital-intensive companies may persuade the Senate to retain some of the incentives, this could be a Pyrrhic victory for American business. By a variety of measures, the cost of capital in the United States remains extremely high compared to levels of the past and to levels abroad. These special investment incentives, while lowering the cost of capital for some, raise the basic price of money for all businesses.

Stimulating investment has worked as a short-term measure in the midst of recession. But over the long term, the nation's economy would be better off if the underlying interest rate was lowered and investment decisions were left to the free market. Notes Allen Sinai: "What drives investment are sales and expectations of sales relative to capacity utilization. Policies that drive the economy faster will have a bigger impact on business fixed investment than any of these tax incentives."

# A FAIR TAX ACT THAT'S BAD FOR BUSINESS[†]

*Lawrence H. Summers**

The last 15 years have not been happy ones for the U.S. economy, and the 1986 tax law threatens to deepen the unhappiness. While making great progress in forging a more equitable tax system, the latest tax act will not help solve our problems of growth and competitiveness and may, in fact, exacerbate them.

In pursuit of an abstract goal of neutrality, reformers have sacrificed the principal forward-looking investment incentive contained in current law (the investment tax credit) and

*Lawrence H. Summers is professor of economics at Harvard University where he teaches courses in macroeconomics and the economics of tax policy. From 1982 to 1983 he served as domestic policy economist at the Council of Economic Advisors. He has been a consultant to the U.S. Department of Labor and the President's Commission on International Competitiveness as well as to the governments of Canada, Jamaica, Indonesia, and Mexico, and to a number of prominent U.S. corporations. He is a member of the Brookings Panel on Economic Activity and research associate at the National Bureau of Economic Research.

†*Harvard Business Review*, March-April 1987. Copyright © 1987 by the President and Fellows of Harvard College; all rights reserved. Reprinted by permission of *Harvard Business Review*.

failed entirely to address the problem of low national savings that lies at the heart of our current competitive difficulties.

My analysis of the reform package shows that it:

- Reduces incentives to save and invest.

- Gives substantial windfalls to companies with capital investment in place but few incentives to companies making new investments.

- Worsens the bias in the tax system toward intangible rather than tangible investments.

- Raises the tax rate on most classes of investments by about 20 percentage points.

- May reduce real GNP in ten years by up to 5%.

- Helps international competitiveness in the short run but weakens it in the long run, ultimately reducing the standard of living in the United States.

- Adds to, not alleviates, the burgeoning federal deficit.

While the president, Congress, and the public have been debating the details of the tax package for more than two years, they have ignored the fundamental economic issues of slow growth and rising trade and budget deficits. They have even pushed us backward in the struggle against these problems. In the long run, the product of their reform efforts will reduce U.S. competitiveness and our standard of living. It is time to work out a new economic policy that addresses the deficit and other problems and undoes the damage the 1986 tax act may well cause.

## WHAT THE ACT TRIES TO DO

While the new tax code is enormously complex and will ultimately affect almost everyone in some way, only a handful of its changes are macro-economically significant. Understanding them requires a grasp of the act's animating philosophy. (See the insert entitled "What the New Law Says.")

The basic objective of the reformers was to reduce tax rates and broaden the tax base while keeping the total level of tax collections constant, a constraint imposed by political reality, despite continuing large federal deficits. The reformers hoped to strengthen both economic efficiency and equity by taxing more income at lower rates. They argued that productivity could be increased by avoiding tax subsidies to unprofitable projects and reducing marginal tax rates and that fairness could be enhanced by limiting the use of tax shelters and imposing tough new minimum taxes.

Evaluating the tax act requires a comparison between the gains made from reducing tax rates and the losses sustained as we broaden the tax base. Certainly the new individual tax system is fairer than the former one. Removing millions of poor families from the tax rolls is a heartening accomplishment, as is the wholesale attack on tax loopholes. The assault on tax shelters is especially desirable because it prevents the diversion of scarce

savings into investment projects that are profitable only because of tax breaks, and it makes it much more difficult for affluent people to avoid paying taxes. Most important, at a time when tax cheating costs the government almost $100 billion every year, the attack on shelters will raise taxpayer morale by increasing the perceived legitimacy of the tax system.

Whether the 1986 individual reforms will increase economic efficiency is doubtful. It is not clear that reducing individual marginal tax rates will help economic performance very much. One careful empirical evaluation estimates that the rate reductions in the 1986 act will raise labor supply by only .9% for the average person in the economy (about 25 minutes a week, or about two days a year).[1]

While the generalized reductions in individual marginal rates will provide few incentives, those changes designed to broaden the tax base may do great harm. Eliminating IRA deductions for many taxpayers will probably reduce personal saving even below its current low level. Eliminating preferential tax treatment for capital gains may simplify the tax code and prevent some shelter activity, but it will also discourage investors from holding corporate equities. And it will make the capital markets less efficient by creating a "lock in," as individuals forgo recognizing large capital gains in order to avoid paying taxes on them.

On balance, the reforms affecting individuals improve tax fairness at a large revenue cost but do little to enhance incentives to work, save, and invest.

### The Chimera of the Level Playing Field

To pay for the large reductions in marginal tax rates for individuals, the 1986 act adds tax burdens on business investment. Reformers argue that the abolition of the investment tax credit and the scaling back of depreciation allowances will "level the playing field" and make the system's allocation of investment more efficient. But this argument cannot withstand scrutiny. In fact, the 1986 act will raise the cost of capital and significantly reduce investments in new equipment that might enhance productivity. It is also likely to reduce economic growth sharply over the next two decades.

Reformers advocated the repeal of the investment tax credit (ITC), the accelerated cost recovery system (ACRS), and corporate rate reductions in the name of neutrality; instead they have created a major bias in the tax system. By reducing the corporate income tax rate that applies to the profits earned on past investments while burdening new investment, the system now favors old capital at the expense of new. Even the most ardent supply-sider will acknowledge that tax incentives don't spur the creation of old capital. But they can and do have an important impact on new capital investment.

The 1986 act raises corporate tax revenues by a total of $120 billion over five years but confers substantial windfalls on capital that is already in place (see *Exhibit I*). Investment in place actually receives tax benefits totaling $68 billion, whereas the burden on new corporate capital rises by $188 billion. Biasing the tax system in favor of capital already in place

helps entrenched companies that have invested heavily in the past but will do little to spur the new investment needed for economic growth.

The reformers have focused on the wrong problem. The Reagan administration and congressional reformers have repeatedly stressed the need to equalize the tax burdens placed on different types of capital goods rather than the need to stimulate overall investment. They defend abolishing the ITC and ACRS by arguing that the tax system now favors equipment investments at the expense of other categories. The 1985 *Economic Report of the President* clearly articulated this level-playing-field argument: "The effective tax rate...is lower for equipment than for structures. Because different industries utilize different mixes of capital goods, differential taxation of assets results in differential taxation of capital income by industry. The average effective federal corporate tax rate on fixed investment varies widely by industry."

The premise that the tax system is biased in favor of equipment investment is untenable. The system has always been biased *against* such investments. Look at tax shelter activity. A prejudice in favor of equipment investment would have made it a common choice as a tax shelter. In fact, real estate investment is the most popular tax shelter, with oil

Exhibit I  **Corporate Tax Reform — New and Old Capital**
(in billions of dollars)

|                                      | 1987    | 1988    | 1989    | 1990    | 1991    | 1987-1991 |
|--------------------------------------|---------|---------|---------|---------|---------|-----------|
| Change in taxes on old capital       | $ 0.8   | $- 8.6  | $-17.1  | $-20.1  | $-23.3  | $- 68.3   |
| Change in taxes on new investment    | 24.3    | 32.5    | 39.6    | 43.5    | 48.5    | 188.4     |
| Total                                | $25.1   | $ 23.9  | $ 22.5  | $ 23.4  | $ 25.2  | $ 120.2   |

Source: Author's calculation. Taxes on new capital include capital cost, minimum tax, and some accounting provisions of the 1986 act. The tax reduction on old capital refers primarily to the corporate rate reduction.

## What the new law says

The tax bill reduces marginal tax rates on individuals and removes some 6 million people with incomes below the poverty line from the tax rolls. In an era when the government has scaled back its assistance to the disadvantaged, this is an important achievement.

Generating political support for such reductions was easy; gaining acceptance to broaden the tax base to replace the revenue lost from the reductions was not. Individual tax rate reductions and increases in the standard deduction sacrificed about $360 billion in revenue over the 1987 to 1991 period. Corporate tax rate reductions sacrificed another $116 billion.

Recouping almost $500 billion over the next five years required a number of measures that will broaden the tax base and raise:

☐ A projected $154 billion from changes in provisions affecting the recovery of investment outlays most importantly the abolition of the investment tax credit.

☐ About $200 billion from closing loopholes like corporate and personal minimum taxes, individuals deductions for tax shelter losses and accounting rule changes, revised tax rules governing financial institutions, and improved incentives for compliance.

☐ A little more than $100 billion from eliminating various incentives like deductions for IRA contributions, state sales taxes, and some employee business expenses.

and gas investment running a distant second. Unlike most types of machinery, buildings are easily transferable and can carry heavy tax-favored debt. They can be resold by their original owners and depreciated several times for tax purposes. The reformers' neutrality calculations have entirely ignored these important factors.

Proponents of the 1986 reforms have taken a narrow view of investment in alleging that equipment investments are tax favored. Contrary to their claims, large categories of investment are now subject to very preferential tax treatment. For example, the system doesn't burden owner-occupied housing, which accounts for more than a third of national wealth. Reducing the tax stimulus to equipment investment actually widens the gap between business investment and investment in owner-occupied housing.

Investments in intangibles, like research and development, advertising, marketing, or goodwill, all receive the ultimate in accelerated depreciation—expensing. Last year such investment totaled more than $200 billion—far more than companies put into industrial structures. These intangible investments may yield benefits only over time (just like capital investments), but companies can write them off in the year in which they are undertaken. Coca-Cola could fully expense all its outlays for developing and marketing New Coke. In contrast, companies must amortize outlays for physical capital over several years. Until now, the ITC and accelerated depreciation have mitigated this bias toward intangible investment, but the 1986 act will reintensify the bias.

Failure to recognize that outlays on intangibles are a form of investment accounts for the widespread misconception that the new tax law will undo the previous law's bias toward capital-intensive industries. Accounting conventions perpetuate this misconception. The ability to write off intangible investments immediately, while amortizing tangible investments in calculating net income, means that reported profits of companies with heavy investment in intangibles are understated relative to those of capital-intensive businesses, and their tax burden, therefore, appears larger.

Since there has never been any quantitative demonstration that neutrality is important for economic growth, the reformers' fixation on this belief is regrettable. A recent study of Don Fullerton, deputy assistant secretary for tax policy, finds that the tax reform changes made in 1986 will raise GNP by less than 1 percent, even after the capital stock has been fully adjusted. That translates into gains in economic efficiency of only several tenths of a percent of GNP each year—less than the statistical discrepancy in the GNP accounts![2]

## REFORM & GROWTH

Reformers have suggested that investment incentives should be scaled back because they do not work. This is not a fair reading of recent history. We have lived through a period of unusually high real interest rates, large federal deficits, and increasing foreign competition. If they had been asked several years ago, most observers would have predicted that this combination would crowd out investment to an unprecedented degree. Yet business fixed investment has proven remarkably robust during the current recovery, and it has grown more strongly than one might have predicted during such a cycle. Indeed, the share of gross business fixed investment in GNP reached its postwar high in 1985. It has fallen off over the last 12 months as it became clear that the investment tax credit would be retroactively repealed.

No one can claim accuracy in predicting the consequences of the tax bill for business investment decisions, but some tentative judgments are possible. *Exhibit II* shows the effective tax rate on various classes of investment under previous law and under the 1986 act. The tax bill raises the effective tax rate on most classes of investment by about 20 percentage points and increases the rate of return

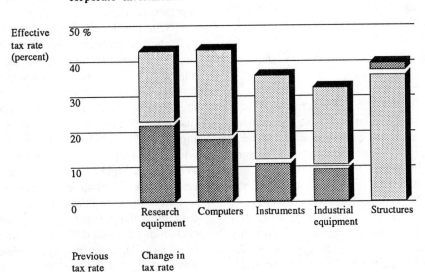

Exhibit II  **Effective tax rates on corporate investments**

Effective tax rate (percent)

Previous tax rate

Change in tax rate

required on a typical investment project by 10% to 15%. In the long run, this may well reduce the stock of plant and equipment by 10% to 15% and reduce the economy's potential output by about 3%.

Beyond this direct impact, shrinking capital investment will slow the rate of technical progress in the economy and this could indirectly reduce real GNP by another 2% or 3% over ten years. It is reasonable, therefore, to estimate that the 1986 act will reduce real GNP in 1996 by up to 5%.

## Competitiveness Problems

The issues of GNP growth are closely linked to international competitiveness. These links may be better perceived by understanding some fundamental truths of economics:

• A nation's trade balance is equal to the difference between its national savings and investment.

• When investment exceeds savings (as has recently happened in the United States), countries must borrow from abroad.

• Because the balance of payments must balance, the mirror image of the United State's rising surplus on the capital account must be a current account deficit.

• Therefore, we must export less than we import.

This is a straightforward economic conclusion. Capital inflows raise the demand for dollars and the exchange rate. In turn, American producers of tradable goods become less competitive in world markets.

Ironically, and perversely, the 1986 act may actually increase the competitiveness of U.S. industry in the short run. It will, as I have argued, reduce investment and probably will not much affect national savings. So for the time being, the trade balance will improve.

Reduced investment incentives will make investing in the United States less attractive to foreigners (as well as to us). With less capital flowing in (and more flowing out), the dollar will continue to weaken and make exports cheaper and imports more expensive.

To improve competitiveness through a reduction in investment is shortsighted. In the long run, with less modern equipment at their disposal, U.S. workers will be less productive. Lower productivity means a lower standard of living. Simply exporting as much as we import is not enough. Countries like Brazil and Argentina, whose economic performance we do not envy, meet this standard. The challenge for economic policy is to achieve balanced trade as well as improvement in the standard of living.

The only way we can simultaneously raise investment and international competitiveness is to increase national savings. There is no alternative. If we don't do this, we will have to finance higher investment from abroad at the expense of improving our trade balance. Reducing the flow of funds from abroad will bring the dollar down and improve our trade balance, but it will also lead to higher interest rates and reduced investment unless we increase savings.

Our low level of national savings poses still another problem. Because we save less than our foreign competitors, the supply of capital to U.S. businesses is lower and its cost higher. The contrast with Japan is most striking (*Exhibit III*). Besides the direct competitive disadvantage this situation imposes, the differing costs of capital help explain the myopia for which our companies are so often criticized. With much higher costs of capital, it makes sense that U.S. business executives give more weight to the present than the future. The 1985 data imply that a manager here would trade 37 cents today for one dollar six years from now, whereas a Japanese manager would trade 66 cents.

Exhibit III: **The U.S. Cost-of-Capital Problem 1985**

|  | Real Interest rate | Price-earnings ratio | Cost-of Capital |
|---|---|---|---|
| United States | 6.6% | 8.5% | 12.9% |
| Japan | 3.2 | 3.8 | 8.4 |

*Source:* George N. Hatsopoulos and Stephen H. Brooks. "The Gap in the Cost of Capital: Causes, Effects and Remedies" In *Technology and Economic Policy,* Ralph Landau and Dale Jorgenson (Cambridge, Mass.: Ballinger, 1986). Price-earnings ratios are from statistics published during 1985 in *Capital International Perspectives.*

## Savings Problems

Raising the national savings rate is the key to achieving the twin goals of greater growth and competitiveness. In the last few years, national savings have plummeted. While the savings rate never fell below 4.5% between 1950 and 1981, it dropped to an anemic 2.9% of GNP in 1981, and it has never regained earlier levels. We face a cruel choice between borrowing from abroad—with the associated dislocations in the traded goods sector—and scaling back investment.

Dissaving by the federal government is clearly the main reason for today's low national savings rate (see *Exhibit IV*). While net private saving has remained roughly constant and declined slightly during the 1980s, federal deficits have mushroomed. Exceeding 4% of GNP in each of the last five years, the deficits have substantially reduced national savings and, in the process, reduced investment and increased the deficit in the current account.

The 1986 tax act does little to address our chief economic problem—the low level of national savings that large federal deficits have caused—and may well intensify it. Designed to have no effect on the deficit, the new law may well lose revenue and increase the deficit.

Exhibit IV: **National Savings, National Investment, and the Trade Deficit (Percent of GNP)**

|  | Federal Savings | Other Savings | Net Invest-ment | Current Account Deficit |
|---|---|---|---|---|
| 1971-1980 | −1.8% | 8.8% | 6.7% | −0.2% |
| 1981 | −2.1 | 7.8 | 5.5 | −0.3 |
| 1982 | −4.6 | 6.6 | 2.0 | 0.0 |
| 1983 | −5.2 | 7.1 | 3.1 | 1.0 |
| 1984 | −4.5 | 8.7 | 6.6 | 2.4 |
| 1985 | −4.9 | 7.8 | 5.6 | 2.9 |

*Source: Economic Report of the President, 1986*

The new bill will inevitably drive households out of tax shelters, so that over time the gains made from limiting deductions will be smaller than forecast. My guess, and it is only a guess, is that the tax bill will end up losing as much as $20 billion in revenues a year by 1990. Even if this opinion proves too pessimistic, the reforms willl not solve the federal deficit problem.

Nor will the tax bill help increase private savings. It limits the attractiveness of IRAs and other forms of tax-sheltered savings. By adding to the corporations' tax burden, the bill will reduce retained earnings and thereby directly reduce savings. This impact will not be offset by extra personal saving engendered by the reduction in personal income tax collections, since consumers spend an overwhelming fraction of the income they receive. Finally, the tax bill will reduce private saving because the increased tax burden on capital income will tend to depress posttax rates of return.

## WHERE DO WE GO FROM HERE?

My diagnosis points to the need for increased tax collections to help reduce the deficit and restore investment incentives. Almost any tax boost would be desirable over the next several years. But the most attractive method would be new federal taxes on consumption, either through value-added taxes, sales taxes, or business transfer taxes. Each of these options taxes consumption in the same way; they differ only with respect to where in the distribution channel the tax is collected.

In the context of our current problems, consumption taxes:

• Do not reduce incentives but do encourage savings and help increase American competitiveness.

• Can generate great potential revenue while preserving low tax rates.

• Offer some important equity advantages and, unlike our current taxes, burden people based on what they withdraw from the economy, not on what they contribute.

Skeptics have argued that the consumption tax is a "money machine" that would fuel government spending. Given the present enormous budget deficit, Congress is unlikely to dedicate any large portion of a tax increase to new spending programs. In fact, we could legally dedicate new tax revenues to deficit reductions by modifying the provisions of the Gramm-Rudman legislation to prohibit spending of any such revenues.

Skeptics also argue that consumption taxes hit the poor harder than the rich. We can address this concern by excluding necessities and providing income tax rebates for the working poor. Most important, the alternatives to a tax increase—slow growth and declining competitiveness—also hurt the poor.

Raising consumption taxes would significantly increase national savings and go a long way toward alleviating our national growth problem. The rate of national savings and productivity growth are closely related (see *Exhibit V*). During the past 20 years, France and West Germany have had about twice the net investment rate of the United States and enjoyed twice as great a productivity growth rate. Japan has invested three times as much as we have and enjoyed almost three times as great a productivity growth rate. Of the most important OECD nations, only the United Kingdom has suffered an investment and productivity growth rate as low as ours.

The Tax Reform Act of 1986 made the tax system fairer and eliminated a number of significant abuses. But it did not address the national savings problem, and it compromised future economic growth by scaling back investment incentives. Clearly, we need a "Taxation for Growth and Competitiveness Act" in 1987.

Exhibit V    **Savings and economic growth**

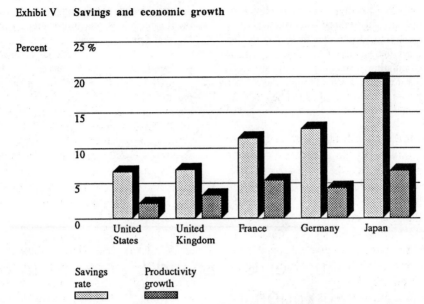

Savings
rate

Productivity
growth

## Notes

1. Jerry Hausman and James Poterba, "Individual Taxpayers' Response to the 1986 Tax Act," forthcoming in *Journal of Economic Perspectives*. For a more pessimistic view about the effects of a change in tax rates on labor supply, see the stud-

ies surveyed in Mark Killingsworth's *Labor Supply* (Cambridge, England: Cambridge University Press, 1983).

2. Don Fullerton and Yolanda Henderson, "The Impact of Fundamental Tax Reform on the Allocation of Resources." National Bureau of Economic Research working paper no. 1904, 1986.

## QUESTIONS

1. On which of the following issues do Levinson and Summers disagree? In each case of disagreement, do they look at different data or simply interpret the same general measures differently?
(a) More investment means more growth.
(b) Tax breaks to investment are uneven across kinds of investment, and abolishing the ITC will reduce the resulting distortions in the kinds of capital invested in.
(c) It is important that we increase national savings.
(d) Repealing investment incentives helps reduce the trade deficit, at least in the short run.

2. Exhibit 1 in Summers suggests that the average effective tax rate on corporate investments before the

1980 reforms was about 20 percent. This implies that an investor kept four-fifths of the return on the investment. To make a $1.00 investment attractive, the investment must generate an economic return of $1.25, one-fifth of which goes to the government.

Levinson estimates that $23 billion in tax revenues were foregone to generate $14.4 billion of investment. At a tax rate of .20, what do you estimate was the pretax value of this investment? If $1.00 in tax revenue can be invested by the government in a project worth exactly $1.00, does this simple cost-benefit exercise support the tax breaks?

3. Economists largely agree that temporary taxes or tax breaks lead people to change the timing of their activities. Summers reports that gross business fixed investment's share of GNP was exceptionally high

in 1985 and much lower in 1986. He attributes the high level in 1985 to tax incentives and the low level in 1986 to the removal of those incentives.

If you're trying to interpret these data to figure out whether tax breaks make a good long-run policy for stimulating investment, it matters a lot whether or not investors in 1985 thought there was a good chance the tax breaks would soon be repealed. Explain why this is so.

4. Along with increased investment, we should try to increase national savings, it is argued.

(a) Retirement is one important reason for saving. Do you think moving to a funded Social Security system would increase national saving?

(b) People are saving when they buy homes. Does the tax code promote this kind of saving? Is housing the "wrong kind" of capital to be creating if our concern is economic growth and competitiveness abroad?

# Further Issues and Questions In Federal Taxation

## Sin taxes.

Facing an atmosphere of righteous indignation over any new taxes, legislators can find it tempting to raise needed revenue through "sin taxes" on socially undesirable consumption goods. Although there is protest when Congress debates extra cigarette taxes, it is hard to be too righteously indignant over the cost of a harmful activity that produces such smelly and unhealthful externalities. Sin taxes are minor revenue sources in contemporary America; the Soviet Union, however, taxed alcohol so heavily that, prior to production cutbacks in 1984, taxes from alcohol sales were enough to fund half the Soviet defense budget.

Political expedience is only one reason for sin taxes. Tobacco smoke and drunken driving are negative externalities, so taxing tobacco and alcohol may lead to their consumption at more efficient levels. One may also invoke considerations of fairness. This newspaper article suggests that some people feel the right level of sin taxes is one that covers the government's costs of dealing with the negative consequences of the "sins."

# WHITE HOUSE STUDY SAYS SIN-TAX BOOST MAY BE JUSTIFIED BY HEALTH-CARE COSTS†

*Paul Blustein\**

WASHINGTON—A confidential analysis by the White House budget office contends the cost to government of dealing with smoking- and drinking-related health problems could justify a major rise in "sin" taxes on tobacco and alcoholic drinks.

The analysis makes no recommendations, but it apparently is designed to provide the Reagan administration a rationale to accept a boost in excise taxes on cigarettes and liquor.

Congress has been moving, albeit hesistantly, toward raising those taxes. The analysis says increasing the revenue from tobacco and liquor consumption could be viewed as raising "abuser fees" to finance federal health

\* Staff reporter of *The Wall Street Journal*

† Reprinted with permission, *The Wall Street Journal*, June 1, 1987, p.48, Copyright 1987 by Dow Jones & Company Inc. All Rights Reserved.

programs rather than as a general tax increase, which President Reagan strongly opposes. The term "abuser fee" is a humorous reference to user fees for government services, which the president favors.

In his toughest anti-tax talk to date, Mr. Reagan vowed last Thursday to veto any tax increase that Congress passes. But top administration officials have been hinting for months the president might acquiesce to excise-tax boosts and other revenue-raising measures that don't blatantly violate his campaign pledge to resist higher taxes.

Budget Director James Miller earlier this year told a Senate panel he would favor an increase in the cigarette tax, currently 16 cents a pack, if he saw evidence that the economic costs to society of smoking outweigh the tax take. Mr. Miller emphasized, however, he wasn't sure whether the cigarette tax is too high or too low, and he said his office hadn't done any studies of the issue.

The budget office analysis was prepared by some of Mr. Miller's senior staff members and presented to the budget chief several weeks ago. Edwin Dale, spokesman for the budget office, declined to comment on the analysis or on Mr. Miller's reaction to it.

The analysis, citing academic and other studies, estimates the federal government spends $7.7 billion a year on health care because of illness attributable to smoking, but raises only $4.5 billion from tobacco excise taxes.

It also says the federal government spends $8 billion a year on health care because of illness and injuries attributable to alcohol, but raises less than $6 billion from taxes on beer, wine, and spirits.

Officials who have seen the analysis said it describes a number of other options, besides raising excise taxes, that the government could pursue—including assessing smokers and drinkers higher medicare payroll taxes.

But Walker Merryman, a spokesman for the Tobacco Institute, cited quite different results from a recent study by Virginia Baxter Wright, an economist at Eastern Kentucky University.

"Her conclusion is that if people quit smoking, the government's health-care costs *would increase* because people would live longer," Mr. Merryman said. "If you assume that smoking kills people at an early age, then they end up not using Medicare, Medicaid, and Social Security benefits."

Mr. Merryman stressed the economist's conclusions were her own and were "not something that I can say because then I'd be saying smoking kills people."

John De Luca, president of the Wine Institute, also dismissed the budget office analysis, citing studies showing moderate drinking helps prevent heart disease.

"There's a cholesterol content to meat and eggs. Should we raise excise taxes on meat and eggs?" he asked.

Janet Flynn, director of public affairs for the Distilled Spirits Council, declined to respond directly to the budget office analysis but added: "A tax increase is still a tax increase. President Reagan said he was against any form of tax increase, and we share the president's view.

"If you increase excise taxes on beer in order to serve a health question, you are penalizing 95% of the drinkers who are not causing any problem at all," she said.

A. Achieving efficient levels of economic activity depends on balancing costs and benefits at the margin. The argument here suggests that excise taxes should raise (total) revenue equal to (total) costs to the government from the negative effects. Imagine for a moment that the government's costs accurately reflected levels of externalities. Under what conditions (what shapes of marginal and average external damage curves) would this criterion lead to an efficient level of consumption?

B. The government's costs attributable to smoking and drinking do not measure externalities. They are largely health care costs for the consumers themselves. Two questions arise.

(1) If consumers are rational and informed, might the availability of government medical insurance encourage smoking and alcohol abuse? If so, does this suggest a rationale for sin taxes even in the absence of externalities?

(2) Consumers may not be fully informed. Do Mr. Merryman's remarks suggest that some smokers may not yet acknowledge the medical evidence on the ravages of smoking?

C. "Sin" can be a trendy commodity. With the financial world's reputation clouded by scandal, House Speaker James Wright suggested in March 1987 a transfer tax (essentially a sales tax) on stock trades. Might this be more progressive than most sin taxes?

## Itemized deductions and tax progressivity.

Do itemized deductions reduce the progressivity of the personal income tax? This item from *The Wall Street Journal's* Tax Report column provides some data.

Average Deductions on 1985 returns look like this—for comparison only.[*]

Publisher Research Institute of America figured these averages from fresh IRS statistics on 1985 returns that claimed deductions. Just remember that deductions must be substantiated; these numbers aren't audit-proof. And note that only 10.7 million returns claimed medical deductions.

The averages by adjusted-gross-income group for medical, tax, charitable-gift, and interest deductions are:

| Income (−000) | Medical | Tax | Gift | Interest |
|---|---|---|---|---|
| $ 20– 25 | 1,713 | 1,830 | 809 | 3,220 |
| $ 25– 30 | 1,379 | 2,133 | 800 | 3,591 |
| $ 30– 40 | 1,639 | 2,696 | 891 | 4,121 |
| $ 40– 50 | 1,727 | 3,483 | 1,105 | 5,243 |
| $ 50– 75 | 2,799 | 4,750 | 1,575 | 6,730 |
| $ 75–100 | 5,550 | 6,492 | 2,538 | 10,038 |
| $100–200 | 8,497 | 11,043 | 4,237 | 14,419 |

*Reprinted with permission. *The Wall Street Journal,* April 8,1987, p.1. Copyright 1987 by Dow Jones and Company, Inc. All rights reserved.

A calculator would be helpful in answering these questions.

A. Use the midpoint of each income range to determine whether the deduction for charitable giving represents a generally increasing, decreasing, or constant share of income. (Some studies have found the relationship to be U-shaped.) Repeat these calculations for the deduction of state and local taxes.

B. Progressivity requires that the deductions bring tax savings that represent a decreasing fraction of income as income rises. Use the 1988 tax rates (see Rosen's "The Marriage Tax Is Down But Not Out," table 1 in Part VI) for single taxpayers to find the effect of charitable deductions on the progressivity of the income tax.

## Asset markets and the changing tax treatment of capital gains.

In competitive markets, the tax treatment of income generated by an asset should be reflected in the asset's price. The 1986 tax reform eliminated preferential treatment of realized capital gains. This was bad news for owners of assets designed to produce capital gains income.

A. Corporations issuing stock to the public must decide how big a dividend to pay. When capital gains were taxed favorably, it made more sense (to economists, anyway) for a firm to avoid paying taxable dividends by keeping their profits and letting the value of the stock rise (a capital gain) to reflect the retained earnings. After realized capital gains became taxed as regular income, what changes would you have predicted in:
   (1) The size of dividend payments from firms already paying dividends, and
   (2) The number of firms not paying dividends?

B. Now imagine a corporation or individual deciding whether to buy a baseball team. As described by Rosen (*Public Finance*, 2nd edition, p. 439), a big chunk of what you're buying is the contracts guaranteeing that the team's players will play for you. Since these contracts are short, baseball teams are assets that are allowed rapid depreciation. New contracts are negotiated later, of course, and when you decide to sell later on the team is worth much more than its depreciated tax value. This excess value is capital gains, and under the pre-1986 tax law only 40 percent of this was taxed.

(1) What do you predict happened to the selling price of baseball teams after the favorable treatment of capital gains was eliminated?

(2) To test this hypothesis empirically, what other things would you want to control for?

# PART VIII

# Deficit Finance

### How much should we worry about budget deficits?

The official deficit measures the difference between the government's revenues and expenditures in a given year. In everyday discussions, the deficit is often interpreted as an erosion of our financial position; it is seen as the increase in our national indebtedness. Is this really what the deficit measures? Should we look at both assets and debts when we worry about our financial status? The articles in this section address these questions. Jules Prag gives a general overview of public concerns about the deficit and the statistical evidence that supports or refutes these claims. Robert Eisner deals with defining the deficit in ways that measure meaningful changes in our national financial health. Michael Boskin and J. Gregory Ballentine debate the wisdom of accounting for federal investment projects in a separate capital budget.

# THINKING ABOUT GOVERNMENT DEFICITS I:

## Domestic Ramifications

*Jules B. Prag\**

When governments spend more than they raise through taxation, they are running a deficit. Like households, governments can spend more than their income by borrowing against future income. President Reagan drew the analogy between households and governments in many speeches saying that individuals (and most

\*Assistant Professor of Economics, Claremont McKenna College.

state and local governments) balance their books and the federal government should do the same. This comparison is appropriate, but the president misspoke. Households make many purchases (homes, cars, many durables) by borrowing rather than depending entirely on contemporaneous income. Similarly, state and local governments, which balance their operating budgets, have budgetary processes that allow them to borrow for long-term projects.

Many of the publicly stated problems of budget deficits do not stand up to empirical investigation. Describing the potential problems of running deficits requires a broad-based look at the federal government's budget process and the microeconomic as well as macroeconomic effects of taxation and government expenditures. Since many of the potentially important effects may lie in the international sector, we must expand the traditional analysis of budget deficits to include their impact on exports and imports; this is done in the second part of this analysis.

## THE SIZE OF THE DEFICIT

The total federal deficit for 1986 was $220.7 billion, implying that the government had to raise that amount of money by selling bonds (issuing new debt). To get some perspective on the size of the deficit, it is slightly more than 5 percent of the GNP for 1986. In the period 1970-1980, the deficit averaged about 1.9 percent of GNP.

Determining who buys this debt is crucial in the analysis of the effects of federal deficits. These bonds could be purchased by our citizens, state and local governments using their tax revenues, the Federal Reserve using new money, or foreign citizens. If our citizens buy the bonds, they can substitute government bonds for private ones, thus lowering private business purchases (the Keynesian story). They might instead increase their savings by the amount of the deficit because they know future taxes will be greater (the neoclassical story). If state and local governments use their surpluses to purchase federal debt, the federal government is allowing these governments to raise revenue for them. Federal Reserve purchase of government bonds will increase the money supply and this can cause inflation. And bond purchases by foreign citizens represent an unambiguous outflow of goods in the future when our children must repay the debt.

## DOMESTIC EFFECTS: KEYNESIAN ANALYSIS

The most frequently cited problem of government budget deficits is that they displace private business purchases because increasing the deficit raises interest rates. This effect, known as "crowding out," can be seen by imagining a fixed supply of funds available for potential borrowers. These loanable funds come from the savings of our citizens. In the closed economy, savings must equal borrowing by all entities, so we have:

$$Savings = Investment + Government\ Deficit$$

Investment in macroeconomic analysis is the term used for all business purchases. These are assumed to be made directly or indirectly with borrowed funds and are therefore inversely related to interest rates. The deficit is the excess of government purchases plus transfer payments over the government tax receipts.

If the economy's savings pool is constant, because the economy is at its potential GNP and savings depends only on the level of GNP, then any increase in the deficit will come at the expense of business investment. The increase in the government deficit is seen in credit markets as an increase in the demand for a fixed supply of funds. This will raise the rental rate of these funds, the interest rate, sufficiently to displace an equal quantity of private borrowing.

For those familiar with macroeconomic IS-LM analysis, the experiment being conducted is an increase in government outlays or a decrease in taxes at full employment (potential) GNP. This would cause a shift to the right of the IS curve and eventually a shift to the left of the LM curve as prices rise and the real money supply falls. Interest rates would rise exactly enough to crowd out investment equal to the increase in the deficit.

An important question in the deficit debate for those who believe that crowding out occurs is whether crowding out guarantees that deficits are harming the economy. Suppose the government uses deficit financing to build highways or to fund NASA or national defense; these are projects that we know have future returns but that private entrepreneurs will not generally provide due to free rider problems or other market failures. Thus, even though private investment has been crowded out, the economy is not necessarily worse off. If the social value of the government project exceeds the value of the private project that was crowded out, the economy is better off. Deficit-financed government expenditures might even "crowd in" additional investment as future economic growth prospects improve. Modern macroeconomic research along this line can be seen in Barro (1981).

With this in mind, it should be noted that in some circumstances deficit financing is economically superior to taxation. For projects such as highways, NASA, and defense, which have at least some of their benefits in the future, deficits allow costs and benefits to be matched over time. Thus, the argument that by running deficits we are mortgaging our children's future must be reconciled with the fact that we are also providing them with assets such as roads, education, and freedom. This point will come up again when we discuss state and local governments.

Aside from allowing us to match costs and benefits over time, deficits also allow the government to minimize the tax burden that would be associated with any period of inordinately large government expenditures. The federal government's principal methods of raising revenue are through income and payroll taxes. Since these taxes lower the take-home pay workers receive for an hour's work, they distort workers' labor supply decisions. If the government raises tax rates to pay for a short-run increase in expenditures, workers will face an income and a substitution effect from this tax rate hike. Since rates are temporarily higher, take-home pay is lower and the cost of an extra hour of leisure time tem-

porarily falls. The substitution effect then says they will work less. But at all levels of work, higher tax rates make them poorer and they will consume less of all normal goods, including leisure. This income effect leads to more work when tax rates are increased. If the substitution effect exceeds the income effect, raising tax rates will lower work effort and overall output. The effect of temporary tax rate increases could be minimized by using deficits to spread the required tax increase over time. While this use of deficits is theoretically important, empirical evidence indicates that the substitution effect is fairly small and not substantially larger (if at all) than the income effect for U.S. workers (see Pencavel, 1985).

In discussing crowding out, we have assumed that deficits do indeed raise interest rates and lower private investment. In fact, many of the empirical studies of deficits do not find a positive correlation between them and interest rates. (See Evans 1985, 1986, 1987a, 1987b; Plosser, 1982.) Similarly, the relationship between the deficit and investment is not unambiguous. For example, in the period 1982-1986 the deficit rose from $128 billion to $220 billion, but net domestic investment also rose from $383 billion to $455 billion, both achieving all time highs in this period. It is hard to draw conclusions from such data because the economy moved from recession to boom during the same period. If deficits do not cause high interest rates and crowd out private investment, some changes in standard Keynesian macroeconomic theory must be considered or other sources of loanable funds must be included in the model.

## STATE AND LOCAL BUDGETS

Aside from selling bonds to private citizens, the federal government might fund its deficit by selling bonds to state and local governments. During the period 1982-1986, when the federal budget saw record deficits, the state and local government budgets were in surplus overall. In 1986, these entities had a $60.8 billion surplus. Summing over all levels of government leaves a deficit of $160 billion. Only this net amount had to be raised by issuing debt publicly. When this correction is made, recent government deficits are still historically high but much closer to other years since 1960. When state and local surpluses exist together with federal deficits, the federal government is in effect using property and sales taxes to raise revenue. These are the principal means, along with income taxation, of state and local revenue collection.

Another important aspect of state budgets is their balanced budget requirements. The majority of states have some form of balanced budget requirement, but they have provisions for issuing debt to fund specific long-term projects. You will often see bond issues for specific projects such as sewer systems or water works. States balance their "operating" budget but not their "capital" budget. This distinction was being implicitly made in the discussion of federal deficits, but the federal budget has no such distinction in reality. Any sensible federal balanced budget law would have to make such a distinction lest one generation be forced to pay high taxes for government investment projects that will have their benefits in future years. The difficulty with making this budgetary distinction at the federal level is how one classifies human capital social programs such as college aid and welfare. Their direct benefits seem contemporaneous, yet their desired benefits are clearly long term. Deciding whether these should be funded with taxes or debt specifically is a complicated problem.

## DEFICITS AND MONEY CREATION—THE INFLATION PROBLEM

A frequently decried problem of deficits is that they cause inflation. This scenario is most likely when the deficit is funded with new money. Since the Federal Reserve has the exclusive right to issue the money we all use in daily transactions, the government could make deficit purchases by selling bonds to the Fed in exchange for new money. This increase in the money supply must raise prices if it does not increase national output because the higher government purchases must crowd out private purchases. Consider the following example.

There is one good in the world, grapefruit, and the supply of them is fixed at 1000 per year. The money supply is $1000, which is used entirely each year to buy and sell grapefruit. Thus, the price of grapefruit is $1. Now suppose the government wants to acquire some grapefruit, and it prints $100 in new money to do so. Prices in equilibrium will rise to $1.10, and the government, using its privilege as the provider of money (known as seignorge), can acquire 91 grapefruit without taxes or publicly issued debt.

Printing money and raising prices to make government purchases is a roundabout form of national sales tax, which reduces consumption. Strictly speaking, inflation means a persistent increase in prices rather than a one-time rise. This scenario could be repeated on a yearly basis with constantly rising prices equal in percentage to the percentage of grapefruit the government wants to acquire.

While "monetizing" the debt will lead to inflation, most empirical evidence finds no recurrent use of this deficit financing tool in the United States. There are some dramatic examples of governments using this method when debts cannot be adequately funded otherwise. In post-World War I Germany, the government debt due to war reparations was funded through money creation. The German inflation rate between 1914 and 1923 was 126,160,000,000,000 percent (126 trillion percent).

It should be noted that a government with a large cumulative debt (the sum of each year's deficit) has a short-run incentive to raise the money supply, cause inflation, and lower the real value of the outstanding debt. This strategy will cause future problems for the government since the risk of repeating this trick will add a risk premium to the return on future government bonds. At the extreme, the government will be completely unable to issue new debt, as in post-World War I Germany.

## NEOCLASSICAL ANALYSIS

If the primary concern of traditional macroeconomists—crowding out of private investment—cannot be empirically documented, we must consider alternative macroeconomic theories and their predictions about the effects of deficit spending. An important alternative to Keynesian macroeconomic theory is represented by the neoclassical school of thought. Much of the neoclassical research on the effects of deficit spending was done by Professor Robert Barro of the University of Rochester.

In his seminal work, "Are Government Bonds Net Wealth?", Barro (1974) argued that deficit-financed tax cuts, keeping government expenditures unchanged, should have no effect on the level of real interest rates, investment, GNP, or any other real measure of economic activity. This theory is known as Ricardian Equivalence and is named for David Ricardo, the nineteenth-century British economist, who first stated that the choice of debt versus taxes to finance government expenditures should be irrelevant to the level of real activity in the economy.

The basic concept behind Ricardian Equivalence is that economic agents (people) take their entire lifetime's income into account when making decisions about consumption and savings. A deficit-financed cut in taxes would be viewed by such agents as merely a redistribution of taxes over their lifetime. Knowing they will pay higher taxes in the future to repay the deficit, they save the tax cut instead of spending it. Thus, the Keynes-

ian notion that investment must be crowded out because the increased deficit is competing with a fixed pool of savings is not the case here because savings is assumed to rise one-to-one with the deficit. Because savings rises, interest rates do not and investment is not crowded out.

Perhaps a simpler way to see Ricardian Equivalence in action is to consider our simple grapefruit economy again. People have 1000 grapefruits available each year to divide between consumption, savings, and taxes. Let us assume taxes are lump sum so there will be no substitution effect on labor of tax changes (recall empirical evidence indicated this was quite small anyway, so using income taxes should give similar results). The government will need 100 grapefuits per year for foreign aid programs. Individuals choose to save 100 grapefruits, which are used by entrepreneurs as investment to create future goods (ground up and used to fertilize the trees). If we start by assuming the government uses taxation to get its goods, we can calculate consumption as:

$$Consumption = Income - Savings - Taxes$$

So consumption will be 800 units. Now suppose the government decides to lower taxes to 50 units and acquire the 50 remaining units by borrowing. Individuals know that future taxes will rise by 50 plus interest; thus, they will need to save their tax cut in order to repay the bonds. The best way to do so and be sure you have exactly enough to pay the higher taxes is to buy the new government bonds. Thus, savings will rise by an amount equal to the deficit. Investment won't be crowded out because agents won't change their rationally chosen decisions about how much to give entrepreneurs merely because the government renamed its method of procurement. Everyone knows the government is going to take 100 units, and whether they call the taking taxes or bonds is irrelevant. This neoclassical view of behavior contrasts with the Keynesian notion that by using bonds instead of taxes people *feel* wealthier, consume more today, and, instead of raising savings, decrease private investment.

The empirical work on this theory is unfortunately no more convincing than the work that tests the Keynesian approach. We have already stated that there is little support for the notion that deficits crowd out investment or raise interest rates. But the critical test of Ricardian Equivalence is whether savings rise with the deficit. Recently, while the deficit has risen, most measures of savings have fluctuated without clear direction. As the next article by Eisner makes clear, one difficulty in this research is defining the deficit in the appropriate way, that is, as a change in future tax liabilities.

# References

Barro, Robert J., "Are Government Bonds Net Wealth?" *Journal of Political Economy*, November/December 1974, 82, 1095-1118.

_____, "Output Effects of Government Purchases," *Journal of Political Economy*, December 1981, 89, 1086-1121.

*Economic Report of the President*, Washington D.C.: United States Government Printing Office, 1987.

Evans, Paul, "Do Large Deficits Produce High Interest Rates?" *American Economic Review*, March 1985, 75, 68-87.

_____, "Is the Dollar High Because of Large Budget Deficits?" *Journal of Monetary Economics*, November 1986, 18, 227-249.

_____, "Interest Rates and Expected Future Budget Deficits in the United States," *Journal of Political Economy*, February 1987a, 95, 34-58.

_____, "Do Budget Deficits Raise Nominal Interest Rates? Evidence from Six Industrial Countries," forthcoming *Journal of Monetary Economics*, 1987b.

Pencavel, John, "Labor Supply of Men: A Survey," in O. Ashenfelter, ed., *Handbook of Labor Economics*, Amsterdam: North-Holland, 1985.

Plosser, Charles I., "The Effects of Government Financing Decisions on Asset Returns," *Journal of Monetary Economics*, May 1982, 9, 325-352.

# WHICH BUDGET DEFICIT?

## Some Issues of Measurement and Their Implications[†]

*Robert Eisner**

A budget deficit is like sin. To most of the public it is morally wrong, very difficult to avoid, not always easy to identify, and susceptible to considerable bias in measurement.

To the body politic, and perhaps also to many economists, the apparent underlying reality is that every dollar of deficit—of a person, business or government—adds a dollar to debt. And debt is bad!

In commentary on that last, I like to recall pleasurably the late Sumner Slichter, a respected conservative economist of at least a generation ago. Churlishly responding to a pressing questioner on a TV program, he suggested increasing debt could be very good; he would generally counsel young people to go into significant debt to buy homes.

More- and less-sophisticated economists have long come to recognize a number of measures of federal budget deficits and their varied implications. Deficits are not always bad, or at least at certain times their alternatives are worse. And we must distinguish among cyclical deficits, structural deficits and high employment deficits, to name a few. But matters are more complicated than many of us have thought to note. We do not usually measure government budget deficits in economically relevant fashion. When we do, we can get results at variance from much conventional wisdom. Just consider the following sketchy set of issues.

1. Should we have included in the fiscal 1983 budget deficit of $195.4 billion some $17 billion of outlays of off-budget federal entities largely to finance direct loan programs? In fact, we did not.

2. As of the end of the 1982 fiscal year, the Treasury listed "contingency" obligations which totalled $6,982 billion, largely for retirement pay and Social Security. Should

*William R. Kenan Professor of Economics, Northwestern University, Evanston, IL 60201. I am indebted to Paul Pieper for his contribution to joint work on which this paper leans heavily.

†AEA Papers and Proceedings, May 1984. Reprinted by permission of *American Economic Review*.

we try to estimate the year's increase in present value of obligations, net against them the increase in present value of anticipated associated receipts, and add that remainder to the deficit? We do not.

3. In general, when the federal government incurs a liability in order to acquire an asset, whether borrowing to make a loan or to acquire real capital, should we net the additional asset from the additional liability in calculating our deficit? Federal investment-type outlays have been estimated by the Office of Management and Budget at $182 billion fiscal 1983. Should the federal government, like private business and state and local governments, have separate capital and current budgets? It does not.

4. We all know that inflation plays huge tricks on conventional accounting. Paul Pieper and I (1984) have estimated that adjusting for changes in the real market value of federal financial assets and liabilities would change the high-employment budget surplus by large *and varying* amounts, ranging between 2.86 percent and -0.18 percent of GNP in the years 1969 to 1982. Adjustments would be broadly similar for actual budget deficits. Should we make inflation adjustments? We do not.

5. The $195.4 billion deficit for fiscal 1983 cited above, we are told, is a historical record for the United States. We have never had a budget deficit that large. And it is anticipated by the Congressional Budget Office that if no corrective action is taken (even assuming that defense spending will grow at a rate of "only" 5 percent after inflation, lower than administration requests) the deficit will rise to about $250 billion in fiscal 1988 and $280 billion in 1989. But so what? What do these mind-boggling numbers mean? Gross National Product in calendar 1983 will be over $3,300 billion, and, by 1989, according to

one set of forecasts, it will be in excess of $5,400 billion. Should we perhaps recognize that in an economy in which everything is growing—output, income, liabilities, and assets—a quite substantial deficit may leave ratios of financial assets and liabilities in our government and national balance sheets unchanged? We generally do not.

6. With all the questions relative to knowing what budget deficits are or have been, problems are vastly compounded in forecasting deficits in budgets yet to be realized. As is well known, huge portions of federal receipts and expenditures are endogenous, determined not merely by decisions as to rates of expenditures and taxes, but by economic and demographic developments, and, indeed, interactions between the budget and the economy. We can perhaps forecast how many people will be in each category eligible for Social Security, but we do not know how many will choose to draw benefits rather than continue working. What assumptions should we make about employment, unemployment, real growth, inflation, corporate profits, and so many other lesser variables which will so critically affect future budget deficits? Should we have a single forecast of these variables, agreed upon by Congress and the administration, so that differences in deficit estimates and predictions can be separated from differences in underlying assumptions? We do not.

7. Finally, how do differences among the measures of budget deficits, past and prospective, relate to their possible impact on the economy? Have we considered which are relevant for the various issues of so much concern—inflation, employment, investment, consumption, distribution of income, role of government, incentives, efficiency, and the allocation of resources?

Having sketched out a set of questions, I shall be so bold as to offer some comments, including even a few numbers on which to reflect.

## I. OFF-BUDGET ITEMS AND CREDIT EXTENSION

Off-budget items relate almost entirely to credit extension, generally by the Federal Financing Bank to federal lending agencies. It has been argued that direct off-budget loans advanced under federal auspices, $14 billion in 1982, plus a portion of guaranteed loans (the total of which was $21 billion in 1982, and estimated at over $50 billion in 1983) represent unrecognized contributions to the true budget deficit.

Clearly, federal loans or loan guarantees that result in private expenditures which would not otherwise be undertaken must be recognized, aside from possible substitution effects, as augmenting aggregate demand. I should caution, however, against viewing them as, except possibly in small part, elements of a budget deficit in most, economically relevant senses. For Treasury borrowing to finance loans to the public, directly or indirectly, except as a second-order effect, adds neither to the net debt of the federal government nor the net financial assets of the public. (To the extent that the federal government borrows at the market rate of interest but lends at a below-market rate, it is, however, acquiring loan assets whose market value is less than the market value of its liabilities.) Hence (except for the parenthetical qualification), these off-budget federal borrowings do not have the essential wealth effects on consumption usually attributable to true budget deficits.

By another criterion as well, that of net claims on credit markets, federal borrowing to finance loans to the public would also qualify very partially, if at all, as components of a relevant budget deficit. For while, on the one hand, the Treasury borrowing draws on the public supply of credit, the Treasury or agency lending offers an essentially equivalent offset by meeting some of the public demand for credit.

## II. CONTINGENCY EXPENDITURES

Constructing a budget of "contingency expenditures" and associated receipts may well be a useful exercise. The relevant numbers, as we have suggested, are enormous, as may be the associated deficits (or surpluses). I should object, however, to incorporating measures of year-to-year increase in net contingent liabilities in current budget deficits. Proclamations (usually intended to be alarmist) of huge net contingent liabilities and accruals to these net liabilities which might be considered annual deficits are in fact highly conjectural. What expenditures or outlays will finally be will depend frequently upon legislation of the future. Similarly, associated receipts will depend upon future legislation as well as highly uncertain economic and demographic developments. And how to balance projected expenditures and receipts depends further on uncertain and changing rates of discount.

An interesting and major case in point is the whole matter of Social Security, on which many have become exercised. We have been told that huge increases in net Social Security debt were having a major impact on aggregate consumption and saving. But after the initial sensationalist articles and arguments, a number of works (including my 1983 article) raised fundamental doubt as to the existence of any clear, measurable impact. And finally, in a few strokes of legislation, the balance between contingent expenditures and contingent liabilities was changed drastically. Who could even say accurately that the public over the last several decades has perceived annual increases in net Social Security wealth? And who can argue persuasively that they are perceiving such increases now?

## III. CAPITAL BUDGETS

Failure to separate current and capital expenditures in the formal federal budget and the associated failure to account systematically for capital assets contributes to confusion in economic analysis and consequent formulation of policy. It does make a difference whether a budget "deficit" finances transfer payments, current services, accumulation of stocks, or long-term investment. For example, the argument, to which I give little weight, that public perception of assets in the form of government debt is offset by anticipated associated tax liabilities, is negated to the extent that real income-producing government assets lie behind the debt. Federal capital accounts might of course well relate, further, not only to investment in physical assets owned by government, but to investment in the human capital and the private and public resources of the nation.

Objection to separating out capital expenditures from the current federal budget seems to stem considerably from concern that any resultant lowering of measured budget deficits would reduce resistance to excessive government spending. Aside from the ideological and unsubstantiated nature of the premise, however, there is no reason why, as I shall illustrate below, separate current and capital accounts cannot be combined to reach a bottom line showing precisely the unified budget deficit to which so much attention is now given. The separate subtotals, though, would give us a better clue as to the extent government was leaving a burden for future generations or building the houses—and other assets—that Sumner Slichter recommended for the young.

## IV. INFLATION ADJUSTMENTS

The failure to account separately for capital expenditures quite breaks the publicly perceived connection between a budget deficit and spending beyond our means or squandering the public treasure. Recurring budget deficits have in fact been accompanied by *in*creasing federal net worth, as noted in my article with Pieper. What has also until recently been remarkably underplayed, if not ignored, is that in periods of inflation our conventionally measured budget deficits are accompanied by *de*creasing values of real federal net debt. The "underlying reality...that every dollar of deficit...adds a dollar to debt" is simply not true in a real sense if price levels are not constant. And if interest rates fluctuate, the statement is not true even with reference to the market value of nominal debt. Adjustments of the official budget deficit to make it correspond to changes in net financial liabilities entail interest rate effects on market value of federal financial assets and liabilities and price or inflation effects on the real values of the corrected market values.

In general, we may write the adjusted or corrected deficit as

$$D_C = D - \dot{P}_A A + \dot{P}_B B - \dot{P}(B + M - A)$$

where $D$ = the "official deficit," $A$ = federal financial assets (excluding gold), $B$ = federal interest-bearing liabilities held by the public, $\dot{P}_A$ and $\dot{P}_B$ = the relative (weighted average) rates of price change of $A$ and $B$, respectively, $\dot{P}$ = the inflation rate, $M$ = non-interest-bearing federal liabilities held by the public, essentially "high-powered money" or the monetary base, and $B + M - A$ = the "net debt."

As noted in my article with Pieper, the corrected deficit is vastly reduced and frequently converted to surplus in years of rapid inflation and rising interest rates (hence falling bond prices). The real federal net debt as defined above hence fell enormously since

World War II, declining in per capita 1972 dollars from $3,694 at the end of 1946 to $1,445 by the end of 1980, despite a heavy preponderance of officially measured budget deficits in the intervening years.

What is more, turning to the high-employment deficit as a first-order measure of fiscal thrust, while the official measure of generally increasing deficit through the 1970s and up to 1981 suggested a stimulatory fiscal policy, the corrected measure showed quite the opposite. The severe recession of 1981 and 1982 was associated with high previous surpluses in the interest- and price-corrected high-employment budget—2.2, 1.8, 1.6, and 2.0 percent of GNP in the years 1978 to 1981. Interestingly, the recovery of 1983 is well accounted for by the sharp 1982 move to a deficit equal to 1.8 percent of GNP in the corrected high-employment budget; this was the product of a growing official deficit, slowing inflation and lower interest rates.

Recent work of Alex Cukierman and Jorgen Mortensen (1983) suggests that inflation corrections call for similar drastic revisions in perceptions of fiscal policies in Western Europe. In particular, the United Kingdom and Italy, with high official budget deficits, turn out to have had very low budget deficits, or even surpluses, after correction for inflation, perhaps accounting for their high unemployment rates. By contrast, the corrected budgets in West Germany, with relatively low rates of inflation and little or no net government debt, were sufficiently in deficit to have been stimulatory, possibly accounting for the low unemployment and rapid growth in Germany.

## V. EQUILIBRIUM GROWTH

Whatever our measure of the deficit in dollars, pounds, lira, or marks, to what is it relevant in a large, changing, and generally growing economy? Recent work has suggested some apparent—if dubious—paradoxes involving deficits and rates of growth of interest-bearing

securities and "money." We may get some needed perspective by exploring briefly one, simple overall relation. Netting out the acquisition of financial assets, essentially the off-budget items discussed above, we may write the official deficit as $D = \dot{B} + \dot{M} - \dot{A}$. Then, denoting $\gamma = (B + M - A)/Y =$ the ratio of net debt to GNP, and $g = \dot{Y}/Y =$ the rate of growth of GNP, it is readily apparent that $D/Y = \gamma g$ is the "equilibrium" condition for a stable ratio of net debt to GNP.

With the current value of $\gamma$ in the United States approximately 0.3 and the growth of GNP in nominal terms about 10 percent, one notes that the "equilibrium" value of $D/Y$, far from zero, is some 0.03. Thus, at current or immediately anticipated rates of growth, we can accommodate an official deficit of 3 percent of GNP without increasing the relative debt burden. In fact, the deficit for fiscal 1983 ran closer to 6 percent of GNP, but it may be argued that this was largely a cyclical deficit and the structural or reasonably high-employment deficit would be considerably less.

Ignoring interest rate effects, we may write for our inflation-corrected "equilibrium" budget deficit ratio, $D_c/Y = \gamma(g - \dot{P})$ or, more precisely, $D_c/Y = \gamma n$, where $n = (1 + g)/(1 + \dot{P}) - 1$. With $\gamma = 0.3$ and a real rate of growth, $n = 0.03$, an inflation-corrected budget deficit that would keep the ratio of net debt to output constant at its current value of 0.3 would then be in the order of 0.9 percent of GNP. This is in the neighborhood of the current price-adjusted high-employment deficit. Congressional Budget Office projections of an official high-employment deficit approaching 4 percent of GNP by 1988 would imply, on the basis of the concomitantly assumed 5 percent rate of inflation, however, a price-adjusted deficit ratio of some 2.5 percent. Such an *adjusted* deficit might well prove unsustainable. Relations estimated by Pieper and me suggest that resultant inflation and increases in debt would widen the gap between official and adjusted deficits until the latter were back at a more modest, equilibrium level.

## VI. CONCLUSION—A VARIETY OF DEFICITS

A few definitions and associated dollar figures for 1982 can help bring all this together. In Table 1, we note a variety of budgets or accounts to be considered. From them one can concoct a very large variety of deficits, only a subset of which are listed in Table 2. Some will be of greater relevance for certain purposes and some for others.

The current budget deficit, D1, would be most consistent with the more usual private business and state and local government measures, but the current adjusted deficit, D4, would be more economically relevant. In terms of macroeconomic policies for high-employment and stable price paths, my preference would go to D6, the national income account adjusted deficit, which would essentially indicate the change in net debt of the

federal government to the public. As remarked above, in the years leading up to 1981, inflation and rising interest rates had both contributed to reducing national income adjusted deficits sharply or even converting some to surplus, but there was a marked shift in the correction in 1982.

We might also keep a close eye on D7, which would include price or inflation adjustments but not the (partially related) sharply fluctuating interest effects on the market value of debt. For a bottom line on the long-run trend in government activities we might regard D8 and D12, the changes in net worth and "total net worth," the latter including contingent assets and liabilities. We should indeed, for many purposes go much further and recognize the intangible wealth to which government ostensibly contributes by expenditures for research and development, education, and health.

What about D3, the official national income account budget deficit (or its unified budget twin)? We may as well continue

Table 1: **A Variety of Budgets**

| Account (1) | Credits (2) | Debits (3) | Deficit[a] (4) |
|---|---|---|---|
| A. Current | 617 | 744[b] | 127 |
| B. Capital | 43[c] | 63[d] | 20 |
| C. National income | 617 | 764 | 147 |
| D. Net revaluations of Financial capital | −10 | 11 | 21 |
| D*. Price component | −28 | −61 | (34) |
| D**. Interest component | 18 | 72 | 55 |
| E. Net revaluations of Tangible capital | 9 | — | (9) |
| F. Off-budget($\Delta V$) | 18 | 17 | (1) |
| G. Contingent[e]($\Delta V$) | −390 | −256 | 134 |

Note: Calendar 1982 unless otherwise indicated; $\Delta V$ is change in value of balances, and parentheses indicate surplus.

[a]Col. 4 is col. 3 minus col. 2.

[b]Includes capital consumption allowances and $701 billion in current outlays.

[c]Capital consumption allowances.

[d]Capital expenditures.

[e]Fiscal 1982.

Table 2: **A Variety of Deficits**

| Deficit Components[a] (Designation) | Deficit[b] (1) | (2) |
|---|---|---|
| D1 = A (Current) | 126.7 | 4.1 |
| D2 = B (Capital) | 20.4 | 0.7 |
| D3 = A + B = C (national income) | 147.1 | 4.8 |
| D4 = A + D (current adjusted) | 147.8 | 4.8 |
| D5 = A + D* (current prices–adjusted) | 93.1 | 3.0 |
| D6 = C + D (NI adjusted) | 168.1 | 5.5 |
| D7 = C + D* (NI prices–adjusted) | 113.4 | 3.7 |
| D8 = A + D + E (net worth) | 139.1 | 4.5 |
| D9 = C + F (NI plus off-budget) | 146.1 | 4.8 |
| D10 = C + F + G (total) | 280.1 | 9.1 |
| D11 = C + D + F + G (total adjusted) | 301.1 | 9.8 |
| D12 = A + D + E + F + G (total net worth) | 272.1 | 8.9 |

Note: Calendar 1982, except for D10, D11, and D12, which includes the G component for fiscal 1982; NI = National Income

[a]As designated in Table 1.

[b]Col. 1 is billions of dollars; col. 2 is percent of GNP.

to calculate it. We need the basic data in orderly form, and we should have the series for continuity. But it may not merit prime focus. If we are concerned with economic analysis and consequences, we should not be shy about looking further.

# References

Cukierman, Alex and Mortensen, Jorgen, "Monetary Assets and Inflation Induced Distortions of the National Accounts— Conceptual Issues and Correction of Sectoral Income Flows in 5 EEC Countries," *Economic Papers* No. 15, June 1983, Commission of the European Communities, Directorate-General for Economic and Financial Affairs, Internal Paper.

Eisner, Robert, "Social Security, Saving, and Macroeconomics," *Journal of Macroeconomics*, Winter 1983, 5, 1-19.

Eisner, Robert and Pieper, Paul J. "A New View of the Federal Debt and Budget Deficits," *American Economic Review*, March 1984, 74, 11-29.

# DOES WASHINGTON NEED A NEW SET OF BOOKS?

## Capital Budget Is a Useful Tool...[†]

*Michael J. Boskin\**

President Reagan has made reform of the budget process, including a line-item veto and balanced-budget amendment, his highest domestic policy priority for the next two years. Several years ago he called for moving federal credit activity onto the budget, and his director of the Office of Management and Budget, James Miller, has wisely revived the call for a separate capital budget.

With capital budgeting, there would be two budgets, a capital and an operating budget, with capital spending placed in the capital budget and a charge for depreciation and obsolescence of the capital stock taken onto the operating budget.

There is a fear that a separate capital account will lead to unnecessary spending, as proponents of specific capital projects delight in the capital spending excluded from the current services budget and deficit. I believe the opposite is the case. First, anyone can add two numbers. The borrowing to finance investment spending will not be hidden. A capital budget properly implemented can bring capital investment spending under control and help us plan for future maintenance and repair costs, development and financing.

## NOT WELL INTEGRATED

Some limited amount of capital budget information is already presented by the federal government, but this is not well integrated conceptually or practically in the budget, per se, and certainly not in the budgeting and appropriations processes.

The federal government's accounting procedures differ greatly from generally accepted accounting principles (GAAP). The unusual features of federal government accounting

*Mr. Boskin, a professor of economics at Stanford University, is author of the forthcoming "The Real Federal Budget" (Harvard University Press).

include a cash rather than accrual basis, failure to separate capital and current accounts, and the exclusion of a variety of items.

Consider what this would mean for the financial reporting of some of our best-known corporations. General Motors had one of the most profitable years in automobile history in 1984. However, if General Motors treated its huge investment expenditures as current expenses, it would have reported a large net loss.

SeaFirst Bank Holding Co. reported a $180 million loss in 1982. Over $100 million of this loss was an increased loan loss provision for expected future losses. If the bank had followed government accounting procedures, recording only net loan losses that actually occurred in 1982, it would have been slightly profitable in 1982.

Our current budget prevents us from properly anticipating future cost. For example, in most years our budget reports negative spending on deposit insurance, as it nets current spending and revenue. In fiscal 1982, in the depths of the recession and at the height of the debt crisis, our budget reported that spending on deposit insurance was a negative $1.4 billion; spending and the deficit were reduced by $1.4 billion, although we probably accrued $20 billion in future payouts.

The need for more comprehensive financial reporting by the federal government has long been felt by accounting professionals. The comptroller general recently issued a report outlining some of the possibilities. Arthur Andersen & Co. periodically provides a very rough cut at "sound financial reporting for the U.S. government," and argues for using GAAP. It estimates that the approximately $200 billion deficit for 1984 would amount to $333 billion under GAAP (the primary difference is the accrued addition to unfunded Social Security liabilities). It estimates total federal liabilities as $4.7 trillion and total assets as $937 billion. My own research indicates this systematically underestimates the value of the assets and inappropri-

ately values liabilities, but it highlights the fact that ignoring these factors can be misleading.

There are many technical problems in implementing a capital budget; some arbitrary decisions will have to be made. But that is true for GAAP in general and the accounting of private firms as well.

And the need for change is great. The federal government capital investment is almost $100 billion, and it has sometimes reached 20 percent of total on-budget spending (a larger fraction of purchases of goods and services). Congress often approves these projects without reviewing meaningful cost-benefit data.

The advantages of a properly implemented capital budget are many: a uniform government-wide policy regarding cost-benefit analyses, such as discount rates and actuarial assumptions; understandable estimates of current and future costs and better-informed choices among capital projects; a more open budget process that decreases the public-works pork barrel, as future maintenance and repair costs would be brought out into the open; more systematic evaluation of capital projects vs. current operating programs. A capital budget, if properly implemented, would thus improve the budget as a reporting, control, accounting, priority-setting and fiscal-policy instrument.

But just separating the investment spending is no guarantee that the investment will have sufficient social returns to merit public financing. There is no substitute for systematic cost-benefit analysis, since the federal government does not undergo a market test that would value the outcomes of the political process. There is no capital market analogous to the stock market, which provides an independent check on the wisdom of capital investment decisions of private firms.

## OTHER IMPROVEMENTS

Thus, capital budgeting, while potentially quite useful, could also be abused. It must be tied to other improvements, such as multiyear budgeting, a line-item veto, and some sensible fiscal-policy rule such as budget balance for current operating expenditures over a time frame longer than a typical business cycle.

The likely benefits of a federal government capital budget substantially exceed the expected costs. It is no panacea for our budgetary woes. It will not eliminate the deficit, nor will it guarantee better spending decisions. But it is potentially valuable as part of an overall package of structural budget reforms that would improve the efficiency of government.

# ...That Special Interests Will Abuse[†]

*J. Gregory Ballentine**

Economists in government are often told that their clever ideas sound good in theory but will not work in the real world. Unfortunately, this is often true. Government fine-tuning of the economy sounded good in theory; in practice it was a disaster. A capital budget for the federal government is the latest "sounds-good" theory that, if adopted, will wreak havoc.

The federal budget is essentially a cash budget. Investment expenditures (such as the

*Mr. Ballentine is a principal with Peat, Marwick, Main & Co. From 1983 to 1985 he served as an associate director for economic policy at the Office of Management and Budget.

purchase of an aircraft carrier) are treated in the same way as current expenses, such as farm-price support payments or interest outlays. Capital-budget proposals would separate the federal budget into two components: an operating budget, much like a private firm's profit and loss statement, and a capital budget, much like a firm's balance sheet. The cash outlay for an aircraft carrier would affect only the capital budget, while current depreciation on the aircraft carrier would appear on the operating budget.

In theory, separate operating and capital budgets give a much clearer picture of the true federal budget and the true budget deficit. Government borrowing to finance current operations—like a firm's borrowing continuously to meet current payroll and expenses—is a sign of trouble. Such deficit financing drains private saving to finance current consumption. Government borrowings to finance public investments, however, need not be a sign of trouble, just as borrowing by a firm to purchase productive assets is not necessarily troublesome.

Of course, many government investments may be nearly worthless—synfuel investments come to mind—but if wise investments are chosen, then a sound fiscal policy would require a balanced operating budget and a capital budget financed by borrowing. In the 1950s and 1960s, for example, such a sound fiscal policy would have balanced the operating budget, but allowed for borrowing—deficit finance—to pay for the construction of the interstate highway system. Such borrowing shifts the cost of paying for the roads to future taxpayers who benefit from the roads when they are completed and in use.

The capital-budget idea sounds good in theory. Why not have the federal government's accounts kept like business accounts with a distinction between current expenses and investments? The problem is how that distinction will be made in practice. In the private sector the distinction between current expenses and capital outlays is established by the marketplace, generally accepted accounting principles, and an independent accounting profession. In the federal government, the determination of whether outlays are placed on the capital or operating budget will be based on political considerations.

Anyone who believes politicians will separate current outlays and capital outlays along objective, intellectually sound principles should note the writings of the most recent Nobel laureate in economics, James Buchanan. The clear incentive for the proponents of each spending program would be to have their program classified as a capital outlay so that it would not have to be paid for by current taxes and would not count against the deficit. The political system will decide

which outlays are which in a way that helps to achieve the goals of various interest groups. As a result, the capital budget will become a new and massive form of off-budget spending.

The conversion of the capital budget into a general receptacle for favored spending programs need not rely on blatant misrepresentation of programs. Objective principles would have outlays for dam projects count as capital outlays; they are investments (though many may not be worthwhile) and would be off the operating budget. But there are other, less clear examples. It is not difficult to imagine proponents of expanded federal spending on education arguing that such spending is an investment in America's future, and there is some validity to that argument. How long will it take for many to argue that agricultural spending is an investment in a way of life that is important to our heritage? Similarly, environmental programs will become investments in our ecology.

The argument that the federal budget should be set up analogously to private firms' profit and loss statements and balance sheets ignores the fact that the cash-flow federal budget is primarily needed as a resource-control mechanism over a system that is prone to vast overspending. The potentially better information from separate operating and capital budgets is already largely provided by Special Analysis D of the federal budget, which separates investment and operating outlays. The key point is that Special Analysis D is *only* an information document. In contrast, the official federal budget is the basis for congressional-appropriations decisions. Cash accounting is needed for that budget to make it easier to hold public officials accountable for their appropriations of taxpayers' cash. Separate, official capital, and current-account budgets may provide better data on the true deficit, but, in the real world, such budgets will become a tool to hide and expand spending.

While the most needed improvements in the budget process—a balanced-budget amendment and a line-item veto—are not related to the cash-budget issue, there are steps that also should be taken to improve the cash budget. In spite of his public reputation as a trickster with budget figures, David Stockman made a lasting contribution to federal budgeting integrity by striving to bring more off-budget spending on budget. That effort should continue. Further, programs such as loan guarantees that provide subsidies without current-cash outlays should be redesigned to require current-cash outlays, thus putting the subsidy explicitly on budget. In the case of guaranteed loans, for example, the government should be required to purchase private loan insurance for the borrower, rather than guarantee the loan directly.

The general thrust of cash-budget accounting reform should be to make the cash budget more all-encompassing. This will let the federal budget accounts better accomplish what they should do: hold officials accountable for taxpayer dollars.

## QUESTIONS

1. How is it possible that deficit financing might, as Prag suggests, "crowd in" private investment? Would even more private investment be "crowded in" if the same government projects were financed by taxation?

2. Prag reports that the deficit in 1986 represented 5 percent of GNP. According to Eisner, is this large enough to increase the relative debt burden?

3. Eisner's corrected deficit makes three adjustments to the official deficit, as shown in his first equation. Explain verbally what each of these adjustments is. Which, if any, might be relevant in the absence of inflation? Explain.

4. Deficit spending is often viewed benignly when it is used to accumulate assets. Eisner's Table 1, account B, gives the capital account figures for 1982, a high-deficit year. Was the government adding to its capital stock?

5. Which of the following would you place on a capital budget?
(a) Federal funding for expanded science laboratories at selected universities.
(b) Federal funding for supplementing faculty salaries at selected universities.
(c) Federal costs of administering the student loan program.
(d) Federal tuition grants to low-income students.
(e) Subsidy costs of school lunch programs.
(f) Cost of the federal food stamp program.

# Further Issues and Questions in Deficit Finance

### *Government investments and the savings rate.*

As we saw in the Levinson-Summers discussion of tax incentives for business investment, there is a chronic worry that the United States saves too little. To support this view, proponents often point to the difference between U.S. savings rates and those of our international competitors, such as Japan. But the United States is alone among major industrial nations in not having a capital budget for its federal government, and this affects measured savings rates.

Income is either consumed or saved. If government saving, via government investment projects, is included in measured consumption instead of saving, show that the measured savings rate is too low by an amount $S^g/Y$, where $Y =$ income and $S^g =$ government saving. Government nonresidential investment in 1985 has been estimated at roughly $150 billion. 1985 GNP was about $4 trillion ($4000 billion).

A. How much do we increase the savings rate if we use these measures of investment and income?
B. Summers reports 5.6 percent as the savings (investment) rate for 1985; how big is your adjustment above as a proportion of the measured rate of 5.6 percent?

### Public choice theory and budget deficits.

The theory of public choice predicts legislators will support projects with benefits concentrat-

ed among their constituents and costs diffused over a larger group.

A. What does such behavior imply for the likelihood of generating significant budget deficits?

### A little revenue is a dangerous thing?

Regressing the deficit as a fraction of GNP on taxes as a share of GNP shows that deficits have risen with the level of taxation.

A. Would you conclude that higher taxes lead to higher deficits?
B. State an alternative hypothesis consistent with this piece of statistical information. Do the two hypotheses have any differences in their implications that you might be able to test empirically? Explain.

# PART IX:

# Fiscal Federalism

---

**Issue:** *Do state and local taxes need to be deductible in order to avoid harmful tax competition among jurisdictions?*

*"Tax Competition: Is What's Good for the Private Goose also Good for the Public Gander?"* Charles E. McLure

*Further Issues and Questions in Fiscal Federalism*

**Issue:** *Eliminating the deductibility of sales taxes.*

**Issue:** *Tax turf.*

**Issue:** *Heterogeneous communities and locally provided goods.*

*Do state and local taxes need to be deductible in order to avoid harmful tax competition among jurisdictions?*

One way states and cities can compete as locations for taxpaying residents and businesses is by keeping taxes low. Since state and local services depend on tax funding, one might wonder whether such "tax competition" might lead to inefficiently low levels of government spending.

In this article, McLure argues that, under certain circumstances, tax competition, like most economic competition in general, can be efficiency enhancing. The view that cities compete for residents and business in an efficient way is the foundation of the Tiebout model of city formation. All views of competition among towns must begin with the assumptions that factors are mobile across jurisdictions and hence can be competed for and that information about the competing locations is easily available and processed. To some extent, these assumptions are probably better approximations to the behavior of businesses, on which McLure focuses, than to the behavior of individuals.

# TAX COMPETITION:

## Is What's Good for the Private Goose Also Good for the Public Gander?[†]

*Charles E. McLure**

## I. INTRODUCTION

During the debate on the Treasury Department's proposals to President Reagan for tax reform (1984), and later in the discussion

*Economist, Hoover Institution, Stanford University.

†National Tax Journal, vol. XXXIX, no. 3. September 1986. Reprinted with permission.

of the President's Proposal (1985), opponents of the elimination of the itemized deduction for state and local taxes often pointed out that eliminating the deduction would cause increased tax competition between states and localities. I did not agree that this self-evident statement provided dispositive proof that deductibility should be maintained; rather,

I said "good," and pointed out that competition among governments should produce the same kinds of benefits in the public sector that we commonly associate with competition among private firms. Of course, the issue is somewhat more complicated than that, and in this paper I examine the pros and cons of the tax competition argument somewhat more systematically, if not dispositively.

At least four lines of reasoning suggest that tax and spending decisions by subnational governments may not be optimal.[1] First, spending may be less than would be required for welfare maximization (as indicated by the failure to achieve a Pareto optimal solution) because of spillovers of benefits between jurisdictions. Second, even if there are no spillovers, if a) property taxes and other taxes on capital are employed to finance government spending that does not benefit production and b) capital is mobile between jurisdictions, tax competition may result in suboptimal levels of expenditures. Third, in the absence of competition between jurisdictions, politicians and bureaucrats may act against the best interests of their constituents, as predicted by the Leviathan model.[2] Finally, interstate migration based on fiscal considerations may be excessive, because of the congestion migration creates.

In my remarks today I want to discuss briefly the implications of the first three of these theories for the costs and benefits of tax competition and/or the deductibility of state and local taxes.[3] In addition, I will direct some concluding remarks to the treatment of the deductibility issue in the tax reform package that was recently endorsed unanimously by the Senate Finance Committee.

## II. TAXATION OF MOBILE CAPITAL

I have been quite surprised—not to say flabbergasted—by much of the formal literature that presumes to examine the supposed adverse effects of tax competition. At the risk of sub-stantial oversimplification, I would describe the problem addressed in much of that literature in the following terms. Suppose that the spending of subnational governments benefits primarily residents of the various jurisdictions, but is financed by a tax on capital that is geographically mobile, presumably via the local property tax or state corporation income tax. In such a situation the mobility of capital between jurisdictions results in tax competition, as the various jurisdictions attempt to avoid driving out business, which would reduce the productivity of labor or employment in the jurisdiction (or both). Tax competition, in turn, results in suboptimal expenditure by the subnational jurisdictions.[4]

The implication that is commonly drawn from this conclusion, either explicitly or implicitly, is that tax competition is undesirable and should be avoided. Wildasin (1986) likens the effects of tax competition to those of benefit spillovers, suggests that a federal subsidy of as much as 40 percent might be appropriate to compensate for the externality, and thereby prevent tax competition and sub-optimal public expenditures. He notes (p. 19), however, that the subsidy provided by existing intergovernmental grants is large enough that "there is only a weak case for further subsidies on fiscal externality grounds." An alternative way to reduce tax competition would be a federal credit for some portion of state and local taxes.[5] This line of reasoning has also been seized upon by advocates of the deduction for state and local taxes to justify their position.[6]

I suspect that virtually all serious economists who write on this topic realize that there is a fundamental objection to this line of reasoning. Surprisingly, they seldom give it prominence, though Oates and Schwab (1985) do so quite clearly and Wildasin has done so in his latest paper (1986). Recall that the issue being examined is whether or not tax competition causes suboptimal spending on public services by subnational governments *if* benefits for residents of the taxing jurisdiction must be financed by taxes on capital that is mobile between jurisdictions. That spending should be suboptimal under these circumstances is hardly surprising. In the extreme case this amounts to asking whether spending on school lunches in Gloucester, Massachusetts would be optimal if financed entirely by a property tax on the fishing fleet docked there.[7] I suspect that most of us would agree that competition from neighboring harbors (in the markets for both fish and dock facilities) would prevent the cost of school lunches in Gloucester from being borne by either consumers of fish or (except in the very short run) owners of boats. Rather, one would expect that boats would be docked elsewhere, little revenue would be collected by Gloucester, the burden of the tax would be borne by owners of the least mobile factors in Gloucester, and school lunches would be supplied at suboptimal levels in Gloucester. If we further constrained all competing harbors to finance school lunches only in this way, without collusion, tax competition would induce underspending in all the fishing centers.

Most of us would not, however, conclude from this simple example that tax competition was the basic cause of suboptimal spending or that such competition should be dampened by providing a federal subsidy to offset the local taxes on fishing fleets. Rather, we would conclude that policies such as this would, at best, be second-best responses forced on us by the adoption of a patently idiotic scheme for the finance of school lunches.[8]

The first-best solution from an allocative point of view would be to charge market prices for the lunches, rather than trying to cover their cost through the taxation of an entirely different and mobile activity. Standard microeconomic analysis would suggest that in the absence of external costs and benefits, and subject to the usual assumptions underlying such analysis, charging those who eat the lunches (or their parents) for the cost of providing them would cause an optimal quantity of lunches to be provided. If, contrary to the basic assumption of much of the litera-

ture of tax competition, the financing of state and local public services reflected more accurately the benefits of such services, the case for reducing tax competition via federal subsidies would be weak and perhaps vanish.[9] Indeed, in a world of user charges and benefit taxes the existence of such subsidies would worsen the allocation of resources, rather than improving it, by reducing the cost of such services to state and local beneficiaries/taxpayers and causing over-production of the subsidized activity.

The natural question to ask at this point is whether it is realistic to suggest that user charges and benefit taxation could be used much more in the finance of the services provided by state and local governments. Even if one agrees that beneficiaries of public services should be charged for benefits received to the extent possible, it is clear that a great proportion of the expenditures of state and local governments must be financed through taxes, rather than through fees and charges. But this does not imply that the case for reducing tax competition has been proven.

Taxes levied by state and local governments could—and should—reflect more closely benefits received by taxpayers. Property taxes levied on homeowners almost certainly reflect the benefits of public education more closely than do those levied on commercial and industrial property.[10] Similarly, individual income taxes and sales taxes probably correspond more closely to benefits of public services than do state corporation income taxes. I submit that greater reliance on these broadbased taxes paid by individuals, and less on taxes imposed on business that do not reflect benefits, would be both feasible and appropriate.[11] If that first-best approach were taken, the second-best question of whether tax competition is good or bad would have substantially less urgency.

Even if there were a shift to greater reliance on taxes that better reflect benefits provided to individuals, on average, the question of tax competition would still arise. Tax competition might, for example, cause migration from jurisdictions whose taxes on families with high incomes and/or no children exceed the value of public services provided to such families. Again, attempting to prevent tax competition in such a case would be a misguided second-best policy. As in the case of non-benefit taxes levied on mobile capital, the more appropriate response would be to adopt financing techniques that reflected even more closely the benefits of public services.

More problematical is the case in which pure public goods (in the Samuelsonian sense) are provided to business. Since the quantity of such services received by a particular business would be largely independent of its own tax payments, tax competition can be expected to result in under-provision of such services.[12] I do not believe, however, that this is the basic problem of tax competition that has motivated much of the recent furor over ending deductibility; in any event, such competition would be reduced by deductibility of taxes on business. Even if a conscious effort were made to shift to taxes reflecting benefits received, including appropriable benefits to business, taxes would be levied on business capital or income. In such cases deductibility would be appropriate—but because all business costs should be deductible, not to reduce tax competition, per se.

## III. BENEFIT SPILLOVERS

Spillovers of benefits between jurisdictions that do not cooperate in the financing of public services will ordinarily be underprovided.[13] For example, no single city has a substantial incentive to finance research on cancer if it believes that its citizens will benefit from the results of research financed elsewhere. The usual prescription for activities such as this is to have them conducted— or at least financed—by a higher level of government that can internalize the benefits that

may be largely external to any given smaller jurisdiction. An alternative is to provide categorical matching grants that reflect the ratio of expected external benefits to total benefits from the activity in question.

Though this particular source of suboptimal spending is not ordinarily identified as resulting from tax competition, two alternative approaches that would reduce tax competition could, at least in theory, move independent subnational decisions closer to the optimal level. First, the federal government could provide credit for a fraction of subnational taxes devoted to the finance of the activity generating inter-jurisdictional spillovers. This is, of course, tantamount to providing a categorical matching grant for such expenditures. Alternatively, all jurisdictions could agree to levy a certain minimal level of taxes for the support of the activity generating spillovers. This would be nearly equivalent to federal imposition of such a tax, with funds earmarked for expenditure on the activity in various jurisdictions. This approach suffers from the practical disadvantage that an agreement between jurisdictions not to compete lacks the enforcement features of either federal taxation and expenditure or a federal matching grant or credit for state taxes.

Deductibility of state and local taxes is often defended as a means of compensating for inter-jurisdictional spillovers between state and local governments. That is, it is portrayed as a kind of matching grant that stimulates state and local government to engage in expenditures characterized by spillovers.

While there is obviously some truth in this description of deductibility, the inaccuracy of the description may be more important than the accuracy. First, the availability of the tax deduction does not depend on the degree of spillovers between jurisdictions. It is equally available for taxes that finance expenditures with virtually no inter-jurisdictional spillovers, such as street lighting, as for expenditures with benefits that flow across jurisdictional boundaries; indeed, deduction available for state and local taxes that finance activities generating negative externalities for neighboring jurisdictions, such as construction of thoroughfares that increase congestion, noise, and automobile accidents in surrounding jurisdictions. In short, the subsidies inherent in deductibility are not targeted toward expenditures yielding positive spillovers, as would be appropriate to compensate for such spillovers.

Second, it is difficult to rationalize a system of implicit subsidies that increase with the marginal tax rate, and therefore the income level, of the residents of the jurisdiction, as do the benefits of deductibility.[14] Let me use an extreme example to make this concrete. It is difficult to understand why, in general, almost half the benefits of public spending in Beverly Hills or Scarsdale should be argued (at least implicitly) to accrue to non-residents, while virtually none of the benefits of spending in Watts or Harlem do so; I would have expected the pattern to be reversed.

In short, while inter-jurisdictional spillover of benefits may result in sub-optimal spending by state and local governments, it is unlikely that using the itemized deduction for state and local taxes is the proper policy response to the problem.

## IV. THE LEVIATHAN PROBLEM

The discussion to this point has contained no description of the decision-making process of governments or the activities of politicians and bureaucrats. So far, sub-optimal behavior by state and local governments occurs simply because governments interested in maximizing the welfare of their constituents act in a way that is inconsistent with welfare maximization for the entire nation, either because of benefit spillovers or tax competition resulting from reliance on taxes not related to benefits of public services. I do not intend to venture into discussion of the propriety of majority voting

models or a discussion of the likelihood that decisions of state and local governments determined through majority voting will be optimal from the national point of view. I must, however comment on the relevance of the likely behavior of politicians and bureaucrats for the appraisal of the costs and benefits of tax competition. I will not attempt a systematic discussion of literature on what might be called the Leviathan problem; rather, I will rely primarily on common sense arguments that suggest that tax competition between subnational jurisdictions may have a salutary effect quite analogous to that of competition between firms in the private sector.

The traditional case for competition among private firms suggests that the combination of profit maximization and perfect competition creates substantial benefits for society. In particular, it induces producers to provide the goods and services that consumers want and to produce them in the most efficient way, in order to minimize costs. If competition is restrained, whether by outright monopolization, collusion between oligopolistic firms, regulation that prohibits competition, tariff protection, or whatever, it can generally be expected that economic welfare will suffer. In the absence of competition there is less incentive to be responsive to the desires of consumers and less pressure to minimize costs. In such a situation it is not uncommon to find powerful labor unions that appropriate for their members part of the surplus resulting from the failure to compete. For reasons such as this, employees of non-competitive sectors, as well as managers, resist attempts to increase competition, for example, through deregulation or elimination of protection.

I see little reason that the analysis just presented is not applicable, in general terms, to the appraisal of the costs and benefits of tax competition. After all, state and local governments are not simply mechanistic black boxes in which the wishes of voters are efficiently converted into the implied public policies. Rather, governments consist of collections of politicians and bureaucrats whose motivations are probably not totally dissimilar from those of managers and employees in the private sector. (We return to discuss this proposition below.) It is reasonable to expect that governments so constituted will not behave in such a way as to maximize the welfare of their constituents, in the absence of the pressures of competition from other governments. Rather, politicians and bureaucrats can be expected to want to further their own agendas through influence over public policy, regardless of whether such policy furthers the objectives of their constituents.[15] Maintenance of employment, salary, and "perks" and freedom from the rigors of cost-minimizing efficiency may be a large part of the agenda, as in the case of employees in non-competitive parts of the private sector.

If jurisdictions compete with each other and taxpayer/consumers are able to vote with their feet, there may be fairly strong pressures for subnational governments to respond to the wishes of the electorate, as expressed in willingness to pay taxes to finance public services (though presumably less pressure than in the private sector to respond to the desires of the consumers, as expressed in the market place). Moreover, competition between jurisdictions would create pressures to increase productivity and reduce costs, in order to avoid becoming uncompetitive, relative to other jurisdictions.[16]

While the brief description of governmental behavior above may sound quite compelling to most Americans, academic critics can almost certainly note points at which it is less than fully rigorous. Moreover, they might ask whether there is any empirical evidence for the proposition that the real world corresponds to the stylized description of political and bureaucratic behavior just presented.[17] Rather than addressing either of these issues in a comprehensive and fully satisfactory way, I

would like to offer a bit of anecdotal evidence from my experience during the debate on tax reform that suggests that the description is not too far-fetched.

First, virtually the only organized opposition to the elimination of the deduction for state and local taxes based on a tax competition argument came from governors, mayors, and public employees; I recall no one not in the public employ raising the possibility that tax competition might be harmful.[18] It is interesting that such objections were expressed even by governors of low-tax states whose residents would benefit, on balance, from the combination .of elimination of the state and local deduction and the reduction of marginal tax rates. Now I recognize that such a stance could be motivated by an honest concern that tax competition would be undesirable, or that the deduction should be retained for some other reason. But again it is interesting that little objection to ending deductibility was heard from representatives of low-tax states who were not politicians or bureaucrats.

Second, I would note that the American Federation of State, County, and Municipal Employees strongly opposed elimination of the deduction for state and local taxes. I presume that the analogy to opposition to deregulation of the airline industry by airline employees is sufficiently clear that it need not be pressed. As in the case of deregulatioin, avoidance of tax competition would help keep secure the protected position of the public employees who are members of that union and allow them greater latitude in furthering their own agendas.

Certain means of combatting tax competition are quite closely analogous to measures that commonly reduce competition in the private sector. Thus, having the federal government undertake a particular activity is similar to monopolization. An agreement among states not to compete in taxation would be similar to a cartel. Given the notorious difficulty of maintaining cartel arrangements, it is hardly surprising that those who are most likely to be hurt by competition between jurisdictions support federal policies that would reduce competition. State and local governments have one advantage not shared by private-sector firms who would seek to reduce competition; the federal government currently softens the impact of competition through the deduction for state and local taxes.[19]

## V. CONCLUDING ASSESSMENT

My consideration of the issues discussed above suggests that the likely benefits of reducing tax competition are relatively slight, particularly if more appropriate means of avoiding suboptimal decisions could be utilized more fully. On the other hand, the benefits of tax competition are potentially quite important. This leads me to conclude that tax competition is, on balance, good and that the case for continued deductibility of state and local non-business taxes is quite weak.

Inherent in this argument is, of course, the view that it might be desirable to expand reliance on matching categorical grants designed explicitly to compensate for spillover of benefits of services provided by state and local governments. Moreover, it would be desirable to rely more heavily on user charges and benefit-related taxes, including broad-based taxes on individuals, and less on taxation of business not related to benefits received, such as state corporation income taxes and property taxes on commercial and industrial property.[20]

Some may object to this conclusion on distributional grounds emphasizing that it would be unfair not to tax business, as well as individuals. To such objections I would offer the following standard replies: first, state and local governments should confine themselves primarily to benefit taxes, leaving income distribution policies to the federal governments.[21] Second, state and local gov-

ernments cannot expect to be very successful in efforts to engage in progressive taxation, even if they are inclined to neglect the above prescription to eschew efforts to engage in redistributive taxation. Taxes levied on mobile capital by geographically limited jurisdictions are likely to be borne by whatever is substantially less mobile—land and perhaps workers and consumers.[22]

Despite the above assessment, I have some misgivings about the Senate Finance Committee's proposal to repeal the itemized deduction for only state sales taxes. I believe sales taxes to be the most appropriate form of tax for state and local governments to use.[23] Repeal of only the sales tax deduction would artificially encourage a shift from sales taxation to income and property taxation.[24] All of the broad-based taxes on individuals (income, sales, or property) should be treated the same way, in order to avoid this type of distortion. Based on the arguments presented above, I believe that none of these taxes should be deductible.[25] All should be made non-deductible, and marginal tax rates should be dropped even further than in the Senate Finance Committee bill.[26] Alternatively, all should be made only partially deductible, or the deduction should be converted to a credit.

## Notes

The author thanks George Zodrow for helpful comments on an earlier draft of this paper.

1. There is no presumption that this list is complete. For more complete discussions of the issues raised here, see the survey by Wildasin (forthcoming) and literature cited there. See Gordon (1983) for a rigorous analysis of several of these and other issues.

2. The Leviathan model is commonly associated with Brennan and Buchanan; see, for example, (1980).

3. The inefficiency of excessive migration is not discussed. Gordon (1983) notes that subnational taxation of activities that produce congestion would cause congestion to be excessive elsewhere. If tax competition were to occur it could beneficially reduce this tendency.

4. See Beck (1983), Wilson (1984, 1985a, and 1985b), Zodrow and Mieszkowski (1986) and Wildasin (1986). The problem is defined clearly, for example, in Wilson (1984, p.1): "...I present a general equilibrium model in which a region's local public expenditures are completely financed by a uniform tax on all of the region's property. Tax competition is then defined as a situation where public service outputs and tax rates are 'too low' in the sense that a federal government could raise the nation's welfare by requiring each region to increase its public service output." In this literature the benefit spillovers discussed in Section III play little or no role.

5. This approach was adopted in 1926 to reduce interstate competition in the area of estate and gift taxes. The federal credit for contributions to state unemployment systems does not seem to be motivated by a desire to reduce interstate tax competition.

6. The discussion in the text concentrates on allocative issues. This argument for deductibility of individual income taxes is susceptible to the objection (spelled out in section III) that the implicit subsidy rate depends on the income levels and marginal tax rates of individuals in various jurisdictions. Of course, the argument presented in this section is substantially more relevant for the corporation income tax, which does not vary between corporations, except for those small corporations subject to marginal rates below the maximum rate. As noted below, there is no suggestion that taxes on business should not generally be deductible.

7. This example is constructed to juxtapose provision of benefits for local residents against a tax on mobile capital used in an industry that serves primarily non-residents. (School lunches are assumed to involve no benefits external to the taxing community.) Oates and Schwab (1985), p. 7, go to the heart of the analytical issue on the benefit side by saying, "It is easiest to think of the tax revenues from capital simply being distributed on an equal per capita basis to the residents of the community."

8. Wilson (1984), p. 18 notes: "In my model, the constraint that local public expenditures be financed by property taxation distorts local government decision-making. In fact, it is easily shown that local governments would behave efficiently if they were allowed to raise revenue by imposing lump sum taxes on their residents." (In the analytical context of Wilson's model lump-sum taxes are not distorting because labor is not mobile between jurisdictions.) Wilson also notes (p. 23); "*I view the results of this paper as an argument against the present system of property taxation in the U.S...* [I]t is also quite possible that decision by local governments to rely heavily on capital taxation rather than some other administratively feasible form of taxation is undesirable from the viewpoint of national welfare... [I]t is not clear that commodity taxes or an income tax might not be preferable to the present property tax system, despite the inefficiencies which they create." (emphasis added)

9. Wildasin (1986), pp. 20-21 notes: "The model employed in this paper is greatly simplified by the assumption that the only tax instrument available to a locality is a single uniform tax on capital...[D]ifferentially lower taxation of highly mobile capital...might blunt or eliminate the tendency to underspend on local public goods that tax competition would otherwise create...Such a tax [on only the immobile factor], being distortionless, would induce an optimizing jurisdiction to achieve a first-best efficient level of public expenditure."

10. Oates and Schwab (1985), p. 6 explicitly identify the tax rate on capital in their model as the excess over the cost of public services consumed by capital. They note (p. 8) that "if capital requires local public services" the efficient outcome "would indicate that the community set a tax on capital which exactly covers the cost of those services."

11. This could be achieved through differentially lower rates on commercial and industrial property and local surcharges on state individual income and sales taxes. An important problem is how to differentiate between "business" and individual income under the income tax. This is one of the primary advantages of state reliance on the sales tax.

12. The problem examined in Zodrow and Mieszkowski (1986) seems to fall in this category.

13. Spillovers of benefits resulting from public services provided to business and financed by ben-

efit taxes on business do not necessarily result in undersupply of the services. Ideally the exporting of taxes just compensates for benefit spillovers in such a case.

14. For one expression of this widely held view, see Gordon (1983).

15. Oates and Schwab (1985), p. 12 note that "government agencies often have their own set of concerns in the political arena that may, in some instances, run counter to their constituents' welfare." The Leviathan literature usually assumes that bureaucrats and politicians wish to see a government larger than desired by their constituents. There is, of course, no a priori reason that the agenda of the government insiders could not be to have a smaller than optimal level of government spending. Experience suggests, however, that the usual assumption is more realistic, as well as the more relevant one for the present discussion. After all, those who favor small government can hardly be expected to oppose tax competition.

16. George Break (1967) p. 178 has described one of the beneficial effects of competition between governments as follows: "...it replaces sloth and inertia with an active search for better and more varied public services and for more efficient ways of providing them." Similarly, Wildasin (1986), p. 19 notes "...the model used here has assumed that...preferences for private and public goods are respected by the local political process. This abstracts from failures of the political process to function efficiently.... Consideration of some of these issues would lead one to conclude that local government spending would be too high in the absence of property tax competition."

Hamilton (1983) has questioned the validity of the Leviathan model. He notes, however (p. 100), "Even if public entrepreneurs pursue technical efficiency with the same zeal and effectiveness as their private counterparts, the effectiveness of the mistake-correcting device is so much lower in the public sector that we can expect lower average efficiency even if public officials are benevolent dictators, so long as we assume them to be no wiser than private entrepreneurs. Thus we get a Leviathan-like result without ensuring it ahead of time by building avarice and deceit into the model." Hamilton concludes from his analysis (p. 104) that there is "...a strong

case that further reliance on explicitly private provision of 'local public services' would be a Pareto-improving move."

17. See Oates (1985) for empirical tests that cast doubt on the validity of the Leviathan hypothesis.

18. U.S. Senators and Congressmen representing high income/high tax states who opposed elimination of the deduction are, of course, in the public employ. The support for continuing deductibility by public sector employees stands in marked contrast to the virtually unanimous view of academic tax experts that deductibility should be eliminated.

19. Of course, income taxation also softens the rigors of competition in the private sector.

20. It should be acknowledged that reducing such business taxes would create undesirable windfall gains.

21. See, for example, Musgrave (1959) pp. 179-83 or Oates (1968). John Shannon has noted in conversation that those concerned about tax competition in the 1960s may have seen it as an obstacle to adequate public spending, as espoused by John Kenneth Galbraith, for example, in *The Affluent Society*. But Galbraith also warned against insistence that all public spending be financed with progressive taxes, since the result of such an attitude might be underprovision of public services of special value to the poor.

22. For further development of this theme, see Mieszkowski (1972) and McLure (1977), (1980), and (1981).

23. See also note 11 above. This assessment would be even stronger if the ridiculously unfair and distortionary de facto exemption of interstate sales by mail-order houses could be eliminated by federal legislation.

24. This suggests that the estimates of revenue expected from repeal of the sales tax deduction are probably over-stated. Partial repeal of all state and local taxes would not suffer from this defect, except as state and local governments shifted reliance from non-deductible taxes on individuals to deductible taxes on business.

25. Eliminating the deduction for taxes paid by individuals would avoid the present-law discrimination against the use of fees and user charges, the

most appropriate way to finance state and local services, where feasible.

26. This might not buy much reduction in the 15 and 27 percent rates, but given the distribution of deductible taxes by income brackets it should make possible a substantial reduction in both the 5 percent surcharge on incomes between $75,000 and about $145,000 and the surcharge used to phase out the personal exemptions.

# References

Arnott, Richard, and Grieson, Ronald E. "Optimal Fiscal Policy for a State or Local Government," *Journal of Urban Economics,* vol. 9, (1981), pp. 23-48.

Beck, John H., "Tax Competition, Uniform Assessment, and the Benefit Principle." *Journal of Urban Economics,* vol. 13, (1983), pp. 127-146.

Break, George F., *Intergovernmental Fiscal Relations in the United States* (Washington: Brookings Institution, 1967).

Brennan, G., and J. Buchanan, *The Power to Tax: Analytic Foundations of a Fiscal Constitution,* (New York: Cambridge University Press, 1980).

Epple, Dennis, and Allan Zelenitz, "The Relation Between Welfare Maximizing and Property-Value Maximizing Governments: The Effects of Jurisdictional Competition," March 1980.

Epple, Dennis, and Allan Zelenitz, "The Implications of Competition among Jurisdictions: Does Tiebout Need Politics?" *Journal of Political Economy,* vol. 89 (1981), pp. 1197-1217.

Gordon, Roger H., "An Optimal Taxation Approach to Fiscal Federalism," *Quarterly Journal of Economics,* vol. 98 (November 1983), pp. 567-86.

Hamilton, Bruce W., "A Review: Is the Property Tax a Benefit Tax?" in Zodrow, George R., editor, *Local Provision of Public Services: The Tiebout Model After Twenty-Five Years* (New York: Academic Press, 1983), pp. 85-107.

McLure, Jr., Charles E., "The 'New View' of the Property Tax: A Caveat," *National Tax Journal,* vol. 30 (March 1977), pp. 69-75.

McLure, Jr., Charles E., "The State Corporate Income Tax: Lambs in Wolves' Clothing," in Henry J. Aaron and Michael J. Boskin, editors, *The Economics of Taxation,* (Washington: Brookings Institution, 1980), pp. 327-46.

McLure, Jr., Charles E., "The Elusive Incidence of the Corporate Income Tax: The State Case," *Public Finance Quarterly,* vol. 9 (October 1981), pp. 395-413.

Mieszkowski, Peter, "The Property Tax: An Excise Tax or a Profits Tax?" *Journal of Public Economics,* vol. 1 (April 1972), pp. 73-96.

Musgrave, Richard A., *The Theory of Public Finance* (New York: McGraw Hill, 1959).

Oates, Wallace E., "The Theory of Public Finance in a Federal System." *Canadian Journal of Economics,* (February 1968), pp. 37-54.

Oates, Wallace E., "Searching for Leviathan: An Empirical Study," *American Economic Review,* vol. 75 (September 1985), pp. 748-57.

Oates, Wallace E. and Schwab, Robert M. "Economic Competition Among Jurisdictions: Efficiency Enhancing or Distortion Inducing?" July 1985.

*The President's Tax Proposals to the Congress for Fairness, Growth, and Simplicity* (Washington: U.S. Government Printing Office, 1985).

U.S. Department of the Treasury, *Tax Reform for Fairness, Simplicity, and Economic Growth,* (Washington: U.S. Government Printing Office, 1984).

Wildasin, David E., "Interjurisdictional Capital Mobility: Fiscal Externality and a Corrective Subsidy." Department of Economics, Indiana University, March 1986.

Wildasin, David E., *Urban Public Finance* (New York: Harwood Academic Press, forthcoming).

Wilson, John D., *A Theory of Inter-Regional Tax Competition,* SSRI Workshop Series 8417, Social Systems Research Institute, University of Wisconsin, Madison (August 1984).

Wilson, John D., "Optimal Property Taxation in the Presence of Interregional Capital Mobility,"

*Journal of Urban Economics,* vol. 17, (1985), pp. 73-89. (a)

Wilson, John D., *Trade, Capital Mobility and Tax Competition,* SSRI Workshop Series 8505,

Social Systems Research Institute, University of Wisconsin, Madison (March 1985). (b)

Zodrow, George R., and Peter Mieszkowski, "Pigou, Tiebout, Taxation, and the Underprovision of Local Public Goods," *Journal of Urban Economics,* vol. 19 (1986).

## QUESTIONS

1. Explain how the deductibility for federal tax purposes of state and local taxes would reduce tax competition.

2. Why does McLure favor deductibility for business taxes but not for nonbusiness taxes?

3. McLure argues that state and local taxes should try to approximate benefit taxes, with redistribution to be performed at a national level. To this end, he favors equal federal tax treatment of broad-based taxes: that is, income, sales, and property taxes on individuals. Do you think these three provide equally good approximations to a benefits tax?

4. McLure states in his conclusion that he views sales taxes as the most appropriate for state and local governments. Since the tax reform act did indeed repeal deductibility only for sales taxes, would McLure have been surprised by the news item reproduced here? Would he have been pleased?

Sales taxes and license fees for cars in New York state would be replaced by a 2.5% property tax under a plan backed by Governor Cuomo. The annual tax's amount would decline with a car's value; most important, it could be deducted on federal returns. An added 0.6% tax in the New York City area would aid metropolitan transportation.*

# Further Issues and Questions in Fiscal Federalism

### Eliminating the deductibility of sales taxes.

A major issue in the 1986 tax reform debate was whether state and local taxes should be deductible. Ultimately, sales taxes lost their deductibility, implying that sales taxes became more expensive to itemizing taxpayers. When sales taxes are deductible, a dollar paid in sales tax saves an itemizer an amount of federal tax equal to the federal income tax rate, $t$, on a marginal dollar of income; the "tax price" of deductible sales tax revenue is $(1-t)$, its net cost to the itemizing taxpayer. As itemizers' tax prices go up, so does the average tax price in the community.

To what extent will sales taxes be curtailed now that they are nondeductible? In "Tax Deductibility and Municipal Budget

Structure," (National Bureau of Economic Research working paper 2224), Douglas Holtz-Eakin and Harvey Rosen estimate that the elasticity of deductible taxes with respect to the community's tax price is in the range −1.2 to −1.6. They find no evidence that non-deductible tax sources are used more heavily as deductible sources become more expensive.

A. Based on these estimates, what do you predict will happen to the level of local expenditures that rely on locally raised revenues now that sales taxes are no longer deductible?
B. Eliminating deductibility for sales taxes will bring extra tax revenue to the federal government. Since the local tax price elasticity is negative, tax revenue to local jurisdictions falls. What can you say about the net effect of eliminating deductibility on the combined level of revenue raised? (Hint: Think about the magnitude of the tax-price elasticity.)

## Tax turf.

When the federal government imposes an excise tax on an item subject to state or local sales tax, sales tax revenues will be affected as quantities demanded react to higher prices.

A. Since sales taxes usually apply to gross prices (including the federal excise tax), what would you like to know about the elasticity of demand before concluding that the federal tax policy was hurting local governments' revenues?

## Heterogeneous communities and locally provided goods.

The Tiebout model predicts a world of homogeneous local jurisdictions whose residents are in basic agreement over the kind and quality of local public services they want. The real world is considerably heterogeneous; in particular, most towns and cities have well-defined richer and poorer sections, as well as areas of lower and higher crime rates. A Tiebout-like policy response to such heterogeneity might be to allow the levels of some publicly provided services to be set by neighborhoods, with neighborhood tax rates varying accordingly.

Los Angeles recently experimented with a proposal to allow certain sections of the city to raise their taxes in order to supplement their level of police protection. The proposal, Proposition 7 on the June 2, 1987 ballot, covered four police department division areas with particularly high levels of crime. Three hundred police officers were to be added to the divisions, at an average cost of $148 annually in increased residential property taxes.

Proposition 7 was overwhelmingly defeated.

A. Why do you think voters were skeptical ("outraged," according to media coverage) of this approach to achieving heterogeneity in the quantities of services provided by local governments?
B. Should parents in high-income neighborhoods be allowed to donate extra resources to the public schools their children attend?

# PART X

# Public Finance in an International Setting

*Issue:* Deficit finance in an open economy.

*"Thinking About Government Deficits II: International Ramifications"*
Jules B. Prag

*Issue:* Agricultural trade wars.

*"Agricultural Subsidies Would Be Jointly Cut Under U.S. Trade Plan"*
Art Pine

*Further Issues and Questions in International Public Finance*

*Issue:* Offshore tax havens.

*Issue:* Externalities and the global environment.

*Issue:* Unitary taxes on multinational corporations.

### *Deficit finance in an open economy.*

If the national debt is held by American citizens, repayment of the debt constitutes an income transfer from American taxpayers to American debt holders. If debt is held outside the United States, repayment removes resources from our economy. Does this distinction change the way we should think about the appropriateness of deficit finance?

Prag's review of macroeconomic models of the deficit's impact is continued, here taking into account the possibility of exporting our debt to other countries.

# THINKING ABOUT GOVERNMENT DEFICITS II:

## International Ramifications

*Jules B. Prag\**

It is often said that deficits and their accumulation as national debt don't really matter because "we owe it to ourselves." To see whether the deficit matters if we owe it to other countries, let us consider the effects of government deficits on the international sector of the economy. Adding the international sector to the picture allows Keynesian models to explain the statistical lack of evidence of crowding out.

*\*Assistant Professor of Economics, Claremont McKenna College.*

To understand the issues involved here, we need some rudimentary skills in international economics. To buy a commodity produced in another country, we must first acquire the currency of that country. Currencies of the various world economies are traded, somewhat freely, on the foreign exchange market. To a large extent the price of foreign currency, known as the exchange rate, is determined by the supply and demand for the currencies. The demand for a foreign currency, say the yen, is determined by the demand for Japanese products, and the supply of yen is due to the desire by Japanese citizens to trade their currency for dollars. So the demand for yen is related to our demand for Japanese goods, and the supply of yen is a measure of Japan's demand for our goods. The dollar price of the yen is the exchange rate but is best looked at as a price, much like dollars per grapefruit is the exchange rate or price of grapefruit. If Americans increase their demand for Toyotas, they will raise their demand for yen, which will raise the price of a yen. When it takes more dollars to buy a yen, the dollar is said to have depreciated and the yen has appreciated.

Since relative prices determine quantity demanded for most goods, the relative price of imported goods to domestic goods should determine our imports and exports. Foreign goods cost $P^*$ in their own country, so $P^* = $ yen/unit. Since yen cost us $e = $/yen$, imported goods cost us $eP^*$. Our own goods cost us $P = $/unit$. So we will import more and export fewer goods if $eP^*$ falls or $P$ rises. Similarly, net exports ($X-M$) will rise if $eP^*/P$ rises.

Relating this to deficits in the traditional model with crowding out of investment, we see that if the increase in deficits raises U.S. interest rates, foreign investors will want to invest their funds in U.S. bonds. The increased interest rates will therefore cause an increase in the demand for dollars or, in figure 1 above, an increase in the supply of yen on foreign exchange markets. The price of yen will fall, the dollar will appreciate (often referred to

as getting stronger), and this will cause an increase in our imports, which now become relatively cheaper, and a decrease in our exports. When we import more goods than we export we are said to be running a trade deficit. So we see why many economists believe that budget deficits can lead to trade deficits.

The reasons why this should concern us are twofold. Beneath the trade flows is an opposite flow of debt. If we import more goods than we export, we must be exporting more debt than we import. This follows because the only way we can consume more than we produce as a nation (that's what being a net importer means) is to borrow from other nations. If this flow of bonds overseas is due to the deficit, then we don't owe it to ourselves; we owe it to foreigners. Future generations of Americans will get higher tax bills but not the government bonds to pay them with.

If we cast aside xenophobic tendencies, this is not necessarily a problem. As before, if on net the deficit is funding worthwhile government investment projects that will pass along to our children a stronoger ecnomy, then paying some of that future return to foreign citizens can be sound business. The optimist would point out that projects like "Star Wars" are very likely to produce amazing spinoff products much the same as NASA gave us velcro. If the government expenditures being financed with deficits do not improve future productivity, our children will be unambiguously hurt to the extent that foreign citizens acquire our debt.

The second problem with deficits in the international sector in a Keynesian model is that the appreciated dollar displaces workers from our export industries and our import competing industries. American exports become too expensive for foreigners when the dollar has appreciated, and employees in these industries will lose their jobs. Similarly, imports become cheaper for Americans, and employees in industries that compete with these imports will lose their jobs. While new jobs

Figure 1

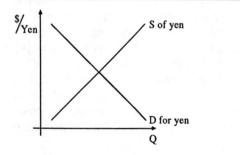

will be created by the deficit in this model, the rearrangement of labor markets due to the deficit can be painful, costly, and inefficient.

These arguments depend on deficits raising U.S. interest rates, leading to an appreciation of the dollar. As stated earlier, little evidence can be found for this effect. Some economists believe that world capital markets are so tightly integrated that even the slightest increase in U.S. rates brings about the inflow of funds and appreciation of the dollar. It is theoretically possible that the deficit crowds out exports and not investment (so that the Keynesian IS curve is horizontal). Evidence indicates that in recent years capital market integration has increased due to technological advances and more open credit markets (see Obsfeld, 1986). But there is no evidence or theoretical reason to lead us to believe that a rise in interest rates in the largest economy in the world could be offset by capital inflows. It is therefore difficult to give credence to the open economy Keynesian notion that U.S. budget deficits crowd out exports but not investment.

Much has been made of this international link recently since, during this episode of record budget deficits, we are also experiencing record trade deficits. Cautious economists point out many other facts to be considered. Our economy has been growing in recent years much more quickly than many of our trading partners. This means that our imports, which are sensitive to our incomes, will rise, but our exports (sensitive to foreign income growth) will not. Also, the largest share of our trade deficit is with Japan and Europe. This could be unrelated to our budget deficit but rather due to the relatively bright investment opportunities in this country and the high U.S. demand for imported luxury goods associated with our relative boom. Finally, a major importer of our products, Latin America, has virtually withdrawn from world markets due to credit problems.

While the link between budget deficits and trade deficits seems as much a coincidence as a causal relationship, there is no denying the flow of funds into the United States from abroad. Since 1980 the holdings of U.S. public debt by foreigners has gone from $129.7 billion to $256 billion, although the percentage of the debt held by foreigners has actually fallen from 21 percent to 16.5 percent. This means that our accumulated deficits will be a net liability to future generations of Americans unless they have been used to finance projects that produce assets worth at least this amount.

# References

Obsfeld, Maurice, "Capital Mobility in the World Economy: Theory and Measurement," Carnegie-Rochester Conference Series on Public Policy, 24, 1986, 55-104.

### Agricultural trade wars.

Subsidies to agriculture cost the United States over $25 billion in 1986. We are not alone; the *Left Business Observer* (February 1987, p. 3) reports a World Bank estimate of $100 billion as the annual farm subsidy cost to governments and consumers worldwide. The costs are high because the United States and Western Europe are competing with each other to make their own products attractive in the export market. Now that the costs of protection and counter-protection have escalated to such large sums, there is growing international interest in joint reduction of agricultural subsidies.

# AGRICULTURAL SUBSIDIES WOULD BE JOINTLY CUT UNDER U.S. TRADE PLAN†

*Art Pine**

WASHINGTON–When U.S. trade representative Clayton Yeutter maps strategy for the current talks with America's main trading partners, he focuses mainly on farmers. For besides being a painful domestic issue, agriculture has become the nation's biggest foreign-trade problem.

For years, the U.S. exported far more farm products than it imported. In the 1970s,

*Staff reporter of the *Wall Street Journal*.

†Reprinted with permission. *The Wall Street Journal*, Tuesday, April 7, 1987 p. 1. Copyright 1987 by Dow Jones & Company, Inc. ALL RIGHTS RESERVED.

in fact, agriculture was the single largest contributor to the trade surplus the country then enjoyed. All this has changed. Although some 30% of the nation's farm output still is sold abroad, the nation last year briefly ran a deficit in agricultural trade.

American trade strategists blame much of the problem on subsidies. In major agricultural countries, farm-support payments have become so generous they spur global overproduction and surpluses that depress prices and squeeze farmers everywhere. They also spawn protectionism.

Mr. Yeutter's prescription is simple:

Reduce government subsidies and trade barriers. "We can't do that unilaterally here in Washington," he says. "It's a global problem that has to be handled globally." For years, however, international trade conferences wouldn't even address the issue.

## COSTS MOUNT

Now the prospects of international action are rising. In the Common Market, subsidy costs are so high they threaten the financial stability of the 12-nation compact. Japan is facing great pressure from abroad to open its agricultural markets. And a longstanding U.S.-European subsidy battle is hurting some other big agricultural producers such as Canada, Argentina, and Australia, galvanizing them into a major political force for overhauling the current system.

The result is that in trade negotiations, farm subsidies have moved to the top of the agenda. Pressed by Washington, the 92-country General Agreement on Tariffs and Trade has agreed on a two-year, fast-track timetable that calls for identifying the issues this year and getting the bargaining under way in 1988.

Washington wants a phased reduction of all countries' farm-support programs and new trade rules to promote peaceful settlement of disputes. To force action, the U.S. has begun an aggressive campaign to make it more costly for other countries to maintain current subsidies.

## HIGH STAKES

Although trade talks in Geneva are finally under way, there is a serious danger that they will drag on so long that countries will lose patience and begin imposing new trade restrictions. "It's going to be a major challenge indeed," Mr. Yeutter says.

But it is an effort the U.S. believes it must make. "Agriculture has become a global problem, affecting both industrialized and developing countries." Secretary of State George Shultz recently told the National Association of Wheatgrowers. "The farming world faces a crisis of over-production.... How we respond to this crisis will determine the future role of American agriculture in the world and the number of farms that survive in this country."

To help make its point, Washington has been using a carrot-and-stick strategy. In 1985, the U.S. began using new farm export subsidies to counter the Common Market's generous export subsidies, which have helped turn Europe from a net importer to an exporter of grain.

Congress also slashed federal price supports, sending crop prices lower worldwide. That policy, combined with the recent decline in the value of the dollar against many currencies, makes it more costly for other countries to maintain crop supports.

## FAT TAX

The U.S. has turned more combative in other ways. Earlier this year, it threatened Europe with huge retaliatory duties and blunted an attempt by the Common Market to raise tariffs on U.S. corn and sorghum. Mr. Yeutter is readying a similar volley against a proposed

Figure 1

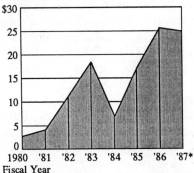

**Cost of U.S. commodity programs (in billions of dollars)**

1980 '81 '82 '83 '84 '85 '86 '87*
Fiscal Year
*Estimated
*Source: U.S. Agriculture Department*

European tax on fats and oils. The new tactics mark a sharp change from a milder—and unsuccessful—1982 American effort to win reductions in subsidies and trade curbs.

Now Washington wants governments to freeze farm programs at current levels and then agree to a world-wide plan to bring subsidies down to a minimal level—perhaps by reducing them 10% or so a year. The U.S. also wants to standardize health and sanitation requirements so these can't be used as trade barriers.

U.S. officials say the ultimate objective of the talks is to write broad rules that will permit governments to continue subsidies but at much lower levels. One idea gaining acceptance among producing countries is to turn farm subsidies into flat income-maintenance programs rather than payments tied to crop prices or to acreage. "This notion of giving a subsidy that encourages production, and then selling it at a lower price, is the inherent nature of the problem," Mr. Shultz says.

Mr. Yeutter has offered to "put everything on the table" in the new negotiations—including a Depression-era U.S. law that enables the U.S. to maintain import restrictions on politically sensitive crops such as peanuts, sugar, and dairy products. But U.S. officials stress that international cooperation is the key. "No country can or will unilaterally disarm its agricultural subsidies overnight." Mr. Shultz says, "We can't just stop ourselves if other people continue, because they'll just make inroads in our markets."

Washington did attempt a unilateral solution several years ago, resulting in an expensive fiasco. In 1983, after failing to launch new global trade talks, the Reagan administration decided to cut U.S. production without waiting for the rest of the world to do the same. The Agriculture Department paid farmers handsomely, in previously harvested grain and other crops, to take large portions of their acreage out of production.

Farmers signed on in droves. Within months 30% of the cropland covered by U.S. subsidy programs—the equivalent to the entire acreage of Western Europe—had been idled by this so-called payment-in-kind program. But when the cutbacks, coupled with a severe drought in the U.S. that year, drove up world prices, other countries increased their production and took export market share away from the U.S.

American farmers also stepped up production as soon as the program expired, and world crop prices sank. The declines helped drive up the cost of U.S. price-support programs. which are designed to bridge a gap between market prices and target prices. In fiscal 1986, farm programs cost Washington $25.8 billion, up nearly tenfold from 1980.

All in all, U.S. policies have given foreign producers an "almost unfettered opportunity for expansion," charges Robbin Johnson, a vice president and economist at Cargill Inc., the grain giant.

But the costs of unfettered expansion are becoming a burden to more and more governments. "There's an increasing realization of the cost being paid for agriculture," says Albert Bressand, the director of Promethee, a Paris-based research group. France, often a spoiler in efforts to cut Common Market farm subsidies, now pays more than it receives from EC farm programs and so is more willing to cooperate.

These conditions are raising the prospects for new global farm rules. Last spring, ministers of the 24-country Organization for Economic Cooperation and Development not only discussed agriculture for the first time but also issued a communique asserting the need to overhaul their farm programs to stem overproduction before it starts a trade war. President Reagan and leaders of the other six biggest industrial democracies endorsed that notion at the Tokyo economic summit last summer.

Then in September, at Punta del Este, Uruguay, the U.S. pushed through a major plank in the new round of trade talks broadening its agenda to include all farm subsidies, not just those that underwrite the cost of exports. Washington followed up by getting GATT to agree to the two-year timetable for trying to resolve the issues.

In another important step, the OECD this year has developed a complex formula that would enable negotiators to calculate a specific dollar value for each country's domestic farm subsides—a move that is expected to make the GATT negotiations a lot more orderly. Washington hopes to push that through at the next OECD ministerial meeting, next month, giving a further boost to the new GATT talks.

The administration also hopes to persuade heads of government to use this year's seven-nation economic summit, set for June in Venice, to provide fresh political impetus for the negotiations.

But the going won't be easy. The U.S. offer to "put everything on the table" hasn't drawn a reciprocal response. Japan, already in turmoil as a result of the dollar's decline against the yen, has been slow to include its sensitive rice-import restrictions in the talks. And Bonn, worried about its tiny but politically powerful Bavarian farms, is a holdout among the Europeans. "The bad-guy these days is West Germany," a U.S. official says.

As a result, some analysts believe that while the nuts-and-bolts negotiations may be done in the GATT, the outlines of any deals will have to be made at higher levels, possibly by heads of government themselves. "The political people have to discuss how to get there because it's really a political question," says Harald Malmgren, a Washington-based trade consultant. "You can't do it in trade negotiations. It requires a commitment at the highest level, to keep the pressure groups from getting through."

One major obstacle is the political calendar. All sides agree that realistically the negotiators can't strike an agreement before the French presidential elections in April 1988 or the U.S. elections later that year, because the farm crisis will be too sensitive an issue in both.

"There's an apprehension in American agriculture that we could be sold short again," says Michael Hall, the Washington representative for the National Corn Growers' Association. Right now there isn't any guarantee that Congress would support a new farm trade pact.

Negotiators for Canada, Australia and even the Common Market already have hinted they will push for an "interim agreement" this year designed to buy time until 1989. But the U.S. opposes any such move, on the ground that it would blunt pressure for a fundamental revamping.

Though farmers used to boast that agriculture was the last bastion of the free market, it now is one of the most heavily subsidized sectors. The U.S. maintains stringent—and quite costly—import quotas on a spate of farm products. Europe and Japan have intricate networks of quotas, managed markets and subsidy payments. Even Canada, Australia and Argentina, which purport to be non-subsidizers, maintain complex government price-setting programs that keep prices high domestically but keep their crops competitive abroad.

Agriculture Secretary Richard Lyng argues that the food-producing nations must work out an accord "or we're all going to have to dip a lot further into our pockets." The alternative to reaching an accord, he says. "is chaos."

Postscript: Did the economic summit in June 1987 provide the hoped-for political progress, or did West Germany and looming elections in France stall the negotiations? *The Wall Street Journal* story (June 11, 1987) filed by Walter S. Mossberg and Philip Revzin reports simply that:

The agriculture language also left out references the U.S. had supported to putting farm-trade talks on a fast track. France and Germany have steadfastly opposed splitting agricultural issues from other trade matters.

# QUESTIONS

1. If deficits cause the dollar to appreciate in world currency markets, how might this affect labor markets in the United States?

2. To protest the presence of their troops in Afghanistan, the Carter administration unilaterally imposed a grain embargo on the Soviet Union. This had the unwelcome effects of increasing market shares for our competitors in international agriculture and of making U.S. supplies seem unreliable. What unilateral solution to agricultural problems did the Reagon administration undertake? Was unilateral action successful?

3. How is it that both the United States and the Common Market can benefit from a global reduction in subsidy levels? Japan has import quotas on rice so strict that rice costs eight times as much in Japan as it would under free trade. Does Japan have any incentive to loosen its import quota on rice?

4. Prag argues that one cause of our current trade deficit is the economic woes of Third World countries, particularly in Latin America, that can no longer afford nonessential imports from the United States. If agricultural subsidies worldwide could be reduced, might our exports of nonagricultural goods to some Third World countries increase?

5. One possible reform of agriculture support programs is to substitute income maintenance programs for subsidies. On separate graphs, show that both price supports (a price floor with the government agreeing to buy any excess supply) and a per-unit subsidy will increase production. Shade in the area showing the cost to the government of this induced overproduction.

   How could you design an income maintenance program that did not depend on production levels?

---

# Further Issues and Questions in International Public Finance

### Offshore tax havens.

In 1987, the U.S. Treasury Department abruptly ended a tax treaty that allowed American investments in the Netherland Antilles to escape most or all income taxes. As a tax haven with tight bank secrecy laws, this Caribbean country of 200,000 people was at the time home to 60 banks and 24,000 corporations (*The Wall Street Journal*, "Netherland Antilles Minus a U.S. Treaty is Tax-Paradise Lost," July 28, 1987). This offshore sector has produced about $250 million in Antillean government revenue annually, or about 40 percent of total government revenues. This income source is now expected to decline by as much as 70 percent in the next few years.

A. Why did the Tresury end the treaty abruptly, rather than announce its intentions well in advance?
B. Creating such a tax haven might be classified as foreign aid. Assuming that corporations are profit maximizers, what do you know about the relative magnitudes of taxes foregone by the U.S. Treasury and revenues generated for the tax haven's government? Is this an efficient form of intergovernmental aid?
C. The island presence of most Netherland Antilles-registered companies is no more

than a file in a lawyer's office. How does the incidence of terminating the tax treaty depend on whether or not similar tax havens are available elsewhere?

D. If treaties can be abruptly and unilaterally canceled, what good are they? Is this treaty cancellation any different from other types of tax reform?

### *Externalities and the global environment.*

Economic activity can have a profound effect on the earth's climate. One major concern is depletion of the atmosphere's protective ozone layer, potentially caused by the use of such chemicals as aerosol propellants and refrigerants. Another worry is deforestation. As many of the world's poorest people search for fuel and arable land, forests are disappearing at an alarming rate, with the potential to change global weather patterns and the climate. Attempts to control the activities that give rise to these externalities are hindered by the free-rider problem and the lack of an intergovernmental body to enforce involuntary solutions.

A. The International Monetary Fund and World Bank have a great deal of power over Third World nations seeking financial assistance. Should this power be used to encourage

responsible management of forested areas?

B. What international pressure can be brought to bear upon industrial nations threatening the ozone layer?

### *Unitary taxes on multinational corporations.*

A multinational corporation must keep track of the exchange of resources among its many divisions and offices. To do so, internal transfer prices are created to tell each division the value of goods received from other branches of the corporation. These costs are used in calculating the profit of the division.

A. These create a dilemma for states wishing to tax multinational corporations doing business within their boundaries. If a state taxes a multinational on profit earned within the state, what incentive does this give the corporation as it sets its internal prices?

B. The alternative is for a state to impose a unitary tax on all of the worldwide profits of corporations doing business within their boundaries. What incentive does this give to the corporation? Which state is more likely to suffer from imposing a unitary tax on corporate profits, California or a somewhat smaller state like Florida?